SCENIC DRIVING
TENNESSEE

D1540291

RUSS MANNING

FALCON®

GUILFORD, CONNECTICUT
HELENA, MONTANA

AN IMPRINT OF THE GLOBE PEQUOT PRESS

/FALCONGUIDE®

Falcon and FalconGuide are registered trademarks of The Globe Pequot Press.

Text design by Debbie Nicolais
Maps created by Brandon Ray and M.A. Dubé © The Globe Pequot Press
All photos are by the author unless otherwise noted.

Library of Congress Cataloging-in-Publication Data is available.

ISBN 0-7627-1138-8

Manufactured in the United States of America
First Edition/First Printing

The routes and sites listed in this guidebook were confirmed at press time. We recommend, however, that you call establishments before traveling to obtain current information.

contents

THE SCENIC DRIVES

acknowledgments

Each day as I traveled across Tennessee, at least one person took the time and had the patience to talk about the past, show me around town, invite me into their home, or explain what I was seeing or should see. I am grateful to them all; without them this book would be less than it is.

MAP LEGEND

Scenic Drive	▬▬▬▬▬	River	
Interstate	〈81〉	Lake	
U. S. Highway	〈58〉	Campground	▲
		Point of Interest	▢
State Route	〈35〉	Dam	▮
Forest/County Rd.	〈108〉	Waterfall	∥
		Pass	) (
Surface Street	McCammon Rd.	Mountain	▲
Railroad	┼┼┼┼┼┼┼┼┼┼	Small Town	○ Rogersville
County Border	Roane County / Loudon County	Large Town	◉ Kingsport
State Line	TENNESSEE / KENTUCKY	State Capitol	✪ Nashville
Forest/Park Boundary	CHEROKEE NATIONAL WILDERNESS	Orientation	N
Scenic Drive Location	TENNESSEE	Scale	0 Kilometers 5 / 0 Miles 5

LOCATOR MAP

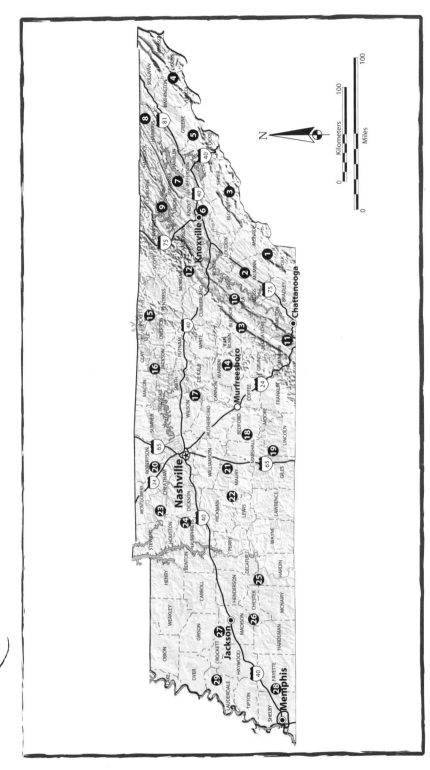

Greeter Falls in Savage Gulf

introduction

Tennessee is a long state, east to west. A drive from Bristol in the northeast to Memphis in the southwest covers 500 miles and crosses nine physiographic regions. Tennessee's elongated shape is tied to the history of its formation.

HISTORICAL OVERVIEW

By the time disputes with France and Spain had been settled, British claim to North America consisted of most of the land east of the Mississippi River. Several colonies had been given "sea-to-sea" grants, and so claimed the lands to the west of the Appalachian Mountains. North Carolina's claim to western lands was determined by surveying virtually straight lines westward from the western border of the colony to the Mississippi River, essentially outlining the future state of Tennessee.

With the end of the American Revolution, the new central government was in need of funds for operating expenses and so asked the states to give up their western lands, which could be sold and the money used to run the government. Along with other states, North Carolina offered its western lands to the government in 1784. But before Congress got around to accepting North Carolina's lands, a newly elected state legislature repealed the act giving up the lands.

In the meantime, the country had become dissatisfied with the Articles of Confederation under which it had been operating and so drew up a new Constitution of the United States. In 1789 North Carolina ratified the Constitution, and three weeks later, the state legislature once more ceded its western lands to the central government. This time Congress acted quickly to accept the land, which became the Territory of the United States South of the River Ohio, more commonly called the Southwest Territory. Once the territory had met certain qualifications and drawn up a state constitution and elected representatives to Congress, the Southwest Territory was accepted as the State of Tennessee in 1796.

Today the state is generally divided into East, Middle, and West Tennessee based on the course of the Tennessee River, which runs northeast to southwest through the eastern half of the state, dips into Alabama, and then turns northwest to cross the state again, ending at the Ohio River in Kentucky.

While the western river valley neatly divides West and Middle Tennessee, the boundary between Middle and East Tennessee is not so distinct. If only the part of the state east of the eastern river valley were considered East Tennessee, that portion of the state would be relatively small. So East Tennessee is generally thought of as the mountainous part of the state, incorporating part of the Cumberland Plateau, which lies to the west of the river.

The more natural way to divide the state into manageable pieces is to look at the physiographic regions. Because Tennessee is not very wide north to south but is long east to west, it cuts across geologic regions, which generally run northeast to southwest—from the Unaka Range of the Appalachian Mountains on its eastern border, through the Great Valley of East Tennessee, across the Cumberland Plateau, down the Eastern Highland Rim, through the Central Basin, up the Western Highland Rim, across the Plateau of West Tennessee, and down to the Mississippi River.

THE UNAKA MOUNTAINS

The Unaka Range of mountains standing on the border with North Carolina contains some of the highest peaks in the eastern United States. The mountains were created through continental collision during the early history of the earth in which the force of the collision moved from the southeast—folding, breaking rock, and pushing up mountains to the northwest. As the initial mountains eroded down to a plain, mountains were created again in a repeating cycle of uplift and erosion until the Unakas of today remain.

These mountains contain some of the most rugged and isolated regions in the country. You can follow hiking trails in Great Smoky Mountains National Park and Cherokee National Forest that wander along clear, cold mountain streams through one of the most biologically diverse regions in the world.

THE GREAT VALLEY OF EAST TENNESSEE

To the west of the mountains lies the Great Valley of East Tennessee, through which the Tennessee River flows. This was an area of weakness that subsided; countless layers of sediment filled the depression and hardened into rock. When the force of the continental collision moved across the land, the rock layers broke and tumbled over themselves and stood on end, creating lines of broken rock running southwest to northeast, like ripples moving across the surface of a pond. Erosion subsequently swept away the softer material between the hills, leaving aligned ridges separated by valleys; so many, in fact, that the overall region running through the eastern United States is called the Valley and Ridge Province.

The Great Valley of East Tennessee was the natural place for early settlement of the state once the pioneers had crossed the Unaka Mountains. Towns such as Jonesboro, Dandridge, Kingsport, and Knoxville became the sites of early Tennessee history. Historic communities, homes, and museums tell the story of this early settlement.

THE CUMBERLAND PLATEAU

Farther to the west, a particularly thick layer of sediment had solidified into an erosion resistant sandstone, which during the last period of mountain-building rose high above sea level. Subsequent erosion swept away overlying sediment layers but then slowed when it encountered this resistant rock, called "Pennsylvanian sandstone." This protective sandstone layer now caps a plateau standing 2,000 feet above sea level.

Called the Cumberland Plateau, the tableland has since become etched with deep river gorges, natural sandstone arches, and slender waterfalls dropping from great heights, creating a geologic wonderland preserved in state parks, natural areas, and national preserves. You can paddle the Obed Wild and Scenic River through a sandstone gorge or drive down the length of Sequatchie Valley between the towering walls of the plateau.

THE EASTERN HIGHLAND RIM

A thousand feet below the plateau on the west lies the Eastern Highland Rim, a strip of land that once encircled a great dome of rock in the center of the state and has now eroded away into a basin. This highland rim is sheltered from erosion by resistant rocks of the Fort Payne Formation, which once extended as flat-lying rock across to the Western Highland Rim, and is now slightly tilted so that it slopes back east due to the dome formation in the center. Around the edges of this central dome, the Fort Payne rock did not fracture during the dome formation and so has resisted the erosion that created the basin.

This highland nurtured Tennessee sons who went out into the world to become statesmen and heroes. You can visit the historic homesites of these native sons, search out waterfalls at the edge of the rim, and camp beside the Cumberland River where it enters the northern part of the state.

THE CENTRAL BASIN

The Central Basin lying in the midst of the highland rim, and 600 feet lower, was created by the formation of a huge arch. In ancient times, a force pushed upward from the depths of the earth forming a dome covering more than

5,000 square miles. This action caused limestone layers deep in the earth to be raised high above sea level and caused the overlying Fort Payne rock to crack as it was stretched over the surface of what came to be called the Nashville Dome. Erosion took advantage of breaks in the overlying rock, and so the dome eroded more quickly than surrounding areas. The surface rock was swept away and the limestone beneath succumbed rapidly, so that today a basin exists where there was once a great mountain.

Limestone makes for rich land, and so it was here, where bluegrass grows thick and tall, that great antebellum plantations were carved out of the land and horse breeding and raising became an integral part of the society. South of Nashville you'll tour one of the largest collections of antebellum homes in the South and watch Tennessee walking horses graze in green fields.

THE WESTERN HIGHLAND RIM

To the west of the Central Basin stands the other half of the highland rim, simply referred to as the Western Highland Rim. This western rim is much wider than the eastern rim and is separated from it only by the Cumberland River, where it cuts through the rim on the northeast, and by the state boundary with Alabama, which carves off a small portion of the Central Basin on the south. The Western Highland Rim slopes down to the west, having also been tilted during the creation of the Nashville Dome. The only geologic difference between the two is that a sea once invaded the western part of the state, covering at least a portion of the western rim but not the eastern.

This sea water contained glauconite, an iron-bearing mineral that deposited into the surface rock of the Western Highland Rim, which gave rise to an iron industry in the 1800s in this portion of the state. Montgomery Bell was perhaps the most prominent ironmaster to set up shop on this western highland. You'll visit one site of his operations at the Narrows of the Harpeth and tour the forge town of Cumberland Furnace.

THE WEST VALLEY OF THE TENNESSEE

To the west of the Highland Rim, the Tennessee River returns on its wandering course from Alabama, flowing north through the state and forming the narrow West Valley of the Tennessee. Obviously, only a complex geologic history could have caused the Tennessee River to change its northeast to southwest course, turning west and northwest and finally north to head for the Ohio River rather than the Gulf of Mexico. One theory has it that the river once flowed through the middle of the state until the Nashville Dome formed; as the dome gradually rose, the river channel was pushed southward down the slope of the dome so that it now dips into Alabama. Another theory says the Tennessee is actually a combination of three rivers; the union occurred as erosion caused one river to capture the flow of another. The reality is likely a combination of both events.

The river, which had been a route for migration during the early settlement of the state, became a route for invasion during the Civil War. Union forces entering the state from Kentucky defeated Confederate troops at Forts Henry and Donelson and then moved south on the Tennessee River to a historic engagement with Southern troops at Shiloh. You can visit several of these battle sites and explore the now peaceful river that is a major flyway for waterfowl.

THE PLATEAU OF WEST TENNESSEE

To the west lies the vast Plateau of West Tennessee. Though the area appears to be more of a plain than a plateau, in fact the region stands 300 feet above the Tennessee River Valley on the east side and, sloping down slightly, 200 feet above the Mississippi River Valley on the west. This area of the state was once covered by a shallow sea, which left the remains of fish, shells, marine turtles, and even giant seagoing reptiles. The deposition of the sea, followed by uplift and additional accumulation of loess, windblown dust laid down at the end of the last ice age, created this large plateau only a few hundred feet high.

The uncompacted layers of sand, silt, clay, and loess lying atop the plateau make this a rich agricultural region known as Tennessee's cotton country. While the region nurtured an agricultural economy, the people working the cotton fields created a music form called the "blues" and perfected the cooking of barbecue.

THE MISSISSIPPI RIVER FLOODPLAIN

Finally, the state ends with the Mississippi River Floodplain that lies below the western edge of the Plateau of West Tennessee. The bluff of this western edge standing above the floodplain is called Chickasaw Bluffs, for the Native Americans that lived here at the time Europeans settled the region. The course of the Mississippi was determined when an arm of the Gulf of Mexico invaded the region during a period of downwarping, creating an embayment. When the land rose and the sea retreated, this area formed a natural drainage channel for the eastern United States; waters from the eastern slopes of the Rockies and the western slopes of the Appalachians flow into the Mississippi River.

Sunk Lake

The Tennessee portion of the river floodplain is relatively narrow because at present the Mississippi River flows near the eastern edge of the plain. Over time the river changes its course, at one time or another occupying virtually all the area of the floodplain. Following the river north, you'll dip in and out of this floodplain that harbors several wildlife refuges. And you'll visit Tennessee's only natural lake, which was created by a ravaging earthquake.

BEFORE YOU BEGIN

Scenic Driving Tennessee describes twenty-nine drives that provide an opportunity to explore the entire state of Tennessee, covering each of the nine physiographic regions of the state and most of the ninety-five counties. While some drives are restricted to a specific geologic region, others traverse more than one region; at times it becomes more interesting to follow the history or a highway or a railroad than a geologic boundary.

The drives cover 3,200 miles of highways and back roads. Varying from 36 miles to 177 miles, the routes provide countryside scenery, shaded lanes, intriguing natural features, outdoor recreational activities, and historic settings. Some of the drives begin in large cities where much of the basic history of the state resides.

The highways and gravel roads included in the drives and side trips are all passable by common passenger automobiles unless otherwise noted. Take care while driving these roads; some are steep and winding and often have other vehicles; at times it may be best for the driver to miss a sight rather than take his or her eyes from the road. If there is no safe pull-out, better to move on to the next attraction. Also watch for wildlife to avoid animals on the roads, especially when traveling through state and national parks and preserves and along forested sections of highway. Birds, deer, raccoons, opossums, turtles, and snakes are the most common animals encountered.

The distances given in the drives have been measured with a vehicle odometer and will very probably differ slightly from the distances given by highway signs, maps, and other vehicle odometers. Total drive mileage is the number of miles of the main route; side trips to nearby places add additional mileage.

Although all these scenic drives can be driven easily in less than a day, most will require additional time to see the sites, walk short trails, and have a meal or two. So in order to fully enjoy the region, plan on taking a full day to cover the route, or invest the time of more than a day, either spending a night or two along the way or breaking the drive into more than one outing.

All attractions and sites along the drives are in bold type, including many historic homes and buildings. Houses open to the public are so stated; otherwise they are private and must be viewed from the street. Many structures are on the National Register of Historic Places; that fact is most often not mentioned in order to keep from frequently repeating this statement. Historic structures not on the register are just as worthy of noting and remembering.

Most small town museums are open only one or two afternoons a week. These schedules may change frequently; so the times and days are not included. Call the local county chamber of commerce or city hall for the days and hours; many museums post phone numbers that can be called to reach someone who will gladly come and open the museum for you.

Many campgrounds are closed during the winter season; so when traveling in late fall through early spring, call ahead to find an open campground. Inns and bed-and-breakfasts are occasionally mentioned when they occupy historic homes and buildings; although staying the night at one of these provides a unique opportunity to experience a historic setting, a mention in the text should not be considered a recommendation. Likewise, a restaurant may be mentioned because it occupies a historic setting or it has been serving meals long enough to be a local landmark itself; a mention should not necessarily be considered a recommendation.

Weather can change quickly in Tennessee, especially in the mountainous regions. Always be prepared for rain, and during the winter, for snow and ice on back roads. Keep in mind that elevation gain means a decrease in temperature; it's not unheard of to go from a sunny valley to snowfall at the top of a high eastern mountain in an hour or two.

The most popular times for scenic driving in Tennessee are spring and fall. Spring brings rain, and so wildflowers and waterfalls abound. In fall, color drapes the backcountry forests and even dapples a lone maple or oak standing in a field. But summer provides a time for families to travel together and participate in outdoor recreation. And in winter, with careful driving, there are scenes of wonder and charm.

Of course, always set out with a vehicle in good running condition and with plenty of gas. Carry along drinking water, especially in summer. When leaving the vehicle for any length of time, conceal all valuables. Respect private property by not trespassing, and respect public property by not littering.

Now get out there. The wonders of Tennessee await.

1

The overhill country

FORT LOUDOUN TO RED CLAY

GENERAL DESCRIPTION: This 153-mile drive through the former home of the Overhill Cherokees explores the mountains and foothills of Cherokee National Forest in one of the most scenic regions of the state.

SPECIAL ATTRACTIONS: Tellico Blockhouse, Fort Loudoun State Historic Area, Sequoyah Birthplace Museum, Chota Peninsula, Cherokee National Forest, Coker Creek, Ducktown Basin, Ocoee Scenic Byway, Red Clay State Historic Area, historic homes and buildings, scenic views, fall color, hiking, biking, boating, fishing, hunting, and wildlife viewing.

LOCATION: Southeast corner of Tennessee. The drive begins at Tellico Blockhouse on US 411.

DRIVE ROUTE NUMBERS: US 411; TN 360, 165, and 68; US 64, TN 60 and 317.

CAMPING: Toqua Beach Campground, Spivey Cove Campground, Indian Boundary Campground, Coker Creek Village, Thunder Rock Campground, Parksville Lake Campground, and Chilhowee Recreation Area Campground.

SERVICES: All services at Tellico Plains, Ducktown, and Cleveland.

NEARBY ATTRACTIONS: Apalachia Dam, Cherohala Skyway, and Chilhowee Recreation Area.

THE DRIVE

Before Europeans came to North America, the mountains and forests of the eastern United States were inhabited by a succession of prehistoric native peoples. By the time of white contact, these Native Americans had coalesced into the historic tribes—the Creeks, Chickasaws, Choctaws, and Cherokees.

The powerful Cherokees called themselves the "Principle People" and were the dominant tribe in the South. They had three concentrations of settlements—in the foothills of South Carolina and northern Georgia, in the western mountains of North Carolina, and along the Little Tennessee River in East Tennessee. Since those in Tennessee were across the Appalachian Mountains from the other groups, they were referred to as the Overhill Cherokee.

THE OVERHILL COUNTRY

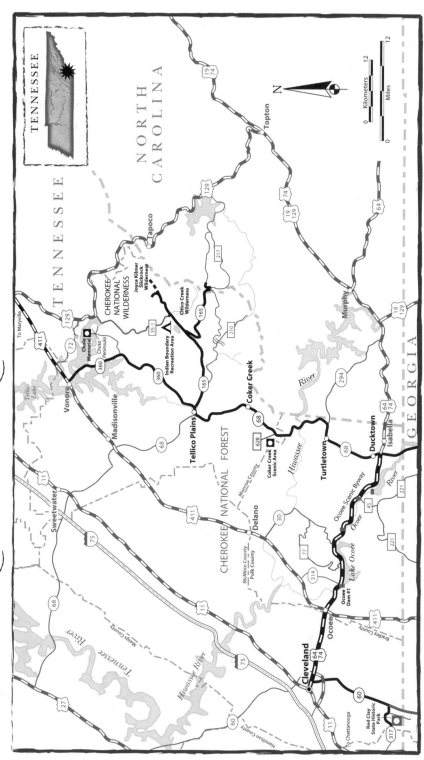

OVERHILL COUNTRY

From Maryville, near the foothills of the Great Smoky Mountains, US 411 heads southwest into the Overhill Country, reaching the Little Tennessee River in 17 miles. Just before crossing the river, turn left on Clear View Drive and then take a quick right on a side road. From a parking area at the end of the road, a paved path leads to the ruins of **Tellico Blockhouse,** built in 1794 as a military fort and a federal store for trade with the Cherokees.

The government agent to the Overhill Cherokees lived here until 1801, and the fort continued to be used until it was removed as a condition of a treaty in 1807. Only the stone foundations remain. Across the Little Tennessee River, you can see the palisade of the reconstructed Fort Loudoun, built from 1756 to 1757 during the French and Indian War. Threatened by France's growing influence in the Mississippi Valley, and wanting to cement relations with the Cherokees, the British colony of South Carolina sponsored the construction of the fort, probably the first planned structure built by whites west of the Appalachian Mountains in the lands that would later become the State of Tennessee.

To reach Fort Loudoun, return to US 411 and cross the Little Tennessee River, here called Tellico Lake with the river backed up by the Tennessee Valley Authority's Tellico Dam far downstream. The building of the dam in the 1970s was the environmental battle of the decade, pitting environmentalists, farmers, and Native Americans against dam builders, politicians, and developers. Conservationists had the battle won when they discovered an endangered fish in the river, the snail darter, and the U.S. Supreme Court ruled the dam violated the Endangered Species Act. But the U.S. Congress voted to exempt the dam from the provisions of the law, and Tellico Dam was completed. The rising waters destroyed one of the last stretches of free-flowing river in the state, flooded some of the finest bottomland farm country, and inundated 200 archaeological sites in the sacred valley of the Cherokees.

Just before the community of Vonore, turn left on TN 360 and cross a bridge over the Tellico River onto an island at the confluence of the Tellico with the Little Tennessee River. The **Fort Loudoun State Historic Area** is just ahead on the left. Behind the visitor center, a path leads to the reconstructed fort resting on an area raised about 17 feet to get it above lake level.

Named for the fourth Earl of Loudoun, James Campbell, who was the British commander in North America at the time the fort was built, Fort Loudoun was manned by British troops and South Carolina militia under Capt. Raymond Demere. In 1757, as the fort neared completion, Demere turned over command of the fort to his brother, Paul, and left. Soon after,

British relations with the Cherokees deteriorated, with skirmishes occurring between the Native Americans and colonists at isolated British settlements; several members of a Cherokee peace delegation to South Carolina were taken hostage and later killed.

In March 1760, Cherokees besieged the fort. By August, food had run so low that Demere surrendered. The garrison of 180 men and sixty women and children were allowed to leave. But the following morning, after camping for the night, the British found themselves surrounded by the Cherokees. Both sides opened fire, and soon all but one of the British officers were killed along with about twenty others. The rest were taken prisoner, some to be tortured and killed, others ransomed by South Carolina and Virginia. Fort Loudoun was occupied for a time by the Cherokees and was then burned. By the time the Tellico Blockhouse was built across the river, relations had settled and trade had resumed with the Cherokees.

Continue east on TN 360 for 0.2 mile to the **Sequoyah Birthplace Museum** on the right. Inside, exhibits tell of George Gist, the child of a Virginia fur trader and the daughter of a Cherokee chief, who was born in 1776 at Tuskeegee Village, now covered by Tellico Lake. Called "Sequoyah" by the Cherokees, Gist was captivated with the idea of reading and writing; he understood the survival of the Cherokees as a nation depended upon adopting some of the ways of the whites, especially using a written language. He began work in 1809 on a Cherokee writing system, using English, Greek, and Hebrew letters that he used to represent sounds in the Cherokee language. In 1821 he presented to his people a syllabary so easy to use that within months the Cherokees became a mostly literate people. In a few years, books were translated into Cherokee, and the *Cherokee Phoenix* was published, a bilingual newspaper in English and Cherokee.

Behind the museum, a long walkway leads to the **Cherokee Memorial,** a burial site for the remains of 191 individuals unearthed during archaeological excavations prior to the flooding of the Little Tennessee River Valley.

TN 360 continues east, crossing from the island to the mainland. To the left, the stretch of land along the lakeshore is set aside in the **Tellico Lake Wildlife Management Area**. Across the lake waters stand the Great Smoky Mountains of the towering Unaka Range. **Toqua Beach Campground** lies on the shore of the lake (no hookups) and several boat ramps provide access for boating and fishing.

In 5.6 miles TN 360 turns to the right, but first stay straight on Co 455 for 5.1 miles and turn left onto the Chota Peninsula.

In 0.7 mile, on the left, stands the **Tanasi Memorial.** Along this south side of the Little Tennessee River, there were once ten villages of the Overhill Cherokee. Tanasi was the capital of the nation from 1721 to 1730, and it is the origin of the name "Tennessee." Tanasi was eventually absorbed by the larger, adjacent town of Chota, which served as the capital for many years. Both townsites are now under the waters of Lake Tellico.

In another mile, the road ends at the isolated tip of the peninsula where a 200-yard gravel path leads to the **Chota Memorial** at the edge of the lake. There you'll stand in silence among pedestals bearing the names of the Cherokee clans: Blue, Long-Hair, Bird, Paint, Wolf, Wild Potato, and Deer.

CHEROKEE NATIONAL FOREST

Return to TN 360, and turn southwest, crossing Ballplay Creek, a tributary of the Tellico River. The road winds through a rural countryside in the foothills of the Unaka Range that stands along the Tennessee–North Carolina border. Wooded slopes flow down to small farms tucked in hollows with pastures, barns, and white farmhouses. Occasional stands of river cane occupy wet areas along streams. In 4.8 miles, at a four-way junction, turn left to stay on TN 360. Continue through forested foothills that occasionally open to settled hollows. In 10.6 miles cross a bridge over the Tellico River to a junction with TN 165.

This drive will continue to the right here, but a side trip to the left leads into **Cherokee National Forest** on the **Cherohala Skyway;** the name is a mix of syllables from Cherokee and Nantahala National Forests. The scenic highway travels along the Tellico River into the mountains with pull-outs offering grand views. In 6.4 miles Forest Service Road 210 to the right gives access to **Tellico Ranger Station,** where you can get maps and information about the national forest; farther along FSR 210 is 100-foot **Bald River Falls** and **Bald River Gorge Wilderness**.

Another 9.4 miles along the Skyway, FSR 345 leads left to **Indian Boundary Recreation Area,** which includes a campground (no hookups); a gravel road from there accesses **Citico Creek Wilderness** and adjacent **Joyce Kilmer-Slickrock Wilderness**. In another 13.6 miles the Skyway reaches the top of the Unaka Range at Beech Gap on the state line at an elevation of 4,490 feet. From here the Cherohala Skyway enters Nantahala National Forest in North Carolina, traveling to Robbinsville in 17 miles.

Back out at the junction of TN 360 with TN 165, continue straight into the community of Tellico Plains, and at a junction with TN 68 in 1.1 miles, turn left. In 3.4 miles TN 68 enters Cherokee National Forest as the highway climbs into the mountains and reaches **Coker Creek Village** in 6.9 miles. The small community of country store, craft shops, lodging, and campground was the location of a gold rush that began in the 1820s, two decades before the famed California Gold Rush. The Cherokees knew of the gold here and occasionally wore gold nuggets as jewelry. When whites asked where the gold came from, they were told Coqua Creek, which the whites called "Coker." Soon, prospectors were trespassing on Cherokee lands, digging mines, and panning for gold in the creek. At one time there were a thousand miners in the area, shipping gold ore to a mint in Dahlonega, Georgia. This discovery of gold was a factor in the eventual forced removal of the Cherokees from their lands. Today you can still pan for gold in Coker Creek, but the gold rush ended soon after the Civil War.

Pass through the coomunity of Coker Creek, and in 6.7 miles TN 68 crosses Coker Creek and then climbs Unicoi Mountain. Continue up TN 68, crossing from Monroe into Polk County, topping the mountain in 2.7 miles, and descending the other side. In 3.4 miles a small parking space on the left is where the John Muir Trail crosses the road. The famed conservationist, who founded the Sierra Club, explored this region of the country as a young man in the late 1860s. Running 19 miles along the Hiwassee River, this trail commemorates Muir's trip through what is now Cherokee National Forest.

The road continues down, curving left along the river beside a picnic area, crossing the Hiwassee, and passing under a railroad trestle. The road then climbs from the river, exiting the national forest. At the top of the next ridge in 2.7 miles, a side road in the small community of Farner leads left to the base of TVA's **Apalachia Dam** in 2.1 miles. This dam on the Hiwassee stands just at the border with North Carolina.

COPPER MINING

TN 68 continues through the mountains 11.8 miles to Ducktown, the center of a copper mining industry for 137 years. Main Street leads left into the old commercial district of the former mining company town; on the far side of the district, the **Company House Bed and Breakfast** now occupies an 1870 company house.

The copper found in the area had been used by the Cherokees before white settlers looking for gold discovered the copper for themselves. The first copper mine opened in 1850. In 1891 rail service reached the basin, allowing an expansion in which more than a dozen American and foreign companies established copper mines. This large industry was fueled by the surrounding forests, which were cut to provide the necessary energy for the industrial processes. Open-pit smelting of the copper ore released sulfur dioxide, which produced the country's first large-scale acid rain, killing what vegetation remained. With the ground bare, erosion swept away countless tons of soil, creating a man-made biological desert of red earth that covered 32,000 acres.

In the early 1900s, mining technology was developed to capture the sulfur dioxide, converting it to sulfuric acid that could be sold as a by-product. Combined with the introduction of electricity and other fuel sources, the new method halted the environmental impact, although erosion continued to be a problem. When the Tennessee Valley Authority was formed in the 1930s, the federal utility along with the mining companies and other agencies began experimental projects in reclamation. The result has been phenomenal, especially in the last two decades, in which millions of pine trees have been planted and grass and black locust seeds have been scattered by plane across the landscape. The area is now once more nearly covered in vegetation.

Just past Main Street, turn left on Burra Burra Road to climb the hill through the old buildings of the **Burra Burra Mine Historic District** and reach the Burra Burra Mine. The adjacent mine superintendent's office is now the **Ducktown Basin Museum,** which tells the story of copper mining and reclamation of the basin. This mine site has not been reclaimed to show the once devastated land. The water-filled pit in midst of the blasted landscape is a cave-in of the underground mine.

OCOEE RIVER

Continue south on TN 68 0.4 mile to US 64 and turn west following the general route of the Old Copper Road, which connected the mining operations in the Ducktown Basin with the nearest railroad in Cleveland to the west. In 1851–53 mostly Cherokee laborers built the road over which the ore wagons traveled.

US 64 follows the Ocoee River, a tributary of the Hiwassee River and one of the most popular white-water streams in the Southeast. A number of commercial outfitters along the way offer white-water rafting trips on the river. Reentering Cherokee National Forest, the highway is designated the **Ocoee Scenic Byway.**

The highway climbs the ridge of Little Frog Mountain, reaching Boyd Gap in 4.2 miles. A turnoff on the left leads to **Vista Point** with views to the west of the Ocoee River Valley. Down from the gap in 0.5 mile, a road to the left provides river access for the commercial outfitters running the upper part of the Ocoee. In another 0.4 mile a short road on the right leads to trailhead parking for the Rock Creek Trail that travels into the **Little Frog Mountain Wilderness** that lies north of the highway.

In another 0.8 mile turn left into the **Ocoee Whitewater Center,** where the white-water events for the 1996 Olympics were held. Now the focus for river and land recreation in the region, the center hosts white-water events and serves as an information center for visitors. The river channel was artificially enhanced for the Olympics, creating additional rapids to challenge paddlers. Walkways and foot bridges aid spectators in viewing the events, providing a mile-long walk along the river. Here is also a 2.4-mile segment of the original Old Copper Road, now maintained as a trail. On this trail you can walk upstream along the river to TVA's Ocoee Dam No. 3, which controls the waterflow in the river.

In 0.7 mile the service road rejoins US 64; continue west. In 0.9 mile TVA's **Ocoee No. 3 Powerhouse** stands beside the river. A tunnel brings water from the lake behind the dam upstream to the powerhouse downstream. The purpose in separating the two is to gain an advantage in elevation loss. The tunnel inclines only slightly while the river channel drops more noticeably; so by the time the water reaches the powerhouse, it is much higher above the ground than when it enters the tunnel upstream, creating the effect of a higher dam at the powerhouse. When electricity is needed, a valve is opened and water from the tunnel rushes down a huge pipe to generators in the powerhouse.

A road across the river and past the powerhouse becomes gravel and reaches a junction with the **Thunder Rock Campground** to the right (no hookups). To the left, FSR 45 leads to FSR 221, which borders the **Big Frog Wilderness** with several trailheads for access to this wilderness and **Cohutta Wilderness** to the south.

Return to US 64, and continue west along the Ocoee River. In 0.3 mile the **Rogers Branch River Access** is on the left at the top of **Ocoee Dam No. 2**; this access is the take-out for the upper run on the Ocoee. A ramp leading down the side of the 30-foot dam provides put-in for running the lower section of the river. Notice a large wooden flume on the far side of the dam. It carries water from the lake behind the dam downstream, gaining an advantage in elevation loss just like the tunnel for Ocoee No. 3. As you continue west on US 64, you'll have several places along the road to glimpse the flume as it passes along the edge of the river gorge, seemingly getting higher as the road and the river descend. In 4.9 miles **Ocoee No. 2 Powerhouse** rests across the river to the left, where water from the flume drops through huge pipes to generators at the powerhouse.

The road continues along Lake Ocoee (also called Parksville Lake) backed up by a third dam downstream. In 3 miles TN 30 turns to the right to

View from Chilhowee Mountain

Parksville Lake Campground (no hookups) and heads for Reliance, which is on the Railroads and Hiwassee River Drive.

Along US 64 to the west, in 0.5 mile, **Mac Point Beach** on the left provides for picnicking and lake swimming. Boat ramps provide lake access.

In 2 miles FSR 77 turns to the right to ascend Chilhowee Mountain on a branch of the Ocoee Scenic Byway. Several overlooks offer expansive views from the top of the mountain ridge west to the Great Valley of East Tennessee. This paved road ends in 7.6 miles at **Chilhowee Recreation Area** where trails lead into **Rock Creek Gorge Scenic Area.**

Just past the junction with FSR 77 lies the Ocoee Ranger Station where you can get information about the national forest. Continue west on US 64. **Parksville Beach** provides for more swimming, and the **Lake Ocoee Inn and Marina** stands at the edge of the lake.

In 2.5 miles **Ocoee Dam No. 1** stretches across the river, forming Lake Ocoee. In another 0.5 mile, a road to the left leads to a recreation area below the dam with walking trails, picnicking, and access to the river for fishing. Here is also a fascinating small-scale model of the Ocoee River that was used for planning when the channel was enhanced for Olympic white-water events.

US 64 leaves the national forest, passing more white-water outfitters, and in 2 miles crosses the Ocoee River, where the stream turns north to head for the Hiwassee. Continue west, entering Bradley County.

CHEROKEES' LAST STAND

In 11.8 miles US 64 reaches US 64/TN 60 Bypass around the City of Cleveland. US 64 continues straight into the town to the **Museum Center at Five Points,** a history museum of the Ocoee River region; turn right on Ocoee Street to explore the historic town center.

Back at the Bypass, turn southeast and travel for 2.3 miles, exiting onto TN 60 south. Passing through a rural countryside, turn right in 9.4 miles on Weatherly Switch Road, which is also TN 317. In 1.4 miles turn left on Red Clay Road, which leads 1.7 miles to the **Red Clay State Historic Area.** Here at a council house beside Blue Hole Spring, the Cherokees made their last stand.

With continuing pressure from whites to take the lands of the Overhill Cherokees, the Native Americans shifted their capital in 1825 from Chota to northern Georgia, calling their capital city "New Echota."

In 1830, with the support of the State of Georgia, Pres. Andrew Jackson pushed through Congress the Indian Removal Act that called for the remaining tribes in the east to relocate to Indian Territory west of the Mississippi River. Georgia passed especially egregious laws affecting Cherokees, forbidding them to dig for gold in the newly discovered gold fields on their own lands and banning all political activity other than meeting to consider removal.

Many in the American public were outraged at this treatment of the Cherokees, with voices raised in public meetings and editorials written deploring the actions of Georgia and the federal government. The Cherokees held their council for one year in Alabama and then relocated the capital to Red Clay in Tennessee. Here the council met from 1832 until 1838 under John Ross, who, though only one-eighth Cherokee, had been elected chief in 1828.

The Cherokees eventually were betrayed by a faction of their own people who thought it best to relocate to the west. The leaders of this faction, who were later assassinated, signed the Treaty of New Echota that called for the removal of the Cherokees. The treaty was ratified by the U.S. Congress in 1836, and when the deadline came in 1838 for the Cherokees to be gone, the U.S. Army rounded up the thousands who had not relocated. A few Cherokees escaped into the mountains, and some who had earlier relinquished their land claims and had become U.S. citizens were allowed to stay; these became the Eastern Band of the Cherokees, which still exists on the eastern side of the mountains in North Carolina.

The rest were marched to the west or were transported by river. An estimated 4,000 Cherokees died along the way from disease and cold weather, including the wife of Chief Ross. Because of the hardships and the unnecessary deaths, the route became known as the "Trail of Tears."

At the state historic area, an interpretive trail leads from the visitor center to the council spring. On a hillside, an eternal flame commemorates the struggle of the Principle People in these last days.

From this end of the drive, you can return to Cleveland or continue west on TN 317 to I–75.

2

Railroads and Hiwassee River

LENOIR CITY TO RELIANCE

GENERAL DESCRIPTION: This 66-mile drive follows routes of railroads that traveled down the Great Valley of East Tennessee and then turns into the Unaka Mountains along the scenic Hiwassee River.

SPECIAL ATTRACTIONS: Fort Loudoun Dam, Tellico Dam, Lenoir City, Loudon, Sweetwater, Niota, Athens, Etowah, Hiwassee State Scenic River, Cherokee National Forest, Reliance, Apalachia Powerhouse, historic homes and buildings, scenic views, fall color, hiking, biking, boating, fishing, hunting, and wildlife viewing.

LOCATION: East Tennessee. The drive begins at Lenoir City on US 11.

DRIVE ROUTE NUMBERS: US 11, TN 30, US 411, and TN 315.

CAMPING: Gee Creek Campground and Quinn Springs Campground.

SERVICES: All services at Lenoir City, Loudon, Sweetwater, Athens, and Etowah.

NEARBY ATTRACTIONS: Lost Sea, Englewood Textile Museum, Gee Creek Wilderness, Fort Marr, and Nancy Ward Gravesite.

THE DRIVE

The easiest way for railroads to pass through Tennessee is down the Great Valley of East Tennessee, which is traversed by the Tennessee River and its tributaries, including the Hiwassee River. The Hiwassee is one of the most scenic rivers in the state, flowing west out of the Unaka Mountains to its confluence with the Tennessee to the northwest. The river is a favorite fishing stream and a relatively easy float stream with just enough thrills to make it interesting but with plenty of time to just sit back and enjoy the scenery.

FORT LOUDOUN AND TELLICO DAMS

Begin this drive at Lenoir City, which is on US 11 southwest of Knoxville. From Exit 81 on I–75, take US 321 east 2.7 miles to an intersection with US

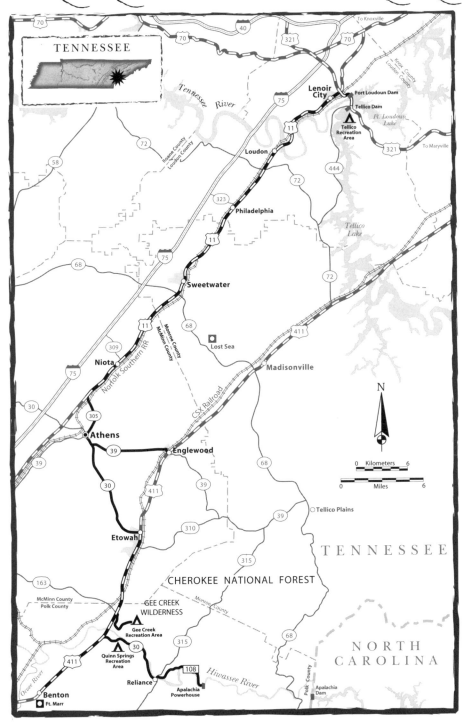

11. First stay straight on US 321, crossing railroad tracks; a right turn leads to TVA's **Fort Loudoun Dam** with overlooks of the lock and dam and the lake, a marina, a picnic area, and boat access for fishing.

Continue on US 321, crossing Fort Loudoun Dam to a junction with TN 444 in 1.2 miles. To the right, this highway crosses the Little Tennessee River in 0.9 mile below the infamous **Tellico Dam,** the last TVA dam, completed in 1979 at a time when most of the public thought no more dams were needed. Environmentalists fought completion of the dam, ostensibly to save an endangered fish, the snail darter, but lost the struggle when the U.S. Congress paved the way for TVA to finish the project by exempting it from the Endangered Species Act. Straight across TN 444 you can enter the **Tellico Recreation Area,** with boat access to Tellico Lake. A channel to the left links the two lakes; Tellico Dam has no electricity generators, so the water from Tellico Lake flows into Fort Loudoun Lake to help power the Fort Loudoun Dam generators.

LENOIR, LOUDON, AND NIOTA

Return down US 321 to US 11 and turn southwest into Lenoir City. In the early 1800s William B. Lenoir established several cotton mills here, which the Lenoir family operated until 1890. The property was then acquired by a group of developers who established Lenoir City Company to create a planned town that would take advantage of the proximity of the Tennessee River and the East Tennessee, Virginia, and Georgia Railroad that passed through the town, now part of the Norfolk-Southern Railroad.

Turn left on A Street and drive 1 block to Depot Street to the old town square where the **Lenoir City Museum** occupies the 1890 Lenoir City Company Office. To the left, past the fire hall, stands the **Lenoir House,** built by William Lenoir around 1820; the white brick home has been converted to apartments. Beside the house, a drive leads down to the site of the last Lenoir Cotton Mill, also built around 1820; the mill stood here until it burned in 1991.

Return to US 11, which is Broadway, and turn southwest to leave the city, entering the countryside. Before I–75 was constructed to the west, US 11 was a major north-south thoroughfare, called the Lee Highway after Confederate Gen. Robert E. Lee; now the highway sees less traffic. In 4.9 miles US 11 crosses the Tennessee River. To the right you can see a railroad trestle that was a strategic link between Knoxville and Chattanooga during the Civil War. When Confederates withdrew from Knoxville during Union Gen. Ambrose Burnside's invasion of East Tennessee in 1863, they crossed the river here and burned the bridge just before Union troops arrived. Later in the year, they burned the bridge a second time. After the war, the bridge was repaired and is still in use.

Immediately across the river, enter Loudon, a historic river town settled in the early 1800s. The Blair family were influential early settlers, and for a time the city was called Blairsville. The city was later renamed for historic Fort Loudoun located to the east.

US 11 enters the city as Mulberry Street. Turn left on Grove Street to pass in front of the **Loudon County Courthouse,** an Italianate structure built in 1872. Turn left on Cedar Street and left again to go behind the courthouse to parking. Near this spot you'll find the **Carmichael Inn.** The first part of this old stagecoach inn was constructed around 1810. The inn was originally located on the north side of the river, and so passengers were ferried across to spend the night and catch another coach north in the morning. To preserve the structure, the city moved the inn to this location and converted it to the **Loudon County Museum and Visitor Center.**

To the left of the inn stands the **Orme-Wilson Storehouse,** built around 1850 as one of the commercial buildings located on the Loudon waterfront. Steamboats plying the waters of the Tennessee stopped at Loudon to load and unload cargo in the busy river trade of the time. The river business declined when the East Tennessee and Georgia Railroad, later the East Tennessee, Virginia, and Georgia, was built through the community, crossing the river on the railroad trestle, which was built in 1855.

Back out on Cedar Street, continue north 2 blocks to Main Street and turn right along the old waterfront. On the right stands the two-story brick **Blair's Ferry Storehouse,** built around 1835. Blair's Ferry operated well into the 1900s, even after the highway bridge was constructed in 1927. The bridge had a toll charge until 1947, and for a while it was cheaper to ride the ferry than pay the toll.

Return to Mulberry Street (US 11) and turn left to pass through commercial and residential areas to leave town. To the southwest, enter pastoral Sweetwater Valley, which is drained by Sweetwater Creek, a tributary of the Tennessee River. The road through the valley passes large farms with barns, silos, and green fields. In 4.8 miles **Sweetwater Valley Farm** on the right makes its own Tennessee cheddar cheese and offers tours of its dairy and cheesemaking plant.

In 0.4 mile turn right on TN 323 and left on Elm Street to enter Philadelphia, settled in the 1820s but largely shaped by the railroad that came in the 1850s. Turn right on Christian Street to cross the railroad tracks and bear left into the old downtown of early 1900s commercial buildings facing the tracks. At Spring Street, turn left to recross the tracks and return to US 11 in 1.1 miles.

Continue southwest to enter Monroe County. In 3.9 miles cross the railroad, which shifts to the left side of the highway, and enter the outskirts of the Sweetwater community. In 0.5 mile you'll see **TMI Academy** to the right. A military school when it was founded in 1874, it relocated here in 1909. After the academy closed in the late 1900s, it became a Japanese high school. In 0.8 mile enter the old downtown at a junction with TN 322 to the left. A small park with a gazebo lies adjacent to the rail line; on the right notice the three-story brick **Masonic Lodge** built around 1875.

Leaving town, US 11 intersects with TN 68 in 1 mile. Here you can turn left and travel 4.9 miles to the **Lost Sea.** Designated a National Natural Landmark, this underground lake covers four and a half acres; tours include rides on glass-bottom boats.

US 11 reenters a countryside of large farms. In 1.8 miles turn right on a small lane to see the **Browder Memorial United Methodist Church,** a brick church with steeple built in 1888. This side lane rejoins US 11, entering McMinn County.

In 4.5 miles pass TN 309 to the right, and soon after, turn left on Burn Street to enter Niota. Bear left to the old commercial district with the **Niota Depot** beside the railroad tracks. Built by the East Tennessee and Georgia Railroad in 1854, this is the oldest depot in the state that's still standing. The brick building now houses the city hall, and the trains still come rolling by.

Return to US 11 and continue southwest, once more passing through farmland. In 2 miles the highway becomes four lanes as it approaches Athens. In another 0.6 mile watch on the left for the **Cleague House,** a brick structure with stepped gables. Built in 1826, it is now virtually abandoned. Samuel Cleague was an itinerant contractor from Virginia who built several homes in the Niota and Athens area.

ATHENS AND ETOWAH

In 0.9 mile turn left to enter Athens on TN 305, which is Ingleside Drive. In 1.4 miles notice the library on the left, an interesting modern construction in the shape of a barn. Turn left on Mayfield Lane to visit the **Mayfield Dairy,** where you can take tours of the milk production or just stop in for ice cream.

Ingleside continues into Athens, passing through a neighborhood of older homes to a junction with TN 30 in 1 mile. This drive will turn left here, but first stay straight across the highway onto Washington Avenue, which is also

TN 39. On the right, the Majestic Mansion Bed and Breakfast occupies the 1909 **Foster Home,** built by George Foster. In 2 blocks at the corner of Jackson Street, is the town square with the **Mcminn County Courthouse.** Turn right up Jackson; on the left is another **Cleague House.** In 1836 the house became the headquarters of the Hiwassee Railroad, which soon foundered in the economic depression of 1837; eventually the East Tennessee and Georgia Railroad assumed operations through the town. To the north, **Tennessee Wesleyan College** occupies this end of town; originally founded as the Athens Female College in 1857, it's now a coeducational institution. The original school building, **Old College,** still stands on the campus.

Return to the town square and continue west on Washington Avenue to the **Mcminn County Living Heritage Museum** on the right with three floors of exhibits on the region's history. You can continue out Madison and turn left on Keith Lane to see the **Keith House,** a Greek Revival mansion built in 1858 by a local farmer and businessman, Alexander Keith; the home now houses Woodlawn Bed-and-Breakfast.

Return through the center of Athens to the junction with TN 30, and turn right to continue this drive. In 1 mile TN 39 leads left for a side trip of 5.8 miles to Englewood. The **Englewood Textile Museum** tells the story of the textile industry in the region and the role of women in the workforce; textile manufacturing was one of the few industries that employed women in the 1800s and early 1900s.

Continue south on TN 30. In 9 miles, at a junction with US 411, turn right to enter downtown Etowah with older commercial buildings on the right. The **Gem Theater,** a 1927 movie house, has been converted to a performing arts theater and the home of the Gem Theater Players. This row of commercial buildings faces the rail line to the left in a traditional layout of a railroad town.

In the late 1800s a consolidation of railroads began as the Southern Railway took over several branch lines including the East Tennessee, Virginia, and Georgia Railroad. The L & N Railroad, which had enjoyed a dominant position in the South, felt threatened and began their "March to Georgia," creating a new line that ran virtually parallel with the old East Tennessee, Virginia, and Georgia Railroad through Tennessee. Etowah was created as an administrative center for this new route, and here the L & N constructed maintenance shops, roundhouses where locomotives were repaired, freight depots, and a magnificent passenger depot, which still stands on the left in the center of town, surrounded by expansive grounds. Constructed in 1906, the renovated **L & N Depot** houses a railroad museum. The grounds include a walkway along the rail line, now owned by CSX, and a bandstand constructed

Nancy Ward Gravesite

of stone in 1937 that is still the focus of community events.

Continue southwest on US 411. To the left stands the main range of the Unaka Mountains. In 4.3 miles enter Polk County. In 0.8 mile, in the community of Delano, watch for a turn to **Gee Creek Wilderness** to the left. Here you can follow a rough paved road and then a gravel road 2 miles to this wilderness area with hiking trails in **Cherokee National Forest.**

In another 0.6 mile on US 411, you can turn left for 1.1 miles to the **Gee Creek Recreation Area** with a campground on the Hiwassee River (no hookups). On US 411, cross the **Hiwassee Scenic River.** In another 1.1 miles this drive turns left on TN 30 along the river, but you can first stay straight on US 411 for a side trip to Benton. In 6.4 miles pass the **Polk County Courthouse** in the town center. In 0.6 mile on the left stands **Fort Marr,** one of the last two known blockhouses remaining in Tennessee; the other is Swaggerty Blockhouse in the northeast section of the state. Built in 1814, Fort Marr was originally located on the old federal road that ran from the Tellico Blockhouse into northern Georgia; the fort stood near the present-day community of Old Fort on TN 68.

In another 1.1 miles on US 411, cross the Ocoee River, a tributary of the Hiwassee, and turn left to the **Nancy Ward Gravesite** at the top of a knoll. Nancy Ward was born in 1738 of a Cherokee woman and a man who is unknown; perhaps he was a British trader, perhaps an Indian from another tribe. Her Cherokee name was *Nanye'hi*. She married a Cherokee warrior, and when he fell in battle in 1755, Nanye'hi took up his weapons and fought alongside the men. For her actions, she became a prominent "War Woman" and later a "Beloved Woman" who assisted the elders in ceremonies and negotiations. A Beloved Woman had the authority to free prisoners, a right she practiced frequently to protect whites who had been captured; she even warned white settlements of imminent attacks. Despite these actions, she remained a Beloved Woman to her people. She married Bryan Ward, a British trader, and eventually moved to this location near Benton where she operated an inn and stock pen at a ford of the Ocoee River. She died in 1822 and was buried on this hill along with her son and a brother.

HIWASSEE SCENIC RIVER

Return northeast on US 411 to TN 30 and turn east to continue this drive. The road enters Cherokee National Forest in 1.4 miles. **Quinn Springs Recreation Area** on the right has a picnic area and campground (no hookups). One of the prettiest drives in the state, TN 30 winds along the Hiwassee River into the mountains. Be aware that this is a narrow roadway. Pull-outs beside the road offer access to the river, a popular float stream that's also known for trout fishing.

In 4 miles enter the community of Reliance with the **Vaughn-Webb House** on the right, a two-story frame house constructed in the 1880s. Joseph Vaughn arrived in the small farming and lumber community in 1880, purchased farmland, and constructed this house for his family. Mail for the community was dropped off at the Vaughn house where Vaughn's wife, Sara, was the "keeper of the mail"; Sara probably gave the community its name. A daughter of the Vaughns married into the Webb family and subsequently lived in the home. In 0.3 mile reach the center of the community at a junction with TN 315 where the **Webb Brothers' Store** stands at the junction. Grandsons of Joseph and Sara Vaughn, the Webbs first opened a store here in 1936. That business now occupies a 1955 building.

This drive turns left on TN 315, but first stay straight on TN 30 to see the **Hiwassee Union Church and Masonic Hall** on the left, built in 1899. The church met in the first floor and the Masons on the second floor of this frame building until the mid-1960s. Just beyond the church, a road on the left leads to **Hiwassee Outfitters** that runs raft and canoe trips on the river.

Return to TN 315 and cross the Hiwassee Scenic River on a highway bridge. On the other side, cross railroad tracks. In the late 1800s the L & N Railroad constructed a branch line through the community to connect its main line at Etowah with Ducktown to the east, which was the center of the flourishing copper mining industry. The rail line, which crosses the river upstream, has been abandoned by CSX, but local officials hope to come up with an alternative use.

On this side of the river, turn right where just at this corner stands the 1891 **Watchman's House.** In earlier days an attendant here would watch for fires on the wooden railroad bridge when the coal-fired engines would cross, spewing hot cinders; barrels of water stood ready to douse the flames. Soon after on the left stands the **Higdon Hotel,** built around 1889 by Calvin Higdon. This two-story frame building provided accommodations for rail personnel and visitors to the mountains. Higdon also operated a ferry across the river.

In 0.6 mile the **Childers Creek Recreation Area** lies on the right at the confluence of Childers Creek with the Hiwassee; there's access to the river. Here you'll find the beginning of the John Muir Trail, which crosses a footbridge over the creek and travels upstream along the Hiwassee Scenic River 18 miles east to connect with TN 68 and the Overhill Country Drive.

In another 0.7 mile turn right on Forest Service Road 108 to continue along the Hiwassee with picnic areas and boat access. In 3.4 miles the road ends at a turnaround at TVA's **Apalachia Powerhouse;** a tunnel brings water to the powerhouse from Apalachia Lake, created by Apalachia Dam about 10 miles upstream on the Hiwassee.

This drive ends here with no connecting roads, so you must return the way you came to Reliance. From Reliance, return along TN 30 to US 411. You may also turn southwest on TN 30 to reach US 64 and join the Overhill Country Drive in 10 miles.

③

Great Smoky Mountains

MARYVILLE TO CLINGMANS DOME

GENERAL DESCRIPTION: This 60-mile drive travels through Appalachian foothills and ascends the Unaka Range to the highest peak in Great Smoky Mountains National Park with some of the best views in the southeast.

SPECIAL ATTRACTIONS: Maryville, Townsend, Great Smoky Mountains National Park, The Sinks, Metcalf Bottoms, Elkmont, Chimney Tops, Newfound Gap, Clingmans Dome, historic homes and buildings, scenic views, fall color, hiking, biking, and wildlife viewing.

LOCATION: East Tennessee. The drive begins in Maryville on TN 35.

DRIVE ROUTE NUMBERS: US 321; TN 73, and Laurel Creek, Little River, and Newfound Gap Roads.

CAMPING: Look Rock, Abrams Creek, Cades Cove, and Elkmont Campgrounds (no hookups).

SERVICES: All services at Maryville and Gatlinburg.

NEARBY ATTRACTIONS: Sam Houston Schoolhouse, Foothills Parkway, Tuckaleechee Caverns, Tremont, and Cades Cove.

THE DRIVE

As the Appalachian Mountains extend into the southern United States, the numerous peaks split into two ranges, with the Blue Ridge extending into North Carolina and the Unaka Range running along the border of Tennessee with North Carolina. In the central part of the Unaka Range stand the Great Smoky Mountains. With the distant peaks appearing in a blue haze, the Cherokees called these mountains Shaconaqe, "place of blue smoke." Recognizing the special scenic value of these mountains, the federal government established here one of the first two national parks in the eastern United States, setting aside 520,000 acres in Great Smoky Mountains

3 GREAT SMOKY MOUNTAINS

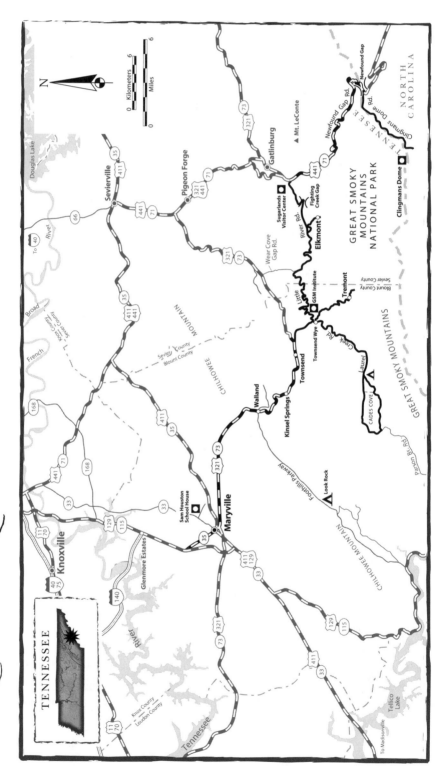

National Park, including the main range of the Unakas with sixteen peaks rising above 6,000 feet. This is America's playground, the most visited national park in the country, with some of the best scenery and some of the best hiking and backpacking in the East.

MARYVILLE

Begin this drive at Maryville, which is 17 miles south of Knoxville on Alcoa Highway, which is also US 129. Past McGhee-Tyson Airport, US 129 turns off to the right while TN 35 curves left to pass through the community of Alcoa, a town created by the Aluminum Company of America, which has a huge plant nearby. TN 35 becomes Washington Street in Maryville and reaches a junction with US 411 to the west and TN 33 to the northeast. The Blount County Chamber of Commerce is on the right just beyond the junction.

You can turn east on TN 33, which is also East Broadway Avenue, for a side trip to the **Sam Houston Schoolhouse.** In 4.2 miles turn right on Sam Houston School Road. In 2.3 miles turn left to reach the schoolhouse. A small museum and gift shop occupies a former residence; the small log schoolhouse rests at the end of a walk at the back of the property next to a spring from which the schoolchildren dipped their drinking water.

Born in Virginia, Sam Houston arrived in Tennessee at the age of thirteen and settled with his widowed mother, brothers, and sisters south of Maryville. Not long after, he ran away to live with the Cherokees at their village on Hiwassee Island at the confluence of the Hiwassee River with the Tennessee River. Later returning to Maryville, he taught school for the 1812 term at this little log schoolhouse. He served as Tennessee's governor from 1827 until he resigned in 1829, probably despondent over his new wife leaving to return home to her parents. Houston lived again with a group of Cherokees who had relocated to the West before heading for Texas where he commanded revolutionary troops that won their freedom from Mexico. Houston became president of the Texas Republic and, after Texas became a state, U.S. senator and governor.

Return to Maryville and turn north again on Washington Street; travel 1 block and turn left down Parham Street, where you'll find parking on the left for the **Maryville-Alcoa Greenway,** which runs 9 miles from Alcoa through Maryville along Pistol Creek. Turn right on Harper Avenue, and in 0.3 mile turn left down Cusick Street to the town square with the 1906 **Blount County Courthouse.** Turn left on Court Circle to a junction with Court Street; turn right on Court and travel 1 block to Lamar Alexander Parkway (US 321), named for Maryville's native son who served as governor of Tennessee and was later U.S. Secretary of Education. Turn left, passing **Maryville College** on the hill to the right; a private school founded in 1819, the college was one of the first schools in the south to accept Native Americans, women, and African Americans. You can turn into the entrance to see **Anderson Hall** on the left, a Second Empire building erected in 1869.

In 0.3 mile the parkway merges with Washington Street and continues to the east. In another 0.4 mile the **Thompson-Brown House** stands on the right; an old two-story log home, it houses the Keep Blount Beautiful organization. Continue southeast on US 321, leaving Maryville. In 5 miles look ahead to the Great Smoky Mountains towering above the foothills.

WALLAND

In 2.3 miles enter the small community of Walland, once the site of the Schlosser Tannery, established in 1900. A rail line was needed to bring the hides from meatpacking houses of the Midwest and to transport the tanned hides to market. The Knoxville and Augusta Railway was extended from Maryville to Walland to serve this need; US 321 basically follows the route of the old railway. Bark from black oak and chestnut trees supplied the tannin that was needed for the tanning process. With the number of hides the tannery expected to process, they needed a large supply of bark. So the founder and general manager of the tannery, John W. Fisher, encouraged lumbermen from Pennsylvania to come to the mountains to supply his tanbark. The group, headed by Col. W. B. Townsend, was amazed at the untouched forests of the Smokies and soon established the Little River Lumber Company to not only supply tanbark to the Schlosser Tannery but to produce lumber for the growing nation. To transport the lumber and bark, the company chartered the Little River Railroad as a common carrier to run from Walland into the mountains.

Continue southeast on US 321, entering the foothills of the Smokies while following the old route of the Little River Railroad. In 1.5 miles you can take a side trip on the **Foothills Parkway** to the west, which runs along the border of the national park. This section climbs Chilhowee Mountain for 11 miles to Look Rock, a prominent peak with an observation tower offering a wide-ranging view of the Smokies. Nearby lie a picnic area and campground (no hookups). Another 7 miles to the west, the parkway ends at US 129 on Chilhowee Lake on the Little Tennessee River. There you can turn left a short distance to Happy Valley Road on the left that leads to the **Abrams Creek Ranger Station and Campground** (no hookups).

Retracing your route back to US 321, continue on US 321 past the Foothills Parkway. In 1.5 miles there's a picnic area beside the river. In 2.6

miles the highway enters Kinsel Springs, a small community that is the gateway to Tuckaleechee Cove, a valley in the foothills of the Smokies. Another roadside picnic area stretches along the river to the left.

TOWNSEND

In 1.7 miles enter the community of Townsend, which bills itself as the "peaceful side of the Smokies," in contrast to the bustling communities of Pigeon Forge and Gatlinburg to the east. You can turn right on Old Tuckaleechee Road and follow the signs to **Tuckaleechee Caverns;** tours include onyx formations and the Big Room.

On US 321 continue into Townsend, the former lumber town of the Little River Lumber Company and named for Col. W. B. Townsend. In 0.9 mile the **Little River Railroad and Lumber Company Museum** lies on the left at the site of the Townsend Mill, where giant old-growth trees hauled out of the Smokies were cut into lumber. The museum includes in its collection the old depot that was relocated from Walland and Shay Engine No. 2147 that operated on Little River Railroad. The Little River Lumber Company operated from 1902 to 1939, producing 560 million board feet of lumber. In 1926, the company sold 80,000 acres of its mountain land to the State of Tennessee for the establishment of the Great Smoky Mountains National Park, although the company retained the right to harvest timber for another fifteen years.

In 0.4 mile the Townsend Visitor Center stands on the right. You can stop here for information about the area, including the timing of spring and fall festivals. A paved bike trail paralleling the road to the right offers an easy ride through the community.

NATIONAL PARK

In 0.6 mile US 321 turns to the left into Wear Cove. Stay straight on TN 73 for 1.8 miles to enter **Great Smoky Mountains National Park,** and in another 0.6 mile, reach the Townsend Wye at the forks of the Little River, with Little River Road to the left and Laurel Creek Road to the right. Just before the Wye is parking on the left for access to Little River, a popular swimming and tubing spot on hot summer afternoons. Across the road from the parking area is the Chestnut Top Trail that for the first half mile is one of the best spring wildflower trails in the park.

At the Wye, this drive turns left on Little River Road, but you can first turn right on Laurel Creek Road, following the West Prong of Little River toward Cades Cove. The West Prong and Laurel Creek drainage was the first to be timbered by the Little River Lumber Company.

In 0.2 mile on Laurel Creek Road, cross the Middle Prong of Little River just above its confluence with the West Prong. On the other side, you can turn left to **Tremont,** the site of a former lumber camp. In 1926 the tracks of the Little River Railroad were extended up the Middle Prong watershed, the last area to be cut by the company. The road into Tremont crosses the Middle Prong twice and in 2.2 miles reaches a left turn into the **Great Smoky Mountains Institute at Tremont,** an educational facility offering workshops about the natural and cultural resources of the Great Smoky Mountains for school groups and adults. A visitor center offers information about the institute and the park.

Beyond the institute turn, the road becomes gravel as it follows the old logging railbed. During the time of the lumbering operations, steam-powered skidders dragged logs down the mountain slopes where steam-powered loaders stacked the logs on the railroad cars. The gear-driven Shay steam engines, which could handle the steep grades, hauled the logs down into the flats along the main line where the loaded cars were switched to the more typical rod and piston engines for the trip to Townsend. The road ends in 3.2 miles at the site of the old community of Tremont. Car shacks once lined the railway where worker families lived; these were portable houses that could be loaded on railroad cars and moved to the next location where timber was to be cut. The community included an all-purpose civic building that served as a school, church, and movie theater. From the end of the road, the Middle Prong Trail crosses a bridge over Lynn Camp Prong and follows the creek, passing **Lynn Camp Prong Cascades** in 0.3 mile.

Return to Laurel Creek Road and continue to the southwest for 7.4 miles, reaching **Cades Cove,** a valley in the mountains that once supported a large agricultural community. The park preserves several pioneer structures as a historic exhibit representing early settlement of the mountains. At a junction to the left lies a picnic area and the Cades Cove Campground (no hookups), where there is a camp store and a horse stable that offers guided horse rides.

Straight ahead from the junction is parking on the left that's a staging area for the beginning of the Cades Cove Loop Road, an 11-mile one-way loop through the cove. This is one of the finest scenic drives in the southern United States, but on a spring or fall weekend the road can be clogged with traffic; so come on a weekday if possible. On Saturday and Wednesday mornings, the road is closed to motorized vehicles until 10:00 A.M. so you can bicycle without worrying about traffic; you can rent bicycles at the camp store. Along the loop are several historic structures representing the early

John Oliver Cabin

settlement of the valley, including several churches and pioneer cabins, such as the **John Oliver Cabin;** John and Lucretia Oliver, with their daughter, Polly, were the first white settlers in Cades Cove; when they came in 1818, they first lived in an abandoned Indian hut but in 1820 built the log cabin that still stands today. Trails lead off from the loop; the most popular is the Abrams Falls Trail, which travels 2.5 miles to 20-foot **Abrams Falls** on Abrams Creek, which is the main drainage for the cove.

LITTLE RIVER ROAD

Return to the Townsend Wye and head northeast on Little River Road. In 3.1 miles the road passes under a rock overhang called "Indian Head," which it resembles when viewed from a distance. In another mile the road crosses a bridge over Little River.

In 0.8 mile a pull-out on the right offers a view of the confluence of Meigs Creek with Little River. Just upstream, the creek drops 30 feet over a rock shelf, forming **Meigs Creek Falls.** In another 1.1 miles the road crosses the river again. There's a parking area on the right for **the Sinks,** a drop in the river that produces a churning pool, as if a stopper has been pulled out of a sink of water. During the logging days, the riverbed here was dynamited to break up a log jam; the resulting blast cut a new channel across a meander of the river, creating this drop in the riverbed. From the parking area, you can walk to viewing spots above the Sinks; take care among the rocks at the edge. This is also the beginning of the Meigs Creek Trail, which follows Meigs Creek upstream.

In another 2 miles along Little River Road, **Metcalf Bottoms Picnic Area** lies on the left. You can pass through the picnic area on Wear Cove Gap Road, crossing Little River for access to the Metcalf Bottoms Trail on the right, which leads 0.6 mile up the mountain to the **Little Greenbrier Schoolhouse,** a log structure built in 1882 and used as both school and church. You can also drive to the school by continuing up the road for 0.5 mile and turning right on a narrow lane to its end in another 0.5 mile. From the schoolhouse, you can continue your walk up the mountain on the Little Brier Gap Trail for 1.2 miles to the **Walker Sisters' Cabin.** Five daughters of John and Margaret Walker continued to live in the cabin after the national park was established, preferring the pioneer existence to which they were accustomed. The last of the sisters died in 1964.

Continue east on Little River Road, crossing Little River again in 2.4 miles. In another 2.5 miles turn right on Elkmont Road, which was the original route of the Little River Railroad.

This watershed of the main stem of Little River comprised more than half of the Little River Company landholdings and so served as the major timbering area of the company for two decades. Construction of the railroad up the gorge of Little River from the Townsend Wye began in 1906 and was completed in 1908 as it reached Elkmont, a newly constructed company town. From there, rail lines snaked up Mids Branch, Little River, and Jakes Creek to bring logs down the mountain to sidings at Elkmont where the loaded cars were switched from the geared engines to rod and piston engines for the long haul to the mill at Townsend. In addition to railroad and lumbering facilities, the Elkmont camp contained housing for the workers and shops and offices.

In 1.2 miles along Elkmont Road, the remains of the **Wonderland Hotel** stand on the knoll to the left at the top of a flight of stone stairs. When the Little River Railroad began operating, it was not long before visitors arrived by train to view the logging operations and to enjoy a day in the mountains. By 1912 the Wonderland Hotel was completed to accommodate these sightseers. In 1919 a group of businessmen purchased the hotel and formed the Wonderland Club, selling memberships that included a lot on which to build a cabin. In the 1920s the hotel was sold to the state for inclusion in the national park, and the owners were given a lifetime lease. In exchange for being allowed to upgrade the facilities, this lease was later swapped for two twenty-year leases, which ran out in 1992 when the owners had to vacate the property. The hotel is now abandoned.

In 0.4 mile Elkmont Road reaches a junction where the Elkmont Campground lies straight ahead. You can continue into the old Elkmont community by turning left and following the road around the campground. In 0.3 mile parking on the left gives access to the 0.7-mile Elkmont Nature Trail, which wanders up Mids Branch, the first area logged at Elkmont.

In another 0.3 mile cross Little River, and in 0.1 mile reach a fork in the road. The left fork is now closed and is part of the Little River Trail that follows Little River into the mountains; the river is one of the best trout fishing streams in the park. The trail passes through the **Elkmont Cabins,** an area that was part of the Wonderland Club where members built their summer homes. These cabins were bought by the state for the national park; owners were also given lifetime leases and were involved in the lease exchanges that expired in 1992. The cabins are now abandoned.

Take the right fork to pass through more of the cabins. At a junction, you can turn left to reach the end of the road and trailhead parking for the Jakes Creek Trail. On the left, stone pillars still mark the entrance to the site of Happy

Landings, the home of W. B. and Alice Townsend, which burned; across the road is the carriage house, which in later years was converted to a residence.

At the junction, turn right on a one-way lane to pass through a street of cabins where a second group, the Appalachian Club, constructed rows of cabins that came to be called "Club Town." In 0.1 mile, the road loops down to the Elkmont Road. Turn left to leave the area, returning to Little River Road. Turn right to continue northeast.

In 0.5 mile, a pull-out on the left gives access to a quiet walkway. Several of these walkways are scattered along the roads through the national park to encourage visitors to take a stroll in the woods. The road then ascends a ridge, reaching **Fighting Creek Gap** in 0.7 mile. On the right, the 12.3-mile Sugarland Mountain Trail climbs the mountain to the crest of the Smokies. To the left, the Laurel Falls Trail leads 1.3 miles to the 75-foot two-step **Laurel Falls** and heads on up the mountain, passing through old-growth forest of tulip poplars and hemlocks.

Little River Road descends from Fighting Creek Gap. In 0.4 mile a series of three overlooks form **Maloney Point,** named for Frank Maloney, an early proponent of the national park and a civil engineer who participated in designating the proposed park boundaries. The view takes in the valley of Fighting Creek.

Little River Road continues descending the mountainside, eventually leveling out in the bottomlands. In 2.5 miles **Sugarlands Visitor Center** lies on the left. Here you can get information about the park and view exhibits on the natural history of the Great Smoky Mountains. Behind the visitor center, you can walk the 1-mile Fighting Creek Nature Trail that visits the **John Owenby Cabin** along Fighting Creek.

NEWFOUND GAP ROAD

Little River Road ends at a junction with Newfound Gap Road. To the left, you can reach the community of Gatlinburg in 1.8 miles. Turn right to continue this drive, passing up Sugarlands Valley, named for the once numerous sugar maple trees that yielded sap for making maple syrup. In 0.4 mile parking on the left gives access to the 0.5-mile Sugarlands Valley Nature Trail, a universally accessible path that loops by the edge of the West Prong of Little Pigeon River.

At **Campbell Overlook** in 1.8 miles, two overlooks offer views of Mount LeConte, a prominent mountain that stands apart from the main range of the Smokies. At 6,593 feet, it is the third highest peak in the park. LeConte Lodge at the summit is accessible only by long hikes of several miles; reservations are required long in advance. This overlook is named for Carlos Campbell, an early park supporter.

In 2.4 miles, in a curve to the left, the **Chimney Tops Picnic Area** lies on the right. The picnic area contains the 0.8-mile Cove Hardwood Nature Trail, which passes through an old-growth forest and, in spring, an abundance of wildflowers. The picnic area is named for two prominent peaks where bare rock juts above the trees. Early settlers thought the summits looked like cabin chimneys rising above surrounding forest. At **Chimney Tops Overlook** in 0.8 mile, three pull-outs offer views of the mountain peaks.

In 1.4 miles Newfound Gap Road passes through a short tunnel. On the right in another 0.3 mile, trailhead parking gives access to the Chimney Tops Trail, a steep 2-mile hike to the summit of **Chimney Tops.**

The road loops over itself in 0.2 mile in a 360-degree curve popularly called "The Loop." This construction was necessary to lessen the steep grade up the mountain.

In 1.5 miles two parking areas on the left give access to the Alum Cave Bluffs Trail, which travels up the side of Mount LeConte, passing the giant overhang of **Alum Cave** and reaching the summit and LeConte Lodge in 4.9 miles.

As Newfound Gap Road climbs higher into the mountains, the road passes from cove and northern hardwood forests into a spruce-fir forest. The evergreen red spruce and Fraser fir dominate the higher elevations of the mountains, but these trees are in decline because of the double impacts of air pollution and insect infestation. Red spruce tries to hold its own against acid rain while nearly all the mature Fraser fir have been killed by the balsam woolly adelgid.

From **Morton Overlook** in 3.7 miles, a panoramic view looks down on the valley of the West Prong of Little Pigeon River, with Anakeesta Ridge on the right and Sugarland Mountain to the left. The overlook is named for Ben Morton, another early supporter of the national park.

In 0.7 mile the road reaches the top of the Smokies range at **Newfound Gap.** At one time, other gaps in the mountain were thought to be lower. But in the 1850s this gap was "newly found" to be the lowest gap along the ridge-line. A large parking area here overlooks the North Carolina side of the mountains. In 1940, Pres. Franklin D. Roosevelt stood on the stone platform to the left of the parking area during the park's dedication ceremonies; the structure is called Rockefeller Memorial to commemorate a large donation from the Rockefeller Foundation for the purchase of lands for the national park. The Appalachian Trail, which follows the ridgeline through the park, passes through Newfound Gap as it travels 2,100 miles from Maine to Georgia.

The Great Smoky Mountains

CLINGMANS DOME ROAD

Where Newfound Gap Road heads southeast down the mountain, turn right on Clingmans Dome Road, which follows the border with North Carolina along the ridgeline of the Smokies. This road is closed in winter, beginning with the first snowfall.

On the left in 2.7 miles, the 0.5-mile Spruce-Fir Nature Trail takes you through a remnant of the high-elevation spruce-fir forest. In another mile, parking on the left is the trailhead for the Fork Ridge Trail that descends off the ridgeline into an old-growth forest of red spruce and hemlock in 2 miles.

Clingmans Dome Road ends in 3.3 miles at a parking area on Forney Ridge. Here a 0.5-mile paved path leads steeply up to the summit of **Clingmans Dome,** at 6,643 feet the highest peak in the national park and in the entire range of the Unaka Mountains. The peak is named for Thomas L. Clingman, a U.S. congressman who explored this region in the 1850s.

At the summit, an observation tower carries you above the surrounding trees for a 360-degree view of the Great Smoky Mountains. Here, seemingly innumerable mountain peaks and a host of plants and animals create a parkland that is one of the most scenic and most biologically diverse regions in all of North America. The national park possesses one hundred kinds of trees, 1,500 species of flowering plants, sixty-one mammals, and 200 bird species in addition to other plants and animals. Over the years it has become the crown jewel of eastern national parks.

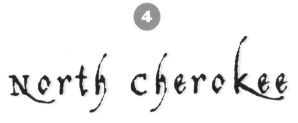

North cherokee

SYCAMORE SHOALS TO HIGHLANDS OF ROAN LOOP

GENERAL DESCRIPTION: This 127-mile drive travels from the site of three important events in Tennessee history through national forest lands around Watauga Lake to the Highlands of Roan.

SPECIAL ATTRACTIONS: Sycamore Shoals State Historic Area, Elizabethton, Cherokee National Forest, Shady Valley, Mountain City, Watauga Lake, Roan Mountain State Park, Highlands of Roan Scenic Area, historic homes and buildings, scenic views, fall color, hiking, biking, boating, fishing, hunting, and wildlife viewing.

LOCATION: Upper East Tennessee. The drive begins at Johnson City on I–181.

DRIVE ROUTE NUMBERS: US 321 and 19E; TN 91 and 133; US 421; TN 167, 67, 173, and 107.

CAMPING: Watauga Dam Campground, Backbone Rock Campground, Johnson County Campground, Cardens Bluff Campground, Dennis Cove Campground, Roan Mountain State Park, Limestone Cove Campground, and Rock Creek Campground.

SERVICES: All services at Johnson City, Elizabethton, and Mountain City.

NEARBY ATTRACTIONS: Watauga Dam, Backbone Rock Recreation Area, Laurel Bloomery, Trade, and Erwin.

THE DRIVE

Along the border with North Carolina, open grasslands stretch along the ridgeline of the Unaka Range at a mountain fastness called the "Highlands of Roan." These mountain lands that make up the northern section of Cherokee National Forest served as the gateway from North Carolina and Virginia into the western frontier. Settlers at the foot of the mountains established the first independent government of Europeans on the continent, the forerunner of the State of Tennessee.

ELIZABETHTON

Begin at Johnson City, which is at the edge of the North District of Cherokee National Forest. From Exit 31 on I–181 on the southeast side of

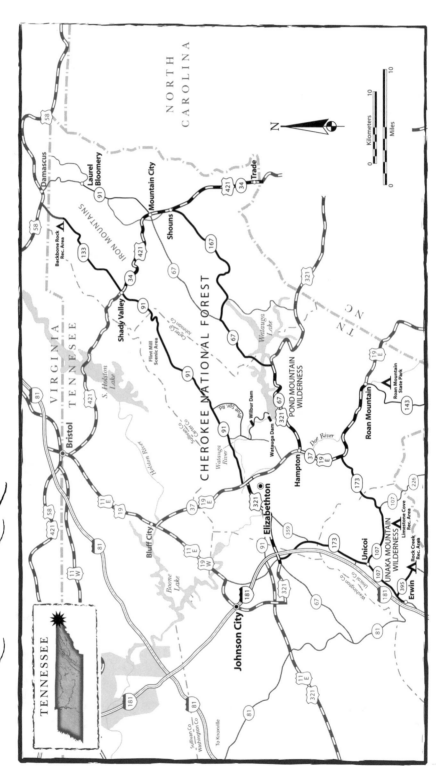

the city, turn northeast on US 321 toward Elizabethton. In 1.3 miles enter Carter County, and in another 3.5 miles notice **Sabine Hill** on the right. This two-story frame house was completed in 1818 by Mary Patton Taylor, the widow of Nathaniel Taylor. Her great-grandsons Robert and Alfred Taylor were both governors of Tennessee.

Just beyond Sabine Hill is a junction with TN 362 to the right and TN 91 to the left; stay straight on US 321. On the left stands a wing of a house where Pres. Andrew Johnson died on July 31, 1875, after suffering a stroke. This was part of the home of his daughter in Elizabethton, which has been moved to this location.

In 1.5 miles turn left into **Sycamore Shoals State Historic Area.** One of the most historic sites in Tennessee, Sycamore Shoals saw three significant events in the early history of the state: formation of the Watauga Association, the Transylvania Purchase, and the muster for the Battle of Kings Mountain.

When Britain still controlled the thirteen colonies, it designated a boundary at the top of the Unaka Mountains as the western border of North Carolina. To the west was Indian land, and whites were not to settle there. Yet families came, south from Virginia and west over the mountains from North Carolina, stopping in what they disingenuously declared they thought was part of Virginia. They settled along the Watauga River, and at Sycamore Shoals, a frequently used ford, they built Fort Watauga. The settlers banded together in 1772 in the Watauga Association, the first independent government established by Europeans on the North American continent. The Association preceded by four years the formation of the United States. After the United States formed, the Association petitioned to become part of the new State of North Carolina, and in 1777, the Watauga and surrounding settlements became Washington County. When North Carolina ceded its western lands to the federal government, the Watauga country became part of the Southwest Territory and, in 1796, the State of Tennessee.

In 1775 Judge Richard Henderson, representing the Transylvania Company, arrived at Sycamore Shoals to negotiate a land purchase with the Cherokees; 1,200 members of the Nation arrived to participate in the negotiations, which resulted in the sale of 20 million acres between the Kentucky and the Cumberland Rivers for a trifling sum of 10,000 pounds in money and goods. A contingent of Cherokees objected to the deal because they saw the semblance of a purchase as a first step in the eventual occupation of all Indian lands. Dragging Canoe, who would later lead the Chickamauga faction in a war against the whites, withdrew from the negotiations, warning the whites were purchasing a "dark and bloody ground." The purchase was actually illegal; only the British Crown could purchase land from the Native Americans. Henderson sent Daniel Boone to blaze the Wilderness Trail through Cumberland Gap for the settlement of Kentucky. But the Virginia colony refused to recognize Henderson's claim to the land. He then sent James Robertson and John Donelson on their historic journeys to the Cumberland River to the west and the founding of Nashville.

Sycamore Shoals was also the gathering place for a battle that was a turning point in the Revolutionary War. When the fighting began at Lexington and Concord, the Wataugans were determined to defend the western frontier. Major Patrick Ferguson, commander of the left wing of Cornwallis's army and of Tory militia, sent a message to the frontier that if the settlers did not "desist from their opposition," he would "hang their leaders and lay waste their country." In response, 1,100 frontiersman mustered at Sycamore Shoals on September 25, 1780, and, led by John Sevier and Isaac Shelby, went in search of Major Ferguson. They found Ferguson's army on October 7 at Kings Mountain, South Carolina. In a battle that lasted just over an hour, the ragtag army of frontiersmen soundly defeated the British, with Major Ferguson dying in the fight. The Battle of Kings Mountain is thought to be an essential victory that with subsequent events led to the surrender of the British and the independence of the United States. The route these "overmountain" men took from Sycamore Shoals to Kings Mountains is now designated the Overmountain Victory National Historic Trail, which consists of a motor route and hiking trails.

For these three events, Sycamore Shoals has been designated a state historic area. A reconstructed Fort Watauga stands on the grounds, and a graveled path leads along the Watauga River to Sycamore Shoals, a relatively shallow crossing of the river marked with rapids. The shoals likely gave the name to the river, which came from a Creek word, *wetoga*, meaning "broken waters."

Continue on US 321 into the community of Elizabethton. In 1.3 miles, where US 321 turns to the left, stay straight on East Elk Avenue into the old downtown. The avenue curves left into the commercial center with buildings dating from the late 1800s and early 1900s. At an intersection with Riverside Drive, just before a bridge crossing of the Doe River, a riverfront park stretches along this tributary of the Watauga, and to the right the **Doe River Covered Bridge** spans the river. Constructed in 1882, the 134-foot-long bridge is still in use, supporting vehicles up to three tons. Covered bridges were once quite common, the covering added to protect the bridge from

Doe River Covered Bridge

weathering and to prevent horses from getting agitated while crossing water. This bridge is one of the few still in use in the state.

Stay straight on East Elk Avenue to cross the river to reach the **Soldiers' Monument** on the courthouse square, a 60-foot monolith erected in 1912 to honor Carter County soldiers. The **Carter County Courthouse** stands to the left, originally built in the 1850s and altered over time. Continue east on East Elk. Notice the **Alfred Moore Carter House** on the left, an 1819 Greek Revival home; Carter's son, Samuel was both a major general in the U.S. Army and later a rear admiral in the U.S. Navy. During the Civil War, as an officer in the Union Army, he led raids into his home state.

At a junction with US 321 at the end of the block, you can stay straight across to the chamber of commerce, which is in a small park with picnic area and walking trail. Turn left on US 321/19E to a junction with US 321 to the left and US 19E straight ahead. Turn right on Old Route 91 to the **Carter Mansion** on the left. John Carter settled first in Carter Valley along the Holston River and then here along the Watauga. When the Watauga Association was formed, Carter was elected chairman of the five-member court that carried out the duties of government. He built this home in the years 1775 to 1780. The mansion is thought to be the oldest frame house in Tennessee. When Carter died in 1781, his son Landon occupied the home with his wife, Elizabeth, for whom Elizabethton is named. When Carter

County was carved out of Washington County, it was named for Landon Carter, who like his father served as representative from the Washington District to the North Carolina General Assembly.

CHEROKEE NATIONAL FOREST

Return to the junction with US 321 and turn north on US 19E and cross the Watauga River to exit onto TN 91 and bear right to head northeast. In 3.2 miles you can turn right on Blue Springs Road for a side trip along the Watauga River to **Wilbur Dam** in 3.8 miles and **Watauga Dam** in another 2.1 miles. The Appalachian Trail crosses on the top of Watauga Dam to enter Cherokee National Forest's **Big Laurel Branch Wilderness.**

Return to TN 91 and continue to the northeast through small mountain communities as the highway threads a valley between Holston Mountain on the left and the Iron Mountains on the right. In 4.7 miles enter **Cherokee National Forest** along a small cascading stream and wind up Cross Mountain. In 2.9 miles the AT crosses the road as the trail passes through this part of the state; the trail to the west provides access to **Flint Mill Scenic Area** on Holston Mountain.

Crossing Cross Mountain, you enter Johnson County and wind down from the top of the mountain 1.1 miles into **Shady Valley,** a mountain cove of rolling fields, grazing cattle, small farmhouses, barns, and silos. The valley is a world unto itself, surrounded by misty mountains in this isolated corner of the state. Shady Valley is known for its cranberry bogs, one of the few places in the state that still grows cranberries; the community holds its Cranberry Festival the second weekend in October.

At a junction with US 421 in 2.5 miles, this drive will turn right, but you can first stay straight on TN 133 for a side trip to **Backbone Rock Recreation Area.** In 9.4 miles the highway passes through a short tunnel in Backbone Rock. Around 1900 the Beaverdam Railway Company constructed a rail line between Shady Valley and Damascus, Virginia, for hauling timber, minerals, and farm products to the main line of the Virginia-Carolina Railway in Damascus; the line was popularly called the "Virginia Creeper." Here where Beaverdam Creek skirts a spur ridge running east from Holston Mountain, the railway blasted a tunnel through the rock. TN 133 now follows the route of the railroad. At the tunnel, a parking and picnic area on the left is the trailhead for the Backbone Rock Trail that leads through the **Beaverdam Creek Primitive Area** to a connection with the AT. Passing through the tunnel, TN 133 leads to Backbone Rock Campground (no hookups) on the left.

MOUNTAIN CITY AND LAUREL BLOOMERY

Return to Shady Valley, and at the junction with US 421, turn east to climb Iron Mountain. US 421/TN 91 winds up the mountain, reaching the top of the ridge in 4.1 miles in Sandy Gap. From here the Iron Mountain Trail runs along the ridge of the mountain, entering the **Iron Mountain Primitive Area** to the northeast. From Sandy Gap, wind down the mountain 5.4 miles to Mountain City. Turn left on Main Street (TN 91) to pass into the downtown area to a junction. This drive will turn right on TN 418, but here you can first turn left on TN 91 for a side trip to Laurel Bloomery.

North on TN 91, which is Church Street, the **Butler Mansion** stands on the left in 0.6 mile, a magnificent brick Italianate home built in 1870 by Roderick Random Butler. A tailor's apprentice when he arrived in upper East Tennessee from Virginia, Butler married a local planter's daughter, Emmeline Jane Donnelly, studied law, and was elected to the state legislature and the U.S. Congress. The home remained in the Butler family until 1992 when new owners restored the home and opened it as Butler House Bed-and-Breakfast.

Continue north on TN 91 following the valley into the mountains. In 3.1 miles notice the **Donnelly House** on the right, a large frame house that is now an antique shop. Richard Donnelly built this house in 1811, incorporating a log cabin that was constructed in the late 1700s. Donnelly's daughter married Roderick Random Butler.

In another 0.3 mile, notice the **Wills–Sutherland House** on the right, a two-story brick home that dates from the Civil War period. To the north along the highway stand more older homes, including the **Morrison-Russell House** built in 1840.

In 2 miles the old **Iron Mountain Stoneware Factory** rests on the left. Iron Mountain Stoneware was once known throughout the United States and other countries. Nancy and Joseph Lamb founded the pottery that turned out especially durable tableware because the pieces were fired at high temperatures. The Lambs closed the factory in the 1990s. Iron Mountain Stoneware is now considered a prime collector's item.

In 0.7 mile enter Laurel Bloomery to a junction with Gentry Creek Road, which leads east for access to the **Rogers Ridge Scenic Area** in Cherokee National Forest. Laurel Bloomery gets its name from iron forges that operated on Laurel Creek in the early 1800s; a mass of wrought iron from a forge was called a "bloom," and so a forge was a "bloomery." The iron ore in the area became depleted and operations ceased in 1870.

Just beyond the junction with Gentry Creek Road is a stone marker on the left commemorating the Daniel Boone Trail Highway. Born in Pennsylvania

Watauga Lake

and reared in North Carolina, Boone became a noted longhunter and frontiersman, entering the Watauga country in the early years of settlement, and at least on one trip, exploring north here along Laurel Creek.

At the Boone Highway monument, turn left on a small lane to the **Old Mill Music Park** where outdoor concerts are held on the grounds of an 1898 two-story frame mill that stands on the bank of Laurel Creek. Part of the mill works and the remains of the dam that created a reservoir of water to power the mill are still here.

Return to Mountain City to the junction with Main Street and stay straight on TN 418 to a junction with US 421 and turn left. Immediately on the right is the **Johnson County Welcome Center and Museum** with exhibits on the region's history. Behind the welcome center, the county has a campground on Town Creek.

Continue east on US 421. In 1.5 miles in the community of Shouns, this drive will turn right on TN 167. But you can stay straight on US 421 for a side trip to Trade in 7.8 miles, following the historic route of the first English traders who ventured over the mountains. James Needham and Gabriel Arthur are thought to be the first in 1673. Arthur stayed with the Cherokees for more than a year and is thought to be the first non-Indian to pass through Cumberland Gap, the route later blazed by Daniel Boone as the way into Kentucky.

The highway climbs into the mountains to the community of Trade, thereafter crossing a mountain gap into North Carolina. The settlement was established as a resting place for travelers, considered the oldest unincorporated community in Tennessee. The town hosts the annual Trade Days, a festival of crafts and performances held the last weekend in June.

Return down US 421 to the community of Shouns and turn south on TN 167 to travel down Roan Creek Valley with broad fields, rolls of hay, old barns, and farmhouses. In 11.4 miles at a junction, turn right to stay on TN 167 along an embayment of Watauga Lake with boat access down a gravel road to the left. The highway passes upstream along Doe Creek. In 1.7 miles cross the creek and reach a junction with TN 67. Turn left to head southwest, passing through the communities of Pine Orchard in 1.4 miles and Butler in 2.3 miles. In another 1.3 miles reenter Carter County.

WATAUGA LAKE

Pass over a ridge and descend 0.9 mile to a bridge crossing of Watauga Lake where boats leave wake lines on the water's surface. Along the lake, you'll pass numerous picnic areas, overlooks, and boat access points. Trails lead into Cherokee National Forest's **Pond Mountain Wilderness**. In 4.7 miles, **Cardens Bluff Campground** offers camping on a bluff above the lake (no hookups). In 3.2 miles, at **Laurel Falls Access** on the left, a trail leads 2.4 miles into the wilderness for access to the AT and Laurel Falls, a broad 50-foot waterfall on Laurel Creek.

ROAN MOUNTAIN

In the community of Hampton in 0.4 mile, continue southwest another 0.8 mile to a junction with US 19E and turn left to cross the Doe River and head into the mountains. In 3.6 miles this drive will turn right on TN 173, but first stay straight on US 19E.

Cross the Doe River again, following the stream up the mountain. In 7.4 miles turn right on TN 143 to enter **Roan Mountain State Park** in 1.1 miles. The park road follows the Doe River, now a small stream, past picnic and recreation areas, cabins, and a restaurant to the left. In 1 mile, the state park campground lies on the right.

Continue ascending the mountain on TN 143, entering Cherokee National Forest in 3.3 miles. Higher into the mountains, you can look down on the Doe River Valley to the right. The road enters the higher elevations where fir and spruce trees predominate and in 4.6 miles reaches Carvers Gap at the top of Roan Mountain at the border with North Carolina. Here the AT crosses the road as it passes through the **Highlands of Roan Scenic Area;** along this mountain range lie grassy balds with expansive views along the mountain ridge. There's a parking area on the right where you can leave your vehicle and walk the AT to the left quickly ascending to the top of Round Bald. The origin of these balds remains a mystery, but most likely they occurred through a combination of weather and geology, burning by Native Americans, and later, grazing of cattle and sheep by early settlers.

The end of June, catawba rhododendron sprinkle these mountain meadows with rose-pink color. A road to the right leads 2 miles to **Rhododendron Gardens** on the North Carolina side of the mountains where trails pass through heath thickets of the blooming bushes. Nearby is the site of the Cloudland Hotel, a resort inn that stood on the mountain in the late 1800s, built by Gen. John T. Wilder. A Union cavalry leader during the Civil War, Wilder settled in Tennessee after the fighting was over, founding the town of Rockwood in East Tennessee and establishing an iron works there. He later settled in Johnson City and constructed the Tweetsie Railroad from Johnson City to his mine holdings in North Carolina.

Return down the mountain to US 19E; the old commercial center of the Roan Mountain community lies to the right with several commercial buildings dating from the late 1800s. You can turn right down Main Street to see the **Wilder Home** on the right, an 1880s wood-frame, Italianate dwelling that is now a bed-and-breakfast.

ERWIN AND TIPTON HAYNES

Return down US 19E to the junction with TN 173 and turn southwest to continue this drive, following Simerly Creek up a mountain valley. At the top of a ridge in 4.4 miles, enter Unicoi County and descend the other side of the ridge into Limestone Cove, reaching a junction with TN 107 in 2.3 miles. Turn right, following Indian Creek downstream.

In 0.6 mile pass through the small community of Davis Springs, and in another 1.5 miles reach **Limestone Cove Recreation Area.** A side road to the left leads to a campground (no hookups); the Limestone Cove Trail off the campground road leads into the national forest's **Unaka Mountain Wilderness.**

TN 107/173 crosses Indian Creek and reaches a junction in 3.6 miles with TN 173 to the right and TN 107 to the left in the community of

Unicoi. This drive will turn right here, but you can take a side trip left to the historic railroad town of Erwin. In 3.1 miles the **Erwin National Fish Hatchery** on the right has a visitor center and a picnic area, and to the rear stands the old superintendent's Victorian home that now contains the **Unicoi County Heritage Museum** with exhibits on the region's history, including railroad memorabilia.

In another 2.0 miles you can turn left on TN 395 to enter national forest lands and reach **Rock Creek Recreation Area** in 2.3 miles, with picnicking and camping (no hookups) on Rock Creek. TN 395 continues into the mountains, reaching Indian Grave Gap on the mountain ridge at the border with North Carolina in 5.1 miles. There the gravel Unaka Mountain Road to the left leads along the ridge of the mountain, past the Unaka Mountain Overlook and the balds of Beauty Spot. The road emerges on TN 107 to the north in 12 miles; this road is narrow, winding, and rough in places.

Back on TN 107, you can continue into Erwin where even newer buildings are constructed to look like railroad buildings. To the right, the CSX Railroad lines pass through the town, once part of the Clinchfield Railroad that ran from Erwin to Kingsport. The town library occupies the 1925 **Clinchfield Depot** near the tracks, and beside it is the old three-story **Clinchfield Central Office.**

Return up TN 107 to the junction with TN 173 and head north on TN 173. In 0.8 mile TN 173 turns left to a junction with US 19W/23; stay straight on Unicoi Drive. Just on the right sits the Watauga Ranger District Office of Cherokee National Forest where you can stop in for information. Stay north on Unicoi Drive. In 4.4 miles enter Carter County. In 2.2 miles pass under US 19W/23 and enter Washington County.

In 0.8 mile the **Tipton-Haynes Historic Site** lies on the left. In 1784 John Tipton built a log cabin on this site. Around 1840, David Haynes, a local landowner, purchased the Tipton cabin for his son, Landon Carter Haynes, whom he named for Landon Carter, the son of John Carter. The log cabin was covered with weatherboards, and Landon Haynes practiced law in an adjacent office building; both structures still stand on the property. Haynes later served in the Confederate Senate during the Civil War.

Continue on Unicoi Drive into Johnson City where the highway becomes South Roan Street. In 1 mile, reach a junction with US 321. Turn right to a junction with I–181 (which to the south is US 19W/23) to complete this loop drive.

Early settlements

ROCKY MOUNT TO DANDRIDGE

GENERAL DESCRIPTION: This 93-mile drive visits Tennessee's earliest settlements, tracing the route of the old Washington Post Road.

SPECIAL ATTRACTIONS: Rocky Mount, William Bean Cabin Site, Jonesborough, Washington College, Davy Crockett Birthplace State Park, Chucky, Tusculum College, Greeneville, Andrew Johnson National Historic Site, Swaggerty Blockhouse, Parrotsville, Newport, Dandridge, historic homes and buildings, fishing, scenic views, fall color.

LOCATION: East Tennessee. The drive begins at Rocky Mountain on US 11E north of Johnson City.

DRIVE ROUTE NUMBERS: US 11E/19W; TN 354, 81, and 353; Old State Route 34; TN 107; and US 321 and 25.

CAMPING: Davy Crockett Birthplace State Park.

SERVICES: All services at Johnson City, Jonesborough, Greeneville, Newport, and Dandridge.

NEARBY ATTRACTIONS: DeVault Tavern.

THE DRIVE

During the early settlement of the western lands of North Carolina, several towns were established as county seats, including Jonesborough, Greeneville, Newport, and Dandridge. In the quest for statehood, this region of East Tennessee attempted to create the State of Franklin, which was rejected by North Carolina. Eventually the land was turned over to the federal government, which established the Southwest Territory with a capital at Rocky Mount.

ROCKY MOUNT AND BEAN CABIN SITE

From Exit 36 on I–181, near Johnson City, take TN 381 to the north, and in 1.3 miles bear left on US 11E/19W. In 2.4 miles cross Boone Lake on the Watauga River, created by the Tennessee Valley Authority's Boone Dam on the South Fork of the Holston River. In 0.8 mile enter Sullivan County, and

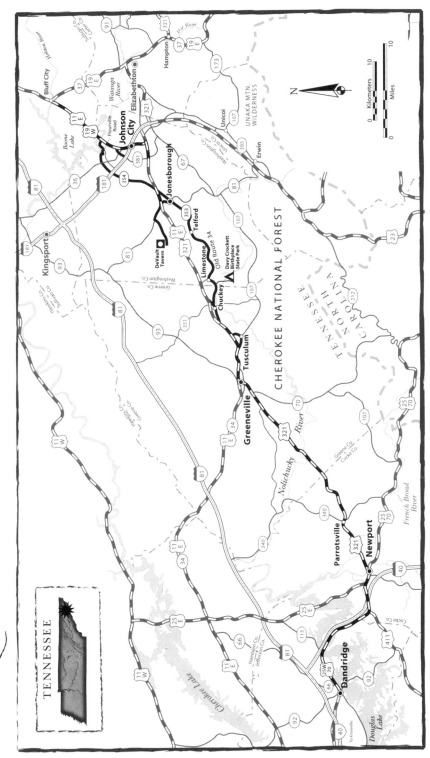

in another 0.7 mile turn right on Hyder Hill Road and bear right to **Rocky Mount,** the 1772 William Cobb home that temporarily served as the territorial capital of the Southwest Territory. The state acquired the property in the 1950s; it is now a living history museum of the late eighteenth century. Accomplished actors impersonating the Cobb family recreate the setting of the time and offer tours of the Cobb home and farmstead.

When the Territory of the United States South of the River Ohio was created from the western lands of North Carolina, Pres. George Washington appointed William Blount as governor. In 1790 Blount arrived in the Southwest Territory, as it was called, to take up his duties, staying at the home of William Cobb. Blount remained at Rocky Mount for eighteen months, periodically occupying a bedroom and an office when not away on business. During this time, Blount selected White's Fort near the confluence of the French Broad and Holston Rivers as a more centrally located place to establish the territorial capital. He relocated there in 1792 in what became the City of Knoxville.

From Rocky Mount, return down US 11E/19W, reentering Washington County and crossing Boone Lake once again. Turn right on Carroll Creek Road. **Winged Deer Park** on the right provides recreation and swimming on Boone Lake. In 1.6 miles turn right on Cedar Point Road, a narrow lane that winds through neighborhoods along the lake. In 1 mile there's boat access on the right on an embayment of Boone's Creek; across the water, boats gather around Sonny's Marina. The road reaches a junction with Flourville Road. On the left stands the old **Flourville Mill** that once produced flour and cornmeal; the waterwheel is still attached at the back of the building.

This drive will turn left here, but first turn right on Flourville Road to reach the **William Bean Cabin Site**. Cross Boone's Creek, and turn right on Cabindale Road to Sonny's Marina at the end of the road. Ask permission at the marina and then make your way along the water's edge past some houses and then into the woods on the left. Follow a makeshift path around a peninsula of land to the cabin site, which is marked by a stone monument.

Thought to be the first permanent white settler in Tennessee, William Bean erected a cabin here in 1769. The actual site lies 90 feet to the southeast, under the waters of Boone Lake; when TVA flooded the Watauga River corridor with the construction of Boone Dam in the 1950s, the agency moved the marker to its present location on the shore of the lake. Bean and his family built this cabin at an old hunting camp that he had once shared with Daniel Boone. At this cabinsite, the last of the Beans' children, Russell, was born, becoming the first known white child to be born west of the Appalachian Mountains in what would become Tennessee. A noted gunsmith, William Bean passed his skill on to his sons, and in the 1780s the family began producing rifles that were the finest of the time; five generations of Beans were subsequently known for their famed Tennessee rifles as they moved out and settled East Tennessee.

Return to the junction of Flourville and Cedar Point Roads, and continue south on Flourville Road. In 0.4 mile join Pickens Bridge Road straight ahead, and in another 0.4 mile stay straight through an intersection with TN 36 onto Boone's Creek Road, which is also TN 354. In 1.3 miles pass under I–181, and continue southeast on TN 354, reaching a junction with US 11/321 in 6.4 miles.

JONESBOROUGH

Stay straight across the highway to enter Jonesborough on Boone Street. At the visitor center on the left, you can pick up a walking tour to forty of Jonesborough's historic sites.

Established in 1779 by the General Assembly of North Carolina, Jonesborough is the oldest town in Tennessee. While Greeneville, Dandridge, and Blountville each claim to be the second oldest town in Tennessee, and Parrotsville takes itself out of the running by claiming to be the third oldest, Jonesborough is the undisputed first town to be staked out in the western lands of North Carolina. Named for North Carolina Assemblyman Willie Jones, Jonesborough was also the first town in Tennessee to be listed on the National Register of Historic Places. Today thousands of visitors come to tour historic Jonesborough, especially the first weekend in October when the town hosts the National Storytelling Festival.

At a junction with Main Street, bear right into the downtown where some of the most historic homes and buildings in Tennessee line the street. Left up Fox Street stands the **Salt House,** built in the late 1840s. During the Civil War, salt was rationed from this warehouse; today it houses retail shops. Just before the railroad tracks, a side road on the right leads to the **Old First Christian Church;** built in the 1870s, the building now houses the Parson's Table Restaurant. Past the Salt House, at the corner of Fox and Woodrow Avenue, the **Rees-Hawley House** stands across Woodrow to the left; the interior log home, now covered with board and batten siding, was constructed in 1793, making it the oldest house in Jonesborough. Today the home is the Hawley House Bed-and-Breakfast. Take a right on Woodrow Avenue and travel 1 block to the **Shipley-Bledsoe House,** which stands on the left.

Built in the 1830s by Shelby T. Shipley, it was later the home of Dr. William R. Sevier, a nephew of John Sevier. Today the house is operated by the Bledsoes as the Jonesborough Bed-and-Breakfast.

On Main Street, the **Washington County Courthouse** on the left stands on the site of five previous courthouses. The first was a small log structure that housed the county court for the settlements in the western lands of North Carolina. Here the early settlers gathered to create the short-lived State of Franklin in 1784, wanting to separate from North Carolina politically since they were already separated physically by mountains, which were at the time nearly impassable. The first general assembly was held in Jonesborough in March 1785 and selected a reluctant John Sevier as governor. A constitutional convention was held in November in Greeneville to the south, and the capital of the state remained there because of Greeneville's more central location.

North Carolina demanded that the new state be dissolved. Franklin appealed to the U.S. Congress for recognition but was turned down. When Sevier's term of office expired in 1788, no one was elected to fill his place; by now most recognized that the state would not survive. In 1789 Sevier and others took an oath of allegiance to North Carolina, and soon after, he was elected to the North Carolina senate. When the western lands of North Carolina, later the Southwest Territory, became the State of Tennessee in 1796, Sevier was elected the first governor.

Perhaps the most noted structure in town, the **Chester Inn** stands on the right side of Main. Built in the late 1790s, the inn is the oldest frame building in Jonesborough. As a stop on the stagecoach road, the inn sheltered three presidents traveling between Tennessee and Washington, D.C.—Andrew Jackson, James K. Polk, and Andrew Johnson. Next door is the **Christopher Taylor House,** a circa 1778 log cabin that was moved from the countryside to this location for restoration. Andrew Jackson boarded in the home while he practiced law in the town for a short time; prior to arriving in Jonesborough, Jackson stayed a few weeks with the Cobbs at Rocky Mount.

The **Jonesborough Presbyterian Church,** an 1840s Greek Revival building, still has the original pulpit, pews, and slave gallery. Adjacent to the church is the **May-Ledbetter House,** a Victorian frame home built in 1904; today it is a bed-and-breakfast and restaurant. This was the location of the print shop of Jacob Howard, who printed a newspaper, *The Manumission Intelligencer,* the first paper in the country devoted to the abolition of slavery. The paper was written by Elihu Embree, a member of the Quakers, who were early opponents of slavery.

Christopher Taylor House

The **Mansion House** is a brick dwelling constructed in 1849; it was once an inn on the stagecoach road. The **Blair–Moore House** on the left, a Greek Revival home built in 1832, is now a bed and breakfast inn. Also on the left is **Sisters' Row,** a row house that is one of the oldest brick buildings in town, constructed in 1820 by Samuel D. Jackson; Jackson's daughters lived in the three units. The **Jonesborough United Methodist Church,** a Greek Revival building constructed in 1846, still has its original slave gallery.

Main Street passes more historic homes as it climbs a hill and reaches a junction with TN 81. Here you can turn right for a side trip to see the **DeVault Tavern.** At a junction with Cobb Street turn left and pass under US 11E. In 2.5 miles, turn left on Old Stage Coach Road and travel another 2 miles to drive in front of the grand old home on the left. Built between 1818 and 1820 by Frederick DeVault, the two-story brick house with white portico was a stop on the Washington Post Road; the stage road entered Tennessee from Abingdon, Virginia, and passed through Blountville, Jonesborough, Greeneville, Newport, Dandridge, and Knoxville before turning west toward Nashville. Many stage passengers stayed at the DeVault home, including Pres. Andrew Johnson, who was a friend of the owner and a frequent guest. In 1864 Confederate Gen. John H. Morgan stopped here for the night on his way south to engage Union forces moving north from Knoxville. Spending the next night in Greeneville, he and his men were ambushed the next morning, and Morgan was killed.

TELFORD, WASHINGTON COLLEGE, CHUCKY

Return to the junction of TN 81 and Main Street, and turn right on TN 81 to leave Jonesborough. In 0.7 mile cross a bridge over Little Limestone Creek and railroad tracks, and bear right on TN 353. The highway passes through a countryside of farms with barns, silos, and old farmhouses, and in 4 miles enters Telford.

To the right across the railroad tracks stands the **Eureka Roller Mills,** built in 1876 as the Telford Agricultural Manufacturing Company and renamed Eureka in 1894. In 0.8 mile, to the right on Stayers Lane, you can see the old **Telford Milling Company** building beside Little Limestone Creek. Both Telford mills have long been silent.

Outside of Telford, glance to the right to see the 1791 **Thomas Embree Stone House,** built by Seth Smith, a Quaker stone mason. Embree influenced his son, Elihu, to take a stand against slavery.

Continue southwest on TN 353, which is also Old State Route 34. In 2.3 miles enter the small community of Washington College, which grew up around **Washington College Academy.** The school was founded as Martin Academy in 1790 by Rev. Samuel Doak, a Presbyterian preacher. In 1795 the school was named Washington College for Pres. George Washington and for a time was the only school of higher learning west of the Appalachians. The eighth oldest school in the country, the college became a high school in 1923 and added "Academy" to its name. The private boarding school of today is temporarily closed.

Old State Route 34 passes through the countryside and in 3.2 miles enters the small railroad town of Limestone. The old **Limestone Depot** sits beside the tracks to the right. As the road leaves the community, the **Gillespie Stone House** stands on the left where the road curves right. Stone mason Seth Smith built the house in 1792 for George Gillespie, an early settler; the house is now virtually abandoned.

In another 0.6 mile, turn left on Davy Crockett Park Road. In 1.3 miles, bear right to stay on this road, and in 0.4 mile cross Limestone Creek into Greene County. In 0.9 mile stay straight across Charles Johnson Road to enter **Davy Crockett Birthplace State Park.** The park includes a campground, picnic areas, and a swimming pool.

On the park grounds beside the Nolichucky River is a reconstruction of a cabin like the home where David Crockett was born. The actual cabin stood at the confluence of Limestone Creek with the Nolichucky, which is just south of this site. A stone marker at the present cabin encases what is thought to be a foundation stone from the original cabin. As a young man, Crockett relocated to Middle and then West Tennessee where he emerged as a political leader, eventually becoming a representative to the U.S. Congress. When he lost a reelection bid, he went to Texas to fight for its independence from Mexico. Along with 186 others, he died at the Alamo in 1836. The legend of David Crockett grew after his death, culminating in the mostly fictitious character of Davy Crockett, "King of the Wild Frontier," in the popular television series of the 1950s; Crockett never referred to himself as "Davy." A monument in front of the cabin erected in his memory contains stone native to each of the fifty states.

Exiting the park, turn left on Charles Johnson Road, and in 2 miles, reach a junction with TN 351 in the old railroad community of Chucky. The 1908 **Southern Railway Depot** still stands beside the railroad tracks, boarded up and forlorn. You can turn left on TN 351 through the community to reach a crossing of the Nolichucky River in 0.6 mile. Just before the crossing, the **Earnest Fort House** stands on the right, built from 1780 to 1783; one of the oldest structures in Tennessee, the three-story stone and log home provided protection from attacking Indians. Across the river is the **Henry Earnest Home,** built in the 1820s. Earnest settled here and established Elmwood Farm around 1777; descendants still own the farm, making it the oldest family farm in Tennessee.

Return to the center of Chucky and stay on TN 351 past the old depot. Just across the railroad tracks, an unusual brick building on the right was originally a bank and later the **Chucky Post Office.**

TUSCULUM AND GREENEVILLE

Turn left on Old State Route 34, which here is also Chucky Highway. In 2.2 miles turn left on US 321/11E, and in another 2.2 miles turn left on Samuel Doak Drive to enter the community of Tusculum. In 2.4 miles bear right on TN 107 to pass **Tusculum College** on the left, the main entrance marked by a stone archway. Rev. Samuel Witherspoon Doak founded Tusculum Academy in 1818, assisted by his father, Rev. Samuel Doak, who had founded nearby Washington College. In 1868 the academy combined with Greeneville College, which had been founded by Rev. Hezekiah Balch in 1794; the two schools formed the nucleus of today's Tusculum College. The campus contains eight buildings dating from 1841 to 1928.

At the far end of the campus, turn left to reach the **President Andrew Johnson Museum and Library.** Designated by Congress, the presidential library is housed in Old College, built in 1841, the first permanent brick building for the school. The library collection includes papers and artifacts from the life of Johnson, whose hometown is Greeneville to the west.

Return to TN 107 and continue west. The **Doak House,** the home of Samuel W. Doak, stands on the left. Built in 1818 and now fully restored, the house is open for tours.

Leaving Tusculum, TN 107 joins US 321E in 0.8 mile; turn left. In 2.8 miles, where the US 321/11E Bypass continues straight, turn left on US 321 Business to enter Greeneville on Main Street.

In 0.4 mile, at the near corner of Church Street on the right, stands the **Greeneville Cumberland Presbyterian Church.** Built in 1860, the church stood in the midst of a Union attack on Confederate forces during the Civil War; a cannonball from the battle remains embedded in the facade of the building, over the light on the right-hand side of the front door. In this attack, General John H. Morgan, who commanded Morgan's Raiders, was ambushed and killed and his staff was captured in 1864 in the center of the next block, which was the garden of the **Dickson-Williams Mansion.** Up Church Street to the right is the 1850 white frame **St. James Episcopal**

Church, where Morgan took refuge during the first part of the surprise attack. The Federal-style Dickson-Williams home is on the hill; William Dickson, the county's first postmaster, built the home between 1815 and 1821 as a wedding present to his daughter, Catherine, on her marriage to Alexander Williams. Famous people of the time were entertained at the home, including Presidents Jackson and Polk; during the Civil War, both Confederate and Union officers headquartered there. The home is open by appointment.

On Main Street, on the right, stands the **General Morgan Inn,** which is a complex of four interconnected hotels dating from the late 1800s; the four-story edifice in the center was the Hotel Brumley, built in 1884. Across Main is the **First Presbyterian Church,** built in 1848 with a steeple added in 1928. Beside the church is a beautiful chapel.

At the corner of Main and Depot on the far left stands the **Greene County Courthouse.** Behind the courthouse is the **Old Greene County Gaol.** Built in 1805, the single-story stone jail was moved to this location in 1838; a second story of brick was added in 1882. The gaol is maintained as a historic structure and is open to visitors.

Turn left down Depot Street and travel 1 block to the **Andrew Johnson National Historic Site** on the left at a junction with College Street. The site commemorates the controversial president.

As a boy in Raleigh, North Carolina, Johnson was apprenticed to a tailor after his father died. Moving to Greeneville, he eventually opened a tailor shop and met and married Eliza McCardle. Johnson's political career began when he was elected alderman for the town of Greeneville in 1829. He went on to be elected mayor of Greeneville, state representative and senator, U.S. representative, governor of Tennessee, and U.S. senator. At the outbreak of the Civil War, he opposed the southern states' secession from the Union, calling it unconstitutional. Because of his pro-Union stand, Johnson was appointed Military Governor of Tennessee in 1862 when federal forces drove the Confederates out of Middle and West Tennessee and occupied the region for the remainder of the war. Pres. Abraham Lincoln selected Johnson as his running mate for the 1864 election, and Johnson became vice president. The following year, Lincoln was assassinated, and Johnson became the seventeenth president of the United States.

Johnson endured a turbulent presidency because of an increasingly hostile confrontation with the U.S. Congress. He saw the purpose of Reconstruction after the war as a method to bring the Confederate states back into the fold as easily and as quickly as possible. But the majority in Congress, led by

Republicans, viewed the South as conquered territory, to be put under military rule and remolded by the federal government.

Many in Congress wanted Johnson removed from office. They finally found a reason—a violation of the Tenure of Office Act, which forbade the president from removing from office, without the consent of the Senate, federal office holders previously confirmed by the Senate. Johnson thought the act unconstitutional and ignored it when he removed from office Secretary of War Edwin M. Stanton, who opposed his Reconstruction policies.

On February 24, 1868, Andrew Johnson became the first president in U.S. history to be impeached by the U.S. House of Representatives. Johnson was found not guilty by the Senate and went on to complete his term as president and was later reelected to the Senate, the only president to return to Congress.

The historic site visitor center contains Johnson's tailor shop, and across College Street stands the Johnsons' Home from 1838 to 1851. Up the hill from College Street on Depot is the Greene County Chamber of Commerce where you can pick up a walking-tour guide to Greeneville, which is the best way to see the thirty-six historic sites. Left on College Street takes you by a replica of the log cabin that was the **Capitol of the State of Franklin.** Behind the cabin is Bicentennial Park, which contains **Big Spring** that provided water to the town for 150 years.

Return to Main Street, turn left and travel 2 blocks to the **Andrew Johnson Homestead,** where the Johnsons lived from 1851 until his death in 1875. Part of the national historic site, the house contains furniture and artifacts from the period. Across Main is the **Sevier-Lowry House,** a log house covered with clapboards. Built by Valentine Sevier around 1795, it is the oldest structure in Greeneville; Sevier was a nephew of John Sevier, Tennessee's first governor. Also on that side of Main, across McKee Street, is the **Nathanael Greene Museum,** containing artifacts and exhibits on Greene County history; Nathanael Greene was a Revolutionary War hero for whom the county was named.

In 0.3 mile turn left on Monument Avenue to reach the **Andrew Johnson National Cemetery** and drive up a narrow road to circle the brow of the hill to parking on the right. On the knoll, Johnson is buried with his wife and other family members; an Italian marble monument, 27 feet tall, stands over the couple's graves.

PARROTSVILLE AND NEWPORT

Stay on US 321 Business to leave Greeneville. In 0.8 mile rejoin US 321 straight ahead after the highway has bypassed the city. At this point you'll enter a pastoral countryside. Barns dot the landscape; dozens are along this section of road through scenic farmland. If you try to keep count, don't miss the barns on the surrounding distant hills.

In 7.5 miles cross the Nolichucky River, a tributary of the French Broad River and one of the most scenic streams in the state, with forest draping down to low rock bluffs standing at the river's edge. In another 3.2 miles enter Cocke County.

Continue through a pastoral countryside of barns, silos, cattle, and occasional houses and old stores that once operated along this old thoroughfare. This is tobacco country, where large and small plots of the large-leaf plant are grown. Upon harvesting, tobacco must be dried before being delivered to market. Many of the barns have plenty of space between the wallboards for air to circulate among the hanging leaves inside. A more recent method of drying tobacco is to hang the leaves on a frame covered with black plastic sheeting, which is less expensive than building a barn.

In 3.6 miles the **Swaggerty Blockhouse** stands on the right. Built around 1787 by James Swaggerty, the fort was one of many constructed throughout the frontier for protection against hostile Native Americans who objected to whites taking their land. This is one of only two known blockhouses that remain in Tennessee; the other is Fort Marr at Benton in the southeast corner of the state.

Continue southwest on US 321, entering Parrotsville in 1.1 miles. Watch on the left for the **Yett/Ellison House,** a brick Federal-style home built in 1857 by Hamilton Yett, a son of German immigrants who settled the region in the 1780s. After the Civil War, the house was sold to John Ford Ellison, who was a sheriff. He occasionally housed prisoners in outbuildings that still can be seen behind the house. Where TN 340 turns off to the left is the **Parrotsville Library and Museum.** On the right is the **Dr. Darius Nease Office,** a small white frame building, and then the **Parrotsville Post Office,** another small white frame building on the right, constructed in 1936.

Continue southwest on US 321, winding through the countryside with the Unaka Mountains of Cherokee National Forest to the southeast. In 4.6 miles, cross the French Broad River, with views up and down the valley. The **Gilleland/O'dell House** stands on a side road to the right, a two-story brick home built in 1814 by Abel Gilleland. This area, now called Old Town, was the original site of the new port located at the upper end of the navigable portion of the French Broad. John Gilleland, father of Abel, donated land for the town to be established in 1799. The town of Newport relocated from here to the nearby railroad tracks when the Cincinnati, Cumberland Gap, and

Charleston Railroad was constructed betwen 1866 and 1869 and became the main form of transportation; later it became part of the Southern Railroad.

In another 2 miles cross a bridge over the Pigeon River, a tributary of the French Broad, and enter Newport. To the right stands the **Southern Railroad Depot,** constructed around 1923. Across the tracks and to the right stands the **Newport Milling Company,** which began milling flour in the 1800s and continued until the 1980s.

Enter the downtown to a junction with Broadway, which is also US 25/70. This drive will turn right, but first turn left through the town. The abandoned **Rhea Mims Hotel** on the right has been a Newport landmark since it was constructed in the 1920s. In another 0.5 mile on the left stands the Hunts/Van Camp/Wolf canning factory. The canning company started small in 1898 when Anna Stokely and her sons founded the business. Will, James, John, Hugh, and George soon took over operation of the business and with hard work and enterprise created a large corporation that sold Stokely canned products all over the country. The small gray building in the center of the complex was the **Stokely Brothers Headquarters;** by 1941 the company operated thirty-four factories in fourteen states.

Return along Broadway to the junction with US 321 and continue straight through town on US 25/70/321. In 0.3 mile US 321 turns left off Broadway; 0.5 mile down that highway, you'll find the chamber of commerce in a new building that houses the **Cocke County Museum** on the third floor. Stay straight on US 25/70 to leave Newport. In 1.2 miles pass US 25E to the right, staying straight on US 25W/70. In 2.8 miles pass under I-40 with US 411 to the left, and in 1.8 miles enter Jefferson County. Continue through a pastoral backcountry, and in 6 miles cross a bridge over Douglas Lake, created by TVA's Douglas Dam on the French Broad River; the interstate bridge spans the lake to the right.

In 0.4 mile turn left on Spring Creek Road. In another 0.4 mile pass through a junction with another backcountry road and stay straight on a narrow, one-lane road to the **French Broad Baptist Church,** an old brick church on the shore of Douglas Lake. When this site was to be flooded by the construction of Douglas Dam, elderly Fanny Swann, who lived in a large plantation house overlooking the river, appealed to Eleanor and Pres. Franklin Roosevelt to save the farm she and her husband had created here on the French Broad River. Although most of the farm was eventually flooded, Pres. Roosevelt ordered a levee to be built to save Fanny's church. You can drive around the front of the church on the levee that now holds back the lake when the water is high. This is one of the prettiest spots in Tennessee with the church beside the lake and, across the water, English Mountain and the Unakas beyond.

DANDRIDGE

Return to US 25W/70 and continue west through farmland with cattle and horses grazing in fields below tall silos. In 4.7 miles the highway enters the community of Dandridge as Meeting Street, passing homes dating from the 1800s. The first settlers arrived here around 1783 when this region was still part of the western lands of North Carolina. The population grew to the extent that Jefferson County was formed in 1792 and Dandridge was established as the county seat, making it one of the oldest towns in Tennessee. The new community was named for Martha Dandridge Washington, the wife of Pres. George Washington.

On the left stands the **Seabolt/Harris House,** a two-story brick home with white portico, built in 1848 and used as a hospital during the Civil War. Just after, the **Hopewell Presbyterian Church** on the right was built in 1872.

Turn left on Gay Street, where TN 92 turns south. On the left corner stands the **Thomas Tavern,** built in 1843 by James Mitchell as a tavern and boardinghouse. Dandridge was a stop on the stage road between Knoxville and Washington, D.C., and also a stop on the west-east route for stock traders traveling to markets in the Carolinas, as well as a boat landing on the French Broad River. As the town grew, several taverns/inns were established to serve the many travelers; five of the taverns still stand in Dandridge.

Just down Gay Street on the left is the **Hynds House,** built around 1845. In the yard to the left side of the house, the **Town Spring** still flows, which was the attraction for settlers in this region; a good source of water was always a requirement. Across the street on the right stands the **Old Jail,** the rear portion built in 1845.

At the corner with Main Street, the **Jefferson County Courthouse** stands on the right. This Greek Revival building, completed in 1845, also houses the Jefferson County Historical Museum; photos and artifacts from the county's past adorn the halls of the courthouse. Across the street on the corner is the **Roper Tavern,** a brick structure built in 1817.

A high levee on the south forms a backdrop for the historic town. When Douglas Dam was constructed on the French Broad River in the 1940s, the town of Dandridge was to be flooded. But responding to the appeals of the local people, President Roosevelt saved the town by having this dike constructed. It now holds back the lake's waters. TN 92 continues to the top of the levee and crosses a bridge over the French Broad, which is one of the two primary tributaries that create the Tennessee River.

In town, turn left on Main Street past several historic buildings. The narrow **Hickman Tavern Coach House** on the right was built in 1845 for stagecoach drivers and now houses the Dandridge Public Works. Just beyond is the **Hickman Tavern** also built in 1845; it houses City Hall, which has a circular staircase that winds from the basement to the top floor, and where you can pick up a walking tour of the city that visits thirty-six historic sites. Across from City Hall is **Shepard's Inn,** originally a log house built in 1820 and now a private residence covered by a Victorian frame facade; Tennessee's three presidents stayed here while traveling back and forth to Washington.

Return along Main and Gay Streets to Meeting Street, and turn left to leave Dandridge, passing more old homes. US 25W/70 passes through small farms with scattered fields and, in 3.7 miles, reaches a junction with I–40 at Exit 415 east of Knoxville.

6

Forks of the River

KNOXVILLE TO MARBLE SPRINGS LOOP

GENERAL DESCRIPTION: This 36-mile drive through the early history of East Tennessee leads from the capital of the Southwest Territory to the home of the state's first governor.

SPECIAL ATTRACTIONS: Knoxville, Forks of the River, Ramsey House, Marble Springs State Historic Farmstead, Fort Dickerson, historic homes and buildings, scenic views, fall color, hiking, biking, boating, fishing, and wildlife viewing.

LOCATION: East Tennessee. The drive begins in Knoxville at the corner of Gay and Hill Streets at Blount Mansion.

DRIVE ROUTE NUMBERS: Riverside Drive, Boyds Bridge Pike, Thorngrove Pike, Asbury Road, TN 168, Neubert Springs Road, Tipton Station Road, Martin Mill Pike, Maryville Pike, and US 441.

CAMPING: Private campgrounds in the Knoxville area.

SERVICES: All services at Knoxville.

NEARBY ATTRACTIONS: Ijams Nature Center, Riverdale, Kimberlin Heights, and Seven Island.

THE DRIVE

When North Carolina turned over to the federal government its western lands that then became the Southwest Territory, the new governor decided to establish the capital at the forks of the great rivers flowing through East Tennessee. Knoxville served as the territorial capital and then the state capital when Tennessee was formed in 1796. The growing city remained the capital until 1812, when it was temporarily moved to Nashville; Knoxville was the capital again from 1817 to 1818 before it was moved to Murfreesboro and then permanently to Nashville in 1826.

BLOUNT MANSION

Begin this drive in downtown Knoxville on Gay Street. At the corner of Gay and Hill Avenue stands a visitor center for **Blount Mansion.** Turn east on

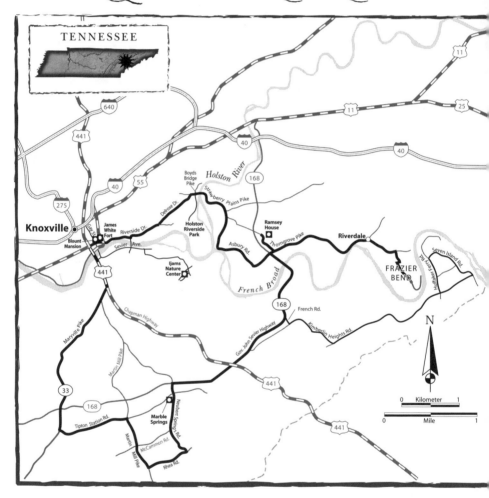

Hill to pass in front of the mansion, and turn right into an alley beside the house to drive around back to the visitor center.

In 1790 William Blount, who had been a member of the North Carolina state legislature and a delegate to the U.S. Constitutional Convention, was appointed by Pres. George Washington to be governor of the Territory South of the River Ohio. Blount first headquartered at the Cobb home, called Rocky Mount, in upper East Tennessee but soon decided that the capital for the new Southwest Territory should be located near the confluence of the French Broad and Holston Rivers, which combine to create the Tennessee River.

The settlement near this confluence was James White's Fort. Blount moved to the fort in 1791, and with land purchased from White, established the territorial capital. He called it Knoxville in honor of Henry Knox, U.S. Secretary of War and head of Indian affairs at the time.

To help his wife and family adjust to life on the frontier, Blount built a two-story house that was one of the first frame houses west of the mountains, and so the home was called Blount's Mansion. Behind the mansion is the governor's office where Blount wrote the Tennessee Constitution, with the help of Daniel Smith who served as secretary of the Southwest Territory. When the state was established, Blount became one of the first two senators from Tennessee to the U.S. Congress. Today Blount Mansion is open to the public as a house museum.

KNOXVILLE

The Blount Mansion Visitor Center can be a base from which to explore the center of Knoxville before heading out of the city. Directly across Hill Avenue from the entrance to Blount Mansion, State Street leads 3 blocks to the **First Presbyterian Church** on the right at the corner of Church Avenue. The adjacent church cemetery contains many early settlers of Knoxville, including James White and William Blount.

On Gay Street, 1 block north at the corner of Main Avenue, stands the **Knox County Courthouse** on the left. The courthouse was built in 1885 on the original site of a blockhouse where federal troops were garrisoned when Knoxville was the capital of the Southwest Territory.

Another block north, also on the left, at the corner of Cumberland Avenue, is the **Lamar House–Bijou Theater,** originally built in 1816 as a residence. The home became a hotel under various names, until in 1856 it became the Lamar House. The hotel was occupied by Union troops during the Civil War; it was here that Union Gen. William P. Sanders died after being wounded in the Battle of Fort Sanders in November 1863 when the

Confederates under Lieutenant-General James Longstreet failed to retake the Union-occupied city. On Kingston Pike to the west, you can visit **Bleak House,** an Italianate home built in 1858. It is now a house museum called Confederate Memorial Hall. From the tower of the house, Confederate sharpshooters wounded General Sanders; in response, Union troops shot at the house, which still shows the scars of federal bullets. In 1908 an addition to the Lamar House became the Bijou Theater, which in later years served as a movie house. Today the restored theater has reassumed its place as a cultural focal point for the city center.

Another 2 blocks north on Gay Street, at the corner of Clinch Avenue, is the **Burwell Building** on the right, erected in 1908 on the original site of Blount College, the forerunner of the University of Tennessee; the college was founded by Rev. Samuel Carrick in 1794. Carrick also founded the First Presbyterian Church on State Street and is buried in the church cemetery. The adjacent **Tennessee Theater** was added to the Burwell Building in 1928. The theater, with its elaborate interior of domed ceiling and plaster moldings, has been restored and is once more a place for shows, movies, and performances.

Clinch Avenue to the west passes between the **U.S. Post Office and Custom House** on the left and **Krutch Park** on the right. You can take a walk through the park named for Charles Krutch, a local photographer who donated funds for the park construction; the open space of native plants and simulated mountain stream leads to **Market Square,** where commercial buildings dating from the late 1800s and early 1900s surround the historic marketplace where vendors still sell a variety of products during the week. The northern end of the park is anchored by the twin towers of the head-quarters of the Tennessee Valley Authority, the giant federally owned utility.

The U.S. Post Office and Custom House was built in 1873 in the Second Renaissance Revival style with local Tennessee marble. After the post office was moved to newer facilities, the building was eventually transferred to the Knox County Public Library System. It is the location of the library's East Tennessee Historical Center. The Center maintains the Knox County Archives and the Calvin M. McClung Historical Collection. Named for a wholesale industrialist who gathered much of the material that formed the basis of the library, the collection contains information and records on East Tennessee and the state. Around the corner on Market Street, the Custom House also contains the **Museum of East Tennessee History,** with exhibits and artifacts on this part of the state, including a rifle made by Russell Bean, the first white person born in Tennessee, and another by

Charles Bean, Russell's son. The Beans, starting with grandfather William, the first permanent settler in Tennessee, were famous gunsmiths.

From the junction of Gay Street and Hill Avenue, you can head south on a side trip to **Ijams Nature Center.** To get there, cross the Gay Street Bridge over the Tennessee River, here also called Fort Loudoun Lake, backed up by TVA's Fort Loudoun Dam far downstream. To the right you can see Volunteer Landing, a linear park on the river, and Henley Street Bridge in the distance. On the other side of the river, stay straight through an intersection and bear left on Sevier Avenue, which travels east along the river. In 0.7 mile at a fork where Sevier Avenue bears to the right, stay straight on Island Home Avenue. Pass under the South Knoxville Bridge, and in another 0.7 mile, turn right to stay on Island Home Avenue where Maplewood Drive enters the community of Island Home Park. In 0.2 mile turn left to again stay on Island Home Avenue, and in 1.3 miles turn left into the nature center.

In 1910 Harry and Alice Ijams built a home here and set about turning their surrounding twenty acres into a wildlife sanctuary they shared with the community. After the death of the Ijams, the Knoxville Garden Club and the Knox County Council of Garden Clubs banded together to acquire the property and establish a nonprofit environmental education center. Today, Ijams has expanded to eighty acres of trails and gardens.

JAMES WHITE FORT

Return to Blount Mansion and head east on Hill Avenue from Gay Street, crossing the Hill Avenue Bridge over the James White Parkway. In 0.2 mile, on the left, stands **James White Fort,** just before a junction with Hall of Fame Drive to the left and Volunteer Landing Lane to the right.

Born in North Carolina of Scotch-Irish immigrants and a veteran of the Revolutionary War, James White came to the western lands following North Carolina's confiscation of Cherokee lands in retribution for their siding with the British during the war. White purchased lands from the state at the junction of the Holston and French Broad Rivers and brought his wife, Mary Lawson, and their children to settle here in 1785; they first settled at the Forks of the River but soon relocated here at the future site of Knoxville.

White erected a cabin on a hill near the place where a creek, once called White's Creek, now First Creek, joins the Tennessee River. Soon White's cabin became a first stop for other settlers moving into the region. To accommodate these guests and to provide better protection, White built three smaller cabins that with his own formed the four corners of a stockade.

The fort originally stood on what is now the east side of State Street between Union and Clinch Avenues. With the passing of time, only White's log cabin remained. It was eventually moved to its present location; with other donated structures, the fort was reconstructed and is now open to the public.

Across Hill Avenue, a walkway leads to the top of the **Gateway Regional Visitor Center** where you can descend into the building for information about the region. The center serves as a gateway to the Southern Highlands, showcasing the various national parks and recreation areas surrounding Knoxville and the technological resources of the region.

At the junction just beyond the fort, you can turn right on Volunteer Landing Lane to drive down to the Gateway Regional Visitor Center. From there you can follow walkways into Volunteer Landing along the edge of the Tennessee River.

To the left at the junction of Hill Avenue with Volunteer, at the far corner, is the **Women's Basketball Hall of Fame;** its presence in Knoxville is a recognition of the several national championships held by the women's basketball team at the University of Tennessee, which resides to the west of the city center. The Hall of Fame, with exhibits and videos about the history of women's basketball, includes a Ballgirl Athletic Playground where visitors can shoot baskets.

Continue straight on Hill Avenue, curving left to a junction in 0.4 mile with Riverland Drive; turn right to a fork and bear right down to Riverside Drive and turn right. In 0.2 mile **Riverside Landing Park** lies to the right at the edge of the Tennessee River; there's a picnic area, playground, and boat access.

Riverside Drive then passes under the South Knoxville Bridge and curves left up to Laurans Avenue to the left in 0.2 mile, at which point the drive curves back right. At this side road junction, a plumbing company occupies the **McCammon House,** the 1850 home of Samuel McCammon, who was Knox County Sheriff in 1842. This was the site of James White's second home in Knoxville. Probably wanting to escape the bustle of the new city center, White moved to this location and built a two-story log house, which was dismantled between 1852 and 1853. A marker on the southwest corner of the lot, along Laurans Street, designates the spot.

Continue out Riverside Drive through a neighborhood of scattered older homes. In 1 mile bear left on Delrose Drive as Riverside continues straight. In 1.5 miles bear right as Delrose joins Boyds Bridge Pike. At a junction with Holston Hills Road, you can turn right to the **Holston Riverside Park** in 0.6 mile. The park lies next to a narrow channel of the Holston River that separates Boyd Island from the shore; the park has picnic areas, recreation fields, and a walking trail along the river.

Continue on Boyds Bridge Pike to cross a bridge over the Holston River. On the other side, the road becomes Strawberry Plains Pike. In 1 mile bear right on Thorngrove Pike, and in another 0.3 mile turn right on Asbury Road.

FORKS OF THE RIVER

In 1.1 miles, as Asbury Road reaches the point of land at the confluence of the Holston and French Broad Rivers, the site of the **Lebanon-in-the-Fork Presbyterian Church** lies on the left. This was the first church in Knox County, organized in 1791 by Rev. Samuel Carrick, the founder of Blount College. The original stone church on this site was replaced in 1903 with a new frame building that burned in 1981. As a memorial, a pavilion supported by the columns from the church covers the old church bell. The cemetery surrounding the church site contains some of the pioneers of the area, including F. A. Ramsey, who accompanied James White on his first exploration of the region in early 1780s. Ramsey's son, J. G. M. Ramsey, is also buried here, as is Elizabeth M. Carrick, the wife of Samuel Carrick.

Past the church site and cemetery, the road curves to the left under a railroad trestle just at the **Forks of the River** where the waters of the Holston to the right and the French Broad to the left mingle to form the Tennessee River.

In 0.8 mile notice the large marble quarry on your left. Quarries once operated in this region, beginning around 1871, supplying Tennessee marble for buildings throughout the eastern U. S. The rock walls of the quarry show the square spaces where blocks of marble have been cut out. Pass through an industrial area, and cross National Drive in 0.5 mile.

An owner of marble quarries in this area built the 1890 Victorian house with neoclassical columns on the right; notice the carriage blocks by the front gate that were used to step into carriages or to mount horses. In 0.3 mile past the house, the **Asbury United Methodist Church** stands on the left, a Gothic Revival church built originally in 1855 and rebuilt in 1898 in a style similar to many Methodist churches built during the period. Francis Asbury, a Methodist bishop and circuit-riding preacher for whom the church and this community are named, conducted the first Methodist service in Knoxville in 1800.

In 0.6 mile cross Gov. John Sevier Highway, and soon after, Asbury Road joins Thorngrove Pike. This drive will turn left here, but you can continue out Thorngrove Pike on a side trip to explore the farming region along the French Broad River. In 1.3 miles bear right at a fork to stay on Thorngrove Pike and enter the community of Riverdale. James White first settled here before moving with his family to the site that would become Knoxville. In

Riverdale Mill

1.4 miles as the road descends a hill, the Greek Revival **Kennedy House** stands on the right; it was built in 1830 by James Kennedy, a Presbyterian minister who emigrated from Ireland.

At the corner of Wayland Road stands **Riverdale Mill,** built in 1858 and once owned by James Kennedy, the son of Rev. James Kennedy. The red two-story frame mill of post-and-beam construction passed through several owners since Kennedy. In 1908 it was modernized with the addition of roll mills to replace the millstones and a 30-foot overshot steel Fitz wheel to replace the original wooden wheel. A long flume brought water to the top of the wheel from a dam upstream along Wayland Road.

Continue east on Thorngrove Pike. In 0.9 mile the **H & H Service Mart** is on the right, a typical country store built about 1880. Scenes in the movie *The Dollmaker* were filmed at the old store. Turn right on Kodak Road into the farming countryside where barns, silos, and grazing cattle dot the landscape. In 0.8 mile, the **Riverdale United Methodist Church** stands on a hill to the left, built about 1890 in a Gothic style of Methodist churches of the time.

The river is no longer in sight here because it has meandered to the right, creating a broad peninsula of land that's called Frazier Bend. Early settlers often settled in these bends in the river to farm the rich bottomlands and to use the river to transport products to Knoxville. Through the generations, Frazier Bend has remained a farming community with broad fields and large old farmhouses dating from the early 1800s.

Return from Frazier Bend along Kodak Road and Thorngrove Pike to the junction with Asbury Road. Stay straight on Thorngrove Pike to continue this drive. In 0.7 mile the **Ramsey House** stands on the right; the home of Francis Alexander Ramsey, it was built between 1795 and 1797. Ramsey, along with James White, was a member of the early team of surveyors that explored the region in the early 1780s. Ramsey settled here in 1792 or 1793. The Ramsey family first lived in a log house before constructing the two-story home of red marble and blue limestone with attached kitchen, considered the finest house of its day. James G. M. Ramsey, the son of F. A. Ramsey, became a physician and author of the state's first history, the *Annals of Tennessee.* Ramsey House today is administered by the Association for the Preservation of Tennessee Antiquities and is open to the public.

KIMBERLIN HEIGHTS AND SEVEN ISLAND

Continue on Thorngrove Pike to a junction with Gov. John Sevier Highway and turn left, crossing Asbury Road in 0.9 mile. The highway, which is also

TN 168, crosses a bridge over the French Broad River in 0.6 mile. In another 0.9 mile French Road turns to the left, where you can take a side trip to the farming community of Seven Island, a lovely pastoral countryside in another bend of the French Broad. In 0.5 mile turn left on Kimberlin Heights Road. **Beulah Methodist Church** stands on the left; the church is another of the Methodist churches built in a similar Gothic design in the 1890s. In 1.7 miles Kimberlin Heights Road bears left as Herndons Chapel Road joins on the right.

Kimberlin Heights was named after Jacob Kimberlin, an early settler. In 1887 a great-grandson of Kimberlin, Dr. Ashley S. Johnson, who had established a correspondence Bible college in Knoxville, acquired the old Kimberlin homestead. There, in 1893, he opened **Johnson Bible College,** originally called "School of the Evangelists," for the training of Christian Church ministers. The college lies to the left as the road curves to the right, 2 miles from the junction with Herndons Chapel Road.

Continue east on Kimberlin Heights Road. In 3.5 miles at a junction with Seven Islands Road, turn left into the Seven Islands Community along the French Broad River. As the road descends toward the river, the **Seven Islands Church** stands on the right, built about 1880. An old cemetery lies adjacent to the church. The river flows by at a distance behind the cemetery.

In 0.6 mile from the church, turn left on Woodlawn School Road. In another 0.6 mile the **Keener–Hunt House** stands on the left at the corner of Woodlawn School and Huffaker Ferry Roads. Along with the two-story brick Federal home built in the 1850s, notice the servants' quarters, smokehouse, and other outbuildings.

Huffaker Ferry Road to the right deadends at the river at the place where Justus Huffaker once operated a ferry crossing. Turn left on Huffaker Ferry Road and travel 0.7 mile up to a junction with Kimberlin Heights Road. Turn right to retrace your route back to Gov. John Sevier Highway and continue this drive to the west.

MARBLE SPRINGS

In 3.4 miles this drive will exit left onto Neubert Springs Road, but first stay straight another 0.3 mile and turn left into **Marble Springs State Historic Farmstead,** the home of Gov. John Sevier. Among the several log structures in the compound stands the original two-story log cabin Sevier built in 1792 and where he and his family lived periodically until his death in 1815. He named the home for the marble deposits and numerous springs on the property.

Sevier and his father, Valentine, were early settlers of upper East Tennessee, then part of the western lands of the North Carolina colony. John Sevier quickly became a leader among pioneer communities and was one of those who led the Overmountain Men in the Battle of Kings Mountain that helped to win the Revolutionary War. He was later selected governor of the State of Franklin when the Watauga settlements attempted to establish their own state. When Tennessee became a state in 1796, Sevier was elected the new state's first governor. He rented a residence in Knoxville and spent his spare time at the country home, Marble Springs.

Sevier and his second wife, Catherine Sherrill, are buried on the grounds of the Knox County Courthouse in Knoxville. The original tombstones of Sevier and Catherine, known as "Bonny Kate," are in the wall of the northeast corner of the courthouse. There is also a marker on the grounds for Sevier's first wife, Sarah Hawkins, who died in 1780 during an Indian uprising, which perhaps partially explains Sevier's later antagonism. In more than thirty battles that Sevier fought with the Native Americans, he earned the epithet "Scourge of the Cherokees."

Return up Gov. John Sevier Highway and exit onto Neubert Springs Road, and turn left to continue this drive, passing behind Marble Springs. In 0.4 mile cross Tipton Station Road to the left to stay on Neubert Springs Road, a small country lane that travels through a farming valley with old barns and farmhouses. In 1.3 miles a gazebo of twisted tree roots stands on the left, all that remains of **Neubert Sulphur Springs,** one of the many spas that operated in the area around the turn of the century.

In another 1.5 miles, at a junction with Rhea Road, turn right for 1.1 miles to Martin Mill Pike. Turn right there, once more passing old farmhouses in a pastoral setting. In 2.9 miles the drive returns to Tipton Station Road. Directly across the road, a drive leads to **New Salem United Methodist Church,** built in 1893 in a similar architectural style as other late 1800s Methodist churches; this one is nearly identical to Beulah Methodist Church earlier on this drive.

CANDORO MARBLE AND FORT DICKERSON

Turn west on Tipton Station Road to continue this drive. In 0.4 mile bear left to stay on Tipton Station. In 2.2 miles turn right on Maryville Pike, which is also TN 33. In 0.3 mile the **Maxey House** stands on the left, an 1830 two-story house with 1860 additions.

Heading back to Knoxville, Maryville Pike passes more older homes and travels under and over railroad tracks. Stay with Maryville Pike through an intersection, and in 4.2 miles **Candoro Marble** is on the left, the old headquarters of Candoro Marble Company. The marble structure was built in 1923 for the John Craig Family of marble dealers and quarriers. Candoro Marble became the largest producer of Tennessee marble in the region, supplying marble for many public buildings in Knoxville and other cities, including the National Gallery of Art in Washington, D. C.

In 0.9 mile Maryville Pike emerges on Chapman Highway, which is also US 441. Turn left, and in 0.1 mile turn left uphill on Fort Dickerson Road to **Fort Dickerson** in 0.5 mile. This fort on a knoll overlooking the Tennessee River and the city of Knoxville was one of sixteen Union earthen forts and battery emplacements protecting Knoxville. The fort was occupied by federal troops from 1863 when Union Gen. Ambrose Burnside took the city and held it until the end of the war in 1865.

Return to Chapman Highway and continue north into Knoxville, crossing Henley Street Bridge over the Tennessee River in 0.8 mile, with the University of Tennessee campus to the left. In 2 blocks you can turn right on Main Avenue for 4 blocks to Gay Street where the Knox County Courthouse stands on the corner. A right turn on Gay Street will return you to Hill Avenue and Blount Mansion in 1 block.

7

Mineral Water, Flying Machines, and Melungeons

KNOXVILLE TO BULLS GAP LOOP

GENERAL DESCRIPTION: This 140-mile drive explores the valley of the Holston River, visiting small communities and towns that figured in the early history of Tennessee.

SPECIAL ATTRACTIONS: New Market, Jefferson City, Panther Creek State Park, Morristown, Crockett Tavern, Bulls Gap, Tate Springs, Rutledge, House Mountain State Natural Area, historic homes and buildings, scenic views, fall color, hiking, biking, boating, fishing, and wildlife viewing.

LOCATION: East Tennessee. The drive begins at Exit 394 on I-40 east of Knoxville.

DRIVE ROUTE NUMBERS: US 11E; TN 66, 113, and 344; and US 11W.

CAMPING: Cherokee Dam and Panther Creek State Park.

SERVICES: All services at Knoxville, Jefferson City, and Morristown.

NEARBY ATTRACTIONS: Mascot, Cherokee Dam, Elrod Falls, and Sneedville.

THE DRIVE

The Holston River travels southwest through the Great Valley of East Tennessee to its confluence with the French Broad, where the two streams combine their waters into the Tennessee River. Cherokee Dam on the Holston backs up Cherokee Lake, which is encompassed by the route of this drive. This loop traverses the rural countryside along the Holston and passes through historic communities. Along the way, you can sample mineral water, learn about a flying machine that predates the Wright Brothers, and take a side trip to visit Melungeon country.

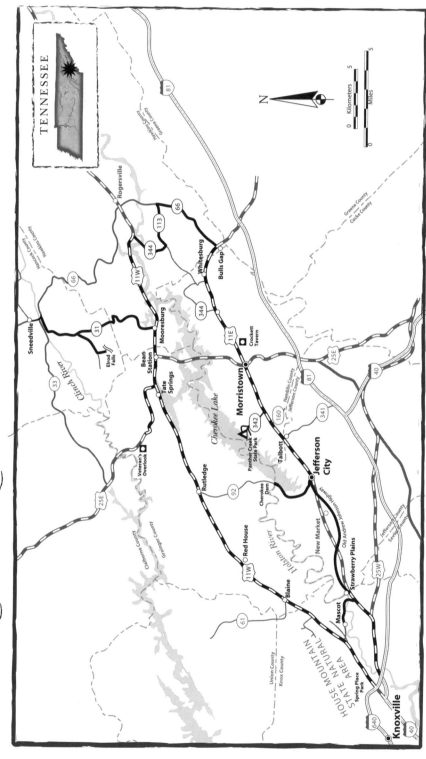

MASCOT

East of Knoxville on I–40, take Exit 394 onto Asheville Highway, which is US 25W/11E and head northeast on the four-lane road. In 0.7 mile cross the Holston River. From that point, travel 5.6 miles, then bear left on US 11E (Andrew Johnson Highway) as US 25W (Asheville Highway) turns off to the right. In another 2.8 miles, you can turn left on Mascot Pike for a side trip to the mining town of **Mascot.** Mascot Pike crosses the Holston River on **McBee Bridge,** built in 1930 with three open-spandrel concrete arch spans. In 2.1 miles turn left to stay on Mascot Pike while Mine Road stays straight. Cross railroad tracks at a junction, and stay right to enter the community of Mascot. Zinc was discovered here in the 1850s and some surface mining took place. Then around 1906, the Holston Zinc Company opened the first zinc mine. The American Zinc Company acquired the mines in 1910, and Mascot became a company town. In the 1970s, ASARCO purchased the mines.

In Mascot, several homes with pyramidal hipped roofs stand along the road; these were once worker cottages. At Library Road on the left, you can turn up to the **Mascot Library,** which is housed in an old post office and jail. Past Tipple Road, the large home on the left dates from the early 1800s. Flat Creek, which runs through the town, is lined with concrete to keep water from getting into Mine No. 2, but now the abandoned mine is flooded. Up from the creek, Staff Road turns off to the right to pass through a group of white cottages that served as housing for the mine staff.

Return to US 11E and continue to the northeast with the Holston River to the left. In 0.4 mile bear left on Old Andrew Johnson Highway, which was the main route before the four-lane was constructed to bypass the small communities. A railroad bridge spans the river to the left; the old East Tennessee, Virginia, and Georgia is now part of the Norfolk–Southern Railroad.

The road passes into Jefferson County and enters Strawberry Plains. In the early years settlers often used fire to clear the land; here the fire got out of control and created a barrens, and on this empty plain, wild strawberries grew, hence the name. A few large old homes and cottages line the road through town. Follow the highway then through farmland to enter Friends Station in 6.8 miles. Here a little gravel road to the right leads to the **Lost Creek Friends Quaker Church;** Quakers settled this area in the late 1700s and in 1815, being opposed to slavery, organized the Tennessee Society for Promoting the Manumission of Slaves.

MINERAL WATER

Old Andrew Johnson Highway reaches US 11E. Turn left and soon after turn right to get back on Old Andrew Johnson Highway. In 1.4 miles enter New Market, with the 1850 **Houston House** on the right. The next house marks the spot of the log home of Frances E. Hodgson, who came here with her family from England in 1865; she later married Dr. Swan Burnett and under the name Frances Hodgson Burnett became a noted author; her children's books include *Little Lord Fauntleroy* and *The Secret Garden.*

Next on the right is a gazebo and wellhouse marking the site of **Houston's Mineral Water.** In 1931 William Avery Houston was so ill with a kidney disease he began preparing for death by getting his affairs in order. Then one morning, Houston reported that he had had a dream in which he was told to drill a well 252 feet deep and drink the water. He brought in someone to drill the well, and even though they struck water at a shallower level, they kept on drilling to the depth Houston had been told, where they found a mineral water. After drinking the water for several days, Houston was cured. He later sold the bottled water throughout the country until the Federal Trade Commission and a court judge ordered him to no longer advertise the water as a curative. Afterwards, Houston sold the water as "good drinking water." Today Houston's grandson, Bill, maintains the old well, having installed a modern pump and filtration system plus ultraviolet light purification. Just past the well stands an old stone-faced concrete block building that William A. Houston operated as a grocery store. Turn in the drive on the far side of the building and drive behind to parking in back of the wellhouse. Go on in and have a drink; it's all on the honor system—25 cents a gallon and drinks from the water fountain are free.

At Churchview Street, just beyond Houston's, the **New Market Presbyterian Church,** a brick church built in 1847, stands on the far corner on the left. Other old homes stand along the street ahead, but turn left up Churchview past other churches and cross US 11E to continue up Churchview to Depot Street on the left. On the corner stands the old **New Market Hotel** facing the railroad tracks ahead. The building started as a two-room house with loft that was the home of the Minnis family, constructed sometime between 1815 and 1820. In the 1880s, George and Elizabeth Dempster arrived from Scotland, and Elizabeth converted the house to a hotel, adding the porch. The hotel business virtually ended with the New Market train crash of 1904, a head-on collision of east- and west-bound trains that killed sixty-four people, including the engineers and firemen. After being derelict for many years, the old hotel has been restored as a private residence.

JEFFERSON CITY AND CHEROKEE LAKE

Return to US 11E and turn left to continue the drive to the northeast. Into the countryside, the highway passes old farms with barns, silos, and outbuildings. In 2.1 miles turn left on TN 92, which is the continuation of Old Andrew Johnson Highway, and in 1 mile pass between pillars at the entrance to Jefferson City. Before entering the town, you can turn left to stay on TN 92 and reach TVA's **Cherokee Dam** on the Holston River in 3.8 miles. A road on the right leads to boat access to **Cherokee Lake** and a campground (no hookups). Just beyond is a visitor center, picnic area, and lake overlook. You can continue on TN 92 another 0.7 mile to a right turn that leads to boat access to the river on the left and the bottom of the dam straight ahead.

Return to Jefferson City and turn left to enter the town. In 0.3 mile on the left stands the wonderful **Hampton Hall,** a brick Second Empire home with red tile roof and green shutters built in 1860. In 0.6 mile enter the old downtown. **Carson Newman College** is on the hill to the right. Watch for the old city hall on the right in the center of town; it is now the Moose Creek Masonic Lodge. In another 0.4 mile **Glenmore Mansion** crowns the hill to the right, a magnificent Second Empire home, it was built between 1868 and 1869 by John R. Branner, who was president of the East Tennessee, Virginia, and Georgia Railroad. Jefferson City was created by the railroad in the 1850s. Branner called his home The Oaks. When the Milton P. Jarnigan family purchased the home in 1882, they renamed it Glenmore for a baby son who died. The home is now a house museum and open for tours May through October.

Continue on Old Andrew Johnson Highway out of Jefferson City, crossing the rail line. In 2.3 miles notice a third large Second Empire home on the left at a distance. In another 0.9 mile rejoin US 11E and turn left. Enter Hamblin County in 0.8 mile. In 2 miles in the community of Talbott, the **Watkins–Witt House** stands on the left; it is a white brick Italianate villa, with a widow's walk, built around 1857.

In 2.2 miles you can turn left on TN 342 to reach **Panther Creek State Park** on the shore of Cherokee Lake in 2.5 miles. Panther Creek and nearby Panther Springs get their names from a story that a panther, or mountain lion, was killed here and fell into the spring. The park has a swimming pool, tennis courts, a campground, and a 25-mile trail system that includes 12 miles of mountain bike trails on the west end of the park. A scenic drive in the park leads to the top of a hill where a picnic area overlooks Cherokee Lake.

Glenmore Mansion

MORRISTOWN

Return to US 11E, turn left and travel 3.5 miles to enter Morristown at a junction where US 11E turns right to bypass the downtown. Stay straight on First North Street into Morristown.

In 0.3 mile the **Hamblen County Courthouse,** an 1874 Second Empire building stands proudly to the left. Turn left up Jackson Street for 1 block to Second North Street. On the far corner stands the **Rose Center,** a Richardsonian Romanesque school built in 1892; it is now a center for historic preservation and a cultural center. The Hal A. Noe Historical Gallery contains the collection of historical photographs taken by Noe, who worked for the *Morristown Daily Gazette and Mail* newspaper. The gallery also contains the remains of the Murrell flying machine. Melville M. Murrell grew up in Hamblen County near Panther Springs. Experimenting with flying contraptions, he eventually created a machine that operated like a bird's wings, stroking up and down by use of cords and pulleys. The wings had horizontal flaps that opened on the upstroke for least air resistance and closed on the downstroke for the most lift. After several flights of 100 yards, he was granted a patent in 1877, twenty-six years before the Wright Brothers had their first successful flight.

On Second North Street you can continue east to explore **Millionaire's Row** of fine old homes dating from the 1880s to the 1950s, part of the Olde Towne Historic District. Four blocks to the north, on Sixth North Street stands **Morristown College,** a school for African Americans founded in 1881 by the United Methodist Church; the school is now a branch of Knoxville College. Ahead lies the old **Morristown Cemetery** where more than 200 headstones and monuments have been uncovered and restored.

Return down James Street to Second North Street and turn right to Henry Street. Turn left down Henry to cross First North Street one block to Main Street. On the corner stands the old **Daily Gazette and Mail Building.** Turn left on Main to pass through the downtown. The street becomes Morningside Drive and in 1.6 miles reaches **Crockett Tavern** on the right, a reconstruction of the late 1700s tavern run by John and Rebecca Crockett, the parents of David Crockett. David was born near Limestone to the east, and when the Crocketts moved here, the tavern became David's boyhood home. David remained in East Tennessee until at twenty-five years of age he moved to Middle Tennessee with wife Polly and their two sons.

Crockett Tavern

Continue on Morningside Drive for 0.5 mile to where the road curves left to Old Andrew Johnson Highway (US 11E) that has passed through town as Second North Street. Turn right to pass under US 25E and head to the northeast. In 3.9 miles enter the small community of Russellville and bear left on TN 344, which is also Old Russellville Pike. You can turn left on Three Springs Road and right on North Second Street to reach the **Russellville United Methodist Church,** built in 1859. During the Civil War, the church was used as a hospital; the basement served as a school until 1875. Return to TN 344 and continue through Russellville. Where TN 344 curves to the left, stay straight on Old Russellville Pike to rejoin US 11E and turn left. Where US 11E curves to the left and Old Stage Coach Road bears off to the right stands the **Coffman House.** The original log cabin here was built in 1783–84 on the land grant of David Coffman. The cabin is now enclosed in clapboard siding in the present house.

BULLS GAP AND MOORESBURG

Stay with US 11E another 2.3 miles into Whitesburg where the **Bent Creek Church** stands beside the road on the left. The brick church was built in 1878 and later served as a Masonic Lodge. In another mile the highway crosses Bent Creek. In 1.2 miles enter Hawkins County. In 1 mile, at a junction with TN 66 to the left, turn right to enter the community of Bulls Gap. South Main crosses a bridge over railroad tracks and descends into the town nestled in the gap. On the left is the **Archie Campbell Homeplace;** country music comedian Campbell gained notoriety on the television program *Hee-Haw.* The street descends past the adjacent Town Hall, which contains the small **Bulls Gap Museum.** The town was created as a junction on the old East Tennessee, Virginia, and Georgia Railroad which passed through this gap, named for John Bull, a noted gunsmith who settled here around 1794. Bulls Gap is a classic railroad town, with several tracks running through the downtown and old buildings facing the rail line. The town's historic district contains twenty-seven structures, including the old **Gilley's Hotel** that once served rail passengers.

Return to US 11E and stay straight across on TN 66. In 9.8 miles turn left on TN 113; if you were to stay straight on TN 66 to Rogersville another 4.2 miles, you would connect with the Country Music, Boatyards, and Journalism drive. On TN 113, in 4.4 miles, turn right on TN 344, which is also called Malinda Ferry Road. In 3.9 miles cross a bridge over the upper end of Cherokee Lake on the Holston River, and in another 0.8 mile, at a junction with US 11W, turn left.

The four-lane highway heads southwest as it parallels the Holston, crossing tributary streams through a rural section of scattered homes; there's a lined bike lane on the shoulder of the highway. You can occasionally glimpse the river through the hills to the left, and signs direct anglers to boat access. In 9.7 miles bear right on Old Highway 11 to enter the small community of Mooresburg. In 1 mile turn right on Church Street; a gravel drive to the right leads to the **Homeplace Bed and Breakfast,** originally an 1850s log cabin that has been expanded and renovated over the years into a white clapboard cottage by the Rogers family, direct descendants of Joseph Rogers, the founder of Rogersville, and Hugh G. Moore, who established Mooresburg. Church Street is aptly named for the old churches along here, the brick **Bentley's Chapel** and the white frame **Mooresburg United Methodist** and **King James Baptist.**

ELROD FALLS AND MELUNGEONS

Church Street reaches a junction with TN 31. You can turn right on TN 31 for a side trip to **Elrod Falls** and **Melungeon** country. TN 31 leads north, crossing two mountain ridges and entering Hancock County. In 9.8 miles, while descending the second ridge, turn left on a side road that curves down to a gravel road and turn left, even though it might look like a driveway through a farm. In 0.8 mile, turn left on another gravel road to its end in 0.4 mile, where a small park has picnic tables; a 100-yard path leads straight ahead to the three-step Elrod Falls. From the parking area, you can look ahead to the lower two waterfalls of 30 and 20 feet, and as you walk along the trail you get a glimpse of the top falls of about 15 feet.

TN 31 climbs a third ridge and descends to the Clinch River in 4.9 miles; there is boat access at this point. The highway curves right along the river to a junction in 1.6 miles with TN 66 straight ahead; turn left here to cross a bridge over the Clinch and stay straight on TN 33 into Sneedville, nestled in a valley among the hills of northeast Tennessee. You might feel isolated and hidden in this Tennessee backcountry, which is what the Melungeons intended when they settled this region. A dark-skinned people with European features, the Melungeons have themselves forgotten from where they came. The French encountered the people in the western Carolina mountains in 1690. Scotch-Irish settlers found them in southwest Virginia and northeast Tennessee. Each time, the Melungeons retreated farther into the hills to escape racial prejudice.

The most recent theory of Melungeon origin is that they are descendants of Spanish and Portuguese colonists who settled in the New World, establishing forts in the Southeast. Some of these colonists also carried Middle Eastern and North African genes, because in A.D. 711 Muslim armies conquered the Iberian Peninsula and occupied Spain and Portugal for 600 years. Some of the New World colonists migrated inland and joined with Native Americans, so that Melungeon ancestry is a complex mix, a true "melange," from which the Melungeon name derived. The greatest concentration of Melungeons is in the area of Sneedville. Over time, others have settled the region so that today the people range from light- to dark-skinned as in any other Tennessee town. In Sneedville, pass in front of the **Hancock County Courthouse** and turn right on Jockey Street one block to the old **Hancock County Jail** that many locals hope to turn into a regional museum.

BEAN STATION AND RUTLEDGE

Return on TN 31 to Mooresburg and pass Church Street on the left to a crossing of Old Highway 11; turn right to a junction with US 11W. Turn right. In 1.6 miles enter Grainger County, the only county in the state named for a woman, Mary Grainger Blount, the wife of William Blount, governor of the Southwest Territory that became the State of Tennessee.

In another 0.8 mile bear right into **Bean Station.** The original Bean Station, the site now inundated by the waters of Cherokee Lake, was one of the earliest settlements in Tennessee, founded in 1776 by Robert and Jesse Bean, sons of William Bean, considered the first permanent white settler in Tennessee. A fort was constructed here at the intersection of the Great Indian Warpath that traveled south through Virginia into Tennessee and the Wilderness Road that headed northwest through Cumberland Gap into Kentucky. Later, the Washington Post Road passed through here and in 1813, Thomas and Jenkins Whiteside built Bean Station Tavern, the largest inn between Washington, D.C. and New Orleans. By the 1830s, the inn consisted of fifty-two rooms, several parlors, and even a ballroom; as many as 200 guests could be housed for the night, and Presidents Jackson, Polk, and Johnson often stayed here. Most of the inn was destroyed by fire, so only a few rooms remained when the Tennessee Valley Authority built its Cherokee Dam and created the lake. The remaining structure was dismantled but was later destroyed when the building in which it was stored burned.

The Bean Station of today is a modern community with virtually no connection to its illustrious past. Through the town, in 1.7 miles, the street curves left to join US 25E. Turn right on the four-lane highway for another 1.7 miles and exit to get back on US 11W. You can stay straight on US 25E for a side trip up Clinch Mountain for 5.1 miles to **Veteran's Overlook** on the left that gives a sweeping view of the Holston River Valley.

On US 11W in 0.5 mile, turn right into the campus of the **Kingswood School.** The narrow road curves left to a large gazebo that marks the spot for **Tate Springs.** In the late 1700s Samuel B. Tate purchased land around the spring and constructed a hotel. In 1876 Thomas Tomlinson acquired the property and added cottages, a swimming pool, golf course, landscaped lawns, and the gazebo over the spring while expanding the hotel. Tate Springs soon became the premier resort of its kind in the late 1800s and early 1900s. Tomlinson bottled water from the spring; he was soon selling the water by mail order nationwide. The resort closed in 1941, and in 1943 the Kingswood School was established on the property. In 1963, the old hotel burned.

Straight up from the spring, the narrow lane rejoins US 11W. Turn right to pass the Kingswood School offices, which are housed in the old resort bathhouse. The highway continues to the southwest, crossing creek embayments off Cherokee Lake to the left and passing down a valley with Clinch Mountain to the right and the ridge of Richland Knobs to the left. In 6.3 miles notice the barn on the left with the sign proclaiming SEE ROCK CITY. By the 1950s, there were 800 Rock City barns throughout the Southeast advertising the nature park that is atop Lookout Mountain above Chattanooga, just across the state line in Georgia.

In 5.5 miles US 11W enters the community of Rutledge where the **Grainger County Courthouse** stands on the right. On the lawn of the courthouse is a replica of **Andrew Johnson's First Tailor Shop.** As a young man, the future president apprenticed as a tailor in his home state of North Carolina. Moving to Tennessee with his family, he settled for a short time in Greeneville before leaving to wander around, working as a tailor. Arriving in Rutledge, he set up his own tailoring business in a small brick building that was also the sheriff's office. But within six months, Johnson returned to Greeneville where he opened a tailor business, married, and began a political career that would lead him to the White House.

At the courthouse square, you can turn left on Marshall Avenue to the **Old Grainger County Jail,** constructed in 1848 and restored by the Grainger County Historical Society. Return to US 11W, and turn left to leave Rutledge. On the right is the **Rutledge United Methodist Church** and up the hill to the right stands the old **Rutledge Presbyterian Church,** a white frame structure with tall, narrow, stained-glass windows.

HOUSE MOUNTAIN AND SPRING PLACE

The highway reenters a rural valley with scattered farms and large old farmhouses in this pastoral setting of rolling hills and fields. Notice the old **Cedar**

Grove United Methodist Church on the right in 3.7 miles. In 6 miles pass through the small community of Red House; in the early 1800s, a tavern painted red stood here on the stagecoach road.

Shields Station lies on the left in 3.4 miles; beginning in 1833, Dr. Samuel Shields ran the large white frame residence as another stop on the stagecoach road. Later the structure served as a post office, store, medical dispensary, and private residence. US 11W then passes through the community of Blaine. In 1.6 miles pass TN 61 to the right. Locally known as Emory Road, TN 61 has long been a route to the west, connecting the Holston River with the Emory River.

Enter Knox County, and in 6.5 miles turn right on Idumea Road to a junction with Hogskin Road in 0.6 mile, and turn left on Hogskin to enter **House Mountain State Natural Area** to parking on the right. Six miles of trail lead from the parking area up House Mountain, a prominent outlying peak that stands apart from the southwest end of Clinch Mountain. Overlooks provide views of the Great Smoky Mountains to the southeast and Clinch Mountain and the Cumberland Plateau to the north and northwest.

Return to US 11W and continue to the southwest. In 0.7 mile turn left on Mine Road to a junction with Old Rutledge Pike, which was once the main route between Rutledge and Knoxville. You could continue straight here to reach Mascot, which was visited on the first part of this drive. Turn right on Old Rutledge Pike to pass in front of **Chesterfield,** a pre-Civil War home and its outbuildings; built by Dr. G. W. Arnold. In 0.5 mile Old Rutledge Pike curves right to rejoin US 11W.

Turn left, and in 3.5 miles watch for the **Legg-England House** on the left. The large white frame house was built in the 1830s as a stagecoach inn. James K. Polk spent the night at this house in 1845 on the way to his presidential inauguration. In another 4.4 miles you can turn right on Loves Creek Road to pass under a railroad overpass and in 0.3 mile reach **Spring Place Park** on the right, a small community park containing springs. Parking beside the road gives access to a spring where folks still get water. Another 0.5 mile up Loves Creek Road is the **Buffat Homestead.** As a boy, Alfred Buffat came from Switzerland with his family in 1848. The Buffats established a farm and erected the grist mill that was known as Spring Place Mill; the mill supplied cornmeal and flour to much of Knoxville and northeast Knox County. Alfred eventually became the operator of the mill and in 1867 built this home, known as The Maples, for his wife, Eliza. Return to US 11W and continue into Knoxville, passing under I–640; there is no access to the interstate here. In another 1.1 miles US 11W reaches a junction with I–40 on the east end of Knoxville.

8

country music, Boatyards, and journalism

BRISTOL TO ROGERSVILLE

GENERAL DESCRIPTION: This 72-mile drive starts at the birthplace of country music, enters the historic boatyard district at the Long Island of the Holston River, and ends at the cradle of Tennessee journalism.

SPECIAL ATTRACTIONS: Bristol, Blountville, Warrior's Path State Park, Kingsport, Rogersville, Pressmen's Home, historic homes and buildings, scenic views, fall color, hiking, biking, boating, fishing, and wildlife viewing.

LOCATION: East Tennessee. The drive begins in Bristol, east of I–81 at Exit 74.

DRIVE ROUTE NUMBERS: TN 126, US 11W, TN 346, 347, 70, 94, and 66.

CAMPING: Warrior's Path State Park.

SERVICES: All services at Bristol, Kingsport, and Rogersville.

NEARBY ATTRACTIONS: South Holston Dam, Steele Creek Park, Exchange Place, Bays Mountain, and Ebbing and Flowing Spring.

THE DRIVE

Settled first as pioneers trudged over the Appalachian Mountains and down into the western frontier, East Tennessee was granted the inevitable honor of being the first in many areas. From the Appalachian songs that metamorphosed into country music to the first newspapers, the eastern part of the state rightly claims to be the beginning of Tennessee. And from here, pioneers followed the rivers and old Indian trails to the eventual settlement of Middle and West Tennessee.

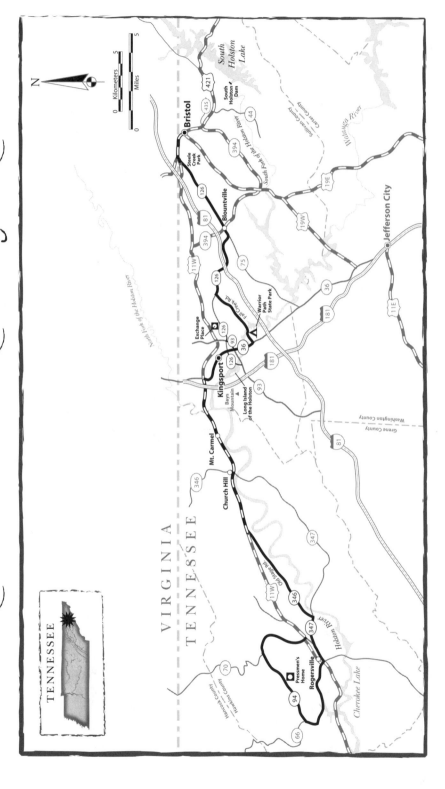

BRISTOL

Begin this drive in Bristol at the corner of Volunteer Parkway and State Street. From I–81 at Exit 74, take US 11W to the east. In 2.4 miles pass TN 126 to the right, and in another 0.7 mile, turn right on US 421, which is State Street. In 1.2 miles, at the junction with Volunteer Parkway, the Chamber of Commerce lies to the right. To the left at the junction, the parkway is Commonwealth Avenue. The city lies on the Tennessee-Virginia state line, and State Street separates Bristol, Virginia, to the north from Bristol, Tennessee, to the south.

Stay straight on State Street to enter the old downtown. In 0.2 mile turn into a parking area on the right to see the **Country Music Mural** on the side of a building. The mural depicts Ralph Peer, the Carter Family, the Stonemans, and Jimmie Rogers. In 1927, Peer, a talent scout for the Victor Recording Company, came to Bristol to record these local musicians. Peer's sessions produced the first commercial recordings of Appalachian music and began the phenomenon that is today's country music. Bristol correctly calls itself the "Birthplace of Country Music." The fledgling industry slowed during the 1930s Depression when people could not afford to buy records. By the time the economy recovered, country music had moved to Knoxville and eventually to Nashville, which is today's "Home of Country Music."

Continue up State Street. The Art Deco **Paramount Theater** on the right, built in 1931 and restored in 1991, is now a performing arts center. The **Country Music Monument** on the right at the corner with Edgemont Avenue also commemorates the 1927 country music recordings, which took place in a brick warehouse that once stood on State Street. Ahead, across the railroad tracks, the **Bristol Sign** arches over State Street; erected in 1910, it declares Bristol "a good place to live." To the left, the 1902 **Union Railway Station** stands beside the tracks; plans call for renovating the station as a community building.

You can take a side trip to **South Holston Dam** by continuing out State Street. In 0.4 mile turn right to stay on US 421; the road curves left and then right. In 4.8 miles turn right on Emmett Road; stay right at a junction in 0.6 mile to cross the South Holston River in another 1.2 miles and enter the reservation surrounding TVA's South Holston Dam. On the left is the **Osceola Island Recreation Area**. Here the South Holston Labyrinth Weir Dam stretches across the river to Osceola Island in the middle of the river and on the other side. The low zigzag dam maintains a constant level of water upstream for fish and waterfowl and helps to aerate the water as it spouts into the lower level of the river. A footbridge crosses to Osceola to where a tree

Country Music Mural

identification trail loops around the island. Another 1.2 miles up the road stands TVA's South Holston Dam. To the right, you can drive to the top and cross the earth and rock-filled dam, with South Holston Lake to the right against a backdrop of the Unaka Mountains.

Return to Bristol and turn south on Edgemont Avenue. Turn right on Anderson Street, and watch for the **E. W. King House** on the left, a wonderful brick mansion with white trim and a wraparound porch built about 1903. Now owned by the Bristol Historical Society, the house sits on the approximate location of Fort Shelby. Bristol occupies a tract of land originally known as Sapling Grove. Evan Shelby purchased part of the tract in 1770 and built a store and stockade and later became brigadier general of the Washington District, as the western lands of North Carolina were known. It was here at Fort Shelby that planning took place for assembling of the Overmountain Men, lead by Shelby's son, Isaac, and John Sevier, who defeated the British at the Battle of Kings Mountain in South Carolina in 1780.

Continue down Anderson to a junction with Volunteer Parkway and turn right to return to State Street and turn left to leave Bristol. In 1.2 miles bear left on US 11W and in another 0.7 mile turn left on TN 126. In 0.9 mile pass through old stone pillars that pose an entrance to the city on this old state route. You can turn left on Steele Creek Drive to visit **Steele Creek Park** on Steele Creek Park Road. This city park has a golf course, hiking trails, picnicking, a nature center, a lake hemmed in by hills, and a one-way scenic drive that loops through the area. Herons, wood ducks, gadwalls, mallards, and other waterfowl are found on the lake in season. Return to TN 126 and continue to the southwest.

BLOUNTVILLE

In 5.2 miles enter historic Blountville, established in 1792 as the seat of Sullivan County. Named for William Blount, the territorial governor, Blountville became a stop on the Washington Post Road. During the Civil War, half the town was destroyed in the Battle of Blountville, in which Federal forces on the west side of town and Confederate forces on the east shelled each other. But several historic buildings remain to give testament to the early town.

On the right is the two-story **Dulaney House,** built by Dr. Elkanah Dulaney in 1800; it is the oldest brick building in Blountville. When William S. Anderson purchased the home, it became known as Anderson Hall. Across the street is the **Miller-Haynes House,** a two-story white frame house built in 1848 by Dr. Elbert S. Miller. In 1855 the home was purchased by Matthew T. Haynes, who was a supporter of the Confederacy during the Civil War. During the Battle of Blountville, Union troops fired on the house and several cannonballs hit the side; some of the damage can still be seen and so the home is called the Cannonball House.

Also on the left is the **Anderson Townhouse,** a log structure built in the years 1792 to 1795 and used as a residence by the first town commissioners when they were in Blountville; Commissioner John Anderson stayed here most often. Today, it is the headquarters for the Sullivan County Historical Commission.

Across the street is another log cabin, the **Snapp-Fain-Taylor House,** built in 1796. The long building on the right is the **Old Deery Inn,** begun as a storehouse in 1785. Before it was completed, William Deery, an Irish peddler, purchased the building and property and constructed the inn, which became a prominent stop on the stagecoach road. Later it was a residence and then operated as an inn into the 1920s. Several log, frame, and brick outbuildings stand behind the inn, many brought here to be saved by Virginia Byars Caldwell, who for a time lived in the inn.

The prominent **Sullivan County Courthouse** stands on the right. The original 1853 west end of the building burned during the Battle of Blountville and was rebuilt in 1866. The east wing was added in 1956. Behind the courthouse is the **Old Town Jail,** built in 1870, that was later used as the sheriff's home.

WARRIOR'S PATH AND KINGSPORT

From Blountville, continue west on TN 126. In 4.8 miles pass under I-81, and in 0.8 mile turn left on Fall Creek Road. In 4.4 miles, cross a bridge over the South Fork of the Holston River, backed up from a TVA dam downstream. Where the road makes a sharp curve to the right, **Warrior's Path State Park** is on the left, named for the old Cherokee war and trading route that passed through this region of East Tennessee to link Cherokee lands with the Iroquois regions to the north. The park has a swimming pool, campground, and a fishing pier and marina on Fort Patrick Henry Lake.

From the park, continue on what is now Hemlock Road. You can turn up left to reach **Warrior's Rest,** a turn-of-the-century farmhouse that is now a bed-and-breakfast. Stay straight for 0.9 mile to reach a junction with Fort Henry Drive, which is also TN 36, and turn right on the four-lane highway. In 0.8 mile cross the South Fork of the Holston River, and on the other side turn right to reach an observation area at the top of a hill overlooking TVA's **Fort Patrick Henry Dam** and the lake behind. Fort Henry was erected on the bank of the South Fork of the Holston River in 1776 as protection against warring Native Americans who hoped to prevent the settlers from taking their lands.

Continue northwest on Fort Henry Drive. At a junction with TN 93 in 1 mile, you can turn right for a side trip to the **Exchange Place**. In 1.6 miles, exit onto Orebank Road. To the left in 0.3 mile is the restored farm complex in the former settlement of Eden's Ridge. The self-supporting farm was also a stop on the old stagecoach road where horses and currency were exchanged. Six of the eight farm buildings are original, dating from 1820–50. The **Kingsport Greenbelt** begins near the Exchange Place and travels west to the other side of the city into Heritage Park.

Return to Fort Henry Drive and continue into Kingsport. In 1.1 miles, TN 126 joins on the right, and in 0.9 mile the drive joins Center Street. In another 0.5 mile, TN 126 turns off to the left as Wilcox Drive. Here you can turn left for a side trip to **Bays Mountain Park.** After 2.6 miles on Wilcox, turn right on Meadow View Parkway for 0.5 mile to pass under I–181 and continue west on Reservoir Road. In 2.2 miles turn right on Bays Mountain

Road and ascend the mountain to the 3,000-acre nature park operated by the city of Kingsport. There is a fee to enter. The park contains 25 miles of trails that wander through the preserve of plants and animals.

Return to Center Street and continue into the Kingsport downtown. In 1 mile turn left on Cherokee Street to Main Street and turn right to the Chamber of Commerce and Visitor Center on the left in the **Old Freight Depot;** beyond stands the **Carolina, Clinchfield, and Ohio Passenger Train Station.** Both structures were built in 1909 when the railroad was built through the town, linking the coal fields of eastern Kentucky and southwest Virginia with manufacturing centers in South Carolina; the rail line is now part of the CSX Railroad. At the visitor center, which also has a twenty-four-hour information kiosk, you can pick up a brochure for a self-guided tour of the historic downtown.

Continue on Main Street to pass in front of the old train station, which now houses a bank. To the right up Broad Street through the center of town in four blocks is **Church Circle,** a semicircular drive where four Colonial Revival churches dating from the early 1900s anchor the northeast end of the downtown.

LONG ISLAND OF THE HOLSTON

Main Street curves to the right and in 0.6 mile joins Center Street, which is still TN 36. Turn left to pass through a section of the city dominated by the printing industry; publishers from throughout the country have books printed in Kingsport. Where TN 36 turns to the right on Lynn Garden Road, stay straight on TN 355; then curve left to pass under a railroad overpass and immediately turn right on Netherland Inn Road to travel along the South Fork of the Holston River to the left.

Pass under I–181 to **Heritage Park** along the shore of the river. Walkways and picnic areas invite you to spend some time in the river environment where you might see herons and other waterfowl and shore birds. To the left, you can walk across a high suspension bridge over the river to the **Long Island of the Holston,** which is indeed long, stretching for almost the entire length of the city between two branches of the river. The island had long been a sacred ground for the Cherokees, but with the encroachment of white settlers, the Native Americans eventually relinquished this region and the island by treaty. Recognizing the Cherokees' tie to the island, the city of Kingsport returned 3.61 acres to the Eastern Band of the Cherokees in 1976. A stone monument was erected on this site, which is accessed by the pedestrian bridge over the river; rock carvings depict the symbols of the seven clans of the Cherokees.

In the early years, Indian Agent Joseph Martin established a trading post on the island with his wife, Betsy Ward, daughter of Nancy Ward, "Beloved Woman" of the Cherokees. This west end of Long Island soon became a point of embarkation for boats and rafts heading down the Holston. In December 1779, John Donelson left Fort Henry with his flotilla of flatboats bearing settlers en route to the settling of Middle Tennessee. James Robertson had left two months before with a party of men driving livestock overland to the future settlement. Donelson made it only as far as the small settlement of Christiansville where Gilbert Christian had established a boatyard here on the north bank of the Holston at this western end of Long Island. Cold weather and other difficulties caused Donelson to delay his departure until February; at that time he and the others made a thousand-mile journey down the Holston and Tennessee Rivers, up the Ohio, and down the Cumberland River to the future site of Nashville, where they reunited with Robertson's group.

In 1802 William King bought two lots in Christiansville and founded King's Boatyard for building rafts while constructing wharfs, warehouses, and a store. By 1812 freight agents crowded along the river bank as they arranged for the shipment of salt, iron, and other products on flatboats down the river.

Continue west on Netherland Inn Road into the **Boatyard Historic District,** which remained the head of navigation on the Holston until 1850. In 0.3 mile the **Netherland Inn** stands beside the road on the right. In 1818 Richard Netherland converted an older boardinghouse built by King into this three-story inn that served people visiting the boatyard and traveling on a branch of the Washington Post Road. The Netherland family operated the inn until 1906 when the Cloud family took over operation; in 1967, the Netherland Inn Association purchased the building and preserved it as a historic house museum. Other historic structures are on the hill behind the inn. You'll also find there a small replica of the flatboats that were built in the boatyards; this was one of three used in a reenactment of John Donelson's thousand-mile voyage in celebration of the country's 1976 Bicentennial.

Continue past the Netherland Inn with Heritage Park and the South Fork of the Holston to the left. In 1.1 miles, just before a bridge crossing of the North Fork of the Holston River, turn left on a one-lane road that circles left around a hill. Here at the end of Heritage Park, you can climb steps to the top of the knoll for a platform overlook of the confluence of the South Fork and the North Fork of the Holston River. The one-lane road rejoins Netherland Inn Road; turn left to resume the drive to the west, crossing the bridge over the North Fork. On a knoll to the left on the other side stands **Rotherwood,** a large brick edifice with several outbuildings on the grounds. The first home of this name was built by Frederick Ross in the years 1818 to 1820; that house burned in 1865, but in the meantime, Ross had built another home that is the Rotherwood seen today here on the bank of the Holston.

Netherland Inn Drive curves right to a junction with US 11W in 0.4 mile. Turn left; **Allandale** stands on the right, a large white mansion with massive portico. Built by Harvey and Ruth Brooks in 1950, the house served as the focus of a 500-acre working farm. The Brooks family donated the mansion, furnished with antiques and art, and twenty-five acres that includes a large barn, outbuildings, and a formal garden to the city of Kingsport. The home and grounds are used for picnics, weddings, home tours, and barn dances in addition to conventions and meetings.

HAWKINS COUNTY

Continue west on US 11W, entering Hawkins County. In 3.7 miles pass the community of Mount Carmel to the right along the railroad tracks. Settlement to the left is conspicuously absent because the land is part of the federal government's Holston Ordinance Works. In 3.4 miles turn right on Central Street to enter the small community of Church Hill. At a junction with Main Street, turn left and cross Alexander Creek; to the right upstream are the old foundations and mill race of **Patterson's Mill,** built by Robert Patterson, along with a fort, around 1775.

At a junction where TN 346 turns to the left, stay to the right and in 1.4 miles pass the **Hord House,** a square, red-brick mansion with portico built about 1850 by Eldridge Hord; a mill was located nearby. The road soon rejoins US 11W.

In 3.4 miles, turn left onto TN 346. In 1.6 miles cross Stoney Point Creek where a magnificent two-story brick home stands on the hill to the left. This **Armstrong House,** built in the late 1700s, once served as a stop on the Old Stage Road. In another 0.5 mile **Fudge Farm** is on the left; built in 1851, it is a two-story Federal-style house with log outbuildings. In 2 miles, cross Surgoinsville Creek to pass through the small community of Surgoinsville. In 2.9 miles turn left on Old Stage Road, which still follows the original route of the stagecoach road. On the left, the large house with outbuildings is the **Miller Home,** built by Jacob Miller about 1790. He also had a store and post office nearby; the complex was a popular stop on the stage road.

In 4.4 miles, at a junction with TN 347, Burem Pike, turn right. Cross Big Creek, a tributary of the Holston, and in 2.9 miles reach West Bear Hollow Road on the right. There's a small park here with picnic tables across from a dam and public water supply on Big Creek. You can turn up West Bear

Hollow Road for 0.3 mile to where the road curves right and stay straight on a narrow lane for another 0.1 mile to reach the **Ebbing and Flowing Spring.** The spring is on the left behind a building on private land, so it's difficult to locate, but the water from the spring runs across the road, which is how you know you are there. In the space of three hours, the spring almost stops flowing and then surges forth again, reaching a flow of 500 gallons a minute. The cycle has repeated over and over for at least 200 years since the spring was first discovered. The best theory anyone has come up with is that in the hillside a balanced rock tips forward with the force of a pool of water behind it and allows the water to flow forth; when the pool is emptied, the rock settles back into position, blocking the flow until the pool fills again.

Back on TN 347, continue to the northwest, climbing a hill to pass the **Amis House** on the right in 0.8 mile, a stone house now covered in clapboard siding. Capt. Thomas Amis settled on this tract of land that was granted to him for his service in the Revolutionary War. The sturdy house he built in 1780 gave security from Native Americans who still considered the land their own.

ROGERSVILLE

In 2.2 miles TN 347 enters Rogersville at a junction with Main Street on the east end of town. Bear left to head toward the town center. This area was first settled in 1775, but it was not until 1787 that the town of Rogersville was laid out and named for Joseph Rogers, an Irishman who settled here in the early 1780s. Rogers married Mary Amis, daughter of Thomas Amis. Another Irishman, John Augustine McKinney, also an early settler, was a lawyer and judge. In 0.7 mile turn left on Colonial Road to see the **McKinney Law Offices,** which were in the large brick Spring House on the left, built in 1816; the spring was a source of water for Rogersville's early residents, and water still issues forth from the bottom of the building. The adjacent home on the corner is **Three Oaks,** built in 1815 by McKinney.

Return to Main Street and continue into the town. The chamber of commerce is on the right where you can pick up a walking tour to thirty-five historic sites in Rogersville; parking is in back. At the center of town, the four corners around the intersection with Depot Street were given for the founding of the city by Joseph Rogers. On the northeast corner is the **Overton Masonic Lodge,** which was originally a bank building constructed in 1839. On the southeast corner stands the **Hawkins County Courthouse,** a combination of Greek Revival and American classicism built in 1836, making it one of the oldest courthouses still in use in the state. The **Shelburne Law**

Rogersville Depot

Offices, constructed in 1837, are across Depot Street from the courthouse. And on the southwest corner is the **Hale Springs Inn,** built by John A. McKinney in 1824. Originally standing on a stage road, it was called McKinney Tavern.

Turn left down Depot Street and travel 3 blocks to the **Rogersville Depot** on the left, built in 1890 by the Southern Railroad after it acquired the Knoxville, Virginia, and Georgia Railroad. The depot has been restored and now houses a museum with displays on journalism, Rogersville being the "Cradle of Tennessee Journalism." The first Tennessee newspaper was printed in Rogersville in 1791; strangely, it was the *Knoxville Gazette.* The city of Knoxville was only just being established, and so the paper was printed in Rogersville for the first year before being moved to Knoxville. Since then there have been twenty-six other newspapers in Rogersville down to the present paper, the *Rogersville Review.*

Turn right on Broadway, and then right on Rogers Street. Go 1 block to Crockett Street and turn left to parking on the right. A small city park here has a walkway and picnic tables along a small stream. To the left, facing Rogan Road, rests the **Rogers Cemetery.** Here lie David Crockett and his wife, the grandparents of the famous David Crockett who played a prominent role in Tennessee history and died at the Alamo in Texas; the Crockett grandparents were killed by Indians near here in 1777. Also in the cemetery are Joseph and Mary Rogers, the founders of Rogersville.

Return to Rogers Street and turn left to pass on the left the **Pettibone Double House,** combined houses that are log underneath the clapboard siding, built in 1786. Next is the **Rogers Tavern,** a 1786 log and stone inn, now covered with siding, that Joseph Rogers operated on the stagecoach road that passed through the town.

Up to Main at the next block, turn right to pass in front of Hale Springs Inn; across the street stands the 1837 **Kyle House,** made of Kentucky blue brick laid in the common bond style. Pass through the town center to return to the junction with TN 347 where you came into town and bear left to a junction in 0.6 mile, with TN 70 to the left. Here in the median of the junction stands the **Hawkins County Milestone,** one of the few in the 1920s placed along the Lee Highway that traveled from Washington, D. C., to San Diego, California. The highway is US 11, which has now been rerouted to the north, but the marker remains along the original route, which was also the location of the old stagecoach road.

PRESSMEN'S HOME

Bear left at the monument on TN 70 to pass under US 11W and continue to the north. The long ridge of Stone Mountain stands to the left. The sharp, rocky point on this end of the ridge is called Devils Nose. The road curves around this end of the mountain to a junction in 5.5 miles where TN 70 turns off to the right; stay straight on TN 94. The road climbs and drops down into Little Poor Valley between Stone Mountain on the left and Clinch Mountain on the right. All of this region is part of the Great Valley of East Tennessee that has many parallel ridges and valleys running northeast to southwest.

In 3.8 miles a lake appears on the left; it is held back by a dam on Little Poor Valley Creek. Just beyond it is the **Pressmen's Home,** which was the headquarters of the International Printing Pressman and Assistants' Union from 1910 until 1967 when the union headquarters was moved to Washington, D. C. Originally, this valley was called Sulphur Springs for the mineral springs in the area. In the 1830s, James Richardson from Virginia purchased land in the valley and constructed a home near the largest spring. After Richardson's death in 1848, Philip Hale and his wife, one of Richardson's daughters, acquired the property, and the Hales expanded the facilities and opened a resort, Hale's Red and White Sulphur Springs. Visitors arriving in Rogersville by train would first spend the night at the hotel in town and then be transported by horse-drawn hack to the resort; the hotel in Rogersville adopted the name "Hale Springs Inn."

The resort spa passed through several owners until William Berry stayed at the resort and, because of the beautiful valley and peaceful setting, thought this would be the ideal spot for the headquarters of the Pressmen's Union. Berry was the charismatic leader of the union, which had elected him president in 1907. He soon convinced the union to purchase the old resort and begin construction on the new headquarters. The first building was a large home for retired union members and their families, which is how the site came to be known as the Pressmen's Home. Soon after, the union built a sanitarium for tubercular members, a hotel for students and visitors, an administration building, a chapel, a printing trades school that was the finest in the country, and various barns and outbuildings. With its own post office, water and electrical system, farm, sawmill, and carpentry shop, the home was self-sufficient, employing 1,500 people at its peak. Berry died in 1948, but the headquarters remained in the valley for another nineteen years; after the union left, it was virtually abandoned.

This is now private land with no visitor access. But from the road, you can still see many of the old buildings of the Pressmen's Home. A stone arch marks the entryway to the compound. Continue out TN 94. In 2.4 miles stands the **Sulphur Springs Primitive Baptist Church,** a small white church with green roof built in the 1870s.

Continue down the narrow, beautiful valley to a junction with TN 66 in 1.9 miles. Turn left to return to US 11W at Rogersville in 10 miles.

TVA and cumberland Gap

NORRIS TO CUMBERLAND GAP LOOP

GENERAL DESCRIPTION: A 118-mile drive travels from the beginnings of the Tennessee Valley Authority at Norris Dam to Cumberland Gap that provided a passageway through the Cumberland Plateau for early settlers and Civil War soldiers.

SPECIAL ATTRACTIONS: Norris, Norris Dam, Norris Dam State Park, Cove Lake State Park, Harrogate, Cumberland Gap National Historical Park, Tazewell, Big Ridge State Park, historic homes and buildings, scenic views, fall color, hiking, biking, boating, fishing, hunting, and wildlife viewing.

LOCATION: Central East Tennessee. The drive begins at Norris, which is east of Exit 122 on I–75.

DRIVE ROUTE NUMBERS: US 441 and 25W; TN 63; US 25E; and TN 33, 170, and 61.

CAMPING: Norris Dam State Park, Cove Lake State Park, Cumberland Gap National Historical Park, Big Ridge State Park, Anderson County Conservation Park, and Loyston Point Recreation Area.

SERVICES: All services at I–75 junction, LaFollette, Cumberland Gap, and Tazewell.

NEARBY ATTRACTIONS: Chuck Swan State Forest and Wildlife Management Area, Anderson County Conservation Park, and Loyston Point Recreation Area.

THE DRIVE

The Tennessee Valley Authority emerged from Pres. Franklin D. Roosevelt's New Deal Program as a federal utility formed to improve the economic prospects of the Tennessee River Valley. From its first dam at Norris, TVA has grown to become the largest electric utility in the country, dramatically changing the landscape of the region through the building of dams and creating lakes on the river system. Much earlier in the state's history, legions of settlers and soldiers found their way to fortunes and battles through Cumberland Gap, which provided a passageway from Tennessee into the Bluegrass region of Kentucky.

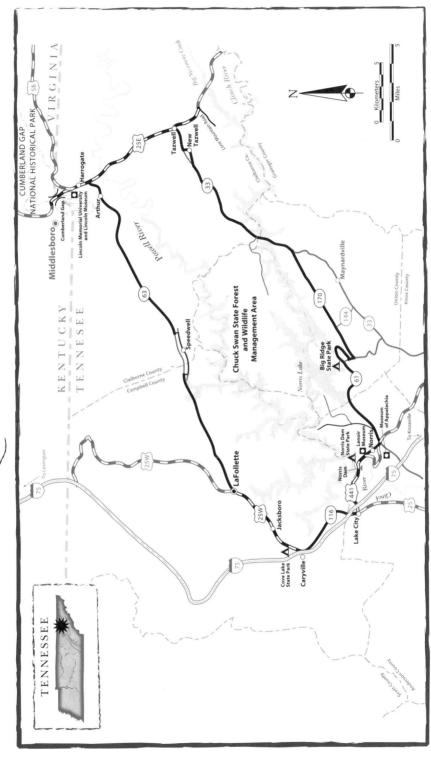

TVA AND CUMBERLAND GAP

9

NORRIS

From Exit 122 on I–75 north of Knoxville, head east on TN 61, a four-lane highway that enters the rural northeast end of Anderson County. In 0.9 mile, the **Appalachian Community Craft Center** stands on the right, the oldest craft cooperative in the state. The craft shop offers pottery, weavings, baskets, jewelry, and other craft items handmade by local artists; the center often has craftspeople at work on-site, and classes are offered in various craft skills.

The **Museum of Appalachia** lies on the left, a collection of cabins, barns, tools, and implements gathered from across this southern Appalachian region by John Rice Irwin, a native of East Tennessee and a former teacher, principal, and superintendent of schools; farm animals graze behind split rail fences as mountain music drifts across the fields; the museum's Tennessee Fall Homecoming in October featuring crafts and music is a major regional event. At a four-way intersection with US 441 to the right, turn left on East Norris Road into the community of Norris.

The Tennessee Valley Authority was conceived as part of the New Deal program to counter the effects of the Great Depression of the 1930s. Sen. George W. Norris of Nebraska had argued for a development program for the Tennessee River Valley. Out of this vision came TVA, with the mission to improve navigation on the Tennessee River, provide for flood control, institute reforestation and rehabilitation of farmland, and assist in industrial development.

The first dam, built between 1933 and 1936, was named in honor of Senator Norris, and the community of Norris was created to house some of the 2,100 engineers and construction workers who would build the dam. This small community was a model of town planning, with homes and streets adapting to the natural terrain and the residents cooperatively working and living together.

In 1948, the federal government sold the town at public auction to a private corporation that in turn sold individual homes and lots to the town residents. In 1949, Norris became an incorporated city. The community was conceived in the garden city style, a scheme of community surrounded by a rural belt that became popular in England and the United States to counter the effects of overcrowding brought on by the industrial revolution.

As you enter the town, East Norris Road climbs a hill, dips through a hollow, and then climbs another hill to enter the historic town center. Notice the distinctive homes to the right; these English-style cottages make the city quite charming. Twelve basic designs were used to construct the homes, and different exteriors were employed to vary the look of the houses—wood, brick, shingles, cinder block, and stone. To the left is the **Norris Religious**

Fellowship, an interdenominational church that maintains the tradition of community cooperation. At the top of the hill, the street bears right and then left to pass in front of the 1935 **Norris School,** the two-story Colonial Revival brick school building where not only children went to classes but workers attended vocational training sessions to learn new skills; today the building is a county middle school. On the right lies the **Norris Commons,** an undeveloped park for playing, walking, or just lying in the grass; this is the largest of several open spaces held in common by the people of the city.

On the right, stands the **McNeeley Municipal Building,** containing the community library and the **Norris Museum** in the old McNeeley Family Clinic building. Dr. S. Gene McNeeley began practice here in 1948 in the former Harriet Hankins house that was converted to a doctor's office for the community. The Hankins house was moved to make way for the first part of the present brick building, which was expanded over the years as McNeeley's physician sons joined him in his practice. In the 1990s, the clinic relocated out of town on TN 61 and the building was donated to the city. The town museum contains an oak cabinet and the implements Dr. McNeeley used in his original office. The museum also traces the history of Norris in photos, videos, and artifacts and contains the city's archives.

The street bears left to pass the small commercial district with a grocery-pharmacy complex on the left that dates from the creation of the town. Since there is no home mail delivery in the community, the U.S. Post Office on the left serves as a meeting place for neighbors who stop by to pick up their mail. You can turn right on Deer Ridge Road and then left on Chestnut Drive to reach **Eric Harold Park,** where you can have a picnic. Just beyond the park is the city office, where you can get information about the town.

NORRIS DAM

As you leave the center of town, the main street through town becomes West Norris Road. The street dips through another hollow where you stay to the right and continues through the surrounding historic neighborhoods to reach a junction with US 441, locally called the Norris Freeway, a limited access highway constructed by TVA. Turn right to pass through forested TVA lands, descending the hill.

The picturesque **Island Home Baptist Church** stands on the right; the white frame structure with steeple and church bell was constructed around 1897. You can turn left on River Road to a parking area beside the Clinch River; a boat ramp provides river access, and you can fish from the streambank.

Norris Dam

US 441 continues from River Road along the scenic Clinch River to the left. In 1 mile a low weir dam in the river channel provides for a constant level of water upstream for fish habitat; this is part of the most popular trout fishery in the state.

To the right is the **Lenoir Museum,** a gathering of old-time farm implements, artifacts, and historical odds and ends collected by Will and Helen Lenoir and donated to the State of Tennessee; the collection provides a look back at how people lived in this region in the late 1800s and early 1900s.

Just past the museum, turn down right on Lower Clear Creek Road to the **Caleb Crosby Threshing Barn** and the **Rice Eighteenth Century Grist Mill,** two historic structures on Clear Creek, a tributary of the Clinch. The threshing barn was built in the 1830s by Caleb Crosby on the Holston River to the east. When TVA created Cherokee Lake with the construction of a dam on the Holston in the 1930s, the barn and threshing machine were dismantled by the family and donated to the National Park Service, which eventually donated the structure to the state, which reassembled the barn here in the 1970s. The nearby grist mill was constructed on Lost Creek in Union County in 1798 by James Rice, an ancestor of John Rice Irwin. Four generations of Rices operated the mill, which has an overshot wheel and carved wooden gears. The Rice land was purchased by TVA in 1935 to make way for the creation of Norris Lake. The mill was dismantled and reassembled on this site, which TVA donated to the state.

Lower Clear Creek Road continues as a gravel road into forested land that makes up the **Norris Watershed,** 2,037 acres set aside on the north side of the city to protect the water supply. The area has 20 miles of trails for hikers, horseback riders, and mountain bikers.

Just past Lower Clear Creek Road on US 441, there's trailhead parking on the left for horse riding. On the right is TVA's **Aquatic Biology Laboratory.** Experimental tree groves stand to the left. Soon after, you can take the road that leads to the bottom of **Norris Dam.** In 0.7 mile parking to the left provides access to the Song Bird Trail and a boat ramp to the river. At the end of the road is a view of the dam and powerhouse, with the river flowing from the bottom of the dam.

Return to US 441 and turn left to drive to the top of the dam in 1 mile. On the left is a picnic area and a visitor center. The highway curves left, and just before the dam, a road to the right leads into the **Norris Dam State Park, East Area,** an older area of the park with picnic areas, campground, rustic cabins, and a hiking trail system that connects with the Norris Watershed trails.

US 441 crosses the top of the dam with views of the lake to the right and the steep drop-off to the river to the left. On the other side, the road curves right and enters Campbell County. A marina rests at the lake edge; the road then curves left to climb a hill above the dam. You can turn left at the top into **West Overlook,** which provides a sweeping view of Norris Dam. Past the overlook, you can turn left on Dabney Lane and immediately turn left again to descend the hill into TVA's **River Bluff Natural Area.** In 0.8 mile there's parking on the right for the River Bluff Trail, a 3.2-mile loop that may be the best wildflower trail in the state; in late March and April the moist slopes along the riverbank are clothed in trout lily, wild geranium, trillium, phacelia, dutchman's breeches, yellow poppy, and more. The road continues on down to the river shore where there is picnicking and fishing.

From the natural area turnoff, continue on US 441, passing back into Campbell County and then reentering Anderson County as the county boundary weaves across the road. In 0.9 mile the **Norris Dam State Park, West Area** lies to the right; this newer area of the park contains a campground, picnic areas, swimming pool, hiking trails, and newer cabins.

COVE LAKE AND LAFOLLETTE

US 441 continues west, descending the hill to pass under I-75 in 2.9 miles and reach a junction with US 25W in Lake City in another 0.4 mile. This town was originally called Coal Creek, for the stream that runs through the town. Lake City lies in the coal fields at this eastern edge of the Cumberland Plateau where mining was once the foundation of the local economy. But with the downturn in the demand for coal and the creation of Norris Lake in the 1930s, the community changed its name to Lake City as it looked to the future.

Turn right to head north on US 25W. Pass under I-75 in 0.4 mile and continue straight on TN 116 to the north. Enter Campbell County to travel through rural countryside bisected by rail lines and enter Caryville in 5.5 miles at a junction with US 25W, which has followed the interstate to this point. Turn right to Cove Lake to the left nestled at the foot of the Cumberland Plateau. The highway crosses Cove Creek, which flows from Cove Lake toward Norris Lake on the Clinch River to the east; downstream, a low constant-level dam maintains the water level in Cove Lake. **Cove Lake State Park** lies along the lakeshore with campground, picnicking, and walking and biking trails. At the park restaurant, **Louie's on the Lake,** dining tables sit at picture windows overlooking a green lawn that slopes down to the water. The lake is known as a wintering area for waterfowl where varieties of ducks and geese gather in flocks on the lake waters.

Behind the park, the **Cumberland Trail** runs along the edge of the Cumberland Plateau near the **Devil's Racetrack.** These giant pillars of rock were once horizontal layers that were pushed up on their sides during the mountain building that created the plateau. Ask for directions at the park to access the trail.

Continue on US 25W to the northeast. In 0.5 mile turn right on Main Street to pass through the community of Jacksboro in 1.7 miles. The **Campbell County Courthouse** stands on the left with a war memorial monument on the courthouse grounds. In 0.3 mile reemerge on US 25W; notice the fine Victorian home on the right, built in 1890.

The four-lane highway passes through a busy commercial district and, in 4.7 miles, enters the town of LaFollette with old commercial buildings lining the street in this coal town founded in 1897. Harvey and Grant LaFollette arrived in the region in the late 1800s and established the Lafollette Coal, Iron, and Railway Company; the community grew up around their operations. In 0.2 mile you can turn left at traffic light #7 to parking on the left for the **Tank Springs Trailhead** for the Cumberland Trail.

Through LaFollette, stay straight on TN 63 where US 25W turns left. At traffic light number 9, you can turn right down Indiana Avenue to **Glen Oaks** on the left, the 1895 home of the LaFollette brothers. The house was built by George Barber, a Knoxville-based architect nationally famous for his elaborate Queen Anne-style houses and for being one of the first architects to sell houses and house plans by catalog. The thirty-room Glen Oaks is thought to be the largest Barber house ever built. Along TN 63, also watch on the right for the **Historic Wedding Chapel,** an old stone church maintained by the Campbell County Historical Society.

ALONG THE PLATEAU

In 0.6 mile, leaving town, TN 63 narrows to a two-lane highway traveling down a valley at the foot of the Cumberland Plateau to the left. Farms with old farmhouses, barns, silos, and rolling fields blanket the landscape. Hawks soar in the lifting air.

In 8 miles enter the community of Well Springs and in another 0.9 mile turn right to the old **Well Spring United Methodist Church,** a white frame building with metal roof sitting at a junction with Old State Route 63. Turn left on the old state route. In 1.5 miles pass into Claiborne County and enter the community of Speedwell. Turn right on Academy Road, a narrow lane passing through a farm to **Speedwell Academy** in 0.3 mile. Originally known as Powell Valley Male Academy, the two-story brick school was constructed in 1827. When girls were admitted to the school, the name was changed. The school is now a community center.

Return to Old State Route 63, and turn right, passing through the community. In 2.3 miles turn left on Cawood Drive to reconnect with TN 63, and turn right to continue northeast through the foothills below the plateau.

In 14 miles, where the highway crosses a bridge over railroad tracks, the community of Arthur lies to the left. The town is named for Alexander Arthur, who came to this area in 1886 to develop the coal fields of the Cumberland Mountains. This was Arthur's second attempt at an industrial enterprise. Earlier he had set up a business to harvest timber in the Newport area near the Great Smoky Mountains; that business failed when logs awaiting transport to market were washed away in a flash flood. Arthur's new venture in the Cumberland Mountains was also destined for failure. With more money poured into developing towns and infrastructure than in the business, investors became disillusioned; the depression of 1893 was the final blow. Arthur founded this small community beside the railroad tracks, hoping to salvage some success from his efforts, but the town never met his expectations.

HARROGATE AND CUMBERLAND GAP

In 1.7 miles reach a junction with US 25E. Turn left to enter the town of Harrogate. To the left lies **Lincoln Memorial University,** a school that grew out of the Civil War. The people of this region mostly remained loyal to the Union during the war, despite the fact that Tennessee had seceded to become one of the Confederate states. During the war, Union Gen. Oliver O. Howard had spoken with President Abraham Lincoln on an occasion in which the President expressed an interest in the mountain people and hoped something could be done to help them. Traveling through this region in the late 1800s, Gen. Howard remembered the President's concern and conceived of a college to educate the young men and women. He, along with Confederate Capt. R. F. Patterson and Rev. A. A. Myers, a Congregational minister, founded a college in 1897, which Howard named in honor of Lincoln. They chose as the site for the university the former site of the Four Seasons Hotel, which Alexander Arthur had established as a resort and sanitarium in this community he named for Harrogate, England; the hotel failed along with Arthur's other ventures. On the campus of LMU is the **Abraham Lincoln Museum,** which contains one of the largest collections of Lincoln and Civil War memorabilia, including many of the President's personal belongings.

Past the university entrance, continue through the community of Harrogate on US 25E, and in 0.9 mile exit off the four-lane highway onto

US 58. Soon after, turn left to descend into the community of Cumberland Gap. Ahead you can see the notch in the mountains that is the famed **Cumberland Gap,** which provided a passageway through the mountains.

The Cumberland Plateau posed a formidable barrier to westward migration for early settlers of the region. Following Indian trails, longhunters and explorers had discovered this gap in the mountains that allowed passage from Virginia and Tennessee to the west into what would become Kentucky. Daniel Boone was one of these early explorers who knew the way through the mountains. Following Richard Henderson's purchase of Cherokee lands in Kentucky, Boone blazed a trail into the wilderness through Cumberland Gap; the route came to be called the Wilderness Road. Thousands of families moved west along this route, passing through Cumberland Gap, making it one of the most crowded thoroughfares for westward migration. During the Civil War, the gap was the main passageway from the Union state of Kentucky into Confederate-held East Tennessee. Both sides vied for control of the gap, with the passage changing hands several times during the war. To commemorate the historical significance of the pass, **Cumberland Gap National Historical Park** was established in 1955, here where the states of Tennessee, Kentucky, and Virginia come together.

The town of Cumberland Gap was founded in the late 1800s by Alexander Arthur to house the workers for his great enterprise. The first task in the business was to construct a railroad tunnel through the mountains to the Kentucky coal fields in order to haul the coal to market. In 1889, after eighteen months of work, the tunnel was completed, and train service began soon after, to and from Kentucky. This small town retains much of its historic character in the old buildings and neighborhoods. In a commercial district in the center of town at a junction with Colwyn Avenue, turn left and go to the end of the street to the old **American Association, Ltd. Headquarters** on the right; this late nineteenth-century building served as the offices for the association formed by Arthur and his investors. Not long after, the headquarters was reestablished at Middlesboro, Kentucky, on the other side of the mountain.

Return along Colwyn Street, and turn left on Llewellyn Street one block to cross Pennlyn Avenue to reach the **Cumberland Gap Iron Furnace.** Originally built in the 1820s and rebuilt in 1870, this furnace, resembling a pyramid of stone, was used to produce iron on the frontier. The iron was used for making such implements as tools, pots, and railroad car wheels. By the 1880s this method of iron production became obsolete, and the furnace was abandoned; the site is now part of the historical park.

The one-way drive into the furnace site circles left back to Pennlyn

Avenue. There you can turn right and travel a short distance to the end of the road at the railroad tracks where they enter the mountain tunnel built by Alexander Arthur's workers. Return along Pennlyn to Llewellyn; notice the **Old Mill** on the right. Turn down Pennlyn to Colwyn, and turn left to pass through town. **Ye Olde Tea and Coffee Shoppe** is on the right in an old bank building. Bear left on Cumberland Avenue where the **Cumberland Gap Towne Hall** is on the right in an old school building. Behind the school, steps lead up to a small monument erected to commemorate Daniel Boone's Wilderness Trail.

The street reaches a junction with the old route of US 25E that once passed through Cumberland Gap into Kentucky; the highway has since been rerouted through a new tunnel in the mountain. The old highway route, now closed, will be returned to the condition of the Wilderness Road that once passed through the gap. The road reaches a junction with US 58, which to the left leads into Virginia; 1.5 miles in that direction lies the national park's **Wilderness Road Campground.** Turn right on US 58, reaching US 25E. You can get on this highway to head north and pass through the 4,600-foot-long **Cumberland Gap Tunnel** into Kentucky. The national park visitor center is located near Middlesboro; there you can get information about the park, access 50 miles of hiking trails, and take a scenic drive to the top of the Pinnacle. This rock promontory on the northeast side of Cumberland Gap presents a grand view of the land and communities surrounding the gap.

The **Cumberland Trail** begins at Cumberland Gap and travels south along the eastern edge of the Cumberland Plateau. This 280-mile hiking trail will pass southwest through the state, ending at Signal Point above Chattanooga. The Cumberland Trail has been designated a Tennessee state park and is about half completed. Parts of the trail will be under construction by the Cumberland Trail Conference for the next several years.

To continue this drive, cross over US 25E to turn down right; you'll see the highway tunnel ahead. The ramp you are on connects with US 25E headed southeast to return through Harrogate to the junction with TN 63 to the right. Continue to the southeast on US 25E.

TAZEWELL

In 2.3 miles cross a bridge over the Powell River, a tributary of the Clinch. In another 7.2 miles enter Tazewell at a junction with TN 345 to the left. In another 0.5 mile US 25E/TN 33 turns to the left while TN 33 continues straight; just past this junction, turn right and travel 1 block to Tazewell Road. Turn right there to enter the old town center of Tazewell. Bear right where the street splits into one-way lanes. On the right in this curve sits **Greystone,** a two-story stone house erected in 1807 by William Graham; the home was later owned by three generations of the Kivett family. To the left at this corner stands the **Tazewell United Methodist Church,** a wonderful stone structure erected in 1908.

Continue through town on Main Street past the **Claiborne County Courthouse** on the left. Beside the courthouse stands the **Hughes Building,** built in 1894 by Judge H. Y. Hughes as attorney offices. On the far side of the town center, the two one-way streets come back together; turn left to go back through town on the one-way street running behind the buildings on Main. Watch for a fine stone home on the right and then pass behind the courthouse to the corner with Montgomery Street. On the far corner on the right is the Claiborne County Library occupying the **James Wier House,** a two-story log home built in 1830 and now covered in weather boarding. Turn left down Montgomery one block to cross Main Street and return to US 25E. Turn right to the junction with TN 33. This drive will continue straight on TN 33, but you can turn left on US 25E for 3.9 miles to the small community of Springdale, and turn right on Lone Mountain Road to **Big Spring Baptist Church,** one of the oldest churches in Tennessee; built in 1796, the log church is still in use.

Return to Tazewell and continue southwest on TN 33, entering New Tazewell in 0.9 mile. When the Southern Railroad came through this region, it missed Tazewell by a mile, and so a new community grew up along the rail line. Bear left on Main Street to head for the old downtown of New Tazewell, passing through an area dominated by tobacco warehouses. On the far side of the town center, turn right to rejoin TN 33 in 0.9 mile, and turn left to continue southwest.

CHUCK SWAN AND BIG RIDGE

Continue through Tennessee backcountry. In 8.2 miles cross Big Barren Creek, a tributary of the Clinch River, and soon you'll see the waters of Norris Lake on the Clinch River to the left. In 2.4 miles a parking area provides boat access to the lake. In 0.5 mile Sharps Chapel Road turns to the right, which heads through farmland to the community of Sharps Chapel in 4.8 miles. You can continue another 5.8 miles on Sharps Chapel Road to the **Chuck Swan State Forest and Wildlife Management Area,** which occupies the peninsula of land at the confluence of the Powell and Clinch Rivers; hunting and primitive camping are allowed here by permit.

In another 0.5 mile on TN 33, enter Union County, and in 1 mile cross a bridge over the Clinch River. In 2.6 miles turn right on TN 170. This scenic highway travels down Hickory Valley between two ridges. Lone Mountain on the left and Chestnut Ridge on the right provide a dramatic example of the parallel ridges and valleys that make up the Valley and Ridge Province. In 11 miles reach a junction with TN 61. Turn right to climb to the top of Chestnut Ridge in 0.7 mile. There turn right on Big Ridge Park Road along the top of the ridge. In 1.7 miles the road turns left off the ridge, and enters **Big Ridge State Park** in 1.1 miles. A turn to the left leads to the main section of the park, but first continue straight to the **Norton Grist Mill** on the left, a mill built in 1825 with an overshot wheel that supplied the surrounding communities until 1930.

Return to the junction, and head for the main section of the park, which has cabins, campground, swimming, picnicking, and boating on Big Ridge Lake. Emerge from the park at the main entrance on TN 61, and turn right to resume this drive. The highway climbs over Bluebird Ridge to the north and descends.

Stay with TN 61 along Norris Lake, and in 4.6 miles, enter Anderson County. In 3.6 miles enter the small community of Andersonville to a junction with Park Road to the right. Here you can take a side trip to **Anderson County Conservation Park** in 7.3 miles with a campground and picnic area. You can also follow signs to **Loyston Point Recreation Area** in another 4.4 miles along a tangle of backroads. The recreation area provides boat access, a campground, picnic area, and a swimming beach on the lake. From the shore of the lake, you can look across a stretch of water that is called the "Loyston Sea." Beneath these waters lies the site of the former community of Loyston; occasionally when the waters of Norris Lake are extremely low, the foundations of the old townsite are exposed, a reminder of the once thriving community that was dismantled to make way for the rising lake when Norris Dam was built.

Return to TN 61 and turn right to pass through Andersonville. Watch for **The Morning Sun Cafe and Gallery** on the right; it serves gourmet coffees, fresh-baked breads, and locally made pastries and displays locally made crafts and art. In 2.2 miles at a junction with US 441 to the left, East Norris Road on the right leads into Norris. Stay straight to reach I–75 in 1.8 miles.

Tennessee River

KINGSTON TO CHATTANOOGA

GENERAL DESCRIPTION: This 140-mile drive travels along the Tennessee River through former Cherokee country past Hiwassee Island.

SPECIAL ATTRACTIONS: Kingston, Fort Southwest Point, Rockwood, Spring City, Watts Bar Dam, Decatur, Hiwassee Wildlife Refuge, Dayton, Chickamauga Dam, Tennessee River Park, Ross's Landing, historic homes and buildings, scenic views, fall color, hiking, biking, boating, fishing, hunting, and wildlife viewing.

LOCATION: Tennessee River Valley in East Tennessee. The drive begins at Kingston south from Exit 352 off I–40 to the west of Knoxville.

DRIVE ROUTE NUMBERS: US 70 and 27; TN 68, 58, and 60; Old Dayton Pike; and TN 153.

CAMPING: Newby Forest Camp, Fooshee Pass Recreation Area, Hornsby Hollow Recreation Area, Armstrong Ferry Recreation Area, and Harrison Bay State Park.

SERVICES: All services at Kingston, Rockwood, Dayton, and Chattanooga.

NEARBY ATTRACTIONS: Roosevelt State Forest, Ozone Falls State Natural Area, Piney River Trail, Stinging Fork Pocket Wilderness, North Chickamauga Pocket Wilderness, and Falling Water Falls State Natural Area.

THE DRIVE

The Tennessee River flows south through the Great Valley of East Tennessee, with the Appalachian Mountains to the east and the Cumberland Plateau to the west. This was once Cherokee land, but several treaties eventually pushed the Native Americans out of the region by 1819, except for the Overhill Country in the southeast corner of the state. Today the Tennessee River consists of a series of lakes impounded by Tennessee Valley Authority dams; so the river placidly flows down the valley through a pastoral countryside dotted with small historic towns.

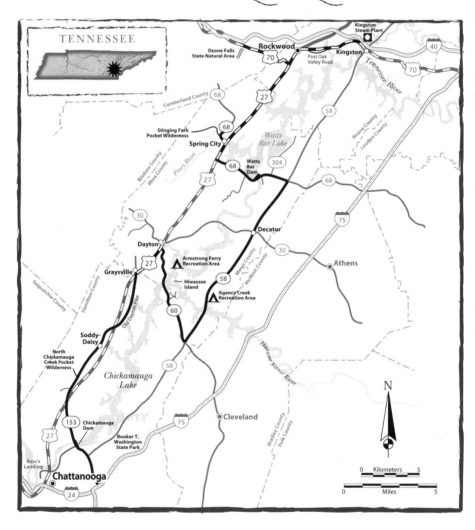

KINGSTON

Thirty-three miles west of Knoxville, take Exit 352 off I–40 to begin this drive. Head south to get to Kingston. Enter the city on TN 58, which is also Kentucky Street. At 0.8 mile on the town square stands the **Old Roane County Courthouse,** a Greek Revival/Federal structure built in 1854 from bricks made on-site by slaves. The building, with its windowed tower, served as a lookout for both sides during the Civil War. When a new courthouse was built to the rear in 1974, the Roane County Heritage Commission saved the old building. It now houses the **Roane County Museum of History,** containing documents and a photographic record of the county's history.

For a day, Kingston served as the Tennessee State Capital. The legislature met here on September 21, 1807, to abide by the terms of a treaty with the Cherokees in which they relinquished Southwest Point, the land at the confluence of the Clinch River with the Tennessee River; the treaty called for the state capital to be located here. At the end of this one-day session, the legislature adjourned and returned to Knoxville.

Across Kentucky Street from the courthouse stands the **Gideon Morgan House,** the oldest residence in the county. The red-brick Federal-style mansion was built in 1812 by Morgan, a Revolutionary War veteran. In 1815 Morgan turned his house into an "ordinary," an inn, along the Walton Road, a federal toll road that ran west over the Cumberland Plateau to the settlements on the Cumberland River where Nashville is today. A young Sam Houston is said to have worked in the grog shop in the basement of the house.

Continue straight on Kentucky Street in front of the courthouse to an intersection with Race Street, which is also US 70. This drive will leave Kingston to the right here, but first continue straight. On the right stands the **Bethel Presbyterian Church,** constructed in 1858 on a nearby hill. It was dismantled and reconstructed at this location from 1883 to 1887.

Leaving the center of town, Kentucky Street parallels the edge of Watts Bar Lake on the Clinch River. The lake was created by Watts Bar Dam on the Tennessee. Kingston's **Waterfront Park** along the shore has a paved walkway along the river. In 1 mile turn right into **Fort Southwest Point.** At the visitor center you can view artifacts and exhibits about the history of the site, and then walk up to the reconstructed fort.

Because of growing hostility between the Cherokees and white settlers, in 1792 Governor William Blount sent John Sevier, in command of the territorial militia, to protect the settlers. Sevier chose to establish a blockhouse on the Tennessee River near the confluence of the Clinch. By 1796 the troops had taken on a reciprocal role of protecting Indian rights, ensuring that whites did not settle on Cherokee lands. This dual role required a larger force of troops. So in 1797 Fort Southwest Point was established on a bluff overlooking the confluence of the Clinch and the Tennessee Rivers, approximately a half mile from the original blockhouse.

In 1801 the job of Cherokee Indian Agent at the fort was given to Col. Return Jonathan Meigs, a Revolutionary War veteran. His first name honors his father's persistence in proposing to his mother; he returned again and again until she agreed. Meigs worked for the rights of the Cherokees, defending them in treaty conferences and encouraging them to establish their own nation. Wanting to be closer to the Cherokees, Meigs moved the Indian agency south near the Hiwassee River in 1807. Fort Southwest Point was abandoned in 1811.

In recent decades archaeological digs have established the layout of the fort and uncovered many artifacts from the early occupation, and the city of Kingston has now undertaken the task of reconstructing the fort. Phase I is complete with a rebuilt blockhouse, a barracks, and 250 feet of palisade walls.

Return from Fort Southwest Point to Kingston and turn west on US 70. The highway generally follows the route of the old Avery Trace, the precursor of the Walton Road. Waterfront Park extends along the Clinch River with the continuation of the paved walk and picnic areas.

As the highway leaves Kingston, the smokestacks of TVA's **Kingston Steam Plant** tower over the trees ahead. In 1.4 miles cross a bridge over the Clinch River above its confluence with the Tennessee while paralleling I–40 to the right. In 0.9 mile you can turn right to pass under the interstate and turn right again to reach the Kingston plant recreation area. Near the plant, train cars line up to unload their coal, which is burned to produce steam for electricity generation. The plant has massive smokestacks, reaching high into the air so that pollution and particulates in the exhaust are widely dispersed. Across from the plant, the recreation area has fishing and boat access to the river; waterfowl congregate on the surrounding waters in winter and a resident flock of Canada geese can be found year-round.

Return to US 70 and continue west. In 2.7 miles **Roane County Park** on the left has picnicking along the Tennessee River, a swimming beach, and a fishing pier. In 1.8 miles a right turn leads to Roane State Community College; just beyond, turn left on Post Oak Valley Road. In 1.2 miles at a fork, bear right on Old Highway 70 to the **Old Post Oak Springs Christian Church.** Built in 1876, the white frame church stands beside an old cemetery; the pews inside were supposedly all made from one large poplar tree. Stay straight to rejoin US 70 and continue west.

ROCKWOOD

In 2.5 miles US 70 joins US 27 and bears southwest, paralleling the ridge of the Cumberland Plateau on the west to enter Rockwood as Gateway Avenue. Rockwood was founded in 1868 to support an iron company. During the Civil War, Union Gen. John T. Wilder camped with his troops at the foot of Walden Ridge, the eastern rampart of the plateau. Noticing outcroppings of iron ore, coal, and limestone, all that was needed for the production of iron, he returned after the war with other northern industrialists to found the Roane Iron Company and established the town, which was named after the company's first president, William O. Rockwood. At first, Roane pig iron was shipped by boat on the Tennessee River; then in 1879, the Cincinnati-Southern Railroad running north to south through the state was built through Rockwood, increasing the number of markets that could receive the iron. The company prospered for many years, but increasing freight costs, several accidents, and the 1930s Depression put the company out of business.

Turn right on Rockwood Street to pass through an old residential neighborhood and cross the railroad tracks that still run through town, part of the Norfolk-Southern. Along the street are large homes that housed the Roane Iron Company officials. At the corner of Hewitt Avenue and Rockwood, on the right, stands the iron company's **Superintendent's House,** a Victorian residence built in 1870. Cross Trinity and Dunlap Avenues to the **Company Store,** an old brick building on the left. At the next block, across Furnace Avenue, stands the **Administration Building** for the **Roane Iron Company.**

Turn right on Furnace, and right on Strange Street to pass through a neighborhood of small, uniform houses that were the company's worker residences. Stay straight on Strange to return to US 70/27 and turn right to leave Rockwood. In 2 miles at a junction outside of town, US 70 turns right while US 27 continues straight to the southwest.

Here you can take a side trip to two state preserves by turning right on US 70, following the route of the old Avery Trace and the Walton Road up the eastern wall of the Cumberland Plateau where sandstone outcrops line the rim. In 2.2 miles turn right on a side road to pass 1.2 miles through **Mount Roosevelt State Forest** to the peak of Mount Roosevelt. Picnic tables at the edge of the plateau offer precipitous views east across the Great Valley of East Tennessee. This is a well-known site for viewing broad-winged and red-tailed hawks in fall; thousands catch the updrafts at the edge of the plateau in their annual migration. The state forest stretches for miles along Walden Ridge, providing opportunity for hiking, mountain biking, and hunting.

In another 5.8 miles west on US 70 in the community of Ozone, cross Fall Creek to **Ozone Falls State Natural Area.** The area protects a waterfall that skips off a lip of sandstone rimrock and arcs 110 feet into a deep narrow gorge.

Return to US 27 and turn right to resume this drive to the southwest. The highway travels straight down the valley between the Cumberland Plateau on the west and the Tennessee River to the east, although a ridge separates the road from the river. Small farms with old farmhouses, barns, and outbuildings dot the landscape; cattle graze the fields. The Norfolk-Southern Railroad parallels the highway on the right. Along the highway several left turns lead to marinas on the river. The marinas also have cabins and camping on the edge of Watts Bar Lake. In 4.5 miles cross Whites Creek into Rhea County.

SPRING CITY

In 9.1 miles US 27 crosses the Piney River into Spring City. In another 0.5 mile, at the first traffic light, a left turn leads 0.4 mile to **Veterans Park,** which has picnic areas and a walking trail. A monument there commemorates the village of Rhea Springs, now under the waters of Watts Bar Lake. The settlement had grown up around a mineral springs and was a stop on the Old Stage Road that ran from Washington, D.C., through Tennessee on its way to New Orleans. The monument in the Spring City park is made of the granite and marble columns from the old Rhea Springs springhouse, a millstone from an old flour mill, and limestone blocks that were the foundation stones for the old Rhea Springs schoolhouse.

On US 70, continue into Spring City, a railroad town created by the Cincinnati Southern as it came through this area; the tracks of the Norfolk-Southern still run through the heart of the community. Across the tracks stands the **Spring City Passenger Station.** Constructed in 1909, this elaborate brick building has been renovated by the city for a chamber of commerce and tourist information center.

From Spring City, you can take a side trip to a couple of preserves set aside by Bowater Inc., a paper company. In 1967 Bowater began setting aside lands that had special scenic value and constructed trails for public use. To get to two of these areas, turn right on Piccadilly Avenue to a junction with TN 68 and turn right. In 0.3 mile turn left on Shut-In Gap Road, paralleling Piney River on the right. In 1.2 miles Bowater's **Piney River Tree Farm Picnic Area** sits beside the river. Across the road, on the left, the Piney River Trail travels for 10 miles along the Piney River and its tributary streams, passing waterfalls, rock formations, and campsites. You can continue straight on Shut-In Gap Road to cross Piney River and make a steep, winding climb up the Cumberland Plateau 4.1 miles to Bowater's **Stinging Fork Pocket Wilderness;** a 1.5-mile trail leads to 30-foot Stinging Fork Falls. Shut-In Gap Road continues another 1.3 miles to a gravel road that leads left to Bowater's **Newby Forest Camp,** which has primitive camping.

YUCHI REFUGE AND WATTS BAR

Return to Spring City and US 27, and continue southwest. In 2.4 miles turn left on TN 68. In 1.7 miles you can turn right on TN 302 for 5 miles to Breedentown Ferry Road (also Boogles Chapel Road) and turn left to reach Smith Bend of the Tennessee River. The Foothills Land Conservancy, the Conservation Fund, and Tennessee Wildlife Resources Agency mounted a campaign to purchase this area, which is now protected as the **Yuchi Wildlife Refuge and Management Area.** Named for the Native Americans who lived here before the Cherokee, this 4,500-acre preserve harbors numerous species of waterfowl during winter; among them is the sandhill crane, the peace symbol of the Yuchi.

As TN 68 continues to the east, you'll see steam rising from the cooling towers at TVA's Watts Bar Nuclear Plant. In 3.6 miles a right turn leads to the nuclear plant and also to the coal-fired plant, but these areas are restricted, so continue straight on TN 68 to reach TVA's **Watts Bar Dam.** Here are all three forms of power generation used by the Tennessee Valley Authority: water, coal, and nuclear. TN 68 crosses the dam on the Tennessee River; you can then turn down right to get below the dam for views across the river to the nuclear and coal plants.

Continue east on TN 68 into Meigs County. In 1.3 miles TN 304 leads left 1.7 miles to the **Fooshee Pass Recreation Area** and another 4.1 miles to TVA's **Hornsby Hollow Recreation Area,** both have camping, picnicking, and river access.

DECATUR AND HIWASSEE RIVER

Stay straight on TN 68. In 2.9 miles, at a junction with TN 58, turn right. Big Sewee Creek meanders along the general course of the highway as it passes through forest and open fields. In 9.1 miles enter the community of Decatur and reach **Meigs County Courthouse** on the left. Built in 1903, it has been restored in recent years. Turn left beside the town square to Main Street and turn left on Main and then right to the **Meigs County Historical Museum,** housed in a small Gothic building built in 1880. Moved from a location closer to the town square, the building was once a law office; the museum contains artifacts from Meigs County's past, including the lawyer's desk.

Return to TN 58 to pass in front of the courthouse and head south out of Decatur along a scenic stretch of rural highway. In 7.1 miles watch for the **Agency Creek House** on the left, a two-story, white frame residence built in 1820; it once had portholes for defense. Just past the house, the highway crosses a tributary of Agency Creek, which parallels the highway south toward the Hiwassee River.

In 3.8 miles, you can turn right and travel 6.4 miles to reach the **Armstrong Ferry Recreation Area,** which has privately operated camping on the Tennessee River. Then watch for **Erwin Grocery** on the left; its an old-time country store. In 1.7 miles the **Agency Creek Recreation Area** on the left has a campground. Soon after, a historical marker commemorates the Cherokee Indian Agency that was located 1 mile east where Agency Creek joins the Hiwassee. Return Jonathan Meigs operated the agency here from 1816 to 1821, having first located the agency farther south after leaving Fort Southwest Point in 1807. The agency was moved again, upstream on the Hiwassee, where it operated from 1821 to 1838.

TN 58 crosses the **Hiwassee State Scenic River** on a long bridge. Watch for a number of waterfowl in winter, and shore birds when the water is down and mudflats are exposed. On the other side of the river, a left turn leads to boat ramp access. **Chickamauga Wildlife Management Area** stretches along the Hiwassee River.

In 4.7 miles turn right on TN 60 to travel toward the Tennessee River. In 4.8 miles pass through the community of Birchwood, and in another 3.9 miles turn right on the old route of TN 60, just before tall twin silos. In 0.8 mile, where the road makes a sharp left curve, Blythe Ferry Road joins on the right. The road continues on down to the shore of the Tennessee River. Here around 1809, a Cherokee, William Blythe, established a ferry connecting white settlements on the east with Cherokee lands to the west; this also became one of the crossings for the Cherokees on the Trail of Tears in 1838 when the majority of the nation was sent to Oklahoma. The ferry operated until 1994 when a new highway bridge was constructed. As a tribute to those who traveled the Trail of Tears, local citizens are working to erect a monument engraved with the names of heads of households recorded in the 1835 Cherokee census; the monument will be on a river bluff in a proposed **Cherokee Memorial Park.**

At the junction with Blythe Ferry Road, turn right and in 0.5 mile turn left on a gravel road to enter **Hiwassee Wildlife Refuge**. At a fork, bear

Hiwassee Wildlife Refuge

right for half a mile to parking. Then walk up to an observation deck; in late fall and winter, you can hear the harsh calls of sandhill cranes. From the deck you can view the congregating cranes along the Hiwassee River where it joins the Tennessee. The sandhill cranes come from their breeding grounds around the Great Lakes. Thousands congregate here, and so the refuge has become a popular place for observing the birds, which stand 3 feet tall and have wing spans of 6 feet. They rise and fall in great flocks when not feeding on the ground. The first full weekend in February is Sandhill Crane Viewing Days, with programs on the cranes and Cherokee heritage. Loads of people are bused from the Birchwood School into the refuge.

In the distance, across the river, lies **Hiwassee Island** at the confluence of the Hiwassee with the Tennessee. The island has been the site of Native American habitation for centuries, starting with a great mound village of the Mississippian culture established around A.D. 1200. In later years, Cherokees had a village here, called "Cayoka." Sam Houston, Tennessee governor and president of the Texas Republic, spent three years here as a teenager. He was the adoptive son of Chief Oolooteka, who named him "The Raven." The chief was also called "Jolly," and so the island is sometimes referred to as Jolly's Island.

DAYTON

Return to TN 60 and continue west. In 2 miles cross the bridge over the wide Tennessee River, here part of Chickamauga Lake backed up by Chickamauga Dam to the south near Chattanooga. As you cross the bridge, look to the right to see the ramps of old TN 60 on both sides of the river, where it came down to Blythe Ferry. Continue to the west 5.2 miles to a junction with US 27. Turn right and bear left on South Market Street to enter Dayton. The **Rhea County Courthouse** is on the town square. Built in 1891 in a Romanesque Revival/Italian Villa style, the courthouse is a National Historic Landmark because the famous Scopes trial took place here from July 10 through July 21, 1925.

The nation watched as John Thomas Scopes was tried for teaching evolution; the defense of Scopes was led by Clarence Darrow, a well-known defense lawyer, while the prosecution was assisted by William Jennings Bryan, Secretary of State under President Wilson and later an imposing orator who defended religious fundamentalism. The trial was actually a setup. The American Civil Liberties Union wanted to challenge the recently passed Tennessee statute that made it unlawful for any teacher in the public schools "to teach any theory that denies the story of Divine Creation of man as taught in the Bible, and to teach instead that man has descended from a lower order of animals." The ACLU offered to pay the legal expenses of any Tennessee teacher willing to test the law. The city of Dayton was eager for the publicity that such a trial would bring; several businessmen, especially a druggist, F. E. Robinson, hatched a plan for hosting the trial in Dayton. Scopes, a coach who also taught math and science, agreed to be the test case. After much debate and deliberation, Scopes was found guilty of breaking the state law and was fined $100. The verdict was later overturned by the Tennessee Supreme Court on a legal technicality.

Although restored in 1979, the Rhea County Courthouse still looks much as it did in the days of the Scopes Trial. The large open courtroom on the second floor contains the original judge's bench, tables, railing, jury chairs, and spectator seats; annually in July, nearby Bryan College produces a reenactment of the trial in the courtroom.

SODDY-DAISY AND NORTH CHICKAMAUGA

Return to US 27 and turn south to leave Dayton. In 3.5 miles pass the community of Graysville, the hometown of Arnim Leroy Fox. "Curly," as he was known, was a champion fiddle player who performed for years at Nashville's Grand Old Opry with his wife, Texas Ruby. The restored Fox homeplace on Fox Street is now the **Curly Fox Museum.**

In 1.5 miles enter Hamilton County. In 9.6 miles, crossing Sale Creek and then Rock Creek, turn left on Old Dayton Pike. In 0.9 mile cross Big Soddy Creek filled with water backed up from Chickamauga Lake on the Tennessee River. A park on the left offers picnicking, fishing, and plenty of ducks and geese. Old Dayton Pike continues along the lake edge, passing under US 27 and entering the community of Soddy-Daisy. In 0.9 mile you can turn left behind a bank to get to the **Soddy Lake Public Fishing Pier** and walk a berm a few yards into the lake to get to the cross-shaped pier to watch the ducks and geese and to fish.

In 2.5 miles, cross the railroad tracks that parallel US 27. In 0.3 mile, Sequoyah Access Road on the left leads 6.5 miles to TVA's Sequoyah Nuclear Plant; it's a mystery why anyone thought the inventor of the Cherokee syllabary would be honored by having a nuclear plant named after him.

Continuing south on Old Dayton Pike, glance to the right to a cleft in Walden Ridge; that formation is Chickamauga Gulch, carved by North Chickamauga Creek. In 3.2 miles you can turn right on Montlake Road to reach **North Chickamauga Creek Pocket Wilderness,** another Bowater preserve with hiking trails.

In 2.5 miles, Old Dayton Pike crosses Falling Water Creek; upstream the state has established **Falling Water Falls State Natural Area.** A proposed trail will lead into Falling Water Creek Gorge to 110-foot Falling Water Falls; you'll turn right on Robertsville Road to a left turn on Levi Road to reach the trailhead.

Pass under US 27 in 0.5 mile where Old Dayton Pike becomes TN 153 that enters the outskirts of Chattanooga. In 5.8 miles, just before reaching TVA's **Chickamauga Dam** on the Tennessee River, you can exit the four-lane highway to get to **North Chickamauga Creek Greenway,** there a walking trail loops through forest along North Chickamauga Creek. A spur trail to the north circles through TVA's **Big Ridge Small Wild Area.**

Continue southeast on TN 153, crossing a bridge over Chickamauga Dam, with Chickamauga Lake to the left and the Tennessee River below on the right. In the distance to the right, you can see the point of Lookout Mountain that stands above Chattanooga.

TENNESSEE RIVER PARK AND CHATTANOOGA

In 2 miles, this drive exits onto Amnicola Highway. But you can take a side trip to two state parks by staying straight on TN 153 to the next exit and heading northeast on TN 58. In 2.2 miles is **Booker T. Washington State**

Park with fishing, picnicking, boating, and swimming on Chickamauga Lake. Another 6.1 miles north on TN 58, **Harrison Bay State Park,** also on Chickamauga Lake, has a marina, campground, swimming, and picnicking.

On Amnicola Highway, you can go left to **Chickamauga Lake Recreation Area,** which has picnicking, boat launch, swimming, and a marina; a paved walking path skirts the water's edge. But continue this drive to the west toward Chattanooga.

In 0.7 mile turn right toward the Chickamauga Dam Powerhouse Visitor Center and turn left down to the river to reach the beginning of Chattanooga's **Tennessee River Park.** An elaborate greenway that stretches southwest from Chickamauga Dam, the park follows the river for miles as it meanders to the north around Chattanooga's downtown.

Back out on Amnicola Highway, continue west for 1 mile and turn right into the Robinson Bridge section of the park. The river park gives access to fishing piers at the edge of the river; it also has playgrounds, picnic areas, and boat launches. The park road passes under the C. B. Robinson Bridge and reemerges back on Amnicola Highway; turn right. The highway becomes Riverside Drive as it approaches the Chattanooga downtown.

In 5.1 miles Riverside Drive passes under the **Walnut Street Bridge,** an old steel-truss bridge that has been converted to a pedestrian crossing of the Tennessee River. The riverwalk crosses the Tennessee here and will extend westward on the north side of the river. Riverside Drive becomes River Front Parkway that continues along this south side of the river into **Ross's Landing,** the site of the ferry described in the Tennessee River Gorge drive. Turn left onto Chestnut Street then left onto Second Street to Broad Street, and end your tour at the **Tennessee Aquarium** and the **Chattanooga Area Convention and Visitors Bureau** on the left. This spot is also the beginning of the Tennessee River Gorge Drive.

11

Tennessee River Gorge

CHATTANOOGA LOOP

GENERAL DESCRIPTION: This 126-mile drive explores the Tennessee River Gorge with Signal Mountain on the north and Lookout Mountain on the south .

SPECIAL ATTRACTIONS: Chattanooga, Signal Point Park, Tennessee River Gorge, Nickajack Cave, Raccoon Mountain, Lookout Mountain, historic homes and buildings, scenic views, fall color, hiking, biking, fishing, hunting, and wildlife viewing.

LOCATION: West of Chattanooga in southeast Tennessee. The drive begins at the Chattanooga Convention and Visitors Bureau on Broad Street.

DRIVE ROUTE NUMBERS: US 127, TN 27, Mullens Cove Road, US 41/72/64, and TN 156.

CAMPING: Marion County Park and Raccoon Mountain Caverns.

SERVICES: All services at Chattanooga.

NEARBY ATTRACTIONS: Prentice Cooper State Forest.

THE DRIVE

The Tennessee River flows northeast to southwest through East Tennessee. Near the southern border of the state, the river abruptly turns west, carving its way through the Walden Ridge portion of the Cumberland Plateau and creating the Tennessee River Gorge, one of the deepest canyons in the eastern United States. Where the river cuts through the plateau, two mountain remain on each side: Signal Mountain on the north and Lookout Mountain on the south. The latter mountain is a prominent peak overlooking the river and forming a backdrop for Chattanooga, which grew up at this passageway west. The name of the city is taken from the Indian name for the mountain, *Chatanuga,* meaning "rock coming to a point."

TENNESSEE RIVER GORGE

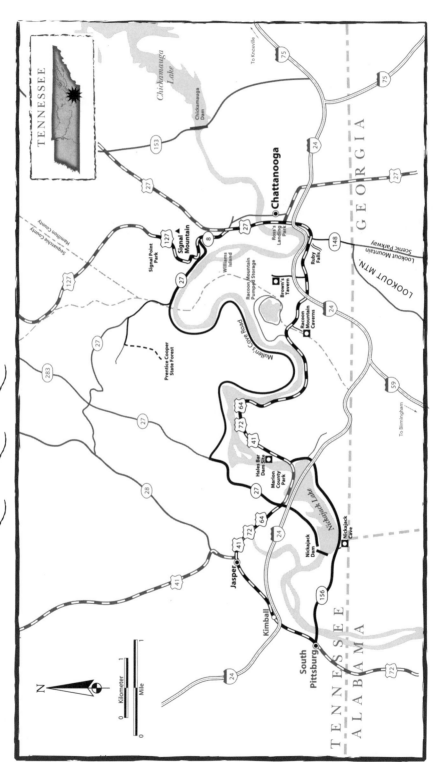

CHATTANOOGA

Begin this drive at the **Chattanooga Area Convention and Visitors Bureau** at the end of Broad Street on the north end of the city's downtown area. The visitors bureau sits beside the **Tennessee Aquarium,** a modernistic building housing one of the world's largest freshwater aquariums. River Front Parkway runs behind the aquarium along the Tennessee River. Between the parkway and the river lies **Ross's Landing Park** at the foot of Chestnut Street on the west side of the aquarium; here is where you can board the *Southern Belle* **Riverboat** for cruises on the Tennessee River.

The settlement that became Chattanooga was originally called Ross's Landing, for the landing and ferry established here by John Ross in 1816. Though he was only a small part Cherokee, Ross left this settlement in 1826 and moved south into Georgia to be near what remained of the Cherokee Nation. Elected principal chief in 1828, Ross argued for the right of his people to stay in their sacred lands. When the Cherokees were banished, he led several detachments on the Trail of Tears in 1838. Other detachments had left by boat from Ross's Landing. A bronze statue of a Cherokee now stands at the park, commemorating the past presence of Native Americans in the region.

On the east side of the Convention and Visitors Bureau, take Market Street north to pass over River Front Parkway and cross the Tennessee River on the Market Street Bridge. Just to the right you can see the **Walnut Street Bridge;** this highway bridge, built in 1891, has been converted to one of the longest pedestrian bridges in the world. Across the river the bridge empties into **Coolidge Park,** where gardens and an indoor carousel are backed up by shops in old commercial buildings to the north. Across the river, at a junction, you can turn right on Frazier Avenue to get to Coolidge Park. This drive turns left on Cherokee Boulevard.

SIGNAL POINT

The boulevard passes through a tunnel into the community of Red Bank. In 1.9 miles turn left on US 127 to pass under US 27 and continue to the northwest. Ahead you can see the bluffs of Signal Mountain. In 2.1 miles this drive turns left on TN 27, but first head up to **Signal Point Park** by staying straight on US 127. The highway makes a steep, winding ascent of Walden Ridge; homes perched on the rim of the plateau have grand views of the Tennessee River below. In 3 miles, the highway tops the plateau in the community of Signal Mountain. Turn left on Signal Mountain Boulevard just before the first traffic light. Turn left on Mississippi Avenue and stay straight through an intersection onto James Boulevard. Then turn left on Signal Point

Native American Statue, Ross's Landing Park

Road; at the corner, the Alexian Brothers retirement complex occupies the old **Signal Mountain Inn,** built in 1913.

In 0.3 mile enter Signal Point Park, part of the Chickamauga and Chattanooga National Military Park, which preserves the Civil War battlefields that gave the Union control of this important transportation center. From the loop parking area you can walk down to the rock promontory of Signal Point. During the siege of Chattanooga, this site was used by the U.S. Army Signal Corps, hence the name. The point offers an expansive view of the Tennessee River in the canyon below.

Signal Point is the southern terminus of the **Cumberland Trail,** which begins just to the right as you walk down to the overlook. It will eventually stretch for 280 miles north to Cumberland Gap National Historical Park on the Kentucky-Virginia border. The trail is being built through the efforts of the Cumberland Trail Conference that coordinates volunteer workers. The state has recognized this effort by designating the long corridor through the state as Cumberland Trail State Park.

PRENTICE COOPER FOREST

Return down Signal Mountain to the junction with TN 27 and turn west. The highway passes through an industrial area and then parallels the Tennessee River. Watch for parking on the left for boat access and wildlife viewing. In 4.2 miles the road crosses Suck Creek to a junction with Mullens Cove Road to the left. The drive follows this narrow winding road through the river gorge. If you have a large vehicle, you may want to stay on TN 27, which is also the route up the plateau for a side trip to **Prentice Cooper State Forest.** The highway follows Suck Creek Gorge up the mountain; the creek is named for a whirlpool that once existed where the creek joins the river. The site is now flooded by waters backed up from TVA's Nickajack Dam downstream. In 3.8 miles the highway tops the plateau where you turn left on Choctaw Trail to Game Reserve Road to enter Prentice Cooper State Forest. The state forest has hiking trails, primitive camping, and hunting in season.

Return to TN 27. If you want to avoid the route through the Tennessee River Gorge, turn left to travel across Walden Ridge and descend the plateau into Sequatchie Valley and reach Powells Crossroads in 10 miles. Turn left to stay on TN 27 another 8 miles to reach the western end of Mullens Cove Road.

TENNESSEE RIVER GORGE

To follow the route into the **Tennessee River Gorge,** return down the mountain to the junction with Mullens Cove Road and turn west. This

Tennessee River Gorge

narrow road runs along the bank of the Tennessee River, here also known as Nickajack Lake. With so little room between the river on the left and the slope of the plateau to the right, the houses along this stretch crowd the road as it weaves through the riverside community.

In 4.4 miles the **Pot Point House** stands on the right. This nineteenth-century log house is the scientific field station and center for education and conservation of the Tennessee River Gorge Trust, a land conservation organization established to protect 26 miles of the river gorge. The trust has been successful in preserving the biological diversity found in the gorge and the traditional cultural ties to the land.

Mullens Cove Road continues west through the river gorge; forested sections are interspersed with houses; the river floats lazily by. In 15.6 miles, the road straightens out somewhat as it emerges from the gorge into Sequatchie Valley. In another 2.6 miles the road reaches a junction with TN 27. If you took the alternative route, you would rejoin the drive from the north at this intersection.

NICKAJACK AND DRAGGING CANOE

Head south on TN 27. Stay with the highway through two sharp turns, and in 5 miles reach a junction with US 41/72/64. The drive turns right here, but first stay straight to get to TVA's **Nickajack Dam.** Pass under I–24 and in 2.5 miles a left turn leads to the **Shellmound Recreation Area,** which has camping, picnicking, and boat access to Nickajack Lake. In another 0.7 mile a road to the right leads to boat access to the river below the dam. Straight ahead is Nickajack Dam. The dam and the lake behind it are named for one of the Five Lower Towns of the Chickamaugas.

Angry over Richard Henderson's swindling of the Cherokees at Sycamore Shoals in 1775, in which Henderson enticed the Native Americans to give up twenty million acres south of the Ohio River, Dragging Canoe withdrew from the Nation. Gathering others around him to form a splinter group, he relocated along Chickamauga Creek at the foot of Lookout Mountain, and so they became known as the Chickamaugas. Supplied by the British during the American Revolution, they became the scourge of settlers along the American frontier. In retaliation, the Chickamauga villages were attacked and destroyed by a force of men under Evan Shelby in 1779, although nearly all the Chickamaugas escaped. Afterward, Dragging Canoe and his people withdrew west of Lookout Mountain and founded the Five Lower Towns at this southern end of Sequatchie Valley. Despite the attempts of the whites to stop the Chickamaugas, Dragging Canoe was never permanently defeated, dying of old age in 1792, probably at Running Water Town, which is thought to now lie under the waters of Nickajack Lake. The Chickamaugas realized they could not keep up their resistance, and so at a peace conference that occurred at Tellico Blockhouse on the Little Tennessee River to the east, the Chickamaugas rejoined the Cherokee Nation.

Return to US 41/72/64 and turn west to reach Jasper in 4 miles, with the old depot on the left and the town square on the right. This drive joins the Sequatchie Valley drive at the junction with US 41 to the right in the center of town. Stay straight on US 72/64. In 4 miles enter the community of Kimball, and in 1.2 miles pass under I–24. In another 1.5 miles exit to the right on Old Highway 72 (also TN 27) toward South Pittsburg. Then turn left on TN 156 to cross the Tennessee River on a prominent arched bridge. In 2.2 miles pass through the small community of New Hope. In 2.8 miles you can turn left to descend to the bottom of Nickajack Dam on this south side of the river.

TN 156 parallels the tracks of the CSX Railroad, which has traveled north from Bridgeport, Alabama, crossed the highway, and turned east to run along a berm on the north side of the road next to the river. In 0.6 mile turn right into the **Maple View Recreation Area,** which has picnicking, swimming, and boat access. From the parking lot a short trail leads to a boardwalk at the edge of the lake. The walkway ends at an observation platform for **Nickajack Cave,** which now is partially filled with water from Nickajack Lake. The rock shelter of the cave had long given refuge to raiding parties of Chickamaugas, river pirates, Confederates digging for saltpeter to make gunpowder, and as legend has it, a group of French Acadians, including the Evangeline of Henry Wadsworth Longfellow's poem. Deported from the Nova Scotia region of Canada because they would not swear allegiance to Great Britain, many Acadians settled in Louisiana and became known as Cajuns. Evangeline's group stopped at Nickajack Cave before building a raft, which they floated down the Tennessee River, the Ohio, and the Mississippi to Louisiana. Today Nickajack Cave is a refuge for bats. Thousands of gray bats, an endangered species, congregate in the cave from late April to early October. At dusk they come streaming out of the cave mouth in search of insects as they fly over the lake waters and over the heads of people standing on the observation deck—a sight not to be missed.

HALES BAR DAM
AND RACCOON MOUNTAIN

As you continue east on TN 156, the highway crosses an embayment of the river where you can look to the right to see the opening of Nickajack Cave. TN 156 winds over a ridge to reach a junction with I–24 in 4.9 miles. Stay straight under the interstate to reach a junction with US 41/72/64. You can turn left here to cross a bridge over the Tennessee River, where you can look to the right to see the sight of the old **Hales Bar Dam,** constructed in 1913. The dam was later acquired by the Tennessee Valley Authority. By the 1960s the dam was leaking and the locks were too small for the growing size of barges. TVA replaced it with Nickajack Dam in 1967. The old powerhouse and parts of the lock of the Hales Bar Dam are still visible. On the other side of the river, in 1.3 miles, **Marion County Park** occupies a peninsula in Nickajack Lake; the park has camping and boat access.

At the junction of TN 156 and US 41/72/64, turn right to continue this drive toward Chattanooga. In 1.3 miles a road to the left leads down to the **Hales Bar Resort and Marina** at the site of the old Hales Bar Dam. US 41/72/64 continues along the bending river. In 5.9 miles **Riverside Catfish House** on the left has been serving up catfish beside the Tennessee River since 1959.

In 5.1 miles you can turn left into the reservation for TVA's **Raccoon Mountain Pumped-Storage Plant.** Raccoon Mountain stands at another bend of the Tennessee River. In the 1970s TVA constructed the pumped-storage plant in the mountain with a man-made lake on top. During times of low demand for electricity, water is pumped from the Tennessee River through tunnels inside the mountain to the top, where it is stored. Then during times of high demand or during emergencies when a generating unit on the TVA system is down, the water is released, pouring down the underground tunnels and turning generators that produce electric power. The access road ascends to the top of Raccoon Mountain to a visitor center where a deck offers a grand view of the Tennessee River Gorge. You can also take an escorted tour of the pumped-storage facility; it begins with a fast descent in an elevator into the heart of the mountain and the underground powerhouse.

Return to US 41/72/64, and turn left to continue east. In 1.2 miles, you can turn right to reach **Raccoon Mountain Caverns** for tours of one of the largest caves in the southeast. There are also hiking trails and a campground.

In 1.5 miles the highway passes under I–24 and enters commercial development on the outskirts of Chattanooga where the road becomes Cummings Highway. In 1 mile, you can turn left on Brown's Ferry Road to pass under the interstate and in 1.8 miles to see **Brown's Tavern,** a two-story log home on the left built in 1803. The Great Warpath passed through here; also a trading route, it once connected the Iroquois Confederacy to the north with the Cherokee Nation to the south. In 1800 John Brown, part Cherokee, established a ferry at the crossing of the Tennessee River and later constructed this tavern.

LOOKOUT MOUNTAIN

Continue east on Cummings Highway to cross Lookout Creek and, in 0.7 mile, turn right on Old Wauhatchee Pike, which is also TN 318. Then turn right on Garden Road to reach the **Tennessee Wildlife Center** and **Reflection Riding Botanical Garden** in 1 mile. The wildlife center contains a number of native animals, including birds of prey and red wolves, plus a boardwalk through wetlands and native plant gardens. A rehabilitation facility attempts to return injured animals to the wild. Adjacent to the wildlife center, Reflection Riding is a 300-acre landscaped park and arboretum with hiking trails and a 3-mile driving loop along a one-lane gravel road; check at the nature center for admittance.

Return to Garden Road, and turn right up the slope of Lookout Mountain. At a junction with TN 148 (also Lookout Mountain Scenic Highway), turn right to ascend the mountain. **Ruby Falls** is on the right.

Here an elevator takes visitors down into Lookout Mountain Caverns to the underground waterfall. Leo Lambert discovered the falls in 1928 and he named it after his wife.

The parkway crosses over the **Lookout Mountain Incline Railway,** the steepest passenger railway in the world, which runs from a station on St. Elmo Street to the top of the mountain. At the top, turn right on East Brow Road in the community of Lookout Mountain. Pass the upper Incline Railway terminal on the right to reach **Point Park,** part of the **Chickamauga and Chattanooga National Military Park** that commemorates the Battles for Chattanooga.

BATTLES FOR CHATTANOOGA

Following the Battle of Stones River to the west that occurred at the beginning of 1863, Confederate forces under Gen. Braxton Bragg withdrew to Chattanooga. Union Major Gen. William S. Rosecrans followed. Fearing he would be cut off from the rest of the Confederacy, Bragg retreated south, allowing Rosecrans to take the city. Rosecrans followed Bragg south, but once Bragg was reinforced, he turned and met the Union forces at Chickamauga Creek at the foot of Lookout Mountain. During the two-day Battle of Chickamauga on September 19 and 20, the Confederates routed the Union troops who retreated to Chattanooga; the battle was one of the bloodiest of the war, with 37,000 casualties.

Bragg pursued Rosecrans and manned Lookout Mountain to the south and Missionary Ridge to the east to begin a siege of Chattanooga. With food growing short, President Lincoln sent Gen. Ulysses S. Grant to assist the Union troops at Chattanooga. Arriving on October 23 and assuming command, Grant immediately opened a supply route by taking the river crossing at Brown's Ferry and holding it against the Confederates. With supplies now flowing into the city, Grant was soon ready to act. On the morning of November 24, Lookout Mountain was clouded in mist and fog as the Union troops scaled the mountain in what became known as the "Battle Above the Clouds." It was not until the next morning when the sky cleared that the Union flag could be seen flying from Point Lookout. Grant then sent his troops against Missionary Ridge where the soldiers raced to the top, forcing the Confederates to retreat into Georgia.

With the decisive victory at Chattanooga, the Union now had a route into the heart of the Confederacy. Grant was given full command of the Union forces, and the next spring, from the Union base in Chattanooga, Gen. William T. Sherman launched his invasion of Georgia that would sever the Confederacy.

At Point Park, walkways lead past interpretive signs, monuments, and Civil War cannon out to Point Lookout, which overlooks Chattanooga beside the Tennessee River. Here the river meanders in the shape of a foot or moccasin, and so it's called Moccasin Bend. An ancient Native American village once stood in this bend of the river and was a contact point for early European explorers. Moccasin Bend is now a National Historic Landmark, and a proposal has been made to either add it to the military park or to make it a national park.

Across the street from Point Park, the visitor center contains a bookstore containing a wide selection of books on the Civil War. And to the left stands **The Battles for Chattanooga Museum,** which contains a diorama of the Battles for Chattanooga.

The road curves left on a one-way lane that emerges back on East Brow Road. Turn right to return the way you came, to the junction with Lookout Mountain Scenic Highway, then turn left down the mountain. In 1.1 miles from the junction, turn left to reach the Cravens House on the left. Built in 1854 by Robert Cravens, the house successively served as headquarters for both sides during the Battle for Lookout Mountain. Some of the heaviest fighting in the battle took place here.

Continue straight past the house and turn right to return to Lookout Mountain Scenic Highway and turn left to continue down the mountain, reaching the junction with TN 318; stay straight to reach Cummings Highway (US 41/72/64). Turn right to complete the descent of Lookout Mountain. In 0.8 mile the road passes under a railroad overpass and enters Chattanooga. St. Elmo Street to the right leads to the lower terminal of the Lookout Mountain Incline Railway.

In 2 miles, pass under I–24 and turn right on West Main Street to Market Street and turn left. On the right stands the grand **Southern Railway Terminal,** built in 1903 and now part of the Chattanooga Choo Choo, a complex of hotel rooms, shops, and restaurants. Continue east on Market Street, passing on the right **Warehouse Row,** a group of railroad warehouses built from 1904 to 1911; these have been renovated as retail shops. Finally, return to the Convention and Visitors Bureau.

12

The Obed River

OAK RIDGE TO MONTEREY

GENERAL DESCRIPTION: A 102-mile drive travels from the once-secret town of Oak Ridge to the Obed River, a nationally designated wild and scenic river, and on to the historic community of Monterey and its Standing Stone.

SPECIAL ATTRACTIONS: Oak Ridge, Oliver Springs, Frozen Head State Park and Natural Area, Lone Mountain State Forest, Wartburg, Obed Wild and Scenic River, Monterey, historic homes and buildings, scenic views, fall color, hiking, biking, boating, fishing, hunting, and wildlife viewing.

LOCATION: Cumberland Plateau in East Tennessee. The drive begins in Oak Ridge on TN 62 west of Knoxville.

DRIVE ROUTE NUMBERS: TN 62, US 27, TN 298, and TN 84.

CAMPING: Frozen Head State Park, and Rock Creek Campground.

SERVICES: All services at Oak Ridge and Monterey.

NEARBY ATTRACTIONS: Harriman, Petros, Catoosa Wildlife Management Area, Deer Lodge, Muddy Pond, and Bee Rock.

THE DRIVE

The Cumberland Plateau harbors deep gorges where rivers flow at the foot of sandstone bluffs. One of these, the Obed River, flows across the northern part of the plateau in Tennessee, carving a 500-foot-deep defile that is one of the most dramatic landscapes in the state. The scenic values and recreational opportunities were recognized by the federal government with the designation of the Obed and its tributaries as a National Wild and Scenic River.

OAK RIDGE

Begin in Oak Ridge, which is at the junction of TN 62 and 95, west of Knoxville and north of I–40. Created by the federal government in 1942, Oak Ridge remained a secret city until 1949 when the fence came down and it was opened to the public. This one-time government installation was established during World War II as one of the locations for the Manhattan

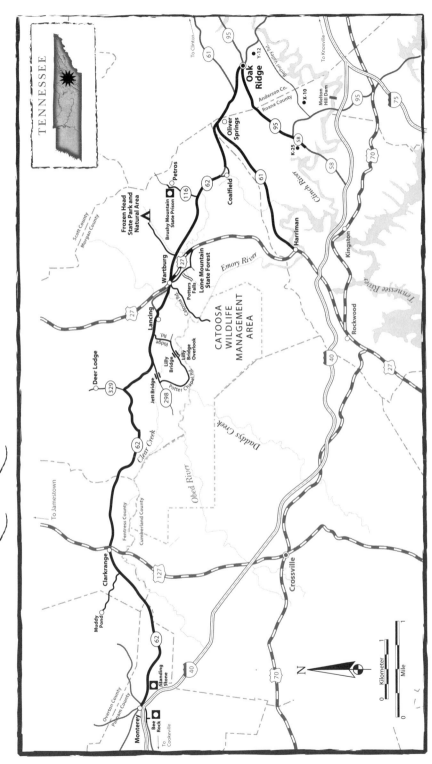

Project to produce the first atomic bombs. News had come that Nazi Germany had successfully split an atom, a process that released huge amounts of energy. The race was on to construct the first bombs. The task at Oak Ridge was the production of fissionable uranium and plutonium that would fuel the bombs. A community was established to house the workers for one of the largest technical projects ever undertaken.

Several historic sites remain in Oak Ridge; you can visit them before heading toward the Obed River. To the southwest on TN 95 (also Oak Ridge Turnpike), one of the gatehouses that guarded the entrances to the town remains, an eerie reminder of the days when the government had to be on the lookout for Nazi spies. From this **Turnpike Gatehouse,** you can continue west 5.3 miles to **K–25,** a sprawling complex that is one of three code-named plants that made up the Oak Ridge operations. At K–25, the more fissionable uranium isotope, U–235, was separated from the more common U–238 in a gaseous diffusion cascade. Because the U–235 is lighter, it would more readily diffuse through a porous barrier when in a gaseous form. Doing this several times in a series of operations (in "cascade") produced the needed concentration for an atomic bomb.

Germany surrendered before U.S. research on the bomb was completed. But Japan continued to fight, so on August 6, 1945, a bomb carrying uranium that had been enriched at Oak Ridge was dropped on Hiroshima, and a bomb powered by plutonium was dropped on Nagasaki three days later, essentially ending the war.

After the war, the Atomic Energy Commission was established to turn the wartime facilities toward peaceful uses. K–25 became the Oak Ridge Gaseous Diffusion Plant. It produced enriched uranium to power the new nuclear navy and the emerging nuclear power industry for production of electricity. With the downtown in the nuclear power industry, the production of enriched uranium ceased in 1985. Today, K–25 has become the East Tennessee Technology Park, where private companies continue scientific research.

In Oak Ridge you can also turn down Illinois Avenue (TN 62) to visit the **American Museum of Science and Energy** on Tulane Avenue. The museum has exhibits, displays, and live demonstrations with many learning experiences for children. Bus tours leave from the museum to visit the Oak Ridge plants, including **Y–12,** where during the war fissionable uranium enriched with the U–235 isotope was produced using an electromagnetic process, and **X–10,** now Oak Ridge National Laboratory, one of the nation's leading research laboratories. At ORNL you can stop at the **Graphite**

Reactor National Historic Site to see the world's first nuclear reactor. During the war, X–10 had the job of constructing this prototype reactor, which used graphite to control the nuclear reaction. Here plutonium was produced, which like U-235 is fissionable. A subsequent larger facility in Hanford, Washington, actually produced the plutonium for the war effort.

To leave Oak Ridge, head northwest on TN 62. In 1.1 miles, at the top of Black Oak Ridge, cross West Outer Drive. The North Ridge Trail follows this ridge along the northern edge of the city; just to the right at the corner, you'll see one of the access points.

OLIVER SPRINGS

The highway descends the other side of the ridge. In 3.7 miles exit the four-lane highway to enter Oliver Springs on Main Street. The town is named for Richard Oliver who settled here in the early 1800s and erected an inn next to a mineral spring. A later inn was erected on the site in the early 1880s; the 150-room Oliver Springs Resort Hotel made the small community nationally known as vacationers arrived by train to partake of the waters. This huge four-story hotel with 60-foot tower burned in 1905, and Oliver Springs once again was a quiet town.

Notice **Colonial Hall** on the left at the corner of Spring Street. The 1830 house was originally built of logs by Lewis Rector and was later covered with weatherboarding; the columned front porch was added in 1898.

Main Street enters the old commercial district of the town. On the right stands **Sienknecht Store,** a 1901 department store that's now an antique shop. You may still see the sign Olga Mining Company painted on the building; Oliver Springs was one of the sites used in filming the movie *The Rocket Boys,* and the sign remains from a fictitious mining company in the movie.

Just down Roane Street on the left stands the odd five-story **Stone Clinic.** The first two floors of the clinic were built by Dr. J. T. Hayes in the 1930s; then Dr. F. O. Stone purchased the clinic. Dr. Stone's hobby was brick-laying, and whenever he had free time, he kept laying brick, building the structure higher and higher. The top three floors became an apartment where he and his family lived.

Continue on Main Street, crossing the railroad tracks and curving left to a junction with Winter Gap Road. Turn left to the **Oliver Springs Railroad Depot.** The 1896 Southern Railway depot now houses the town library and museum, which contains artifacts and photographs on the local history.

Return up Winter Gap Road through the intersection with Main Street to a junction with TN 61/62. This drive will follow TN 62 straight ahead, but here you can turn left on TN 61 for a side trip to visit historic Harriman in 15 miles. The town was founded in 1889 by the East Tennessee Land Company, led by Walter E. Harriman and Frederick Gates, both temperance advocates. In February 1890 the company held a great land sale attended by thousands who wanted to be part of the "Utopia of Temperance." All the lot deeds forbid the "use of the property, or any building thereon, for the purpose of making, storing, or selling intoxicating beverages." The marvelous Romanesque **Temperance Hall** stands prominently in the town; it was built in 1891 as the headquarters of the land company and now houses city offices and the Harriman Heritage Museum.

BRUSHY MOUNTAIN, FROZEN HEAD, LONE MOUNTAIN

In Oliver Springs, take TN 62 northeast to enter Morgan County and climb toward the Cumberland Plateau, following the hollow of a small creek. This is coal country with open pits beside the road and old strip mines slashing across the surrounding mountain slopes. In 4.2 miles descend into the small community of Coalfield, which resides in a cove in the plateau.

TN 62 continues its gradual climb, now ascending the hollow of the Little Emory River, eventually passing rock outcroppings in the narrow passage. In 2.5 miles the highway crosses the upper reaches of the stream and levels off among the Cumberland Mountains, which stand on this northern end of the Cumberland Plateau.

In 1.7 miles you can turn right on TN 116 for a side trip to Petros and **Brushy Mountain State Prison.** The historic prison resides at the base of Frozen Head Mountain; incarcerated here for a time was James Earl Ray, the convicted killer of Martin Luther King, Jr. This prison also saw the end of the use of convict labor to mine coal. In the late 1800s, prisoners were leased from the state by coal companies and used as forced labor in the coal mines. Free miners objected to the practice and eventually rebelled in the 1890s at coal mines near Tracy City, Oliver Springs, Briceville, and Coal Creek, which is present-day Lake City; the miners attacked the stockades where prisoners were kept, setting them free. The state militia was brought in to put an end to the violence in what came to be called the "Coal Creek Wars." The practice of leasing convicts for coal mining ended in 1896, but the state continued to use Brushy Mountain prisoners in state-run mines near Petros into the 1950s.

Return from Brushy Mountain to TN 62, and continue northwest. In 5.9 miles you can turn right on Flat Fork Road to head for **Frozen Head State Park and Natural Area.** A prison farm with red barns and grazing cattle occupies this valley in the mountains. In 3.3 miles, curve right to cross Flat Fork Creek and curve back left to enter the state park with its 50-mile hiking trail system and backcountry campsites. In winter, frost often covers the park's Frozen Head Mountain, hence the name.

Return to TN 62, and continue northwest 1.9 miles to a junction with US 27 to the north at the outskirts of Wartburg. Stay straight a short distance to a second junction with US 27 to the south and turn left. In 2.5 miles turn right on Clayton Howard Road to enter **Lone Mountain State Forest.** A picnic area and trailhead lie on the left; the forest of hardwoods and pines contains 15 miles of hiking and horse trails.

Continue west on Clayton Howard Road to emerge from the forest and travel through rural backcountry. In 1.3 miles at a fork, stay to the left, and in 0.9 mile turn right on Potters Falls Road, which makes a steep, winding descent to a crossing of Crooked Fork Creek. **Potters Falls** is on the left; here a broad waterfall spills over a 15-foot ledge. Across the bridge, a pull-out is on the left. From this point you can walk down an old road to **Lower Potters Falls;** the creek drops 20 feet among rock ledges.

WARTBURG

Potters Falls Road ascends from the creek and eventually becomes Kingston Street as it enters Wartburg in 2.1 miles. The community was once a German colony, founded in 1845 by George F. Gerding. The town was named after the castle in Germany where Martin Luther, German leader of the Protestant Reformation, took refuge and translated the Bible into German. With the close of the Civil War, the colony was in a shambles from marauding solders. Gerding sold much of his land and moved to Oliver Springs in 1872; his daughter and son-in-law also settled there, purchasing Colonial Hall. But Wartburg survived, with German descendants still living in the area.

At the junction with Main Street stands the **Morgan County Courthouse.** Turn left to pass in front of the courthouse to Maiden Street and turn right 1 block to the headquarters and visitor center for the **Obed Wild and Scenic River.** The nearby Obed River and parts of its tributaries, Daddys Creek and Clear Creek, along with a section of the Emory River into which the Obed flows, make up the nationally designated river. Here on the Cumberland Plateau, where erosion proceeds downward into less resistant layers below sandstone caprock, these streams have carved a deep river gorge. The river is known for whitewater paddling; hiking trails that include a section of the Cumberland Trail are being developed. You can get maps at the visitor center that show the river access points and trailheads.

WILD AND SCENIC RIVER

Return down Maiden Street to cross Main Street and travel 1 block to Spring Street. Turn right on Spring, crossing Church Street in another block. Spring Street becomes Catoosa Road as it heads southwest. In 5.3 miles the road begins a winding descent into the gorge of the Emory River. In 0.5 mile, just before the Nemo Bridge crossing of the Emory, you can turn right and descend into **Rock Creek Park,** a picnic area beside the river; this is also a major takeout point for paddlers. An old highway bridge still crosses the river here and has become part of the hiking trail system to provide access to the Cumberland Trail on the other side of the river.

Continue on Catoosa Road across the Emory, and begin ascending from the river. A narrow road on the right gives access to the **Rock Creek Campground** beside the river; the Nemo Bridge Section of the Cumberland Trail travels from the campground along the Emory and then along the Obed River to the north. You can stay on Catoosa Road out of the river gorge and along the plateau for 1.5 miles to enter **Catoosa Wildlife Management Area,** which borders the Obed and Daddys Creek. The gravel roads in Catoosa are closed to everyone February through March and to all except hunters during big game hunts in the spring and fall. Other times of the year, you can enter Catoosa for access to trails and the river system and to see the **Devil's Breakfast Table,** a natural geologic formation where a huge slab of rock lies on a tall pedestal.

Return to Wartburg to Main Street and turn west, taking Main Street out of town, which is also TN 62. In 1 mile turn left on Montgomery Road. Cross the Emory River and reconnect with TN 62 in 3 miles; turn left. In 0.5 mile descend into the old railroad town of Lancing. The road curves right across railroad tracks, virtually making a U-turn to pass through the community. At a distance to the left, notice the **Shady Grove Presbyterian Church,** built in 1884. Pass an old country store on the left that still serves the community. The road then curves left to rise out of Lancing.

In 2.3 miles turn left on Ridge Road. In another 2.9 miles the road makes a winding descent into Clear Creek Gorge to the Lilly Bridge crossing of Clear Creek. There's parking for stream access before the bridge. Across the bridge, steps on the left provide access to a trail that leads up to the gorge wall at an approved place for rock climbing. A side path to the left off this trail offers a view of 20-foot **Melton Mill Branch Falls,** which spills down a rock face as the stream makes its way to Clear Creek. The main trail continues up along the bluff to Lilly Bridge Overlook, but you can also drive to parking for the overlook.

Lilly Bridge Overlook

To do this, continue on the road ascending out of the gorge, and turn left on a gravel road leading to a picnic area from which a path leads to **Lilly Bridge Overlook.** An elaborate boardwalk prevents trampling of fragile vegetation at the gorge rim and makes the view universally accessible. The overlook offers a dramatic view of Clear Creek Gorge.

Return to the road, which on this side of Clear Creek is called Potter Chapel Road, and continue west; on the left is parking for a long walk to the confluence of Clear Creek with the Obed River. Potter Chapel Road continues north to a junction with TN 298 in 5.5 miles. Turn right onto TN 298. The highway descends into the gorge to the Jett Bridge crossing of Clear Creek in 0.8 mile. When the road begins to rise after you cross the creek, you can make a sharp left turn on a narrow gravel road that descends back to the creek. A picnic area and stream access are available there.

DEER LODGE AND MUDDY POND

TN 298 continues out of the gorge of Clear Creek 1.3 miles to a junction with TN 62; turn left to continue west, passing through farmland with barns, fields, and, in season, rolls of hay. In 3 miles, where the highway curves to the left, you can turn right on TN 329 for a side trip to Deer Lodge in 2.4 miles. There was a small community here when Abner Ross came in 1884 to purchase 600 acres of land on which to develop a health resort. Ross had been the manager of the Tabard Inn at Rugby to the north and brought with him a small herd of deer that he had kept on the hotel grounds, so Ross's new community came to be called "Deer Lodge." Several Victorian homes were constructed in the community along with a school, churches, and boarding-houses. Visitors arrived by train at the nearby Sunbright station and traveled overland to the community. The resort declined after 1900, but the town revived with an influx of Polish settlers, primarily from Pennsylvania. Thereafter many of the original settlers left, moving on to other opportunities. On the right stands the **Deer Lodge Congregational Church,** built in 1889, and the **Weidemann Hotel,** which operated around 1900 to accommodate visitors to the town.

Return to TN 62 and continue to the west. You'll be in a rural area with scattered farms and forest. In 1.8 miles cross a high bridge over White Creek, and in 8.2 miles enter Fentress County. The Cumberland Plateau is relatively flat through this section; green fields with grazing horses and cattle are typical here. In another 7.3 miles enter the community of Clarkrange at a junction with US 127. Cross the highway and continue west on TN 62.

In 1.2 miles you can turn right on Campground Road for a 3-mile side trip to **Muddy Pond,** a Mennonite community. The Mennonites are a Protestant sect named for Menno Simms, a Dutch/German religious reformer of the 1500s. Mennonites maintain their faith by leading a simple life that avoids the distractions of modern conveniences; many do not use automobiles or telephones. The Mennonites are known for being fine farmers, and they offer their surplus to the public. In late September and early October visitors are especially welcome to witness the making of sorghum, a light molasses made from pressed sweet sorghum, a cornlike grass similar to sugar cane.

MONTEREY AND THE STANDING STONE

Return to TN 62 and continue west, entering Putnam County in 4.9 miles. In another 7 miles enter the community of Monterey. You'll find Whittaker Park on the left where the Monterey Branch Library is located. Here on a tall pedestal is all that remains of the **Standing Stone.**

When early pioneers followed old Indian trails across the Cumberland Plateau to the Cumberland River settlements to the west, they encountered on one of those trails a stone monument in the shape of a dog. The Cherokees of the region said the stone was carved in ancient times to honor the dog that, according to legend, led their ancestors to this land. The statue stood beside the trail for generations, marking the way west—that is, until the white man came this way. Frontier travelers chipped off pieces of the dog as souvenirs. In 1894, the completion of the Nashville and Knoxville Railroad, later called the Tennessee Central Railroad, linked Cookeville in the east with the coal fields of the western plateau. When the construction team arrived at a small community called Standing Stone, which had grown up near the dog sculpture, the railroad renamed the community Monterey. As the railroad was constructed up the eastern edge of the plateau, the work crew encountered what was left of the Standing Stone and blasted it out of the way. The following year local citizens wanting to preserve the memory of the Cherokees selected the largest remaining piece of the stone and mounted it on the pedestal in the city park. Today Monterey holds its Standing Stone Day on the second Thursday in October with celebrations the following weekend. Cherokees typically travel from North Carolina and Oklahoma to attend the festivities.

From the park, continue on TN 62 into the town of Monterey. Old commercial buildings line Commercial Street. Turn left on TN 84, which is Holly Street. On the left stands the **Imperial,** an old railroad hotel dating from the early 1900s when Monterey was a bustling summer resort. Seven hotels once catered to visitors riding the train up the mountain from Nashville, seeking the cool environs of the Cumberland Plateau; only the Imperial remains.

Continue on TN 84 to the south. US 70 joins the highway from the left before a junction with I–40. You can add a short side trip to this drive by staying on TN 84/US 70 under the interstate for 0.4 mile and turning left on Bee Rock Road to the **Garden Inn at Bee Rock Bed and Breakfast.** This inn occupies a point of land on the western edge of the Cumberland Plateau. During the day, visitors are welcome to park at the entrance and walk into the grounds, which includes Bee Rock at the edge of the plateau, with a view of the Calfkiller River Valley, and the **Campground Bridge Complex,** a rare double arch where two spans bridge a narrow crack in the plateau rim.

sequatchie Valley

CROSSVILLE TO SOUTH PITTSBURG

GENERAL DESCRIPTION: This 108-mile drive travels south through Sequatchie Valley with the towering ramparts of the Cumberland Plateau to the east and west.

SPECIAL ATTRACTIONS: Crossville, Cumberland Homesteads, Cumberland Mountain State Park, Pikeville, Whitwell, Victoria, Jasper, South Pittsburg, historic homes and buildings, scenic views, fall color, hiking, biking, fishing, canoeing, and wildlife viewing.

LOCATION: Southeast Tennessee in the Cumberland Plateau. Begin the drive south from I-40 at Exit 317.

DRIVE ROUTE NUMBERS: US 127, TN 28, Old State Highway 28, and US 72.

CAMPING: Cumberland Mountain State Park and Fall Creek Falls State Park.

SERVICES: All services at Crossville, Pikeville, Jasper, Kimball, and South Pittsburg.

NEARBY ATTRACTIONS: Grassy Cove, Fall Creek Falls State Park, Savage Gulf State Natural Area, and South Cumberland Recreation Area.

THE DRIVE

A caprock of resistant sandstone protects the Cumberland Plateau from erosion. But to the south, this capstone was broken during the formation of the plateau, creating a great anticline, or arch. Uplifted as a long mountain range and exposed, the land quickly eroded. Even after the mountain of rock was removed, erosion continued to scour along the fault line, creating a defile that is one of the longest and straightest valleys in the world. Called Sequatchie, after a Cherokee chief, the 70-mile-long valley is today a pastoral scene of rich farmland and rural peacefulness with scattered communities.

CROSSVILLE

On I–40, at Exit 317 between Knoxville and Nashville, take US 127 south toward Crossville. In 3.9 miles enter Crossville on Main Street. The city was named for a crossroads that was here in the early years when the Walton Road

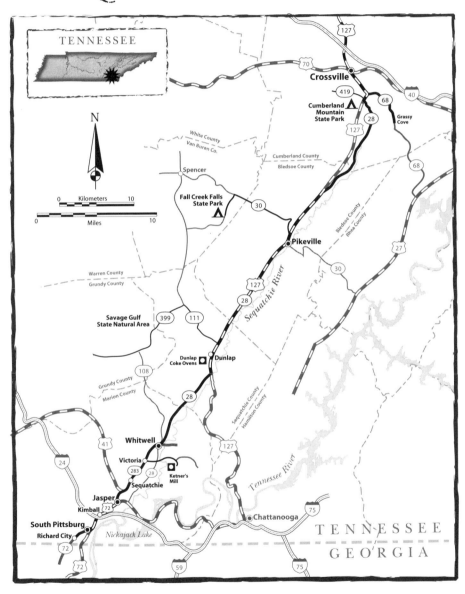

and later the Old Stagecoach Road between Knoxville and Nashville inter-sected with the Kentucky Stock Road that ran north through Tennessee. On the right stands the Tennessee Central Railroad's **Crossville Depot,** built in 1926; now it houses a gift shop and a small railroad museum.

Just before the turn of the century, the Tennessee Central took over the old Nashville and Knoxville Railroad, which previously ran only from Nashville to Monterey. The Tennessee Central completed the line to the east, so that it passed through Crossville. The first train arrived in 1900. From this depot Alvin C. York departed for service in World War I and returned a national hero. (York is described in the Hero, Statesman, and Rolly Hole Chapter.) The Tennessee Central became bankrupt in 1968 and was taken over by the Norfolk-Southern Railway, which ran the train until 1988. A portion of the railroad right-of-way that passes through town has been pro-posed as a biking and hiking trail linking Crossville with Crab Orchard to the east; there it will eventually connect with the trans-state Cumberland Trail.

Also on the right is the **Old Cumberland County Courthouse,** built in 1886–87 from local Crab Orchard sandstone. Many of the buildings in this central core of the downtown are faced with this multicolored sandstone characterized by lines, ripples, and swirls. Found in thin-layered beds only in the area of the Cumberland Plateau around Crossville and Crab Orchard, this fine-grained sandstone has been shipped all over the country for construction ranging from the U.S. Post Office in Philadelphia to the flagstone of New York's Rockefeller Center. The old courthouse has been restored and is now the Museum and Library of Cumberland County. The newer **Cumberland County Courthouse** stands on the left; it was built in 1905.

Watch for a small 1930s building on the left. Covered entirely in sand-stone, including its roof, it once served as a highway patrol station. In the next block, the 1905 **First National Bank Building,** now a home health care facility, has different types and colors of sandstone in its facade; various slabs show the results from different methods of cutting and polishing. Across the street stands the 1936 **Palace Theater,** an Art Deco rendering in Crab Orchard sandstone; the old theater is slated for restoration.

Continue south on US 127 out of town. The third weekend in August each year, this highway becomes "The World's Longest Outdoor Sale," a giant yard sale that started in 1986 as a way of getting people off the interstate and into the small towns along the Cumberland Plateau. Thousands of vendors set up along US 127 from Covington, Kentucky, through Tennessee to Chattanooga and on into Georgia and Alabama. Bargain hunters also arrive by the thousands. This stretch of US 127 south from Crossville and down Sequatchie Valley is one of the most active sections of the outdoor sale.

CUMBERLAND HOMESTEADS AND GRASSY COVE

In 2 miles, the highway enters the **Cumberland Homesteads Historic District,** a former 1930s New Deal community of distinctive English-style cottages. The construction of Pres. Franklin D. Roosevelt's New Deal communities across the country was intended to alleviate the hardships of the '30s depression, providing jobs and low-cost housing. Eleanor Roosevelt visited the Cumberland Homesteads in the 1930s to see how the model community was progressing. The project lasted for twelve years while the economy recovered and World War II ensued. In 1945 the project was terminated, and the families were given the opportunity to purchase their homes at low interest rates. Many of the homes are still occupied by the original homesteaders or their children. You will easily recognize the Cumberland Homesteads houses along the highway, faced almost entirely with Crab Orchard sandstone.

At the intersection of US 127 with TN 68 stands the **Cumberland Homesteads Tower,** an octagonal sandstone structure containing the community's water tank. The base of the tower, which has four wings in the shape of a cross, housed the administrative offices of the homesteads project and is now the **Cumberland Homesteads Museum,** containing exhibits on the history of the community. Across from the tower is the **Cumberland General Store**, a hardware store that has tools and implements for farm and home, everything from windmills and wood stoves to mule bits and cow kickers.

At this junction you can turn left on TN 68 for a side trip to **Grassy Cove.** More homesteads homes are along the road. In 1.2 miles **Homestead Bed and Breakfast** is on the left in an original 1934 homesteads house. In another 3.8 miles, notice on the right a trailhead for the **Cumberland Trail,** which, when completed, will travel from Cumberland Gap to the north along the Cumberland Plateau to Signal Mountain to the south. Here the trail climbs Brady Mountain to pass along the northwest rim of Grassy Cove.

TN 68 descends into Grassy Cove, a pastoral valley of productive farmland. Here in Grassy Cove, and similarly in Sequatchie Valley to the south, where the plateau caprock is missing, the land has eroded down to limestone, which makes for rich, fertile land. The 3,000 acres of Grassy Cove is surrounded on all sides by mountains in the general shape of a triangle—Brady to the northwest, Black Mountain to the northeast, and Bear Den Mountain to the southeast. Luckily, the water that drains from the mountains into the

Cumberland Homesteads Tower

cove has an outlet. Being much more easily eroded than sandstone, limestone bottomlands typically contain caves, sinks, and underground streams—what geologists call a "karst" formation. The waters of Grassy Cove gather in Cove Creek and flow into a cave at the base of Brady Mountain. Cove Creek emerges on the other side of the mountain as the Sequatchie River. Because of the geological significance of the valley, Grassy Cove has been designated a National Natural Landmark.

Traveling along TN 68 through the cove, you'll pass the **J. A. Kemmer and Son Store,** an old country general store containing everything from hardware to groceries. Conrad Kemmer settled Grassy Cove in 1808 and his descendants still farm the cove. At a distance behind the store is the mountain cave that drains the valley. Across the highway stands an old Kemmer homeplace, a brick residence with red barns and outbuildings. On the other end of the cove is also the **J. C. Kemmer and Son Store.** Just before the store, you can turn right on Kemmer Road to the **Grassy Cove United Methodist Church.** Founded in 1803 on land given by John Ford, Sr., the old church has been replaced with a newer red brick building. Ford is credited with discovering Grassy Cove in 1801; he found a valley with grass as high as a person's head, hence the name. Ford, a veteran of the Revolutionary War, is buried in the cemetery beside the church.

Return to Cumberland Homesteads, and turn south on US 127. TN 419 to the right leads into **Cumberland Mountain State Park,** which was once the community park for the Cumberland Homesteads. The park contains a campground, cabins, a restaurant, and hiking trails along Byrd Lake. The lake was created by a dam erected by the Civilian Conservation Corps in the 1930s; the dam is the largest steel-free masonry structure built by the CCC.

SEQUATCHIE VALLEY

Continue south on US 127; Brady Mountain stands to the left. US 127 stays straight to the descent into Sequatchie Valley in 9.2 miles. For a more scenic route, bear left in 2.6 miles on Old State Highway 28. The road wanders across the plateau through a rural area of small farms. In 3 miles, cross Daddys Creek where the road curves right. Notice the foundations remaining from the old Sutton Ford Mill. In another 4.7 miles the road begins a winding descent into Sequatchie Valley. To the left is a cove where the waters of Cove Creek emerge through Devil Step Hollow Cave as the headwaters of the Sequatchie River.

The road descends to a crossing of the Sequatchie River and follows the river downstream through the narrow head of the valley, a forested river hollow.

At a junction with Upper East Valley Road to the left, bear right to stay on Old 28, crossing back over the river. Sequatchie Valley opens up to rolling farmland with scattered barns and houses; slow down and enjoy one of the prettiest valleys in Tennessee as you pass from Cumberland County into Bledsoe County. In 9.7 miles the road reaches a junction with US 127. Turn left to take the main highway straight down the broad valley bounded by the wall of the Cumberland Plateau on the right and Walden Ridge to the left. Named for an early explorer, Elijah Walden, the ridge is actually the entire eastern flank of the Cumberland Plateau as it passes through Tennessee. But here where Sequatchie Valley forms a deep rift in the plateau surface, Walden Ridge stands alone, separated from the rest of the plateau.

Eight miles down US 127, you'll enter Pikeville. On the outskirts of town, you can follow TN 30 to the right for a side trip to **Fall Creek Falls State Park,** climbing the plateau and reaching in 12.5 miles a left turn on TN 284; you'll reach the park entrance in another 2 miles. The park has camping, lodging, and hiking trails in a wonderland of canyons and waterfalls, including 256-foot-high Fall Creek Falls, the tallest in the eastern United States.

At the US 127 and TN 30 junction, you reach the center of Pikeville by staying straight on US 127, which is also Main Street. (If you take the side trip, return on TN 30 and take a right on US 127 to reach Pikeville center.) The **Bledsoe County Courthouse,** built in 1909, stands on the left. Named for explorer Zebulon Pike, the town grew up around a large spring on this high ground west of the Sequatchie River. Turn left on Spring Street, just before the courthouse, to drive around the square and see the old homes that still grace the downtown. On the left is the **John Bridgeman House,** a two-story Tennessee Federal brick home built in the early 1820s and now owned by First National Bank. Behind the courthouse on Frazier Street is the **Dr. James A. Ross House,** a two-story frame residence built around 1875. It was used as a hospital at one time and now contains the offices of Sequatchie Valley Area Tourism. Out back is the small office Dr. Ross used; a garden contains the town spring.

Around the courthouse, reconnect with Main Street and turn left to pass through the **South Main Historic District** of large homes dating from the late 1800s. The **Vaughn House** on the right, a 1890 three-story Victorian, contains an antique shop, and **Colonial House** and **Victoriana** are bed-and-breakfast inns. The **Eliza S. Ault House,** built around 1892, has a log cabin on the property built about 1790.

Leaving Pikeville, US 127 passes a junction with TN 30 to the left and returns to the pastoral countryside of Sequatchie Valley—cows graze and hay, corn, soybeans grow on farmland below the towering walls of the plateau. Along the way, cross into Sequatchie County. In 18.3 miles, the highway reaches a junction with TN 111, a scenic highway that dips across the valley from rim to rim. If you take TN 111 to the left, in 4.2 miles you'll reach a scenic overlook that offers a panoramic view of the valley. If you take TN 111 to the right, you'll have a dramatic climb up the plateau for a side trip to **Savage Gulf State Natural Area,** a virtual wilderness of three converging canyons with hiking trails and primitive camping. To access the canyon areas, turn left off TN 111 in 9 miles onto TN 399.

From the junction with TN 111, stay straight on US 127 to enter Dunlap. In 1.9 miles turn right on Cherry Street, right on Third Street, left on Hickory Street, and then right on Mountain View to reach the **Dunlap Coke Ovens Historic Site.** In the early 1900s the Douglas Coal Company and then the Chattanooga Iron and Coal Company constructed 268 brick ovens here for the purpose of converting locally mined coal into coke, a more concentrated carbon form that burns hotter than coal and so can be used for processing iron ore. The operation was taken over by Southern States Coal, Iron, and Land Company in 1919 and continued until 1922. From the visitor center, constructed to look like the old company store, you can walk among the coke ovens sitting in lines in the woods. A large Victorian building you passed on the way in was the Dunlap Club House for the coal company's visiting officials and managers; the large residence is now the **Club House Bed and Breakfast.**

Return to US 127 and continue south. At a junction, TN 28 turns off to the right to continue down Sequatchie Valley while US 127 bears left to cross the Sequatchie River where Scott and Ernestine Pilkington's **Canoe the Sequatchie** offers canoe trips on the gently flowing river. Back at the junction stay with TN 28, which passes through rural countryside with fields, barns, and farmhouses. Cross into Marion County. In 14.5 miles TN 28 enters Whitwell, named for Thomas Whitwell, a Welsh metallurgist who, with James Bowron, founded Southern States Coal, Iron, and Land Company in 1874. The company opened coal mines on the Cumberland Plateau above the town. Whitwell was killed in a mine explosion in 1878.

Turn right on TN 108 and in a few yards turn left on Valley View Highway. At a junction with TN 283, turn right to stay on Valley View Highway. In 2.3 miles in the small community of Victoria, you can see the small bell tower of **Bethel United Methodist Church** above the trees on the right. Turn right on Bob Mosley Road to get to the white frame church, built in 1887. The Southern States Company turned this former community of Dadsville into another company town, opening coal mines above the town and constructing coke ovens to produce the coke that was used in iron furnaces at a third company town down the valley, South Pittsburg. This early industrialization of the southern end of Sequatchie Valley was financed by a London, England, syndicate. The branch of the Nashville, Chattanooga, and St. Louis Railroad, which gradually extended up the valley from around 1870 to 1891, connected these industrial towns and provided transportation for the coal and coke. The company's operations in Dadsville was under the direction of John Frater, who built the Bethel Church for the community. When Queen Victoria donated a bell for the church, the town was renamed in her honor.

At a junction with Ketners Mill Road, the old **Victoria Depot** stands on the left; it's now a residence. For a side trip to **Ketner's Mill,** turn left to cross TN 28 and in another 2.1 miles cross the Sequatchie River and immediately turn right to reach the mill. Built around 1824 by Ephraim Prigmore, the original wooden mill was acquired by Alexander K. Ketner in 1868; in 1882 Ketner added the brick building that is still standing. Waterpower turns millstones that grind corn and wheat into meal and flour. Four generations of Ketners operated this mill until 1992. A Fall Country Fair is held here each year in October, and the old mill is put into action again to grind corn into meal.

Return west across TN 28 to the junction with Valley View Highway, and turn left to continue south. In 3.7 miles pass through the small community of Sequatchie, originally called Owen Switch. The name was changed when a group of New England investors established the Sequatchee Valley Coal and Iron Company in 1890, using the old spelling of the name. They also formed the Sequatchee Town and Improvement Company. The growth of the community never matched the dreams of the investors.

In 2.8 miles US 41 turns off to the right to climb the plateau to Tracy City in the heart of the **South Cumberland Recreation Area,** a combination of small natural areas featuring waterfalls, hiking trails, and a campground. Tracy City was also a town created during the coal boom; the Sewanee Mining Company, later the Tennessee Coal, Iron, and Railroad Company, operated in this region. Being the more successful operation, the company eventually took over the Southern States operations.

JASPER AND SOUTH PITTSBURG

Continue straight on Old Highway 28 (now also US 41 east), which becomes Betsy Pack Drive as you enter Jasper. Betsy Pack, daughter of Cherokee Chief John Lowery, donated forty acres for the establishment of a town for the seat of Marion County in 1820. The town was named after William Jasper, a sergeant in the Revolutionary War. Originally from South Carolina, he fought in the battle for Fort Moultrie in Charleston Harbor. During the assault he retrieved the fort's fallen flag and rehoisted it. He was later killed at Savannah.

The drive passes a number of historic homes and the 1875 **McKendree United Methodist Church** and reaches the town square, which is the site of the **Marion County Courthouse.** Older commercial buildings surround the square, and at the far left corner stands the **Jasper Depot.** In 1867 a branch line from the Nashville, Chattanooga, and St. Louis Railroad, which ran across the southern part of the state where it dipped south to Bridgeport, Alabama, was completed from Bridgeport to Jasper. The original depot burned in the early 1900s and was replaced with the present structure. The railroad continued building the line up the valley through Victoria and Whitwell, reaching Pikeville in 1891.

At a junction with US 64/72 in Jasper, turn right to continue down Sequatchie Valley. The valley broadens as it nears the Tennessee River. In 4 miles, pass through the community of Kimball. In 1890 a group of investors purchased 64,000 acres and renamed the small community of Wallview after R. I. Kimball, the vice president and general manager of the Kimball Town Company. Bankruptcy soon ended the project. Today's Kimball is a small bustling commercial district that has grown up beside I–24. Pass under the interstate and in another 1.5 miles exit to the right on Old Highway 72. TN 156 turns left to cross the Tennessee River on a prominent arched bridge, which is the route for the Tennessee River Gorge drive.

In 0.5 mile enter South Pittsburg, the former company town of Southern States Coal, Iron, and Land Company, Ltd. When James Bowron came to the United States from Stockton-on-Teas, he had the backing of an English syndicate, the Old English Company, to acquire lands for iron production. The place he selected was here on the Tennessee River at the southern end of Sequatchie Valley. In 1874 Bowron, along with Thomas Whitwell and others, founded the Southern States Company.

As part of the venture, Bowron established South Pittsburg; although the name was spelled differently than Pittsburgh, Pennsylvania, the association was clear. A model town was constructed with worker cottages, managers' homes, offices, hotels, and foundries. Two blast furnaces were begun. Unfortunately, Bowron died in 1877 and Whitwell a year later, followed by two other major investors. Bowron's son, William, who had joined the enterprise, tried to carry on and did succeed in completing the first blast furnace, which began operation in 1879. But the vision and energy of the founders was gone. In 1881, Southern States was acquired by Tennessee Coal, Iron, and Railroad Company.

W. M. Duncan, a Nashville banker involved in the Tennessee Company, took an interest and in 1885 bought the town project. In 1886 he sold the town to a new real estate firm, South Pittsburg City Company; William Bowron was one of the company founders. The City Company promoted the town and sold lots at auction. A number of businesses and industries were attracted, and South Pittsburg finally experienced the boom that had been planned for it.

When you enter South Pittsburg on Old Highway 72 (Cedar Avenue), you'll reach the downtown district. Commercial buildings here date from before the turn of the twentieth century. On the right stands the **Opera House,** built in 1890 for traveling minstrel shows. Now it houses a music shop with a collection of old juke boxes. Turn right on Third Street and drive to the corner of Elm Street to see the **Old First National Bank Building;** built in 1887, it is considered one of the finest bank buildings in the South. The city purchased the old structure and moved it to this location; it is now the city hall. Across Elm is the **Christ Church Episcopal** on the right, a white frame building constructed in 1883; it has a bell tower and a rectory. Cross Holly Avenue and turn left on Oak Avenue to see the **Cook/Headrick House,** one of the large houses built by the Southern States Company and originally the headquarters of the Old English Company. At the next block, turn left on Fourth Street to return to Cedar Avenue where you should turn right.

Old Highway 72 next enters Richard City, now part of South Pittsburg. Richard Hardy came to the region in 1907 to take advantage of the limestone found in the valley. He opened the Dixie Portland Cement Company at the small community of Deptford. As the town grew, it was renamed for Hardy, president and manager of the company. Turn right on Nineteenth Street to its end to see the remains of the once state-of-the-art factory. Tom Mix worked here for a time as labor boss; later he joined Wild West shows, which led to his career as one of the first western movie stars. Turn right and drive two blocks to **Richard Hardy Memorial School.** Hardy recognized the need to educate the children of his workers, and so he had the cement neoclassical building erected in 1926. The school was originally called Dixie Portland Memorial School; the name was changed after Hardy's death in 1927. Return to Old Highway 72, and return north to reach I–24.

Rock Island and Cumberland Caverns

CROSSVILLE TO MCMINNVILLE

GENERAL DESCRIPTION: This 62-mile drive descends the Cumberland Plateau onto the Highland Rim to visit the site of the Great Falls at Rock Island and Cumberland Caverns.

SPECIAL ATTRACTIONS: Pleasant Hill, Rock House State Shrine, Sparta, Rock Island State Park, Faulkner Springs, McMinnville, Cumberland Caverns, historic homes and buildings, scenic views, fall color, hiking, biking, boating, fishing, and wildlife viewing.

LOCATION: Middle Tennessee. Begin the drive south from I–40 at Exit 317.

DRIVE ROUTE NUMBERS: US 70; and TN 1, 287, 288, 56, and 8.

CAMPING: Rock Island State Park.

SERVICES: All services at Crossville, Sparta, and McMinnville.

NEARBY ATTRACTIONS: Virgin Falls Pocket Wilderness and Big Bone Cave State Natural Area.

THE DRIVE

The confluence of the Caney Fork and the Collins River was the site of early industrialization and later hydropower generation. The area is called Rock Island, for a small island in the Caney Fork River. This region of the Highland Rim is also known for its caves. Caves do not form in the sandstone of the Cumberland Plateau, but here at the foot of the plateau, caves appear in limestone layers of rock exposed in outlying mountains. Cumberland Caverns is considered one of the largest in the East, second only to Mammoth Cave in Kentucky.

PLEASANT HILL

From I–40, take US 127 south toward Crossville. In 2.9 miles turn right to a junction of highways and stay straight on US 70. In 2 miles a side road left

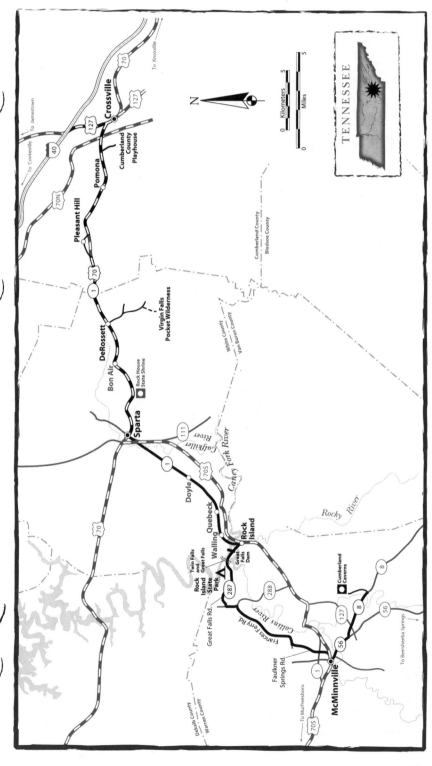

leads to **Cumberland County Playhouse,** Tennessee's premier regional theater. Founded by the Crabtree family, the playhouse stages nationally recognized plays as well as original work grounded in the history and culture of Tennessee. Plays are often sold out, so make reservations.

In 2.5 miles pass through the small community of Pomona, once a retreat founded by John M. Dodge, a famous portrait painter. Dodge planted many apple trees in the area and named his community for the Roman goddess of orchards. Virtually nothing remains of the original settlement but the name.

In 4.6 miles turn right on a side road into Pleasant Hill. Soon on the left stands **Pioneer Hall,** the museum of the Pleasant Hill Historical Society. The 1887 three-story frame building is the only structure remaining from Pleasant Hill Academy, a secondary school founded by the American Missionary Association of the Congregational Churches to provide education for the children of this once remote plateau country. The school was established by Rev. Benjamin Dodge. By 1947 the region had adequate public schools, and the academy closed its doors.

Beyond the school, **Uplands Retirement Village** lies to the left. The village is a former hospital begun by Dr. May Wharton, known as the "Doctor Woman of the Cumberlands." Dr. Wharton followed her husband, Edwin, to Pleasant Hill in 1917 when he accepted the position of principal of Pleasant Hill Academy. She soon began practicing medicine in the region and stayed on after her husband died in 1920, founding a hospital and sanitarium that was at first called Uplands and later Cumberland General. Because of the cooler temperatures and clean air of the plateau country, the doctor considered this an excellent place to retire, and she gave away land to those who would come to live here. When she moved the hospital to Crossville, which was more centrally located, the facilities in Pleasant Hill became a retirement community.

Retirement cottages line a neighborhood street as you leave the town. In 1.5 miles rejoin US 70; continue west.

VIRGIN FALLS AND ROCK HOUSE

In 2.9 miles leave Cumberland County and enter White County. In 3.3 miles in the small community of DeRossett, you can turn left on Eastland Road for a side trip to **Virgin Falls Pocket Wilderness** and **Centennial Conservation Wildlife Management Area**. In 4.4 miles turn right on Chestnut Mountain Road, and in another 1.6 miles turn right on Scotts Gulf Road to access both areas. The land that makes up the WMA was donated to the state by the Bridgestone-Firestone tire company to preserve the region of Scotts

Gulf on the Caney Fork River. The pocket wilderness, containing 110-foot Virgin Falls, has been set aside by Bowater Inc., a timber company that preserves pockets of its outstanding lands for the enjoyment of the public. Hiking trails penetrate both areas.

On US 70, continue west, passing through the communities of BonDecroft and Bon Air. In 1.4 miles, at the edge of the Cumberland Plateau, a pull-out on the right circles a block of sandstone separated from the rim. From here you have an expansive view off the plateau onto the Highland Rim. The highway then descends this steep western wall of the plateau.

In 1.5 miles, just as the highway levels off on the Highland Rim, turn left on a side road to reach the **Rock House State Shrine.** Built in the 1830s, this small sandstone house served as a toll house and stop on the Washington Post Road, the old stagecoach road that ran from Nashville to Knoxville and northeast to Washington, D.C. Presidents Andrew Jackson and James K. Polk would spend the night here on their travels between Middle Tennessee and the country's capital; Sam Houston, governor of Tennessee and later Texas, is known to have stopped here as well.

SPARTA

Continue west on US 70. In 3.7 miles enter the town of Sparta, which straddles the Calfkiller River, a tributary of the Caney Fork. In the center of town Liberty Square is on the left with the **White County Courthouse.** The square is surrounded by early twentieth-century commercial buildings, including the **Oldham Theater** and **American Legion Hall.** The highway then crosses a bridge over the Calfkiller River. A riverfront park runs along the edge of the stream; it has a fishing pier, walkway, and picnic area.

In 0.6 mile turn left on TN 1 to leave Sparta. In 0.5 mile pass under a railroad overpass, which is a branch of the old Nashville, Chattanooga, and St. Louis Railroad, now part of the CSX Railroad; this line, the Caney Fork and Western, joins the main line at Manchester to the southwest.

ROCK ISLAND

Continue to the southwest, paralleling the railroad. The highway passes through several towns that were stops on the rail line—Doyle, Quebeck, and Walling. In 11.3 miles cross a bridge over the Caney Fork River. At the crossing, look upriver to the left where a rock island with a few trees stands in the river near the confluence of a tributary stream, Rocky River. In another 0.8 mile enter the community of Rock Island, which was named for this island in the river.

Spring Castle

Turn right on TN 287 and cross the railroad tracks that have been paralleling the highway. On the right sits the small **Rock Island Depot.** Continue through the community of older homes, and at a fork, stay right on TN 287, which is also Great Falls Road.

Cross the Collins River just above its confluence with the Caney Fork and enter **Rock Island State Park** in Warren County. To the right is the **Great Falls Dam** across the Caney Fork; the dam creates the Great Falls Reservoir.

Continue into the park, where the **Falls City Cotton Mill** stands on the right. This three-story brick mill constructed in 1892 by Clay Faulkner, along with H. L. and Jesse Walling, stands above the Great Falls on the Caney Fork. The owners also established a mill village they called Fall City. The mill produced cotton sheeting until 1902 when a flood washed away the waterwheel; the site was sold to the Great Falls Power Company, which constructed the dam and powerplant.

On the left across from the mill is the **Spring Castle,** a small castlelike structure that is a springhouse. Just past the mill, turn right into a parking area where an overlook on the right provides a view of **Great Falls,** a broad waterfall in the rocky riverbed of the Caney Fork. At the end of the parking area, another overlook offers a view of the Caney Fork River Gorge where **Twin Falls** streams down the rock face on the left. When the Great Falls Dam was constructed, backing up both the Caney Fork and the Collins River, the rising water unexpectedly found a passageway through the ridge that separates the two streams. Now the water pours out of gaps in the rock to create the double waterfall.

Continue on Great Falls Road, climbing along the peninsula of land between the two rivers. The Caney Fork is the waterway on the right, and the Collins is on the left. Tennessee Valley Authority facilities stand along the road; when the federal utility was created in the 1930s, TVA acquired the Great Falls Hydroelectric Plant, adding the site to its vast network of powerplants on the Tennessee River system.

Turn right off Great Falls Road to the state park visitor center on the right and to access the park facilities: picnic areas, campground, cabins, and recreation sites. You can make an appointment to be guided to nearby **Big Bone Cave State Natural Area,** which contains a cave named for the bones of a prehistoric ground sloth that were found in the cave during mining for saltpeter in 1811. Saltpeter mining also took place during the Civil War; ladders and wooden vats left from the operations can still be seen on the cave tours. Big Bone Cave lies under Bone Cave Mountain to the east, an outlier separated by erosion from the Cumberland Plateau.

MCMINNVILLE

Return to Great Falls Road (TN 287) and continue west. To the left a side road leads to boat access on the Collins River. In 3.7 miles turn left at a junction with TN 288. In another 0.9 mile stay straight onto Frances Ferry Road where TN 288 turns left. This back road travels through a beautiful farmland of cattle fields, silos, and tree nurseries, crossing small tributaries of the Collins River. In 7.5 miles cross Charles Creek and reach a junction with Faulkner Springs Road. At the junction stands **Falcon Manor,** the 1896 home of local entrepreneur Clay Faulkner. In addition to the cotton mill at Great Falls, Faulkner had a woolen mill on Charles Creek and later a hotel here near a mineral springs. To entice his wife, Mary, to move from McMinnville and settle near his enterprises, he promised to build the finest house in the county. He succeeded grandly with the Victorian mansion. From 1946 to 1968 the mansion served as a hospital. The current owners acquired the property in 1989 and restored the home to a bed-and-breakfast.

This drive will turn left on Faulkner Springs Road, but you can stay straight another 0.4 mile to see **Falconhurst** on the left. The 1850 brick Federal-style house was the home of Asa Faulkner, Clay's father, and later the home of Charles Faulkner Bryan, a well-known composer and scholar of folk music.

From Frances Ferry Road, turn up Faulkner Springs Road, and in 1.4 miles cross the TN 1 Bypass around McMinnville and enter the city on Spring Street, reaching the town center at E. Morford Street. Turn right on the one-way street, then left on High Street and left again to go back through the center of the town on one-way Main Street. The **Black House** on the right is a red brick house built in 1825 by Jesse Coffee; it was later the home of Dr. Thomas Black and his family. Two Gothic-style churches also grace the center of town. On the right on Main Street is the 1878 **First Presbyterian Church** and on the left the 1889 **First United Methodist Church**. The 1897 **Warren County Courthouse** on the left anchors the town square.

At the far end of the town, stay straight to a junction with TN 56 and turn left. Cross a bridge over the Barren Fork of the Collins River, and in 1.4 miles reach a junction with TN 8 to the left, which is the route for this drive.

TN 56 continues to the southeast, paralleling the Collins River on the left through a wonderland of nurseries. In 1887 J. H. H. Boyd began collecting seeds and plants to sell, settling in the McMinnville area because the soil and climate were ideal for establishing a nursery. From this beginning, the nursery industry has expanded to 400 growers cultivating more than 1,500 varieties of plants; Warren County now boasts of being the "Nursery Capital of the World."

CUMBERLAND CAVERNS

For this drive, turn off TN 56 onto TN 8. In 0.3 mile pass through a junction with TN 127, and in another 3.2 miles cross a bridge over the Caney Fork River. In 0.8 mile turn left on Cumberland Caverns Road and enter the grounds of **Cumberland Caverns** in another 1.4 miles. A National Natural Landmark, the caverns make up the second largest cave system in the eastern United States. Contained in Cardwell Mountain, an outlying mountain of the Cumberland Plateau, the cave was discovered in 1810 by surveyor Aaron Higgenbotham and was then known as Higgenbotham Cave. Another portion called Henshaw Cave was used for the mining of saltpeter during the War of 1812 and the Civil War. Later explorations confirmed that the two caves are part of one great cavern. Tours include the Hall of the Mountain King (600 feet long, 150 feet wide, and 140 feet high), perhaps the largest underground chamber in the eastern United States.

In 1838 the Cherokees' forced migration followed the route of a turnpike Higgenbotham had constructed down the Cumberland Plateau. The 2-mile Collins River Trail from Cumberland Caverns commemorates the Trail of Tears by following the route down the mountain to Shellsford on the Collins River. Several detachments of Cherokees stopped to rest and grind corn at that point at a mill operated by James Shell. You can return down TN 8 and turn right on TN 127 to the Shellsford Bridge crossing of the Collins and look upriver to see the stone ruins of the mill.

Hero, Statesman, and Rolly Hole

JAMESTOWN TO COOKEVILLE

GENERAL DESCRIPTION: This 92-mile drive drops off the Cumberland Plateau onto the Eastern Highland Rim to visit the York homeplace and Hull birthsite while passing through a countryside of Tennessee hill farms and communities.

SPECIAL ATTRACTIONS: Jamestown, Alvin C. York State Historic Site, Cordell Hull Birthplace State Park, Dale Hollow Lake, Livingston, Standing Stone State Park, Cookeville, historic homes and buildings, scenic views, fall color, hiking, biking, boating, fishing, and wildlife viewing.

LOCATION: Northeast Upper Cumberland Region of Middle Tennessee. Begin the drive in Jamestown on US 127.

DRIVE ROUTE NUMBERS: US 127; and TN 325, 111, 52, 136, and 85.

CAMPING: Obey River Recreation Area, Willow Grove Recreation Area, Lillydale Recreation Area, and Standing Stone State Park.

SERVICES: All services at Jamestown, Livingston, and Cookeville.

NEARBY ATTRACTIONS: Old Alpine Institute.

THE DRIVE

Tennessee has had more than its share of famous people who rose from humble beginnings to national and even international renown. Here in this remote Upper Cumberland region of highland valleys and rural communities, two of the state's best citizens went about their lives, fulfilling duty to country and to their fellow humankind, and in so doing, changed the world. In juxtaposition to such lofty accomplishments, Tennesseans also show skill in life's more mundane pursuits, such as playing marbles.

ALVIN YORK

Begin this drive on the Cumberland Plateau in the center of Jamestown at the junction of TN 52 and Old Highway 127. From this intersection, head

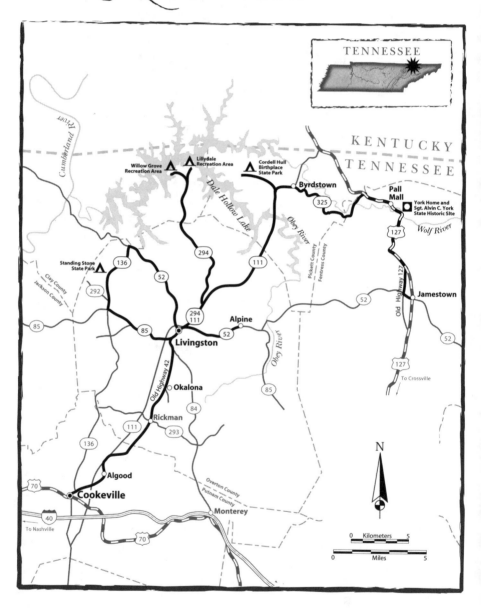

north on Old Highway 127. In 1.2 miles pass the **York Institute** on the left. Named for Alvin C. York, the school was founded in 1929 through York's efforts to improve education in his home area. He traveled the country, giving talks to raise money for the school. Wherever he went, people listened, for York was perhaps the greatest hero of his generation.

Born in the Wolf River Valley to the north, York struggled with his pacifist leanings at the time of United States' involvement in World War I. Finally deciding he should support the struggle, he enlisted and was soon in Europe on the front line. On October 8, 1918, in the Argonne Forest of France, York's platoon had orders to take a nearby railroad that was guarded by a German machine gun installation. In the withering fire from the guns, most of York's men were killed or wounded; the few that remained were pinned down.

The Germans didn't know, however, that the next soldier they faced was perhaps the best marksman in the American and European armies. York had honed his skill with a rifle as a boy hunting in the Tennessee backwoods. From cover, York began to shoot the Germans manning the machine guns. With each crack of the rifle another German soldier fell to the ground. In an attempt to still the deadly fire, seven Germans charged. York first shot the last of the charging men and then the next to last, and then the next. The soldier in front probably did not realize all those behind him were already dead when York's bullet stopped him. With twenty-five dead, the Germans surrendered. York, with seven of his men, herded the captives back to the American lines, gathering others along the way. When York and his men arrived, they had 132 prisoners.

York was hailed a hero, much to the dismay of this quiet and shy young man. Refusing endorsements and other business offers, he returned to Tennessee and married his childhood sweetheart. Finally, at the outbreak of World War II, York agreed to have a movie made about his display of courage, in hopes that it would help inspire America's efforts in the new war. *Sergeant York* opened in 1941, starring Gary Cooper, and once more York became a national celebrity.

In 0.8 mile TN 154 turns off to the right. You can take a side trip here to the **Big South Fork National River and Recreation Area**, a 125,000-acre preserve of steep-walled river gorge, natural sandstone arches, and waterfalls. More than 300 miles of hiking, horse, and mountain biking trails penetrate this remote region of the Cumberland Plateau. Camping is available at Bandy Creek Campground. To head for the Big South Fork, follow TN 154 9.5 miles to a junction with TN 297 and turn east.

For this drive, stay straight 1.2 miles to a junction with US 127, which

Big South Fork Gorge

bypasses Jamestown, and turn left. The highway narrows to two lanes and, in 1.3 miles, drops off the western wall of the Cumberland Plateau. Exposed sandstone marks the plateau rim as the road descends into the Wolf River Valley.

After a long, winding descent, US 127 reaches the valley floor and continues north. With rolling farmland below towering bluffs of the plateau, this is perhaps the prettiest valley in Tennessee. It's not difficult to imagine why Alvin York returned to his home along the Wolf River after the war. In 1.4 miles you can turn right on Wolf River Loop Road to cross the river and reach the Wolf River Cemetery where York is buried.

Stay straight on US 127 into Pall Mall to the York Home on the right. It also serves as the visitor center for the **Sgt. Alvin C. York State Historic Site.** This house and farm was the home of Alvin and Gracie York and their children in the years after World War I. Beyond the home, the highway crosses the Wolf River, and just on the left stands the red grist mill that York operated in the 1940s.

US 127 then leaves Pall Mall. In 2.8 miles descend into the lovely valley of Caney Creek, a tributary of the Wolf. Across the creek, the **Forbus General Store** stands on the right. A white frame country store that opened its doors in 1892, this establishment serves up breakfast and lunch and is known for its homemade fudge. Ascending from the creek, enter Pickett County; in 1.1 miles at the top of a ridge, turn left on TN 325 to descend and cross the Wolf River. This scenic highway precipitously wanders up and down and along ridges past old barns and modest farmhouses, winding through a pastoral countryside. Across the farmland in late fall, tobacco dries in open-air sheds and barns.

CORDELL HULL

In 8.9 miles cross Town Branch and enter Byrdstown to a junction with TN 325. On the town square stands the stone **Pickett County Courthouse** and on the southwest corner is an old **Masonic Lodge,** built around 1880 and now containing a hardware store; the first county court was held in the upstairs. Take TN 325 around the square to the right and then turn off right on North Main at the opposite corner to pass through the old downtown. Turn left to stay with TN 325 on West Main. In 1.4 miles at a junction with TN 111, turn left.

In 0.7 mile turn right to stay with TN 325 on Cordell Hull Memorial Drive. In 1.7 miles is **Cordell Hull Birthplace State Park** on the right, which features a museum and the birthplace of Cordell Hull. It's quite remarkable that a person born in this small log cabin in the Tennessee backcountry would rise to become one of the world's leading statesman. Born in 1871 into a farming family, Hull showed an interest in learning early on while attending a one-room school his father had built. He later received a law degree and practiced law in Celina, where he began a political career. He served first in the Tennessee Legislature and then in the U.S. Congress. Elected to the U.S. Senate, he resigned in 1933 to become Secretary of State under President Franklin D. Roosevelt, serving for almost twelve years, longer than any other Secretary of State. During his term, he instituted the "good neighbor" policy with Latin American countries. With the outbreak of World War II, Hull saw the need for an international organization that would help maintain peace and so laid the groundwork for the creation of the United Nations. Because of illness, he resigned his position in 1944, prior to full ratification of the UN Charter; even so, he is considered the "father of the United Nations." In 1945 this man of humble origins was awarded the Nobel Prize for Peace.

DALE HOLLOW LAKE AND LIVINGSTON

Return to TN 111, and turn south. In 2.2 miles the highway descends to a long bridge crossing of Dale Hollow Lake on the Obey River, a large tributary of the Cumberland River. The lake is the result of an Army Corps of Engineers dam farther downstream. In 0.7 mile on the other side of the river, you can turn right on Obey Park Road to reach the lakeshore. A marina lies to the right and the **Obey River Recreation Area** is on the left, with boat access to the lake, picnicking, swimming, and a campground.

Continue to the south on TN 111. In 3.3 miles enter Overton County while traveling through a pastoral countryside of rolling fields, cattle, and woodlands on the Eastern Highland Rim. In 6.6 miles TN 294 heads north, which you can take for 13 miles to visit the **Willow Grove Recreation Area** and the **Lillydale Recreation Area** on Dale Hollow Lake. Both have picnic areas, boat access, and campgrounds. Lillydale is one of the sites for the Dale Hollow Lake Eagle Watch tours that are held the third and fourth Saturdays in January; reservations must be made with the Army Corps of Engineers for the barge tours, which search for sight of wintering eagles. At this junction, TN 294 joins TN 111; in another 3.7 miles stay with TN 294 as it turns off left to enter **Livingston.**

In 0.9 mile TN 294 ends where TN 52 joins on the left and becomes Main Street. Before heading into the downtown, you can turn left on TN 52 for a 6-mile side trip to the **Alpine Institute,** a mission school established in 1821 by the Cumberland Presbyterian Church. The school operated until the 1940s, during which time students worked on the school's hundred-acre farm to help pay their tuition. The institute became a public school, but is now closed. The campus includes **Alpine Presbyterian Church,** a rustic Gothic stone building still in use.

Return to Livingston and follow Main Street (TN 52) into the town. Turn right on Roberts Street two blocks to University Street to see the site of Livingston Academy, established in 1909. Future governor Albert H. Roberts was instrumental in getting the school located in Livingston; the **Roberts Law Office** stands at the corner of the school grounds.

Main Street separates into one-way lanes into the downtown. The Chamber of Commerce sits on the left between the two lanes. On the other side, Mofield Street branches off to the right to the **Cornucopia Bed and Breakfast,** a large two-story brick house that is one of the oldest homes in Livingston. In the center of town, TN 52 turns to the right while TN 85 continues straight. **Overton County Courthouse,** built in 1868–69, stands on the square, which is surrounded by a downtown of old commercial buildings.

ROLLY HOLE

Turn right on TN 52 to leave the downtown. Cross TN 111, which bypasses the town on the northwest, and climb a ridge to the northwest. In 9.9 miles turn left on TN 136 to enter **Standing Stone State Park.** This park on the northern end of the Eastern Highland Rim is named for the Standing Stone that marked an old Cherokee Trail that traveled to the west; the stone once stood on the edge of the Cumberland Plateau in present-day Monterey to the south. Today a remnant of the stone is preserved in a Monterey municipal park. Standing Stone State Park has ten miles of hiking trails that wander through the forest surrounding Standing Stone Lake, a man-made lake on Morgan Creek. The park also has a campground and a swimming pool.

At the recreation lodge are several marble yards where the National Rolly Hole Marbles Championship is held each year on the second weekend in September. Although the contest is billed as a national championship, participants now come from around the world to attend the tournament here in northern Tennessee where shooting marbles is still a popular pastime. The marble yard is a large compacted dirt rectangle where the play takes place. The game of rolly hole has an elaborate set of rules whereby two teams of two players each shoot flint marbles in an effort to sink them in three holes evenly spaced on the yard while keeping the opposing team from making their holes by knocking their marbles away. Players who have devoted years to learning the game exhibit remarkable speed and accuracy.

Travel through the park to the dam holding back Standing Stone Lake. The road crosses the dam as a single lane and then climbs from the lake. The **Moses Fisk Home** stands on the left, a reconstructed frame house. Fisk came from Massachusetts and settled here on the frontier in 1799. Working as a surveyor, he helped determine the boundary line of Tennessee with Kentucky and Virginia. With Sampson Williams, he established Fisk Female Academy at Hilham in 1806; the original structure burned and was rebuilt in 1817 as a school for boys. Fisk operated the school until his death in 1843.

In 1.3 miles a road on the left leads down to the upper end of Standing Stone Lake. Stay straight to leave the park and reach a junction with TN 85 in Hilham. Turn left to pass through the community.

OLD CHURCHES

In 3.1 miles, you can turn right on Old Union Road and travel 1.6 miles to a four-way junction to see the **Old Union Meeting House,** a log church. Return to TN 85 and continue east 4.3 miles to a junction with TN 111 on the southwest of Livingston. Turn right.

In 0.6 mile turn left on TN 84, and in 0.7 mile where TN 84 turns left, stay straight on Old Highway 42, which is also called Rickman Road. In 2.5 miles at a fork in the Okalona community, Old Highway 42 stays to the right, but you can first turn left to reach the **Okalona Methodist Church** built in 1893; beside the church is the **Okalona Log Church and School,** a small log structure built in 1867.

Back at the junction, stay on Old Highway 42, crossing the Roaring River and traveling through farm country. In 5.1 miles pass through the small community of Rickman. In another 1.4 miles cross Spring Creek, a large tributary of the Roaring River and enter Putnam County. In 3.6 miles curve right to a junction with TN 111. Turn left to continue south. In 0.7 mile turn left to head for Algood. In 1 mile cross railroad tracks to pass through downtown on Main Street, which is lined with old commercial buildings. Watch for **Algood Methodist Church** on the left, a lovely frame church built in 1899. Just beyond the church, turn left to stay on Main Street, which curves right to a junction with TN 111 in 1.4 miles.

COOKEVILLE

Stay straight across TN 111 to enter Cookeville on 10th Street. In 2 miles, at a junction with TN 136, which is also Washington Street, turn left. You'll pass some older homes on this stretch. In 0.8 mile at a junction with Broad Street, turn right to enter the old downtown. The **Putnam County Courthouse** stands on the square to the left; it is a Richardsonian Romanesque style building constructed in 1900. On Jefferson Street, which forms the west side of the square, the **Shopping Arcade** stands in a row of commercial buildings across from the courthouse. Finely restored and now used as an office building, the 1913 Arcade building was patterned after early European malls and is one of the earliest enclosed shopping malls in the United States.

To the right on Jefferson is the **Old Methodist Parsonage.** Built in the 1800s as a one-room log cabin, the old parsonage is now sheathed in siding and houses the Upper Cumberland Tourist Association Regional Office. Stop here for maps, brochures, and further information on the Upper Cumberland region.

Continue west on Broad Street; at Dixie Street at the next block, you can turn right and travel 1 block to cross First Street and find the **Jere Whitson House** on the left. The Victorian-style home was built in 1900 by Whitson, a businessman who owned a general store that was located on the town square and who helped found Dixie College to the north on Dixie Avenue. The school later became **Tennessee Technological University.**

Back on Broad Street stands the **U.S. Post Office and Courthouse,** a fine Italianate-style building constructed in 1916. Broad Street then enters the **Historic West Side,** a row of commercial buildings that has been renovated into a pleasing blend of small shops and businesses. This commercial district grew up with the coming of the Tennessee Central Railroad. In 1902 Jere Baxter purchased the Nashville and Knoxville Railroad that ran through Cookeville and renovated the rail line into the Tennessee Central, which connected with major rail lines to the east and west. At the end of the West Side commercial district, the **Tennessee Central Depot,** constructed in 1909, houses a museum of artifacts, photographs, and memorabilia on the Tennessee Central and on local history. On the grounds is an original Tennessee Central caboose and also a caboose from the L & N Railroad that now owns the old Tennessee Central line.

upper cumberland River

COOKEVILLE TO HARTSVILLE LOOP

GENERAL DESCRIPTION: This 143-mile drive explores the Upper Cumberland River Region, visiting small river towns and pastoral valleys and passing two Army Corps of Engineer dams that create lakes on the river system.

SPECIAL ATTRACTIONS: Gainesboro, Celina, Red Boiling Springs, Lafayette, Hartsville, Carthage, Granville, historic homes and buildings, scenic views, fall color, hiking, biking, boating, fishing, hunting, and wildlife viewing.

LOCATION: Upper Cumberland of Middle Tennessee. Begin the drive in Cookeville on TN 135.

DRIVE ROUTE NUMBERS: TN 290, 56, 53, 52, 10, and 25; US 70; and TN 96.

CAMPING: Salt Lick Creek Campground, Dale Hollow Dam Powerhouse Recreation Area, Pleasant Grove Recreation Area, Defeated Creek Recreation Area, and Indian Creek Recreation Area.

SERVICES: All services at Cookeville, Hartsville, and Carthage.

NEARBY ATTRACTIONS: Fort Blount, Dale Hollow Dam, and Cordell Hull Dam.

THE DRIVE

The Upper Cumberland region of Tennessee encompasses the lands surrounding the Cumberland River and its tributaries. The river flows south from Kentucky into Tennessee where it wanders southwest, passing present-day Nashville. This Upper Cumberland area is a highland region of rolling hills covered in forest and fields, small farms tucked into isolated coves, and historic communities planted along the meandering river.

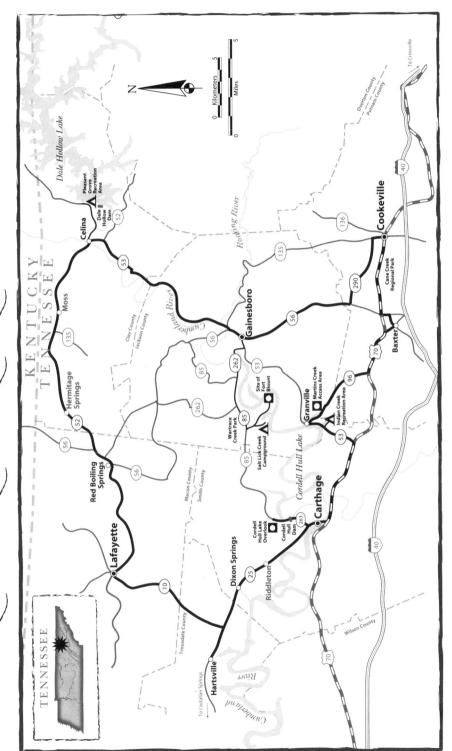

GAINESBORO AND FORT BLOUNT

From Cookeville head north on TN 135 to pass the campus of **Tennessee Technological University.** The school originally opened in 1912 as a high school called Dixie College. Not until 1924 did the school offer a four-year college program; it became a university in 1965. On the north side of the campus, turn left on TN 290, which is also Twelfth Street, to head west. In 6.6 miles enter Jackson County, and in another 2 miles reach a junction with TN 56 and turn right.

The highway passes through a pastoral countryside of small farms and forested hillsides. In 8.6 miles turn left off TN 56 to enter Gainesboro on Main Street. Several large older homes stand along the street. The old **Jackson County Sentinel Building** on the left now houses the Jackson County Museum. Just beyond is the historic town square where old commercial buildings surround the **Jackson County Courthouse.** On the west side of the square, to the back of an open lot, rests a monument to the town's first family, Joseph and Elizabeth Eaton. The first couple to be married in Gainesboro, in 1821, they also had the first child born in the town, they named their baby America. The Eatons lived in a log cabin on this block and operated Eaton's Tavern and Inn, which stood nearby; the Eatons were buried on this spot when they died in the 1870s.

On the north side of the town square, you can turn left on Hull Avenue for a side trip to the site of **Fort Blount** on the bank of the Cumberland River, an important stop on the old Avery Trace. Take Hull Street west out of town, which is also the route of TN 53; in 0.6 mile turn right on TN 262. The highway descends into the pastoral Cumberland River Valley. In 1.3 miles cross the river and continue to the west. In 3.7 miles where TN 262 turns off to the north, stay straight on TN 85. Cross Wartrace Creek to the **Wartrace Creek Park** on the left. This Army Corps of Engineers recreation area is located at the upper reaches of Cordell Hull Lake, which is named for the Tennessee statesman credited with creating the United Nations. The lake is backed up by Cordell Hull Dam far downstream on the Cumberland River. This day-use park has picnic areas, boat ramp access to the river, and a swimming area.

The highway climbs a ridge and descends into a valley to the small community of Gladdice in 2.3 miles. Turn left on Smith Bend Road. In 3 miles you can turn right to reach the Corps of Engineers **Salt Lick Creek Campground** on Cordell Hull Lake. In 3 miles the road becomes gravel and, in another 0.7 mile it ends at the edge of the Cumberland River at the site of Fort Blount.

In 1787 North Carolina authorized a road connecting the eastern towns with the remote settlements on the Cumberland River at present-day Nashville. The next year, Peter Avery, a noted longhunter of the region, guided the crew that blazed the road from Campbell's Station, west of present-day Knoxville, across the Cumberland Plateau and the Highland Rim to the Cumberland River settlements. Avery Trace crossed the Cumberland River at this location, and Sampson Williams soon established a ferry to carry travelers across the river. Because this was still disputed Indian territory at the time, protection was needed for travelers, and so in 1792, a fort was built at this crossing on the far side of the river and named for William Blount, the territorial governor. In 1794 a new fort was built on this side of the river. A second road, the Walton Road, was constructed between 1801 and 1802. It followed much of the Avery Trace but bypassed to the south this crossing of the Cumberland River. Fort Blount was soon abandoned.

DALE HOLLOW AND CELINA

Return to Gainesboro, and stay straight on TN 53 (Hull Street) through town to a junction with TN 56. Turn left to leave Gainesboro. The highway approaches the Cumberland River on the left, and in 1.2 miles TN 56/85 turns off to the left; stay straight on TN 53/85. The **Cordell Hull Wildlife Management Area** stretches along the river. In 0.3 mile cross the Roaring River just before its confluence with the Cumberland. In 0.6 mile TN 85 turns off to the right; stay straight on TN 53. In 9.3 miles enter Clay County. In 7 miles TN 52 joins the highway from the right, and in another 1 mile TN 52 turns left into Celina, which will be the route of this drive. First stay straight on TN 53 and curve east for a side trip to **Dale Hollow Dam.**

In 1.3 miles cross the Obey River, a tributary of the Cumberland, and in another 1.6 miles turn right to enter the reservation around the Army Corps of Engineers Dale Hollow Dam. The **Dale Hollow National Fish Hatchery** lies to the right. Rainbow, brown, and lake trout for stocking rivers and streams are raised here in ground-level tanks. Just beyond the hatchery, a road to the right leads into the **Dale Hollow Dam Powerhouse Recreation Area,** which has a campground and a picnic area below the dam near the Obey River. The road continues on, climbing to the top of the dam and crossing with grand views of Dale Hollow Lake to the left and the Obey River flowing away to the right.

Return to TN 53. You can turn right, and in 0.4 mile turn right on Old Burkesville Road, and in 0.7 mile turn right again on Cedar Hill Road to enter the **Pleasant Grove Recreation Area** on Dale Hollow Lake. Boat access, a picnic area, and a campground are here.

Cordell Hull Law Office

Return to Celina; the community is named for a daughter of Moses Fisk, an early settler in the Upper Cumberland region. At the junction with TN 52, turn right to the **Clay County Museum,** which contains artifact displays and exhibits on the history of the area. Adjacent to the museum stands the **Cordell Hull Law Office;** born near Brydstown to the east, Hull practiced law in Celina before starting a political career that culminated in becoming Secretary of State for Pres. Franklin D. Roosevelt. TN 52 leads into downtown Celina where the **Clay County Courthouse** stands on the town square; built in 1873, the two-story brick edifice is one of the oldest working courthouses in the state. Stay on TN 52 around the square and out of town to the west. In 0.4 mile cross the Cumberland River, passing from the Eastern Highland Rim to the Western Highland Rim. Cattle fields and fine old farmhouses standing on knolls and tucked away in hollows are among the sights on this journey.

RED BOILING SPRINGS AND LAFAYETTE

In 10 miles, pass through the community of Moss, a lumbering community where Honest Abe Log Homes has its national headquarters. In 7.5 miles enter Hermitage Springs, which was a mineral springs resort in the early 1900s; little is left except a few cottages that date from the resort era. In 2.8 miles enter Macon County. In another 2.8 miles descend on North Main Street into **Red Boiling Springs** in the valley of Salt Lick Creek. Turn left on Church Street to pass through a covered bridge over the creek. Church Street circles right to cross back over Salt Lick Creek to a junction with TN 151. Across the road stands a hand pump for one of the mineral wells that once made Red Boiling Springs a famous resort.

The notoriety of the mineral springs in this valley began with an 1840 settler, Shepherd Kirby, who washed his infected eyes with water from one of the springs and was healed. The community soon sprouted more than two dozen hotels and boardinghouses for visitors to take the waters during the resort heyday from the late 1800s into the 1930s. Five types of water are found in the area. Red water, which at one time "boiled" from a spring and gave the place its name, was supposed to help urinary diseases. White water was used for indigestion. Black water supposedly cured digestive tract diseases. These waters have a slight tinge to them, but mostly they are named for the color they give to a silver coin that is left to sit in the water. Freestone water had no substantial mineral content. Finally, there was double-and-twist water, which was used for soaking but not drinking because it would cause a person to double over and twist. Many of the hotels and boardinghouses had bath houses and offered the waters for drinking. The hand pumps around town delivered the various kinds of water.

Turn left on TN 151, which is also East Main Street. On the right stands **Armour's Red Boiling Springs Hotel;** built in 1924, it is one of three hotels that still operate in the town and the only one that still offers mineral baths, using black water. The **Donoho Hotel** sprawls across the far side of Salt Lick Creek on the left; this frame hotel, built in 1914, still retains much of its early charm. Also on the left, the **Thomas House Bed and Breakfast** occupies the old Cloyd Hotel, constructed in 1932 from bricks fired on the property. All three hotels encourage reservations, and the general public can make reservations for meals at the Donoho and Thomas House.

Return along East Main to the center of Red Boiling Springs. Just past Church Street, a small log building on the right serves as a welcome center where you can pick up a brochure detailing a tour of historic sites. The junction of East Main with North Main (TN 151 with TN 52) marks the commercial center of the community; on the right stands the old **Red Boiling Springs Bank.** Turn left on TN 52 to climb from the valley of Salt Lick Creek, leaving Red Boiling Springs.

Donoho Hotel

Continue across the Western Highland Rim. In 11.3 miles turn right on TN 261 into Lafayette where the **Macon County Courthouse** stands on the town square. While the courthouse is a 1930s construction, the town square dates to much earlier, as can be seen from the mighty oak tree on the courthouse grounds. The bottom lobby of the courthouse contains a number of photographs of Macon County history. Around the square, take Church Street to the northwest to **Key Park.** The city park of gardens, walking track, playground, and picnic tables was once part of the grounds of the old Key Home. The land was left to the city by Deliah Key Jackson upon her death. The Macon County Chamber of Commerce occupies the **Key Park Log House,** a log home built in 1842; the log house also serves as a museum with historical photographs and artifacts dating from the 1800s.

Return down Church Street to the square and turn right on College Street, which is also TN 10. Cross TN 52 and continue southwest on TN 10, leaving Lafayette. The highway soon descends off the Western Highland Rim into the Central Basin of Tennessee, traveling down Goose Creek Valley with old barns, farmhouses, and small white churches. In 7 miles enter Trousdale County. In 1.9 miles notice to the right the old **Beech Grove School,** a deserted white frame schoolhouse beside Goose Creek. In 3 miles TN 10 reaches a junction with TN 25. The drive will head to the east, but first turn west to visit Hartsville.

HARTSVILLE

On the right stands the **James DeBow Home.** Construction on the home began in 1854 but was interrupted by the Civil War. The house was completed in 1870, and here local leaders met in the parlor to determine the lines of Trousdale County, which was formed that same year. DeBow was selected as the first chairman of the county commission.

Cross Goose Creek and in 1.6 miles turn left on Main Street, passing large old homes and crossing Little Goose Creek into the **Hartsville Downtown Historic District.** The community is named for James Hart, who operated a ferry here on the Cumberland River beginning in 1798. At the corner of River Street to the left, which is also TN 141, is the town square with the 1906 **Trousdale County Courthouse.** Past the town square another block is a junction with Church Street to the left and Broadway to the right. On the left stands the **Hager Building,** an 1838 structure used as a hospital during the Civil War. Just up Church stands the old **Hartsville United Methodist Church,** a slender red brick church built in 1843. During the Civil War, the building, which had just one story, was also used as a hospital; here less seriously wounded soldiers were treated. In the 1880s, the second story was added on the building; a line with darker brick below and lighter brick above shows the attachment of the upper story.

Turn right on Broadway to the old **Hartsville Depot** on the right. Built in the 1890s, the restored depot now houses the Hartsville-Trousdale County Chamber of Commerce; stop here for a driving tour brochure for the 1862 Battle of Hartsville. After hours, you'll find the brochure in a mail box beside the side-door entrance.

With Union forces occupying Middle and West Tennessee early in the war, federal garrisons were established at Gallatin and Castalian Springs to the west and here at Hartsville. Underestimating the federal troops in Hartsville, which numbered 2,400, Gen. John Hunt Morgan, the famed Confederate cavalry commander, thought he could slip into the town and smash the federal garrison before reinforcements could arrive. Approaching from the south, Morgan and 2,100 troops arrived at the Cumberland River opposite Hartsville at 10:00 P.M. on December 6, 1862. Crossing the swollen river in the bitter cold was taking longer than expected, and so Morgan moved on Hartsville early the next morning with only 1,300 men, leaving the remainder of his troops to cross and follow as quickly as they could. A portion of Morgan's cavalry soon took the town, while Morgan with most of his men approached the federal camp, located south of town near the river. Morgan sent in a small force dressed as Union soldiers to capture the Union pickets; they succeeded, but other Union troops saw what happened and sounded the alarm; the battle ensued. In little over an hour, Morgan's cavalry and infantry outmaneuvered the larger federal force, capturing 1,834 Union soldiers in addition to killing fifty-eight and wounding 204; Morgan's troops suffered only 139 casualties killed, wounded, or missing. Having little time to savor the victory before federal reinforcements would appear, Morgan recrossed the river with his prisoners and retreated to Murfreesboro where he received a hero's welcome.

The driving tour of the battle site visits the Cumberland River crossings, battery emplacements, the Union camp site, and antebellum homes where the wounded received care. You can turn south on TN 141 from the town square and left on Cemetery Road to reach the **Hartsville Cemetery** where Confederate and Union soldiers were buried; some Union dead were later sent to their homes in the North or reinterred in the National Cemetery in Nashville. A monument at the back of the cemetery commemorates the Confederates who died at the Battle of Hartsville.

Return from Hartsville along TN 25 to the east, passing the junction with TN 10 to the north, and continue east toward Carthage. In 2.2 miles the Tennessee Valley Authority's unfinished **Hartsville Nuclear Plant** stands to the right on the Cumberland River. In the 1960s, TVA embarked on an ambitious nuclear power program; those were the heady days when many thought nuclear power would provide cheap, unlimited electrical power. TVA was well into its nuclear program, building several nuclear reactors throughout the Tennessee River Valley, when it became apparent that nuclear power was not cheap nor did the American public require so much power; estimates of future power consumption had been grossly overestimated. Hartsville was put on hold, and later TVA greatly scaled back its nuclear program. Today, the single nuclear plant cooling tower and the skeletal beginnings of a second are testament to how frequently and completely the "experts" can be wrong.

DIXON SPRINGS AND CORDELL HULL DAM

Enter Smith County, and in 0.5 mile watch on the left for **Dixona,** the frontier home of Tilman Dixon, a former captain in the Revolutionary War. Dixon arrived here in 1787 to lay claim to land granted him for service in the war. The land he selected was along the route of the Avery Trace between

Carthage to the southeast and Gallatin to the northwest. He built a log house of at least eight rooms and also constructed barns and other outbuildings. A spring to the southeast, which became known as Dixon Springs, had been a well-known stopping place for travelers; soon many of these travelers chose to stay the night at Dixona, which Dixon began operating as a tavern. As a merchant and tavern keeper, Dixon became one of the wealthiest men in the region. Dixon died in 1816 and is buried in a small cemetery at a distance behind the house. In 1858 James Vaughn added two brick Italianate wings and double porches to the home, giving it the look of a Williamsburg house, but much of the original log cabin is intact. The home is open to the public for tours by prior reservation.

Cross Dixon Creek and bear right on a small side road to enter the community of Dixon Springs. Soon on the right is the old **Dixon Springs Public School,** now occupied by a Missionary Baptist Church. Continue through the **Dixon Springs Historic District** of homes dating from the 1800s. After a small intersection in the center of the community, the **Dixon Springs Union Church** stands on the left, a frame building constructed in 1877. Stay straight on the narrow lane to rejoin TN 25 in 1.2 miles. Continue to the southeast, traveling through a lovely pastoral valley.

In 1.3 miles bear right on another country lane into the small community of Riddleton, also a settlement that grew up along the Avery Trace. Several older homes, stores, and churches make up the present rural village. In 1.6 miles rejoin TN 25. Eventually, the Cumberland River nears the highway where the road runs along a rock wall to the left.

In 5.7 miles enter Carthage at a junction with TN 263 to the left. This drive will turn right into the downtown, but first you can take a side trip to **Cordell Hull Dam** by turning left. TN 263 climbs a ridge to pass through the Turkey Creek Community and descends to a road junction in 1.9 miles where you turn right into the Army Corps of Engineers reservation around the dam. There's picnicking, boat access, and paved walking trails. Return to TN 263 and turn right to climb the ridge for 1.7 miles to a right turn into the **Cordell Hull Lake Overlook.** From the overlook parking, a sidewalk winds up a knoll to the overlook, which offers expansive views of Cordell Hull Lake backed up by Cordell Hull Dam. From the parking area, the Bearwallow Trail leads southeast to **Defeated Creek Recreation Area,** which has a campground, picnicking, boat access to the lake, and swimming. To reach Defeated Creek by vehicle, continue north on TN 263 1.6 miles to a junction with TN 85 and turn right 2.1 miles to the community of Defeated, and turn right on West Point Road to reach the recreation area.

CARTHAGE

Return to the junction with TN 25 and stay straight through the intersection to enter Carthage on Main Street. The town was settled around 1787 when Capt. William Walton accompanied Tilman Dixon into this region. Walton was also a Revolutionary War veteran who had come to claim land granted to him for serving in the war; the land grant he selected was on the banks of the Cumberland River near the confluence of the Caney Fork River to the east. In 1801–02, Walton took charge of building a wagon road from Fort Southwest Point at present-day Kingston over the Cumberland Plateau to the western settlements, including his new settlement of Carthage. The route became known as Walton Road.

On Main Street, notice the grand **Davis/Hull/Moore Home** on the right, a brick house with white trim built by Calvin Davis in 1889. In 1906 the home was purchased by William Hull, the father of Cordell Hull, Secretary of State under Pres. Franklin D. Roosevelt. Following Cordell's birth in a log cabin in Pickett County, William Hull entered the lumbering business. He prospered and for a time lived here in Carthage; by then, Cordell was already on his own, practicing law and beginning his political career.

Other fine old homes stand along Main Street approaching the town center. If you take a left up Fisher Avenue and travel 2 blocks you will reach the **Cullum Mansion,** a two-story brick home with white portico built in 1848 by William Cullum, a lawyer and congressman. On the left side of Main stands the **Carthage United Methodist Church,** a Gothic Revival building constructed in 1889. To the right on Fite Avenue in 2 blocks is the wonderful white brick **Swope/Fite/Ligon Home.** Then continue into the downtown, where the old **Walton Hotel** stands on the left in a row of commercial buildings.

At the corner of Third Avenue and Main is the town square on the right with the **Smith County Courthouse,** a grand Second Empire building constructed in 1879. Through the downtown, passing in front of the courthouse, Main Street ends at a junction with the historic **Cordell Hull Bridge** crossing the Cumberland River to the right. Stay straight on Upper Ferry Road. In 1 mile turn right on Z Country Lane and turn right into the **Carthage Access Area** with boat access to the Cumberland River. The remains of an old lighthouse stand on the riverbank. You can continue on Z Country Lane, which becomes gravel, to pass under the TN 25 Bypass and reach the end of the road at the overgrown site of the **William Walton Home.** Just the stone foundations remain. Walton built this home here on a knoll overlooking the Cumberland River. With the construction of the

Walton Road, he opened stands, or taverns, along the route for traveler accommodations. His own home here was also opened to guests, and from this spot he operated a ferry across the Cumberland River. Walton is buried on this property.

Return to Upper Ferry Road and turn right to a junction with TN 25. Turn right to cross the Cumberland River, and in 0.8 mile, exit onto US 70 and turn east. In 0.3 mile Gibbs Landing Road leads left to **Gibbs Landing Bed and Breakfast** on the Caney Fork River. In another 1.6 miles US 70 crosses the scenic Caney Fork.

On the other side of the river in 0.8 mile, the brick house to the right with a guard gate at the highway is the home of Albert Gore Jr., former vice president of the United States who in 2000 lost his bid for the presidency to George W. Bush in one of the most controversial elections in U.S. history.

GRANVILLE AND BAXTER

US 70 continues east through a pastoral countryside where many of the farmhouses are in the Gothic Revival style, recognized by the gables facing the front of the house. In 3.6 miles US 70 climbs from the Central Basin onto the Eastern Highland Rim. Once on top, in the small community of Chestnut Mound, turn left on TN 53, dropping back off the rim. In 3.7 miles you can turn right on Enigma Road and then left on Webster Road and left to **Indian Creek Recreation Area,** which has a swimming and picnic area, boat access to the Indian Creek embayment of Cordell Hull Lake, and a campground.

Continue north on TN 53 to cross Indian Creek in 0.5 mile and enter Jackson County. In 1.5 miles enter Granville, a historic river town on the Cumberland River. This drive will turn right on TN 96 into the old town, but you can first stay straight on TN 53 to cross a bridge over the Martins Creek embayment off Cordell Hull Lake. Just on the other side to the left lies a portion of the **Cordell Hull Wildlife Management Area** where the Cordell Hull Lake Horse Trail begins. In several miles the horse trail penetrates Holleman Bend of the Cumberland River to the **Holleman Bend Recreation Area,** which has a campground with no hookups and boat access to the lake; the recreation area can also be accessed by Holleman Bend Road to the left off TN 53. The small park at this horse trailhead also has a paved walkway that leads down to benches at the edge of the river across the embayment from Granville.

Return across the bridge to Granville and turn east on TN 96, which is also Clover Street. A few old commercial buildings stand along the street, including the old **Thrift Bank.** On the left side of the street is the small white frame **Freedman Doctor's Office** where Dr. Luther M. Freedman practiced for sixty-seven years. Also on the left stands the **Granville Church of Christ,** built in 1883. It now houses the Granville Museum. Then on the left is the **Granville United Methodist Church,** a vernacular Gothic building.

Continue on TN 96 to leave the community, heading east along this southern shore of the Martins Creek embayment. In 1.5 miles the **Martins Creek Access Area** on the left provides boat access to the lake. The road narrows between the creek on the left and the bluff to the right and enters Putnam County. In 0.8 mile watch for a fine two-story home on the right with gingerbread detailing along the eaves.

The lake embayment narrows to just the channel of Martins Creek, where trees overhang the stream. As the road curves right up Shaw Branch, a tributary stream, it enters a classic Tennessee "holler" with small farms and houses tucked into hillside coves. Goats gambol up the steep slopes. Cows precariously graze on the hillsides. Such hill farms give rise to the joke that the fields are so steep, the cows have developed shorter legs on one side.

The hollow grows even narrower as TN 96 penetrates deeper into the valley, reaching the head of the cove and then climbing in a steep winding ascent back onto the Highland Rim to a junction with US 70 in 5.7 miles. Turn left.

In 4.1 miles turn right to enter the community of Baxter on First Street. At a junction with Main Street in 1.2 miles, turn left to pass through the center of town, which is primarily a row of old commercial buildings across the railroad tracks to the right. A classic railroad town that grew up along the Tennessee Central Railroad, the community was named for Jere Baxter, the founder and first president of the railroad.

Main Street curves left to leave Baxter and in 1 mile reaches a junction with TN 56. Turn left and travel to a junction with US 70, where you should turn right. In 5.3 miles **Cane Creek Regional Park** lies to the right. In addition to a sports recreation area, the park contains a fifty-six-acre lake with fishing piers and a boat ramp, picnic areas, and biking and hiking trails. In 1.7 miles US 70 enters Cookeville to a junction with TN 135 on the west side of town.

Center Hill Lake and Cedars of Lebanon

COOKEVILLE TO LONG HUNTER STATE PARK

GENERAL DESCRIPTION: A drive of 128 miles explores the area around Center Hill Lake, offering expansive views off the Eastern Highland Rim to the Caney Fork River Valley, and ventures into the largest forest of red cedar remaining in the United States.

SPECIAL ATTRACTIONS: Burgess Falls State Natural Area, Center Hill Lake, Smithville, Appalachian Center for Crafts, Edgar Evins State Park, Cedars of Lebanon State Park, Long Hunter State Park, historic homes and buildings, scenic views, fall color, hiking, biking, boating, fishing, hunting, and wildlife viewing.

LOCATION: Eastern Highland Rim and Central Basin of Middle Tennessee. Begin the drive in Cookeville on TN 135.

DRIVE ROUTE NUMBERS: TN 135 and 136; US 70; TN 56, 141, 96, and 265; US 231; and TN 171.

CAMPING: Ragland Bottom Recreation Area, Floating Mill Recreation Area, Edgar Evins State Park, Long Branch Recreation Area, Cedars of Lebanon State Park, Long Hunter State Park.

SERVICES: All services at Cookeville and Smithville.

NEARBY ATTRACTIONS: Holmes Creek Recreation Area.

THE DRIVE

Where the Eastern Highland Rim stands above the Central Basin, Falling Water River spills from the highland into the valley of the Caney Fork River, which has been dammed to create Center Hill Lake. This drive through lake country offers some of the best scenery in the state, with forested slopes leading down to the fjordlike river. It makes a perfect route for a fall-color outing. West of Center Hill Lake, the drive enters the red cedar forests of Middle Tennessee, which harbor rare and endangered plants within their cedar glades.

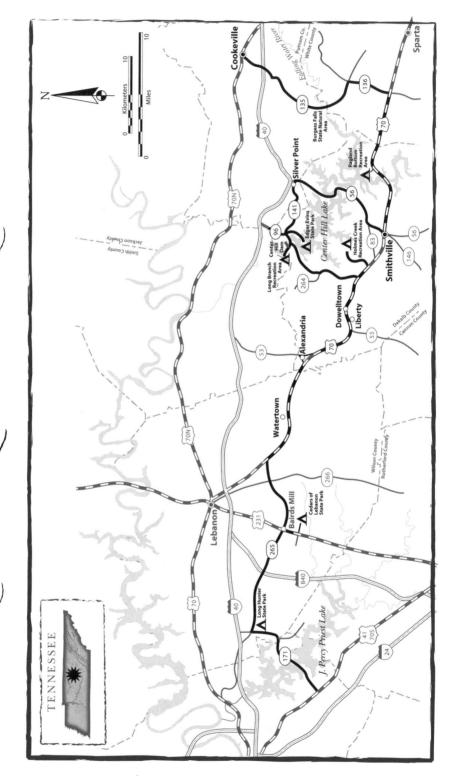

BURGESS FALLS

From Cookeville, take TN 135 (Willow Street on the west side of town) south to cross I–40 in 2 miles. In another 5 miles turn left to stay on TN 135, passing through rural countryside. In 3.7 miles cross a bridge over Falling Water River, here backed up by a small dam to the right where the city of Cookeville had a powerhouse. Electricity was produced at this site until 1944 when the Tennessee Valley Authority had grown large enough to supply the electrical needs of the Tennessee River Valley, making Cookeville's hydropower operation obsolete.

Crossing the river, the highway passes from Putnam County into White County. On the other side, turn right into **Burgess Falls State Natural Area.** The state natural area is named for Tom Burgess, who settled a Revolutionary War land grant here in 1793. Burgess operated a water-powered grist mill along the river. Falling Water River is aptly named, for here are three major waterfalls within a three-quarter-mile walk: 30-foot Upper Falls, 50-foot Middle Falls, and finally 135-foot Burgess Falls. Waterfalls are a characteristic of this region. With the 1,000-foot Cumberland Plateau looming to the east, streams must carve a path to the west, eventually spilling over the edge of the Eastern Highland Rim into the streams and rivers of the Central Basin.

From the Burgess Falls overlook, a steep path leads down to the base of the falls. The river below the falls looks natural and free-flowing here, but it is actually the beginning of the headwaters of Center Hill Lake; Falling Water River is a tributary of the Caney Fork River, which far downstream is backed up by the U.S. Army Corps of Engineers Center Hill Dam.

From the state natural area, reemerge on TN 135 and continue southeast across the Eastern Highland Rim in a bucolic countryside of cattle grazing in green fields. In 3.4 miles, at a junction in Bakers Crossroads, turn right on TN 136 to head south. This stretch of highway is also called Old Kentucky Road, reflecting the Kentucky Stock Road that once passed through this region. Opened in 1806 and also called the Kentucky-Alabama Road, it entered Tennessee from northern Alabama, passing through the state into Kentucky. Farmers to the south drove cattle, sheep, hogs, even turkeys along this road to markets in Kentucky, which is how it came to be called a "stock" road.

CENTER HILL LAKE
AND EDGAR EVINS STATE PARK

In 4.3 miles turn right on US 70, to head west. In 5.4 miles pass from White County into DeKalb County. In another mile Johnsons Chapel Road leads right 3 miles down to the **Johnsons Chapel Recreation Area,** which has picnicking and boat access to the Falling Water River embayment of Center

Center Hill Lake

Hill Lake. In another 0.9 mile along US 70, Ragland Bottom Road to the right descends 1 mile to the **Ragland Bottom Recreation Area** on the Caney Fork River portion of Center Hill Lake; the recreation area has picnicking, swimming, boat access to the lake, and a campground (no hookups).

US 70 soon descends off the Highland Rim to cross a bridge over the Caney Fork River and then climb back to the relatively flat top of the highland. In 7.5 miles US 70 enters Smithville to a junction with TN 56. Here you can turn left to Bryant Street, right to College Street, and left to **Greenbrook Inn Bed and Breakfast.** The inn is a reconstructed antebellum log cabin that once sat on the Caney Fork River; when the river was to be flooded with the construction of Center Hill Dam, the cabin was dismantled and moved to this location.

From US 70, turn north on TN 56. At Main Street you can turn left to enter the downtown and reach the town square where Smithville holds its annual Old Time Fiddlers' Jamboree and Crafts Festival on the weekend closest to July 4. Smithville is also the home of the Evins family. J. Edgar Evins was a local businessman and contractor and also served as the mayor of Smithville for many years; as a state senator, he was instrumental in the development of Center Hill Dam and Lake. His son, Joe L. Evins, became the local U.S. congressman in 1947 and served for thirty years. At the junction of TN 56 with Main Street, you can turn right to pass the Evins family's **Cumberland House** on the left, a large home built in 1890 and remodeled by the elder Evins after he purchased the house in 1907.

Continue north on TN 56, traveling through farmland. In 6.2 miles begin a long descent off the Eastern Highland Rim at the place where it is deeply incised by the Caney Fork River. The road passes along a rock wall to the right with an expansive view to the left of the long, arched Hurricane Bridge crossing of the river. The road curves to the left to meet this bridge in 1.4 miles. But just before the crossing, a right turn leads to the **Joe L. Evins Appalachian Center for Crafts,** which resides on a hill in a bend of the Caney Fork. The road into the craft center passes the Berry C. Williams Overlook; Williams was the founder of the Old Time Fiddlers' Jamboree and was an advocate for the establishment of a crafts center. A short observation tower offers distant views of Center Hill Lake from this knoll. Continue up the road to the Appalachian Center for Crafts, a state facility operated by Tennessee Technological University in Cookeville. The center offers workshops in contemporary and traditional crafts. The crafts gallery located in the administration building offers for sale the work of Tennessee and other Appalachian states artisans and craftspeople.

Return to TN 56 and cross Hurricane Bridge, which gets its name from nearby Big Hurricane and Little Hurricane Creeks. On the other side, you can turn down left into the **Hurricane Bridge Recreation Area,** which has riverside picnicking, fishing, and boat access to the lake. TN 56 climbs from the river, once more mounting the Highland Rim. In 1.3 miles a pull-out on the right offers an overlook of Center Hill Lake. In another 0.4 mile a road left leads down to the **Floating Mill Recreation Area,** which has picnicking, swimming, boat access to the lake, and a campground.

In 3 miles TN 56 reenters Putnam County. In another 0.5 mile cross railroad tracks to a junction with TN 141 just before reaching I–40. Turn left on TN 141, and in 0.8 mile enter the small community of Silver Point. Watch for the **West End Church of Christ** on the right, which was originally the Silver Point Christian College for African Americans. The school operated for only a few years in the early 1900s.

From South Point, TN 141 meanders west across the Eastern Highland Rim for 2 miles before it begins a descent, reentering DeKalb County and bottoming out in a hollow. Traveling through the valley past small farms and old farmhouses, the highway reaches a junction in 3.9 miles with TN 96 to the right and straight and a left turn into **Edgar Evins State Park.**

The park road climbs to the top of the hill above Center Hill Lake. In 1.6 miles the park office and visitor center is on the right. The building has a courtyard in the center where an observation tower rises through the treetops. Climb the winding stairs to the top for a bird's-eye view of the lake and Center Hill Dam. In addition to cabins, a swimming pool, boat dock, picnic area, and boat access to the lake, the park has a campground where platform campsites create level parking on the lakeshore.

Return from the state park to the intersection of TN 141 and 96 and turn left, heading west and then southwest. You can turn right to pass the visitor center for Center Hill Dam and descend into the **Buffalo Valley Recreation Area** where there is boat access to the Caney Fork River below the dam. Continue up TN 141/96 to reach an overlook of **Center Hill Dam** on the right. The road then crosses the dam, with Center Hill Lake stretching away to the left. On the other side is a junction with TN 141 turning right. Down that road you can reach the **Long Branch Recreation Area,** which has picnicking, boat access to the river below the dam, and a campground.

This drive continues straight ahead on TN 96. Just on the left is the **Center Hill Recreation Area** with boat access to the lake. Straight on TN 96 there's ample parking along the road on the left for a picnic area that's just down the hill. Continuing southwest, TN 96 passes along the forested shore of Center Hill Lake, gradually climbing. In 3 miles, a road to the left enters the **Cove Hollow Recreation Area,** with more picnic areas and boat access. TN 96 then leaves the lake as it once more heads out across the Highland Rim.

In 8.1 miles at a junction with US 70, a side trip left leads 2.5 miles to Caseys Cove Road for access to **Holmes Creek Recreation Area,** another Corps of Engineers recreation site on Center Hill Lake; the site has picnicking, boat launch, and camping. For this drive, turn west on US 70 to make a last descent off the Eastern Highland Rim into the Central Basin, reaching the valley floor in 1.5 miles. In 1.9 miles enter the community of Dowelltown. US 70 bypasses such small rural communities, but you can enter Dowelltown to the right on Main Street, passing through the community of old homes to Turner Street. Just ahead stands the **Dowelltown Missionary Baptist Church,** a white frame church built in 1896. Turn left up Turner Street to rejoin US 70 and continue west.

In 0.5 mile turn left on Main Street to enter the community of Liberty. Cross Smith Fork, a tributary of the Caney Fork River, to enter the **Liberty Historic District** of old homes, churches, and commercial buildings. The road curves right to pass through the town center. The **Liberty Town Hall** and **History Room** reside in a stone building on the right. In 1.2 miles the street meets TN 53; turn right to reconnect with US 70 and turn left to continue west through Tennessee farmland.

In 5.5 miles turn right on TN 53 and then left to enter the community of Alexandria on Old Highway 53; in town, turn left on Main Street to pass through the old town center with old homes, commercial buildings, and churches. Watch for the **Gen. John Hunt Morgan Monument.** A famous Confederate cavalry commander in the Civil War, Morgan began a famous raid into Ohio and Indiana on June 11, 1863, leaving from this site. The raid ended July 26, with the capture of a federal force in Ohio a scant 100 miles from Lake Erie. Turn left up Academy Street and right on Locust to rejoin US 70 and continue west, crossing into Wilson County.

In 2.8 miles turn right on Main Street to enter Watertown, a historic railroad town. The street crosses railroad tracks and then a creek to reach the town square, which is surrounded by old commercial buildings. On Depot Street to the left, the **Watertown Bed and Breakfast** occupies a nineteenth-century railroad hotel. Excursion trains bring visitors to the community several times during the year. Continue on Main Street to the west, passing through a neighborhood of older churches, cottages, and large residences.

CEDARS OF LEBANON
AND LONG HUNTER STATE PARK

Reconnect with US 70 in 1.4 miles and continue west. In another 2.8 miles turn left on TN 265. Cross railroad tracks running east to Watertown. Continuing through farmland, notice the increasing number of cedar trees, usually found in fields and fence rows across Tennessee, but growing more frequently here where the soil is rocky and shallow. In 8.3 miles at an intersection with US 231 in the small community of Bairds Mill, turn left 0.6 mile and left again into **Cedars of Lebanon State Park.** The park is named for the region's cedar trees that are reminiscent of the cedar forest found in the Biblical Lebanon; Isaiah refers to "all the cedars of Lebanon, that are high and lifted up."

This Middle Tennessee region harbors some of the last remaining red cedar forests in the world. Where the soil is thin and rocks are exposed, cedars thrive. Growing in the open glades among the stands of cedars are an array of blooming plants, from small annual herbs to herbaceous perennials, including yellow glade cress, pale blue glade phlox, limestone flame-flower, prairie larkspur, leafy prairie clover, Pyne's ground-plum, rose verbena, and pink Tennessee coneflower. Fifteen species exist exclusively in this habitat; another twenty-seven species occur on the state list of endangered and threatened species. These areas also support prairie grasses like little blue-stem and side-oats grama. The cedar glades of Middle Tennessee make up one of the few places in North America where scientists know that all recently evolved plants still occupy their place of origin. Many of these cedar glades are now protected in state parks, forests, and natural areas.

Each spring, usually the third weekend in April, the state park hosts a wildflower pilgrimage that explores the cedar glades in search of flowering plants. The park also offers picnicking, camping, cabins, swimming pool, and hiking trails that loop through the cedar forest with limestone outcrops and sink holes.

Return to US 231. Directly across the road is the **Cedars of Lebanon State Forest;** a narrow graveled lane penetrates the forest for a drive among cedars and a glimpse of glades among the trees.

Turn north on US 231 to return to TN 265, and turn left to continue west, passing through a valley of farms, fields, rock fences, and cedar trees. In 4.5 miles, cross I–840, which when completed will be a regional bypass around Nashville. Then turn left to stay on TN 265, and in 7.4 miles turn left on TN 171. In 3.2 miles a left turn on Couchville Pike leads to the **Bryant Grove Recreation Area** on the Army Corps of Engineers J. Percy Priest

Lake impoundment on the Stones River. The recreation area, which has picnicking, hiking trails, a fishing pier, and boat access to the lake, is part of **Long Hunter State Park.** In another 0.4 mile on TN 171, enter Davidson County, and in 0.9 mile enter the state park, which is named for the early explorers of Tennessee, who were called "longhunters" because they would stay out exploring and hunting for weeks, months, sometimes years at a time. In 0.4 mile a road to the right leads to the **Bakers Grove Primitive Use Area** that has backpacking and primitive camping on the 6-mile Volunteer Trail.

In another 0.7 mile turn left to reach the park visitor center on the right. This section of the park has boat access, fishing, picnicking at Couchville Lake and along the shore of J. Percy Priest Lake. Hiking trails include a quarter-mile Nature Loop Trail that passes through a cedar glade.

TN 171 continues southwest from the state park to cross a bridge over J. Percy Priest Lake and reach US 41/70S in 4.8 miles. To the south on this four-lane highway lie Smyrna and Murfreesboro.

18

Stones River and Walking Horses

MURFREESBORO TO LEWISBURG

GENERAL DESCRIPTION: A 77-mile drive through some of Tennessee's most beautiful countryside begins at the Stones River and wanders through the region that gave birth to the Tennessee walking horse.

SPECIAL ATTRACTIONS: Murfreesboro, Stones River National Battlefield, Bell Buckle, Wartrace, Shelbyville, Lewisburg, historic homes and buildings, scenic views, fall color, hiking, biking, boating, fishing, and wildlife viewing.

LOCATION: Middle Tennessee. Begin the drive in Murfreesboro east of I-24.

DRIVE ROUTE NUMBERS: US 41; TN 64, 82, and 269; and US 41A and 31A.

CAMPING: Henry Horton State Park.

SERVICES: All services at Murfreesboro, Shelbyville, and Lewisburg.

NEARBY ATTRACTIONS: Sam Davis Home, Bridlewood Farm, Henry Horton State Park, and Berlin Spring.

THE DRIVE

At places in Tennessee, the violence of the past is juxtaposed with the peacefulness of the present. The Civil War Battle of Stones River was one of the bloodiest fought during the war, yet it took place on the northern edge of present-day farm country that produced the docile Tennessee walking horse. The emergence of this horse breed has transformed this once contested section of Middle Tennessee into a pastoral scene of gently rolling fields, ambling horses, and welcoming people.

MURFREESBORO

Begin this tour in Murfreesboro at the very center of the state in Middle Tennessee. In 1834 the state sought to find the geographic center in order to

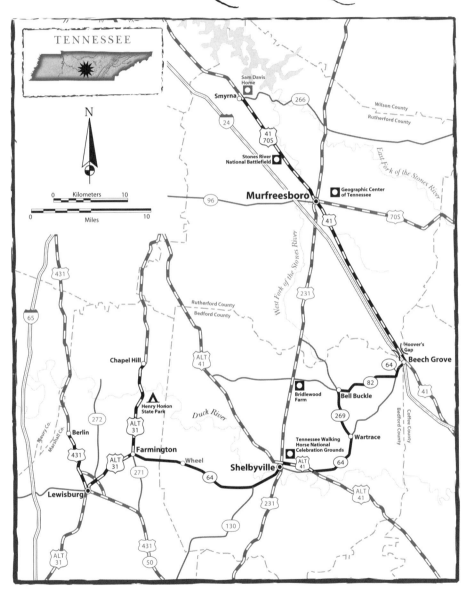

locate the capital as near as possible to the middle of the state. Professor James Hamilton, who was hired for the task, determined the center of the state is located at Murfreesboro. Although the city had been the state capital from 1818 to 1826, the capital remained in Nashville, politics being what it is. An obelisk marks the spot on Old Lascassas Pike, northeast of the town center.

The **Rutherford County Courthouse** crowns the town square at the center of Murfreesboro, which was founded in 1811 and named for Col. Hardy Murfree, a Revolutionary War veteran. The grand Greek Revival/Italianate courthouse was built in 1859, one of the few remaining antebellum courthouses in the state. Commercial buildings dating from the late 1800s and early 1900s surround the courthouse square.

From the square, head down East Main to enter the **East Main Street Historic District.** Homes dating from before the Civil War to the early 1900s grace the street. The oldest part of the **Murfree Home** at 332 East Main was built in 1835 by Mathias Murfree, the son of Col. Hardy Murfree.

At Maney Street you can turn left and drive to the end of the street to reach **Oaklands,** an Italianate mansion that is now a house museum. The original one-and-a-half story home was built for Sally Murfree and her husband, Dr. James Maney; Sally had inherited the land from her father, Col. Hardy Murfree. Four rooms with an Italianate facade were added in the late 1850s for their son, Lewis Maney, and his wife, Rachel, who had inherited the property.

At 511 East Main is the magnificent **Collier-Crichlow House,** an 1879 Second Empire mansion built for Ingram Collier, a mayor of Murfreesboro who died before the house was completed; the Collier family lived in the home into the early 1900s. At University Boulevard, with **Middle Tennessee State University** straight ahead, you can turn left, then turn right on Greenland Drive and left on Old Lascassas Pike to reach the **Geographic Center of Tennessee.**

Turn around at a convenient place, and return to East Main and turn back toward the center of town.

Return on East Main toward the town center and turn left on Academy Street; travel 4 blocks to **Bradley Academy,** a 1918 school building that stands on the site of the first school for African Americans in Murfreesboro; the building now houses a museum of African-American heritage. Continue south on Academy a short distance to Broad Street (US 41) and turn right and then turn left on Front Street to **Cannonsburgh,** a reconstructed pioneer village representing the original settlement that existed here before Murfreesboro was formed. The village includes a grist mill, church, school, and town hall with a collection of antique farm equipment. Cannonsburgh anchors one end of the 1.7–mile **Lytle Creek Greenway,** which travels along this tributary of the Stones River. The creek is named for Capt. William Lytle, a Revolutionary War veteran on whose land grant Murfreesboro was founded; it was he who requested the town be named after Col. Hardy Murfree. The greenway ends at a junction with the **Stones River Greenway** near the confluence of Lytle Creek with the river. The river greenway travels for 2.6 miles along the West Fork of the Stones River, connecting sections of the **Stones River National Battlefield,** the site of a massive Civil War engagement around the New Year of 1863.

STONES RIVER

To get to the battlefield, return to Broad Street and turn left, headed northwest. Pass through a junction with TN 96 and US 231 and turn left on College Street, which is also Old Nashville Pike. Cross the West Fork of the Stones River, which flows through the west side of Murfreesboro. In another 1.1 miles you can turn right to **Gen. Bragg Headquarters Site,** marked by a stack of cannonballs; Gen. Braxton Bragg was commander of the Confederate Army of Tennessee at the Battle of Stones River.

Old Nashville Pike passes under the CSX Railroad, originally the Nashville and Chattanooga Railroad. It was this railroad that made Murfreesboro of strategic importance; with the Federals in control of Middle and West Tennessee, the railroad served as the Union supply line for the inevitable advance on Chattanooga, a major Confederate rail center. In 0.7 mile pass under the overpass of Thompson Lane. Then on the right is the **Hazen Monument** where some of the fiercest fighting on the first day of battle took place; this was the only Union position to hold its ground that first day. Survivors of Col. William B. Hazen's brigade erected this monument in 1863, making it the oldest intact Civil War monument in the country.

Soon after, you can turn right into the **Stones River National Cemetery.** After the Battle of Stones River, most dead were buried on the field. But in 1865 the national cemetery was established, and 6,100 Union dead were reinterred here; among them were 2,562 unknown soldiers. The Confederate dead were taken to their hometowns or some nearby community still held by the South; some were buried in a mass grave but were later reinterred in Murfreesboro's Evergreen Cemetery.

Then on the left is the Stones River Battlefield. From the visitor center, a 2-mile one-way drive passes through the battlefield of the first day of fighting.

In the winter of 1862, Gen. Braxton Bragg settled in winter quarters in Murfreesboro. Earlier in the year, Union forces had invaded Tennessee along the Cumberland, Tennessee, and Mississippi Rivers and now controlled the western half of the state. The next major step for the federal army was to penetrate the South along the rail line leading from Nashville through Chattanooga and into Georgia, thereby cutting the Confederacy in two.

On December 26, a 43,000-man Union Army under Gen. William S. Rosecrans left Nashville, following the Nashville Pike and the parallel Nashville and Chattanooga Railroad. Within four days, Rosecrans' army was camped within half a mile of the Confederate encampment at Murfreesboro. Both positions stretched across the turnpike and the railroad. By coincidence, both Rosecrans and Bragg had decided to attack the other's right flank when battle ensued the next day.

But it was Bragg who moved first. Gaining the initiative, the Confederates attacked at dawn, driving back the Union right flank and part of the center, closing the Union line like a jackknife. The right half of the federal line (the left side from the Confederate perspective) was driven back to the Nashville Pike where Rosecrans told his men to "contest every inch of ground." The Union soldiers, with artillery reinforcements, repelled numerous Confederate attacks, with the Southern soldiers suffering many casualties. The day ended with this stalemate, and the two armies held their positions through the next day.

After completing the battlefield drive, return down Old Nashville Pike (College Street) and turn right to circle onto Thompson Lane and travel to a junction with US 41; turn left to Van Cleve Lane and turn right to the end of the road at **McFadden's Ford,** which is marked by an artillery monument. Here at the river ford is also the upper end of the Stones River Greenway.

On the morning of January 2, General Bragg was surprised to learn that Union troops had crossed the river to the east side and now commanded a rise that threatened his right flank. He ordered five brigades under Maj. Gen. John C. Breckinridge to take the hill. Breckinridge objected, saying that high ground on the west side of the river commanded the eastern hill and that Union artillery positioned there could fire on the Confederate troops; an assault would be suicidal. Bragg replied, "I have given the order . . . and expect it to be obeyed."

Breckinridge sent his troops against the federal position on the eastern hill. They met with some resistance but soon took the hill, with the Union soldiers retreating down the other side and crossing the river to the west at McFadden's Ford. As the Confederates pursued, the Union artillery opened fire in the face of the Southern soldiers, just as Breckinridge had forewarned. In minutes, 1,800 Confederates were killed or wounded; the rest retreated.

Soon the Union troops recrossed the river and once more were atop the eastern hill.

With 13,249 Federal casualties and 10,266 Southern casualties, the battle ended. Bragg withdrew from Murfreesboro, leaving it in Union hands, retreating to Tullahoma. The two armies would meet once again at the battles for Chattanooga.

Return to US 41. You can take a side trip here north along US 41/70S to the **Sam Davis Home;** in Smyrna in 6.7 miles turn right on TN 102, and in 2.6 miles, turn left on Sam Davis Road to the stone gateway on the right. That is the entrance to the home of Sam Davis, a twenty-one-year-old Confederate who earned a place in history through his loyalty and faithfulness. On a scouting expedition in 1863, Davis was captured in possession of Union documents. Refusing to reveal the source of the papers, he was hung as a spy and his body sent back to his home in Smyrna. The 1850s Greek Revival home is now a house museum open for tours.

Return down US 41/70S to Murfreesboro past the Stones River Battlefield, to a junction with TN 96 and US 231. You can turn right on TN 96 and right on TN 99 into Old Fort Park to **Fortress Rosecrans.** After the Battle of Stones River, the Union Army moved to consolidate its strategic advantage by building a train depot and a fortification to defend it; Murfreesboro would become a supply center for the Union troops moving on Chattanooga. The 200-acre Fortress Rosecrans was the largest earthen fortification built during the Civil War. Most of the fort is now gone, but some of the earthworks can still be seen.

Return to US 41 and turn right, passing through town and leaving Murfreesboro. The highway enters the countryside to the southeast, passing fields and farms. Although the highway parallels I–24, it's a scenic drive.

In 13.9 miles pass through Hoover's Gap, and in another 2.9 miles enter Coffee County. Bear right on Old Highway 41 in the community of Beech Grove and turn right on Confederate Cemetery Road to the **Beech Grove Confederate Cemetery.** Here on this small hill between US 41 and I–24 lie Confederate soldiers who died in a defense of Hoover's Gap from advancing Union forces in June 1863. A monument in the cemetery commemorates the unknown dead.

TENNESSEE WALKING HORSE COUNTRY

Return to Old Highway 41 and turn right to TN 64. Turn right to pass under I–24 and enter Bedford County, which contains some of the most beautiful landscape in the state. This is Tennessee walking horse country, where huge

Tennessee Walking Horses

farms spread across rolling hills, wooden fences enclose green pastures, and raising horses is more a passion than a pastime. TN 64 has been designated the Tennessee Walking Horse Parkway where it travels through Bedford County west into Marshall County; brochures for the parkway, available in towns along the way, identify horse farms and horse-related businesses in the region, many of which are open for visits.

In 1.3 miles TN 64 reaches a junction with TN 82 to the right. The parkway continues on TN 64 to the southwest through some of the nicest walking horse country. For this drive, however, turn right on TN 82, a designated Tennessee Walking Horse Trail off the parkway. It passes through more farm country with huge rolls of hay scattered in fields like thrown dice.

In 5.3 miles enter the small community of Bell Buckle, first passing through Webb School, which was founded in 1870 by William R. "Sawney" Webb and moved here from another location in 1886. The private preparatory school of stone buildings still turns out well-educated leaders of their communities, including a U.S. senator, a U.S. attorney general, and Prentice Cooper, a two-term governor of Tennessee. At the other end of the campus, you can turn left to the school office building. Behind that stands the **Junior Room,** a frame school building constructed in 1886; it is now the school museum.

Continue into Bell Buckle whose pleasingly alliterative name is traced to a story that a Cherokee carved a buckle and a bell on a tree, as a warning to white settlers and their cattle to stay away. Pass through an old neighborhood of finely restored Victorian homes, including the **Candleshoe Bed and Breakfast** and the **Bell Buckle Bed and Breakfast.** Emerge into a small commercial area at a junction with TN 269 joining from the north; a strip of shops to the right face the railroad tracks in a traditional arrangement for a railroad town. **Bell Buckle Crafts** occupies a one-hundred-year-old bank building. **Bell Buckle Press** is run by Margaret Britton Vaughn, Poet Laureate of Tennessee; the small press publishes Tennessee writers. At the far end is the **Louvin Brothers Museum;** Ira and Charlie Louvin, stars of Nashville's Grand Ole Opry, have been described as perhaps the "greatest traditional country duo."

Cross the railroad tracks to TN 269 turning off left to the south, which is the route for this drive. You can take a side trip here on TN 82 5 miles to **Bridlewood Farm,** a private equestrian community and Tennessee walking horse stud farm that welcomes visitors six days a week. You'll see mares grazing in the fields with their rollicking foals and get a chance to view some of the world grand champion walking horses that stand at the farm.

Return to TN 269 and turn south. The highway travels through more backcountry to Wartrace in 4.9 miles. As you enter the town, the highway swings right, joining Spring Street, to pass in front of the **Chockley Stagecoach Inn,** a wood frame building on the right constructed in 1852 and now a residence. Just beyond, at a junction with TN 64, stands the **Walking Horse Hotel** on the right, a three-story brick hotel built in 1917; it is still open for business. Wartrace was established as a railroad town in 1852 when the Nashville and Chattanooga Railroad was constructed through the region; the name given the town comes from an Indian war trail that passed through the place. The Walking Horse Hotel was originally the Overall Hotel but was purchased around 1930 by Floyd and Olive Carothers, who later changed the name to recognize the hotel and the community as the "Cradle of the Tennessee Walking Horse."

A combination of thoroughbreds, standardbreds, Morgans, and American saddle horses, the distinctive Tennessee walking horse was originally bred as a farm animal. Breeding for the desirable characteristics for several generations over 150 years resulted in a gentle horse with a particularly smooth gait. The movement that distinguishes a true walking horse is that the horse walks under itself with its back legs and nods its head up and down while the front legs step high and out. This movement has been inbred in the horses and is emphasized with training and at times with thick, lightweight horseshoes and anklets placed on the horses' front feet; a practice called "soring," in which chemicals were used to irritate a horse's forelegs, was banned in the 1970s.

In the 1930s, horse enthusiasts gathered at the Overall Hotel to discuss horses. Carothers, a noted horse trainer, had taken a plow horse and trained him into a walking horse in a field behind the hotel. Although walking horses had been featured in horse shows annually in Wartrace, Davis opined there was a need for national recognition of the distinctive Tennessee horse. In 1939 Davis took his idea to Shelbyville, which soon inaugurated the Tennessee Walking Horse National Celebration. Carothers rode his horse to that first national competition; Strolling Jim, as the horse was called, became the first World Grand Champion. Since then, the national celebration has been held each year in nearby Shelbyville for ten days ending on the Saturday before Labor Day in late summer. The celebration has grown to the largest horse show in the world, with as many as 4,000 horses competing from throughout the U.S. and several foreign countries.

In Wartrace you can walk into the field behind the Walking Horse Hotel where Strolling Jim was trained. The horse is buried to the back of the field, the site marked by a gravestone.

At the hotel, this drive rejoins the Tennessee Walking Horse Parkway. In the center of town, notice the tall brick building that was the **Wartrace Flouring Mill,** built in 1880, and the town **Well House,** built in 1909 in the form of a bandstand over the town water well. Known for its water, Wartrace became a health resort in the late 1800s; bottled water was shipped throughout the region.

Turn right on the parkway (TN 64), headed southwest toward Shelbyville. Wartrace and Shelbyville are also connected by the **Walking Horse and Eastern Railroad,** an excursion branch line that operates on Saturdays and during special events, especially the Tennessee Walking Horse National Celebration. Round-trips are available only from the Shelbyville end.

The parkway travels though a countryside of horse farms; the huge horse stables stretch across the farms like large upscale motels. The parkway has broad shoulders that also make it a good bicycling route. In 5.7 miles enter Shelbyville and bear right on US 41A. In 2.5 miles turn right on Strolling Jim Drive to reach Calsonic Arena, an indoor horse show arena that contains the **Tennessee Walking Horse Museum,** with photographs and exhibits on the history of the Tennessee walking horse.

Back out to US 41A, turn right to continue into Shelbyville. Celebration Drive to the right leads into the **Tennessee Walking Horse National Celebration Grounds,** which contain the 30,000-seat Celebration Arena where the national celebration is held. In addition to the walking horse, Shelbyville celebrates other equine species. The city hosts a Spotted Saddle Horse World Championship Show in the fall and the Great Celebration Mule and Donkey Show the weekend before July 4.

Continue into Shelbyville along US 41A, which is Madison Street. At a junction with Main Street, turn left to head for the town center. You can turn left on Lane Parkway and left on East Lane to see the **Cooper House** on the left; the magnificent home surrounded by stonework was built in 1904 by the father of Prentice Cooper, Tennessee governor from 1939 to 1945. A native of Bedford County, Prentice grew up here and attended Webb School in Bell Buckle before going on to Princeton and Harvard and then returning to serve his home state.

Return to Main Street and continue up the hill to the **Bedford County Courthouse** on the central courthouse square, a design with the courthouse in the center and four equal sides of commercial buildings facing it; the Shelbyville square is thought to be the first central courthouse square in the country. Commercial buildings surrounding the square date from the late 1800s and early 1900s. At the far corner of the square, you can turn left on Depot Street to the **L & N Spur Line Depot,** which has been restored into office spaces.

On the north side of the town square, turn down Holland Street to TN 64/US 231 and turn left to leave Shelbyville. Cross a bridge over the Duck River, and just on the other side you can pull off to the left into a small park beside the river for picnicking and fishing. The low **Duck River Dam,** part of an early hydroelectric project, makes a scenic waterfall in the river.

Continue south on TN 64/231 and then turn right to stay on TN 64. The Tennessee Walking Horse Parkway continues west through Bedford County, passing more horse farms with green fields, grazing horses, and grand stables. In 9.9 miles pass through the small community of Wheel, and in another 1.9 miles enter Marshall County.

HENRY HORTON STATE PARK AND LEWISBURG

In 3 miles reach a junction with US 31A in Farmington where you can turn north and travel 5.5 miles to **Henry Horton State Park.** On the right lies the grave of Henry Horton, Tennessee governor from 1927 to 1932; the state park is located on the former Horton estate. The park has a golf course, inn and restaurant, cabins, picnic areas, and boat access to the adjacent Duck River. US 31A crosses the Duck River at Fishing Ford. Just on the other side, a left turn leads to the park campground. On the right is a pull-out for **Wilhoite Mill.** At this river ford an inn that was constructed in 1845 was purchased by Mrs. William Wilhoite. The next year she had a dam and grist mill constructed on the river. Her son, John, helped with the building and ran the mill; one of John's daughters married Henry Horton. Walk the Wilhoite Mill Trail to the dam and turbine site on the river; all that remain are log footings, a few gears, and a long machinery shaft.

The community of **Chapel Hill** lies another 2 miles north on US 31A. A monument on the west side of the highway there marks the birthplace of Nathan Bedford Forrest, the Civil War cavalry general whose exploits made him one of the most dashing heroes of the Confederacy. After Union forces gained control of the western half of the state in 1862, Forrest led his men on several daring raids that wreaked havoc with federal supply lines. At the end of the war, with the Confederacy defeated, he dismissed his men, saying, "you have been good soldiers, you can be good citizens, obey the law, preserve your honor." Forrest died in Memphis in 1877.

Return along US 31A to the junction with TN 64 and continue southwest. In 4.4 miles, stay straight through an intersection with US 431 (Ellington Parkway), following US 31A/431 Business into Lewisburg. The highway becomes Second Avenue, which leads to the **Marshall County**

Courthouse on the town square. Older commercial buildings surround it, including, on the north side, the 1913 **Dixie Theater,** which is now the home of the Marshall County Community Theater.

Up First Avenue from the northeast corner of the square, stands the **Ladies Restroom;** it is the only building used solely for this purpose known to be in Tennessee. City officials had the restroom constructed for the women of families coming from the country to the county seat to conduct business. The building includes a reception room, bedroom, toilet facilities, and a downstairs kitchen and dining room.

From the southeast corner of the square, head east on Commerce Street, which is also the route for US 431 Business out of town, reaching a junction with Ellington Parkway. Turn left to find the **Tennessee Walking Horse Breeders' and Exhibitors' Association** on the right. The organizers of the association first met in Lewisburg in 1935, and so the city became the official headquarters. The association selected 115 horses for the foundation stock for the Tennessee walking horse; the number one sire was a black stallion named Allan with a blazed face. The stud book was closed in 1947, and so from 1948 onward, for a horse to be registered as a Tennessee walking horse, both parents must be registered horses. Today there are more than 350,000 registered Tennessee walking horses. In the lobby of the association building are photographs of every World Grand Champion, starting with Strolling Jim in 1939.

From Lewisburg you can take a side trip northwest to the **Berlin Rock.** Stay on Ellington Parkway, which is also US 431, around Lewisburg to the junction with US 31A where you entered the city. Stay on US 431 to the northwest for 3.6 miles to enter the community of Berlin. Early settlers of German descent likely gave the name to the community, which grew up around a spring that is now set aside in a small park. The spring flows from beneath a rock ledge. Beside the spring sits the Berlin Rock. This pedestal of stone served as a rostrum from which two presidents, two U.S. senators, four Tennessee governors, six U.S. representatives, and seven judges have made speeches. James K. Polk came to Berlin while campaigning for the presidency in 1844, and the rock was set up at the spring so that he would have a place to stand and have his say. When he was elected president, the rock became a bit famous and was moved to Lewisburg. Many others followed the tradition Polk had started, including Andrew Johnson. Eventually, the rock was moved back to Berlin.

Return down US 431 to TN 50, where you can return to Lewisburg or turn right and travel 6 miles to I–65.

19

The Whiskey Trail

LAWRENCEBURG TO MANCHESTER

GENERAL DESCRIPTION: A 140-mile drive through David Crockett country passes through a land of waterpowered mills and the origins of Tennessee whiskey to a sacred ground of Native Americans.

SPECIAL ATTRACTIONS: David Crockett State Park, Lawrenceburg, Pulaski, Lynnville, Fayetteville, Falls Mill, Winchester, Tullahoma, Short Springs State Natural Area, Manchester, Old Stone Fort State Archaeological Park, historic homes and buildings, scenic views, fall color, hiking, biking, boating, fishing, hunting, and wildlife viewing.

LOCATION: The lower part of Middle Tennessee. Begin the drive at David

Crockett State Park on US 64 west of Lawrenceburg.

DRIVE ROUTE NUMBERS: US 64 and 31; TN 129; US 31A, 431, and 41A; TN 55; and US 41.

CAMPING: David Crockett State Park, Tims Ford State Park, Barton Springs Recreation Area, and Old Stone Fort State Archaeological Park.

SERVICES: All services at Lawrenceburg, Pulaski, Fayetteville, and Tullahoma.

NEARBY ATTRACTIONS: Amish Country, Tims Ford State Park, George Dickel Distillery, Normandy Dam, Ledford Mill, Jack Daniel Distillery, and Lynchburg.

THE DRIVE

The southern part of Middle Tennessee possesses an interesting mix of old mills, historic sites, whiskey distilleries, Amish communities, and an old stone fort. David Crockett spent some time here before moving to West Tennessee. George Dickel and Jack Daniel created world-renowned sipping whiskey. Amish families sought the seclusion of Tennessee backcountry. But it was Native Americans that first settled the region.

DAVID CROCKETT STATE PARK AND LAWRENCEBURG

Begin this drive in Lawrenceburg on US 64 in Lawrence County. On the west side of town is **David Crockett State Park.** Named for the legendary

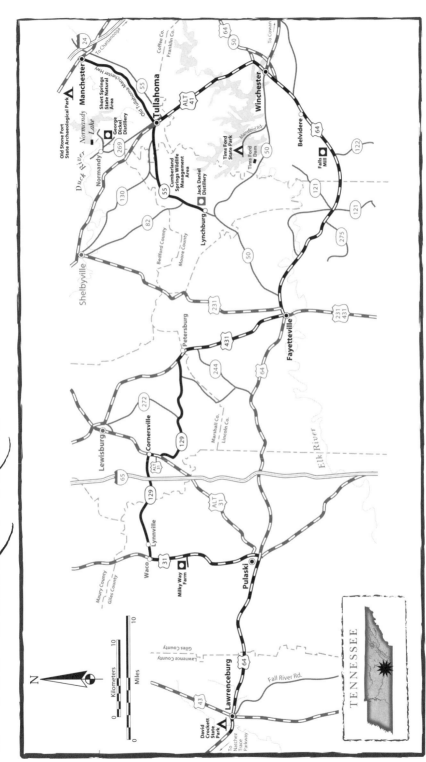

Tennessean, the park offers camping, picnicking, and outdoor recreation, including hiking and biking on several miles of trails. After migrating from East Tennessee and living for a time in Franklin County near Winchester, Crockett settled in Lawrence County in 1817. Along Shoal Creek, which runs through the state park, he established a mix of businesses that included a powder mill, a distillery, and a grist mill. During the time he was in Middle Tennessee, Crockett began his political career, serving as justice of the peace, commissioner of Lawrenceburg, and representative to the state legislature. In September 1821, a flood washed away the buildings and equipment he had accumulated. Crockett moved once again, leaving what remained to his creditors. He settled in Gibson County to the west.

Head east on US 64 into Lawrenceburg. Immediately east of the state park, the road crosses Shoal Creek twice to reach an intersection with North Military Avenue. Turn right and drive 1 block to the historic square, which is ringed with commercial buildings dating from the late 1800s and early 1900s. The center of the square is a park with monuments and markers about the history of the county. A statue of Crockett stands on the south side of the square. The actual frontiersman had little resemblance to the Disney version of Davy Crockett who wore a coonskin cap. This true-to-life statue doffs a hat in greeting.

On the southeast corner of the square, in the third floor of the Sun Trust Bank Building, is the **James D. Vaughan Museum.** In the early 1900s, Vaughan sponsored the first professional southern gospel quartets, published the first southern gospel magazine, and established in Lawrenceburg the first southern gospel music radio station. Lawrenceburg is now recognized as the birthplace of southern gospel music.

On Waterloo Street to the west stands the **Old Jail Museum,** which occupies a jailhouse built in 1800; the museum contains artifacts and exhibits on Lawrence County history. South on South Military Avenue on the left is the **David Crockett Cabin and Museum,** a reconstruction of Crockett's office on the left that contains artifacts and memorabilia from the Crockett era. Near the museum stands the **Lawrenceburg Cumberland Presbyterian Church;** built in 1859, it's the oldest church in the county. East from the square on Pulaski Street, the **Granville House Bed and Breakfast** occupies a grand mansion with porches and portico.

Return to US 64 and continue east through Lawrenceburg. At an intersection with US 43, you can turn north and travel 5.6 miles to Etheridge, which is at the center of an Amish community. Not indulging in modern conveniences, the Amish still drive horse and buggy to town; you'll see sev-

David Crockett Statue

eral along the road. In Etheridge are a number of craft stores; **Amish Country Galleries** is stocked with authentic local crafts, including baskets, furniture, and other items crafted by the Amish.

Continue east on US 64, which is designated Davy Crockett Parkway. In 2.2 miles cross Shoal Creek again. In another 4.2 miles enter Giles County. Just on the left stands **Mama J's Cabin,** an 1800s log cabin that is now a store with local crafts and gifts. In 2.7 miles **Green Valley General Store** on the right in the small community of Bodenham has a collection of old tractors and farm machinery gathered around the store, which offers baked goods and crafts.

PULASKI

US 64 continues through a countryside of farms and scattered forest. In 9.1 miles US 64 turns right to bypass Pulaski, but stay straight into town on College Street to reach a junction with Second Street. On the right corner stands the **Martin House,** now occupied by Community Bank. The home was built in 1840 by Thomas Martin, a local businessman; his daughter

Ophelia added New Orleans-style architecture. The neighborhoods to the south form the **South Pulaski Historic District** with homes ranging from pre-Civil War to the early 1900s.

Turn north on Second Street to the town square, which is dominated by the **Giles County Courthouse,** a French Renaissance building completed in 1909 with a grand interior rotunda rising 110 feet to the top of the courthouse dome. The commercial buildings around the square date from the last half of the 1800s and early 1900s. The neighborhoods outside of the square make up several historic districts; a walking tour booklet is available at the chamber of commerce on the southwest corner of the square. Just down Madison on the left is a one-story commercial law-office building where the Ku Klux Klan was conceived.

The building was the law office of Judge Thomas M. Jones. On December 24, 1865, Jones' son, Calvin, met with some of his friends, all Confederate veterans. The young men decided to organize a social club. Kennedy had been asked to look after the Thomas Martin Home while the Martins were away, and so the group next met there and selected the name Ku Klux, perhaps a play on the Greek word for "circle." They added "Klan" apparently just for the alliteration. Taking the Martin sheets and pillow cases, they dressed in fanciful outfits and went out on the town as pranksters. Soon other young men wanted to join, and so the group developed an elaborate initiation into the Klan. It was probably inevitable that neighborhood pranks quickly turned to intimidation of northern carpetbaggers and newly freed African Americans.

The Ku Klux Klan quickly spread to other cities of the south, and in April 1867, a group gathered at the Maxwell House Hotel in Nashville to combine isolated Klans into a united organization; Gen. Nathan Bedford Forrest was chosen as the Grand Wizard, and wherever he traveled, Klan membership grew. Soon violence toward blacks and unsympathetic whites escalated into beatings, rapes, and murders. The Tennessee State Legislature enacted what came to be called the Ku Klux Klan Act, which outlawed secret organizations that had the purpose of disturbing the peace.

By now even Forrest had become concerned with the level of violence, some of which he attributed to non-Klan perpetrators. In 1869, Forrest issued an order for the Klans to stop their activities, essentially disbanding the Klan, although some individual Klans continued their practices. But even these were abandoned at the end of Reconstruction. The Ku Klux Klan re-emerged in Atlanta as a white-supremacist organization in the early 1900s; probably the only connection to the original group that started at Pulaski was the adoption of the name and the costumes.

On the south side of the courthouse square stands the **Sam Davis Statue** commemorating of one of the Confederacy's youngest heroes. Just twenty-one years old, Davis was a member of a scouting group sent to gather information on Union movements during the Confederate siege of Union forces in Chattanooga in 1863. Davis was captured south of Pulaski in possession of federal documents and imprisoned in a jail that stood on the northwest corner of the town square. Union Gen. Grenville Dodge asked him to reveal the source of the papers: "I pleaded with him . . . to give me a chance to save his life, for . . . he was a most admirable young fellow." Refusing to betray his source, Davis responded, "If I had a thousand lives, I would give them all here before I would betray a friend or the confidence of my informer." The Federals hung Davis as a spy and buried him in a local cemetery, but within a few days his body was sent back to his home in Smyrna. Southerners considered the execution unjust because Davis was wearing his Confederate uniform at the time of his capture; so he should have been considered a soldier performing his duty, not a spy. From the southeast corner of the square, you can take Madison Street east three blocks to Sam Davis Avenue and turn right to the **Sam Davis Memorial Museum,** a small Civil War museum erected on the site of Davis's execution.

MILKY WAY AND LYNNVILLE

From the town square take First Avenue (US 31) to the north to leave Pulaski. In 0.5 mile pass US 31A to the right and enter a pastoral countryside of rolling hills and white-fenced fields. In 6.6 miles the **Olivet United Methodist Church** stands on the right; this small 1871 church building has architectural detailing along the eaves. The highway then crosses a bridge over a railroad and in 1 mile passes **Milky Way Farm** to the left; the Tudor mansion can be glimpsed through the trees at the top of a knoll.

Frank and Ethel Mars, the founders of Mars Candy Company in Chicago, settled here in the early 1930s, investing in 2,800 acres of farmland. The couple established a farm they named after one of their candy bars and which became one of the top five farms in the country, producing cattle, sheep, and horses, including a Kentucky Derby winner. At its peak, the farm had thirty barns, its own railroad depot, and several houses, all centered around the huge Tudor mansion that today is a corporate retreat. Tours are available to groups by appointment.

Many of the outbuildings of the farm are now gone, but you'll see a few of the remaining barns on the hillside as you pass by, continuing north on US 31. In 4.1 miles turn right on TN 129. In 1.4 miles enter the old railroad town

Milky Way Farm

of Lynnville. The **McGregor Hardware Store** built in 1895 contains the local library. **Soda Pop Junction** occupies an old drugstore. The **Lynnville Depot** beside the train tracks houses a railroad museum. Across the tracks on the right stands the old **Iron Horse Hotel,** which is now a restaurant.

Stay on TN 129 through town and back into a countryside of fields and houses. In 4 miles enter Marshall County, and in another 2.3 miles pass under I–65. Notice the large columned house on the left in 1.3 miles, just before the highway curves to the right. It was built just prior to the Civil War by James Ham. The construction bankrupted the Hams and the house became known as **Ham's Folly.**

Continue east, crossing a ridge with a view into the valley to the left and descending into Cornersville in 2.4 miles. In the community, the highway curves left at a city park. Across from the park stands the Greek Revival **Cornersville United Methodist Church** built in 1852; the top floor served as a Masonic Hall until 1939. TN 129 intersects with US 31A in the center of town. Turn right to pass through the small commercial district to the south. Just out of downtown, you'll pass three distinctive homes on the left, all two-story white frame houses possessing porches across the front with spindle detailing.

Pass through horse country for 2.2 miles, then turn left to continue east on TN 129. The highway winds through a scenic countryside of farms with a collection of old homes and barns. In 4.5 miles turn right to stay on TN 129 at a junction with TN 272. At a junction in another 6 miles, turn left to stay on TN 129, which then curves right to a junction with US 431 in another 2 miles. Turn right; in 1.5 miles pass a junction with TN 130 and turn left on Church Street, entering Lincoln County, named for a Revolutionary War veteran, Gen. Benjamin Lincoln. Church Street passes into the historic town of Petersburg, containing old homes, churches, and commercial buildings centered on a small town square. Turn right on High Street to return to US 431.

FAYETTEVILLE

Continuing south, the highway travels through horse country, passing large homes and stables, eventually entering Fayetteville in 11.9 miles on Main Street and reaching the town square with the relatively new **Lincoln County Courthouse** and a junction with US 64. The commercial buildings ringing the square date from the late 1800s through the 1900s, including the art deco **Lincoln Theater** on one side and side-by-side pool halls on the other; **Marbles Mercantile** is a hundred-year-old general store. To the right from the south side of the square, **Cahoots Restaurant** occupies the old jail/firehouse.

Stay straight through town on Main to reach the **Lincoln County Museum and Civic Center,** which occupies the old factory warehouse of the Bordon Milk Plant. You can continue straight to the site of **Camp Blount** in 0.8 mile. In September 1813, during the War of 1812, Andrew Jackson mustered here a group of 3,500 volunteers, who then marched into Alabama to confront the warring Red Stick faction of the Creek Nation, which Jackson defeated at the Battle of Horseshoe Bend; David Crockett was one of the volunteers who accompanied the troops into Alabama. The mustering ground, which was shaded by four giant oak trees, was named for Willie Blount, governor of Tennessee, a half-brother of William Blount, the former territorial governor. Camp Blount served as a mustering ground several more times. Unfortunately, two of the giant oak trees were felled to make way for development, but the other two oaks stand quite prominently on the left with a historical marker.

Return to the center of Fayetteville to explore the historic neighborhoods containing old homes dating from the early 1800s; a tour guide is available from the chamber of commerce. Don't miss the **Douglas-Wyatt House,** a magnificent Steamboat Gothic home on Washington Street to the north; the two and one-half story, white frame home built between 1894 and 1895 with wraparound porches actually resembles a steamboat.

Take US 64 east to leave Fayetteville. In 4.7 miles the highway crosses the Elk River; on the right stand the piers of an old six-arch stone bridge that was erected before the Civil War; Sherman marched his troops across the bridge on his way to reinforce federal troops in Chattanooga in 1863. The span collapsed in the 1960s.

In 1.2 miles, in the community of Kelso, an old general store on the right is the headquarters of **Elk River Canoe Rental,** which offers leisurely float trips on the Elk. You can turn right on Teal Hollow Road to visit the small community, which contains the **Kelso Cumberland Presbyterian Church,** built in 1876, and the **Kelso Depot,** an old board and batten train depot that reflects Kelso's heyday as a railroad town.

Continue east on US 64. In 6.2 miles a shaded picnic area on the left marks the entrance to the **Flintville Fish Hatchery Wildlife Management Area.** The hatchery is 0.7 mile down the road.

Beyond the hatchery entrance, TN 121 joins US 64 from Elora to the south and then turns off to the left. US 64 continues east through farm country; rolls of hay are scattered in the fields; the western edge of the Cumberland Plateau looms in the distance.

FALLS MILL, WINCHESTER, TULLAHOMA

In 5.5 miles enter Franklin County, and in another 4.1 miles enter Old Salem. Turn left on Old Salem-Lexie Road and travel for 1.2 miles, then turn left on Falls Mill Road to **Falls Mill.**

Erected in 1873 by Robert Mann and Azariah David, the three-story brick mill first served as a cotton and woolen factory, powered by water from Factory Creek, which spills down beside the mill. A stone dam built in 1871 stores water upstream, which then flows down a mill race to the 32-foot overshot steel waterwheel; this present wheel replaced a wooden waterwheel in 1906 when the factory was converted to a cotton gin, which operated until the 1940s. The mill then became a woodworking factory for a time. In the 1960s the building was restored, and grain milling equipment from an old mill in Winchester was installed. The mill is fully operational, the turning waterwheel powering machinery inside through a series of gears and pulleys. Millstones grind corn and wheat to produce cornmeal, corn grits, and flour that is shipped to restaurants and specialty stores and may be purchased at the mill or by mail order. The mill is open for tours and contains a museum of textile and milling equipment. The grounds of the mill also contain the reconstructed 1895 **Henry Koger Cabin,** a log house that is a bed and breakfast, and the reconstructed **Rocky Springs Stagecoach Inn,** which was originally erected near Elora around 1836.

Return to US 64 and continue east; a historical marker on the left remembers Polly Crockett, the wife of David Crockett who died prematurely after Crockett returned from the Creek War. The Crocketts lived on Beans Creek in Franklin County. Crockett soon married Elizabeth Patton; the couple with their children later moved to Lawrenceburg.

In 3.1 miles **The Swiss Pantry** on the left offers Mennonite/Amish baked goods, cheeses, and other products. In Belvidere in 1.7 miles, the **Belvidere Market** resides in an old general store that offers antiques and crafts and serves sandwiches. You can turn left on Owl Hollow Road to the **First United Church,** built in 1885 but later renovated with brick and stained-glass. A paved heritage walk beside the church passes the names of Swiss-German families who settled the region.

Continue east on US 64 to the outskirts of Winchester in 4.4 miles, where the highway curves right to bypass the downtown. Exit right and take the ramp over US 64 to the left to travel US 64 Business into town. In 1 mile you can turn left on 100 Oaks Drive to **Hundred Oaks Castle,** built in 1890 by the son of Albert Marks, governor of Tennessee from 1879 to 1881. The huge Gothic mansion was patterned after Abbotsford Castle, the ancestral home of Scottish author Sir Walter Scott; a fire destroyed much of the home in 1990, but it is being renovated by Nashville's Kent Bramlett Foundation.

Past 100 Oaks Drive, the business route splits into one-way streets; stay right to enter the town square of Winchester, named for James Winchester, one of the early settlers of upper Middle Tennessee. Just before the town square, you can turn left on TN 50 for a side trip to **Tims Ford State Park.** Stay with TN 50 through several turns, finally entering the countryside to the west. In 1 mile, the **Antebellum Inn** stands on the right, a grand red brick mansion built in the 1850s. It is now a bed-and-breakfast and contains a pub. In 4.2 miles bear right at a fork on Mansford Road. In 3.7 miles the road crosses a bridge over Tims Ford Lake, created by TVA's Tims Ford Dam on the Elk River. In another 0.8 mile turn left to enter the state park and reach the visitor center on the right in 0.6 mile. The park has a campground, lakeside cabins, picnic areas, trails, and boat access to the lake.

In Winchester, the **Franklin County Courthouse** anchors the town square. Stay around the square to the old **Oldham Theater** on the far corner and continue to the east, leaving town on US 41A, which is also Dinah Shore Boulevard; the popular singer who once had her own television show was born in Winchester. The **Franklin County Old Jail Museum** on the right stands above a Tims Ford Lake embayment. Built in 1897 and used as a jail until 1972, the building now contains artifacts and exhibits on Franklin County history, including mementos from the life of Dinah Shore, who lived in a neighborhood behind the museum.

Continue on US 41A, crossing a bridge over the lake embayment and curving to the north. Enter Coffee County and in 14.2 miles enter Tullahoma, a railroad town established along the route of the Nashville and Chattanooga Railroad and given a Choctaw name for red clay or rock. The **Tullahoma Fine Arts Center** on the right contains a regional museum of art in the 1870 Baillet House. Turn right on Lincoln Street, with the chamber of commerce on the corner. In 1 block lies Atlantic Street with the railroad, now the CSX Railroad, running down the middle of the thoroughfare. Cross the tracks and turn left on the far lane of Atlantic to enter the **Depot Historic District,** with the **Tullahoma Depot** sitting beside the tracks on the left and late nineteenth and early twentieth-century Victorian houses on the right, including **Holly Berry Inn,** which occupies the 1907 Hicks-Jennings House.

SIPPING WHISKEY

From Tullahoma you can take a side trip to Lynchburg by returning to US 41A and continuing northwest to turn west on TN 55. In 2.5 miles enter Moore County and pass through the pine and hardwood forest of **Cumberland Springs Wildlife Management Area.** In 2.3 miles you can turn right on Ledford Mill Road to pass through a five-way intersection and continue 2.8 miles to **Ledford Mill,** an 1884 three-story building on Shipman Creek, a tributary of the Duck River. Water spilling down from the pond above the dam creates a dramatic setting for the mill, which is now a bed-and-breakfast. The community that once existed around the mill included distilleries that operated until 1909.

Back on TN 55, continue to the west. In 6.9 miles enter Lynchburg and reach the **Jack Daniel Distillery,** the oldest registered distillery in the United States.

Jasper Newton Daniel, known as "Jack," was a runaway child who found a home with Rev. Dan Call, a Lynchburg Lutheran minister and whiskey-maker. At the age of 13 Jack joined Call in his whiskey business; however, it wasn't long before the reverend decided to give up whiskey-making and sold the business to Jack, who moved it to a cave spring that had iron-free limestone water, perfect for making whiskey. Over the years, as other distilleries sought to shorten the whiskey-making process, Jack Daniel steadfastly held to the extra step of charcoal mellowing, which had been developed in this part of Tennessee. The whiskey is dripped through 10 feet of charcoal made from sugar maple wood, a process that distinguishes Tennessee whiskey from bourbon, which originated in Bourbon County, Kentucky. The Tennessee version is sometimes called "sipping whiskey," because it's meant to be sipped and savored.

When Jack Daniel died in 1911, the distillery passed to his nephew, Lem Motlow, who hung on to the operation during Prohibition and reopened the distillery when Prohibition was repealed in 1933. Moore County chose to remain a dry county where alcoholic beverages could not be sold, but Motlow, a state senator, managed to get the legislature to pass a bill making it legal to make whiskey in Lynchburg. And so Jack Daniel's continued to be made, and the distillery has become a world-renowned producer of Tennessee whiskey.

Tours of the distillery, offered free to thousands of visitors each year, include visits to a barrelhouse containing thousands of fifty-gallon barrels of whiskey, the rickyard where sugar maple is burned to make charcoal, the cave spring that still supplies all the water for the whiskey-making, and the buildings that house the fermenting tanks of a sour mash mixture of corn, rye, and barley malt, the whiskey stills, and the charcoal mellowing vats. The mash is not actually sour; the term refers to some mash from a previous batch being added to a new batch to maintain consistency. The distillation process separates and purifies the whisky by evaporating the alcohol and recondensing it. The whiskey is then aged in white oak barrels that are charred on the inside to caramelize the wood sugars and give color and flavor to the whiskey.

Beyond the distillery, you can continue on TN 55 into Lynchburg and turn left on Mechanic Street to the town square centered on the 1885 **Moore County Courthouse.** On the far corner of the square, turn right on Main Street to see the old **Moore County Jail Museum,** a two-story brick jailhouse built in the 1800s, and **Miss Mary Bobo's Boarding House,** an 1867 hotel that was converted to a boarding house by Mary Bobo in 1908; the lunches Miss Bobo served to residents and anyone else that dropped by became popular in these parts. She operated the boardinghouse until her death in 1983. Jack Daniel's great-grandniece, Lynne Tolley, now operates a lunch-by-reservation establishment where guests still join together at long tables and help themselves to heaping bowls of fine country cooking.

Back in Tullahoma, you can also take a side trip north to the **George Dickel Distillery** on TN 269, which is the extension of Atlantic Street. The tree-shrouded highway follows the railroad north, entering Bedford County in 4.5 miles. In another 2.8 miles enter the small railroad town of Normandy. Turn right to cross the tracks to a strip of old commercial buildings, then turn right on Cascade Hollow Road and travel 1.2 miles to Cascade Hollow.

In 1870 George Dickel established a distillery here for the manufacture of Tennessee whiskey that, like Jack Daniel's, has since become known throughout the country and parts of the world as a high-quality whiskey. Dickel chose this hollow for his distillery because of the pure water in Cascade Spring that is still used today in the whiskey-making. The process used by George Dickel is similar to Jack Daniel's, except the whiskey is chilled during the charcoal-filtering process. Dickel noticed that batches of whiskey produced during the winter seemed to be noticeably smoother, and so he deduced that because chilled whiskey is slightly more viscous, it therefore filtered more slowly and cleanly. So he introduced a process he called "chill-mellowing," in which the whiskey is cooled to 43 degrees Farenheit before being charcoal filtered.

In Normandy, you can also turn north on Frank Hiles Road and travel 2.1 miles to TVA's **Normandy Dam,** which creates Normandy Lake on the Duck River. In another 1.1 miles the **Barton Springs Recreation Area** lies on the left, offering picnicking and camping (no hookups).

OLD STONE FORT

After these side trips, leave Tullahoma to the northeast on Lincoln Street, which becomes Old Tullahoma-Manchester Road. In 2.5 miles you can turn left on Carter Blake Road and travel 1.4 miles to a right turn on Short Springs Road. Drive for another 1.2 miles to the **Short Springs State Natural Area.** Trails lead into the natural area along Bobo and Newman Creeks, which cascade off the Highland Rim to eventually become part of the Normandy Lake empoundment.

Continue northeast on Old Tullahoma-Manchester Road, paralleling a branch line of the railroad out of Tullahoma and TN 55. To the east lies the vast acreage of the **Arnold Engineering Development Center,** a U.S. Air Force research and test facility that uses a variety of wind tunnels and test cells in aerospace research.

Passing through the countryside for 9.3 miles, the road enters Manchester as Spring Street to a junction with US 41. Spring Street continues into the town square centered on the **Coffee County Courthouse,** an Italianate building constructed in 1871.

Turn north on US 41 to circle the town on the west. In 0.4 mile cross a bridge over the Little Duck River, and in another 0.9 mile turn left into **Old Stone Fort State Archaeological Park,** which contains a campground, picnic area, and a visitor center/museum. A trail from the museum leads to Old Stone Fort, a fifty-acre compound built around A.D. 30 by Native Americans of the Middle Woodland Period. The stone and earthen walls that circled the enclosure appeared to be an old fort to early settlers, but it was most likely a ceremonial gathering place. The 1.3-mile path circles the compound, which stands on a bluff at the edge of the Highland Rim where the Barren Fork on the northwest and the Little Duck River on the southeast cascade off the rim to a confluence below the stone fort where the two stream combine to make the Duck River.

The Duck travels to the west for 269 miles to the Tennessee River, making it the longest river wholly within Tennessee. The river harbors roughly thirty rare aquatic species, including freshwater mussels, snails, and fish. This biodiversity and its recreational opportunities have made it the center of conservation efforts aimed at protecting its water quality and scenic values.

Bledsoe's Lick, Mansker's Station, and Port Royal

CASTALIAN SPRINGS TO ADAMS

GENERAL DESCRIPTION: This 77-mile drive through Middle Tennessee north of Nashville passes some of the most historic sites in Tennessee, including a side trip to Andrew Jackson's Hermitage.

SPECIAL ATTRACTIONS: Wynnewood State Historic Site, Bledsoe's Fort Historic Park, Bledsoe Creek State Park, Gallatin, Shackle Island, Rock Castle State Historic Site, Mansker's Station, Springfield, Adams, Port Royal State Historic Site, historic homes and buildings, scenic views, fall color, hiking, biking, boating, fishing, hunting, and wildlife viewing.

LOCATION: Upper Middle Tennessee. Begin the drive in Castalian Springs west of Hartsville on TN 25.

DRIVE ROUTE NUMBERS: TN 25, 174, and 258; US 31E and 41; and TN 76.

CAMPING: Bledsoe Creek State Park.

SERVICES: All services at Gallatin, Hendersonville, Goodlettsville, and Springfield.

NEARBY ATTRACTIONS: The Hermitage, Glen Raven, and Wessyngton.

THE DRIVE

Bigfoot Spencer, Isaac and Anthony Bledsoe, Hugh and Nancy Rogan, James and Sara Winchester, Daniel and Sara Smith, Andrew and Rachel Jackson, and Kasper Mansker constitute a partial roll call of the first families of Middle Tennessee. These pioneers built forts, log cabins, and finally great stone and brick mansions as they made the transition from frontiersmen to prosperous plantation owners. They carved out of the wilderness the foundation upon which present Middle Tennessee stands. Many of their homes still grace the landscape, testament to their courage and resilience in the settling of the state.

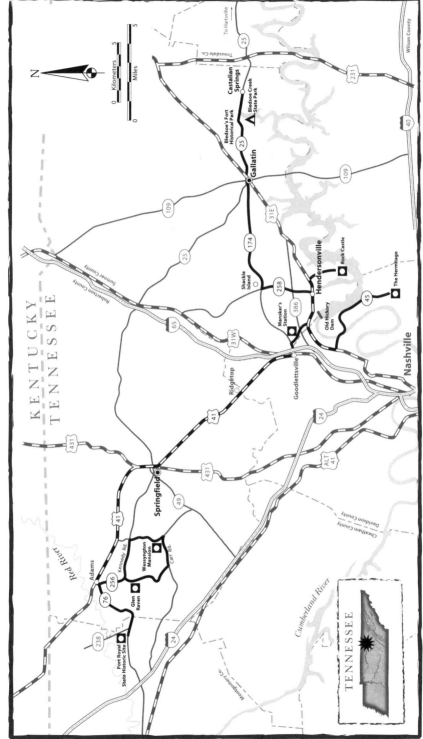

BLEDSOE'S LICK

This drive begins at Castalian Springs on TN 25. Entering the community from the east, turn left on Corn Hill Road to Old Highway 25 and turn right. The **Thomas Sharp Spencer Monument** stands on the left. Spencer, an early longhunter, was one of the first white men to enter Middle Tennessee. By all accounts, he was a huge man. Another hunter, seeing Spencer's large footprints, fled the area saying that the region was inhabited by giants. Thereafter, the longhunter was known as "Bigfoot" Spencer. He helped settle Bledsoe's Lick, now the community of Castalian Springs, and also French Lick, which became Nashville. In 1794 he was killed by Indians near Crab Orchard to the east on the Cumberland Plateau. On this spot, he is said to have spent the winter of 1778 to 1779 in a hollow sycamore tree that stood here at least until 1839.

Soon after on the right stands a shelter over **Bledsoe's Lick,** a mineral spring discovered by Isaac Bledsoe in 1772, a longhunter from Virginia. The sulfur spring was a gathering place for animals that came to drink the water and lick minerals from the surrounding rocks and dirt. Bledsoe and other longhunters found game easily at such licks. This had also been the location of a prehistoric Woodland Indian town with ceremonial mounds and earthworks; a remnant of the principal mound can still be seen north of TN 25.

Just beyond the spring, **Wynnewood State Historic Site** lies on the left. In 1828 Alfred R. Wynne with William Cage and Stephen Roberts erected this stagecoach inn on the Avery Trace that ran by Bledsoe's Lick, connecting East Tennessee with the early Cumberland settlements. Two stories high and 140 feet long, this is probably the largest log building ever constructed in Tennessee. In 1834 Wynne bought out his two partners and moved into the inn with his family. The inn had been constructed on land owned by Wynne's wife, Almira Winchester, the daughter of James Winchester, one of the early settlers of Middle Tennessee who with Andrew Jackson and John Overton opened West Tennessee to settlement and founded the city of Memphis.

In addition to travelers passing through the region, the inn hosted people attracted by the mineral water, thought to be a cure for illnesses; Castalian Springs became known as a mineral springs resort. On his visits to the region, Andrew Jackson often brought a thoroughbred horse to race against Wynne's horses. Wynne operated the inn until his death in 1893, and the building remained in the family until 1971 when Wynne's grandson, George Winchester Wynne turned the inn over to the State of Tennessee to be preserved as a historic site. You may tour the old inn, which has an attached log kitchen. Behind the house is a small log cabin erected in 1780 by Isaac Bledsoe when he returned to settle the area.

Past Wynnewood, rejoin TN 25 and continue west. In 0.4 mile turn right into **Bledsoe's Fort Historical Park,** which preserves the site of a fort constructed by Isaac Bledsoe in the early 1780s; here he brought his family and others to permanently settle the region. Several forts were built on the frontier in the early years to shield the settlers against attacks by Native Americans. Other forts in the region included Mansker's Station and Fort Nashborough. Being so isolated from settlements to the east and the government of North Carolina, these early settlers banded together in the Cumberland Compact, a style of self-government similar to the Watauga Association developed by the early settlers of East Tennessee. Each of the forts had representatives on the Tribunal of Notables, which served as the governing body; Isaac Bledsoe served as the representative for Bledsoe's Fort.

A 1-mile trail circles the open field where Bledsoe's Fort once stood and visits several historic sites. Near the parking area stands **Rogana,** a two-room stone cottage built by Hugh Rogan around 1798 in a small settlement to the north that also came to be called Rogana; to preserve the house, it was dismantled and reconstructed in this historic park. Rogan left Ireland for America in 1775, fearing arrest by the English for his association with Irish defenders. He first arrived in Middle Tennessee as a guard for a survey team marking the boundary between the North Carolina and Virginia colonies, which had been granted all lands west to the Mississippi River, the area that would later become the states of Tennessee and Kentucky. Rogan later returned to Tennessee with the John Donelson party to settle Nashborough in 1780. He soon traded his land in the future Nashville for land on Bledsoe Creek to the north. He did not bring his wife, Nancy, and son from Ireland until 1797 because he had been told she had remarried during his long absence, thinking him dead; she had in fact been waiting faithfully for him for almost twenty years.

The park grounds include the **Nathaniel Parker Cabin,** a log house constructed in 1785, relocated here from the Greenfield Fort area, and the **Belote Cemetery,** which contains the graves of early settlers, including Isaac and Anthony Bledsoe. Anthony joined his brother in settling Middle Tennessee in 1784, building Greenfield Fort to the north. Anthony was killed at Bledsoe's Fort in an Indian attack in 1787; Nathaniel Parker later married Anthony's widow. Isaac was also killed by Indians, 100 yards west of the fort in 1793.

Continue on TN 25 to the west. In 0.8 mile turn right on Cragfont Road to reach **Cragfont.** In 1798 James Winchester began construction of his home, which he named for the fact that it stands on a rocky bluff above a spring. Constructed of gray limestone quarried on site, Cragfont was one of the finest homes on the frontier when it was completed in 1802. Winchester came to Middle Tennessee in 1787 and prospered. He served as one of the five original council members for the Southwest Territory and was later elected speaker of the state senate when the State of Tennessee was formed in 1796. A veteran of the Revolutionary War, he led troops as a brigadier general during the War of 1812. Later, he participated in the founding of Memphis, choosing the city's name; his son Marcus was Memphis's first mayor. The Winchester family occupied Cragfont until 1864; today it is a historic house museum open for tours. Winchester and his wife, Sara Black, are buried in a cemetery behind the house.

Return to TN 25 and continue west, crossing Bledsoe Creek. In 1.1 miles turn left on Zeiglers Fort Road. In 1790 Joseph Zeigler established a station on the Avery Trace in the vicinity of Bledsoe Creek; a station, or inn, as distinguished from a fort, had fewer fortifications for protection against Indian raids. In 1791 an attack on the station by Creeks, Cherokees, and Chickamaugas resulted in ten settlers killed and eighteen taken prisoner; the latter were later ransomed.

In 1.3 miles, turn left into **Bledsoe Creek State Park** on the Bledsoe Creek embayment of Old Hickory Lake backed up by Old Hickory Dam on the Cumberland River. The park has a campground, picnic area, 5 miles of hiking trails, and boating, fishing, and swimming on Old Hickory Lake.

GALLATIN

Return to TN 25 and continue west. In 4.1 miles the road curves left to join Main Street into Gallatin. The junction of these roads is the site where Confederate Col. John Hunt Morgan's cavalry captured a federal garrison of about 200 men in 1862 and severed the railroad line between Louisville and Nashville. Withdrawing toward Hartsville, Hunt encountered another federal force, which he defeated before retreating south.

In 0.6 mile on the right stands **Williamson and Adams Carriage Factory,** a yellow-painted brick building that served as the headquarters for federal forces occupying Gallatin during the Civil War and which later housed a lumber store and later an iron foundry. From here, Main Street enters the historic downtown of Gallatin. In the center stands the **Sumner County Courthouse.** At Water Street, you can turn right to see the **Palace**

Theater on the left, an art deco movie house built in 1913 and, across the street, the 1917 **Gallatin Buggy and Implement Company** that once sold buggies, wagons, and horse-drawn plows and other farm implements.

Just beyond Water Street, the chamber of commerce sits on the right; stop here for information about the town. Across the street stands the **First United Methodist Church;** the main sanctuary was built in 1843. Just beyond it is the **First Presbyterian Church,** an 1836 Greek Revival temple-style building that was used as a hospital for federal troops during the Civil War; during that time the Methodists shared their church with the Presbyterians.

Then on the left is **Trousdale Place,** built after 1813 by John H. Bowen and acquired in 1822 by William Trousdale, who was governor of Tennessee from 1849 to 1851. Trousdale was called the "Warhorse of Sumner County"; a military hero, he fought in four wars: the Creek War, the War of 1812, the Seminole War, and the Mexican War. The house is open to the public and contains Trousdale family furnishings. The **Sumner County Museum,** containing artifacts from the history of Gallatin and Sumner County, is located behind Trousdale Place in a three-story carriage house.

Past Trousdale Place, cross US 31E as TN 25 bears right, crossing CSX railroad tracks that run on the northwest side of the city, and turn left on TN 174, locally referred to as Long Hollow Pike. Head west into the countryside of rolling hills, forest, and large older homes. In 4.7 miles cross Station Camp Creek into the small community of Ocana. More than one creek in Tennessee is called Station Camp, because it was along such creeks that early longhunters camped, or "stationed." For about four months in 1772, Kasper Mansker, Isaac Bledsoe, and others were stationed along this creek.

SHACKLE ISLAND AND ROCK CASTLE

In 3.5 miles TN 174 intersects with TN 258 in the community of Shackle Island where the highway crosses Drakes Creek. You can turn right on TN 258 (Tyree Springs Road) for 0.4 mile to see **Old Brick** on the left, a five-bay, two-story brick home built in 1804 by Robert Taylor, a builder responsible for several structures in Shackle Island; he constructed this home for William Montgomery, a surveyor for the federal government who received land in payment and became a wealthy merchant and landowner.

Return to the junction with TN 174; this drive will continue on TN 258 south (Shackle Island Road), but first turn right on TN 174 and continue into Shackle Island. It's said that illegal whiskey was once available in a shack on an island in a nearby creek, so customers were told to go to the "shack on the island." Eventually the place became known as Shackle Island.

The **Beech Cumberland Presbyterian Church** stands on the right among the trees. The stone building with 3-foot thick walls was erected in 1828 by Robert Taylor. William Montgomery is buried in the church grave-yard along with other early settlers. Also on the right stands the **Kirkpatrick House;** originally a two-story log structure, the home was covered with weatherboard and a portico added. Then on the left is the **Taylor-Montgomery House,** a two-story stone house Robert Taylor built in 1824 for his brother. Turn around after viewing these houses and return to TN 258 and turn south.

Where TN 258 crosses TN 386 in 3.1 miles it becomes New Shackle Island Road. In another 2.5 miles the highway reaches a junction with US 31E in Hendersonville. This drive will turn right, but first turn left to head east. In 0.5 mile you can access **Old Hickory Dam** to the south on the Cumberland River where you have access to Old Hickory Lake. In another 1.5 miles turn right on Indian Lake Road and travel 1.4 miles and stay straight through a four-way intersection onto East Drive to enter the grounds of **Rock Castle State Historic Area.** Ahead stands Rock Castle, a stone Georgian-Federal mansion built around 1780 by Daniel Smith and his wife, Sarah. Smith was a surveyor for North Carolina and received this land in pay-ment for his services. Today the home stands on an embayment of Old Hickory Lake, but it once commanded a 3,140-acre plantation. A leader in the settlement of the future state, Smith served as secretary of the Southwest Territory and so was instrumental in drafting the constitution of the new state of Tennessee, along with Territorial Governor William Blount. He later served as U.S. senator from Tennessee. Daniel and Sarah are both buried in a family plot on the grounds.

THE HERMITAGE

Return to US 31E and turn back west, passing New Shackle Island Road and, in 1.2 miles, passing under access for TN 386. In another 0.3 mile this drive turns right on Center Point Road, but you can first continue straight for a side trip to **The Hermitage,** the home of Andrew Jackson. In 4.4 miles along US 31E, turn left on TN 45. Cross the Cumberland River in 2 miles, and in another 5.4 miles, turn left on Rachel's Lane, which leads to the Hermitage Visitor Center.

Andrew Jackson is one of the monumental figures in United States history. Arriving in Tennessee in 1788 as a twenty-one-year-old lawyer from North Carolina, Jackson spent some time in Jonesborough, but soon relocated to Nashville where he boarded with the widow of John Donelson. There he fell

The Hermitage

in love with the Donelsons' daughter, Rachel, who at the time was unhappi-
ly married. Rachel and her husband had applied for divorce, and thinking it
had been granted, Jackson and Rachel were married. Later, when they
learned the divorce had become official only after they had married, Jackson
and Rachel married a second time. The mistake would haunt the couple;
when Jackson entered politics, his foes accused Rachel of bigamy.

Jackson quickly rose to prominence in Tennessee affairs. He was a member of the state's constitutional convention and was elected Tennessee's first
congressman in 1796 and U.S. senator the following year. He was also a military leader, and it was on an aborted attempt to wrest Florida from the
Spanish that Jackson's men first called him "Old Hickory" for his determina-
tion and toughness, a nickname he proudly bore the rest of his life.

During the War of 1812, Jackson defended Mobile, Alabama, from British
attacks and drove them out of Pensacola, Florida, before taking command at
New Orleans. On January 8, 1815, in the Battle of New Orleans, Jackson and
his army fought off the British who were attempting to take the city, and
Jackson became a national hero.

In the meantime, Jackson prospered financially. The cotton plantation which he established became one of the largest in Middle Tennessee with 140 slaves working in the fields and at the house. At first Jackson and Rachel lived in two log cabins that still stand on property. They stayed there until the first Hermitage was built in 1819–21. This simple Federal-style brick home was the only Hermitage that Rachel knew, for she died in 1828. In 1831 the home was remodeled with library and dining room wings attached and a colonnade added to the front facade. A fire seriously damaged the building in 1834, and it was rebuilt in more of a Greek Revival style.

Serving in the U.S. Senate again, Jackson ran for president against the incumbent, John Quincy Adams. Although Jackson won the vote, he did not have a majority, and so the election was sent to the House of Representatives, who selected Adams. Jackson was enraged and became determined to win the next election, which he did in 1828; he was reelected in 1832. During his presidency he established Jacksonian democracy: government for the good of the common man.

Despite Jackson's earlier battles with the Native Americans, many had been his friends in the early years, and he had unofficially adopted an Indian boy who lived at the Hermitage. Inexplicably, it was Jackson who pushed through the Indian Removal Act of 1830 that eventually resulted in the removal of Native Americans to the Oklahoma Territory, including the Cherokees who were marched along the Trail of Tears in 1838. On their way west, one contingent of Cherokees passed by the Hermitage where the retired president had returned home.

After Jackson's death in 1845, Andrew Jackson, Jr., an adopted son, took over operation of the plantation, but a drought in 1856 caused a massive crop failure that led to the loss of the property to the state. The family lived on in the house for a time. Jackson's granddaughter, Rachel, was instrumental in establishing the Ladies' Hermitage Association, which purchased the house from the state in 1889 and now maintains the property as a museum; the house contains almost all original furnishings. Jackson and his beloved Rachel are buried in the adjacent garden.

You can also visit **Tulip Grove,** which is at the end of Rachel's Lane. The Greek Revival Mansion was built in 1836 for Andrew and Emily Donelson; Andrew was a nephew of Rachel Jackson. The Donelsons accompanied Jackson to the White House, where Andrew served as Jackson's secretary and Emily was the official hostess. Emily died soon after Tulip Grove was completed. Donelson remarried and in 1858 sold the mansion and moved to Memphis. The house remained a private residence until 1964 when the Ladies' Hermitage Association leased the home and opened it as a house museum. On the way to Tulip Grove, you can also stop off at the **Hermitage Church,** the small brick church Jackson built for Rachel in 1823.

MANSKER'S STATION AND SPRINGFIELD

Return from the Hermitage to US 31E in Hendersonville and turn north on Center Point Road to pass under TN 386 and soon turn left on Caldwell Drive. In 2 miles **Moss-Wright Park** lies on the left and just beyond stands the **Mansker's Station Frontier Life Center.** The modern building acts as a welcome center for the reconstructed Mansker's Station, which resides in the park behind the center.

Kasper Mansker, another longhunter from Virginia, came to Middle Tennessee around 1770, leading a group of hunters. Finding it "the goodliest land under the scope of heaven," he returned in 1779 to settle on Mansker Creek to the northwest; the community that eventually grew up nearby became Goodlettsville. The fort he constructed there lasted only a year; hostilities by Native Americans caused Mansker and his settlers to abandon the site. He returned later and built a second fort, which became a major stopping place for the early settlers of Middle Tennessee.

The reconstructed fort is an authentic representation, although it is smaller than the original. The log buildings of the fort are surrounded by a palisade; a blockhouse anchors a corner; each corner would have had a blockhouse from which to fire down on attacking Indians. Reenactors demonstrate life styles and crafts of the period while you tour the facility.

Moss-Wright Park has recreation facilities and picnic areas, as well as the **Bowen-Campbell House,** a two-story brick mansion constructed in 1785–87 by William and Mary Bowen, the parents of John Bowen, who built Trousdale Place in Gallatin. A grandson of William and Mary, and a nephew of John, William Bowen Campbell, who later lived in the house, served as governor of Tennessee from 1851 to 1853, defeating William Trousdale for reelection. The dwelling may be the first brick house in Middle Tennessee.

From Mansker's Station, continue north along Caldwell Drive 0.5 mile to TN 174 and turn west to cross Mansker Creek into Davidson County. In 0.5 mile pass under I–65, and reach a junction with US 41 in Goodlettsville. This drive will turn right on US 41, but first turn left and then right on Memorial Drive to **Kasper Mansker's Grave,** marked by a monument and a mound of stones lying in front of a community center. Mansker lived at his second fort until his death in 1821.

Return to the junction of US 41 and TN 174 and continue north on US 41. In 1.1 miles, cross Mansker Creek and then pass under the access for US

31W. In 3.6 miles enter Robertson County. In 10.2 miles enter the town of Springfield and turn left on TN 49 to enter the historic downtown. The **Robertson County Courthouse** crowns the hill at the town square. A middle section of the courthouse was built in 1879; two wings and a clock tower were added in 1926. At the far side of the square, turn right on Sixth Avenue to the **Robertson County History Museum** housed in an old post office on the left. At the next corner, turn right on Locust to Fifth Avenue. On the left corner stands the **First United Presbyterian Church;** the oldest section was constructed in 1839 and a larger sanctuary was added in 1897. The original building was used as a stable by occupying Union forces during the Civil War; hoof marks can still be seen on the floor.

BELL WITCH AND PORT ROYAL

Return to US 41 and turn left to continue northwest, leaving Springfield and entering a countryside dotted with old homes and barns surrounded by green fields and white fences. In 11.5 miles reach the community of Adams with **Bellwood Cemetery** on the right. You can turn in and drive to the back of the cemetery where a monument to the Bell family stands.

John and Lucy Bell with their children moved to Robertson County in 1804 on land along the Red River. They prospered on their farm until 1817, when strange things began to happen. A noise at the door, but no one there. The sound of dogs fighting in the house, but no animals indoors. The cadence of someone walking down the hall, but no one in the hall. Then a voice could be heard, at first a whisper, then coherent words addressed to the family, and finally full-length conversations. When asked who it was, the voice said it was the witch of a dead neighbor, Kate.

According to family legend, the Bell Witch, as she came to be called, harassed the family for several years, giving special attention to John Bell, whom she said she wanted to kill, and younger daughter, Betsy, whom she slapped, pulled her hair, and stuck with pins. When Betsy was courted by a young man, the witch ran him off. John Bell died mysteriously in 1820, some say of poison. The witch seemed to like Lucy Bell and avoided John Jr. Another son, Richard, later wrote of the incident in a book he called *Our Family Trouble*. The witch left in 1821, saying she would be back in seven years. The voice was heard again in 1828, but for only two weeks. Leaving again, the witch said she would return in 107 years, but in 1935, nothing happened. The Bell home had been destroyed in 1837.

Many visitors to the Bell home experienced the witch for themselves. Andrew Jackson, hearing the stories, decided to visit the Bells. On approaching the farm, the wagon wheels locked for no apparent reason, and during the night, some of Jackson's party were pinched and slapped.

Perhaps the most famous haunting in U.S. history, the Bell Witch is given credence by the presence of a state historical marker in Adams on US 41. There, an old brick school on the right houses a combination antiques and collectibles store and the Adams Museum, and every Saturday night hosts a country and blue grass concert called the "Bell Witch Opry."

Just beyond the school, you can turn right on Keysburg Road and travel 0.4 mile to a right turn on a gravel road. Drive 0.6 mile to get to the **Bell Witch Cave.** The owners offer guided tours of the cavern, said to be the site where the Bell Witch rescued a child that had become stuck in a passageway.

In 0.3 mile farther on US 41, turn left on TN 76. On the right stands the **Red River Baptist Church;** founded in 1791 on the nearby Red River, it was the first church west of the Cumberland Plateau. The church moved to this location and the present building in 1898.

In 0.1 mile TN 256 turns off to the left as TN 76 curves to the right. Here you can take a side trip to glimpse two magnificent plantation mansions. TN 256 travels through beautiful farmland with grazing cattle, old farmhouses, and tobacco fields. In 2.5 miles turn right to stay on TN 256, which passes through the huge plantation of **Glen Raven.** In 1 mile, the massive three-story plantation house stands in the trees to the right. It was built between 1897 and 1902 by Felix Ewing and his wife, Jane Washington. The tobacco plantation they created was virtually a village, with church, school, post office, and power plant. Along the highway still stand some of the tenant houses and the old store. The Ewings operated the plantation until 1931 when they lost most everything in the Great Depression.

In 0.9 mile TN 256 crosses the Sulfur Fork of the Red River. In 2.8 miles at a four-way junction, turn left on Carr Road. In 1.9 miles cross a tributary of the Sulfur Fork, traveling through a beautiful bottomland along the creek. In 2.2 miles **Wessyngton Mansion** stands on the hill to the left, built in 1819 by Joseph and Mary Washington; Joseph was a cousin of George Washington. The Federal-style home has seen many additions over the years. When Joseph and Mary's son, George A. Washington, took over management of the plantation in 1848 upon the death of Joseph, he turned the farm into a thriving tobacco plantation that in 1860 was the second largest producer of tobacco in the world. When George died in 1892, the land was divided among his children. A daughter, Jane, received the land upon which she and her husband, Felix Ewing, established Glen Raven. A son, Joseph E. Washington, received the land that included the house, and he and his descendants lived on at Wessyngton.

The road curves left, passing a right turn that leads to the community of Flewellyn, and ascends the hill to pass the gate entrance to Wessyngton. In 0.8 mile recross the Sulfur Fork, and in 1.7 miles reach a four-way junction with Kennedy Road. Turn left, and in 3.3 miles rejoin TN 256 and continue straight 2.5 miles back to TN 76; turn left to continue the drive.

The highway travels through a countryside of fields and rolling hills. In 3.9 miles cross the Sulfur Fork again, and enter Montgomery County. In 1 mile turn right on TN 238 (Port Royal Road), and in 1.1 miles reach **Port Royal State Historic Site** at a crossing of the Red River. Just before the bridge over the river stands an 1859 **Masonic Lodge** that is now the park office and museum; the Masons met here until 1921, after which the building served as a general store, doctor's office, post office, and later a telephone company office.

The primary attraction here is the old covered bridge that once spanned the Red River. Port Royal became a prosperous trade town in the early 1800s because an old Indian trail, later a stagecoach route, crossed the Red River here at the confluence of the Sulfur Fork. This was the route taken by the overland contingent of Cherokees on the Trail of Tears. They camped at Port Royal to rest and resupply and crossed the Red River on the old covered bridge, continuing northwest into Kentucky and through Missouri and Arkansas to Oklahoma.

The original bridge across the river washed away in a flood in 1866. A second bridge was constructed in 1903 and continued in use until 1955, when the present highway bridge was constructed. In 1972 the neglected bridge collapsed into the river. The area was declared a state historic site in 1977, and the state reconstructed the covered bridge to preserve the historic setting. Unfortunately, a flood in 1998 once more damaged the bridge, and only pieces remain on both sides of the river.

From Port Royal, you can continue for 2 miles on the Old Clarksville-Springfield Road that runs beside the Masonic Lodge. When you reach TN 76, continue west another 4 miles to I–24.

Tɦe Aŋtebelluɱ Traɪ́l

NASHVILLE TO MOUNT PLEASANT

GENERAL DESCRIPTION: Antebellum mansions, horse farms, and Civil War history combine in this 78-mile drive that epitomizes Middle Tennessee culture and experience.

SPECIAL ATTRACTIONS: Fort Nashborough, Tennessee State Capitol, Franklin, Spring Hill, Columbia, historic homes and buildings, scenic views, fall color, hiking, biking, boating, fishing, and wildlife viewing.

LOCATION: Middle Tennessee. Begin the drive in downtown Nashville on Broadway.

DRIVE ROUTE NUMBERS: US 31 and TN 243.

CAMPING: Private campgrounds.

SERVICES: All services at Nashville, Franklin, and Columbia.

NEARBY ATTRACTIONS: Radnor Lake State Natural Area, Chickasaw Trace Park, and Mt. Pleasant.

THE DRIVE

Prior to the Civil War, Nashville had been selected as the permanent location of the state capital amid the large plantations and wealthy residents of Middle Tennessee. The huge mansions that adorned these plantations and the wealth accumulated by these Tennesseans were the result in large part to the availability of slave labor. While the more mountainous East Tennessee had few slaves, the Central Basin of Middle Tennessee where Nashville is located had large plantations more typical of the deep South; cotton, corn, and livestock were raised on the fertile land of the Cumberland River watershed. While these plantation homes were usually built by ignominious means, still they are magnificent structures representative of a period of history that is part of the collective memory of the South. The Tennessee Antebellum Trail is a designated drive through Davidson, Williamson, and Maury Counties.

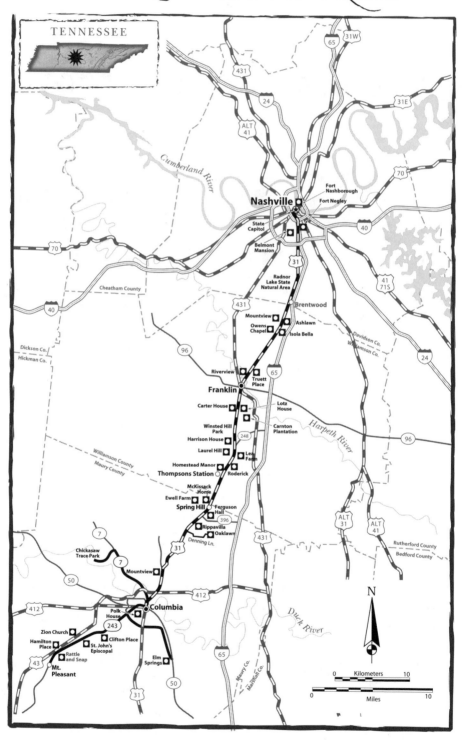

FORT NASHBOROUGH AND FORT NEGLEY

Begin this drive in Nashville on Broadway Avenue. At the corner of Fifth Avenue and Broadway is the **Nashville Arena and Visitor Center** where you can get information about the city. Just up Fifth Avenue to the north is **Ryman Auditorium,** built by Thomas Ryman in 1891 as the Union Gospel Tabernacle for revival meetings. Soon the building was being used for secular performances as well, and in 1905 the name was changed. The auditorium became nationally known in 1943 when WSM Radio began broadcasting its Grand Ole Opry program from here so country music fans could come and watch the stars perform, and thus began Nashville's claim to being the home of country music. Now a National Historic Landmark, the Ryman was the Opry's home until 1974 when it moved to a new hall east of the city.

Down Broadway to the east, First Street runs along the Cumberland River where it flows through the city. On First is **Fort Nashborough,** a replica of the eighteenth century fort built by the founders of the city. Following Richard Henderson's illegal purchase of Cherokee lands south of the Ohio River, he decided to settle the western lands of North Carolina in what would become Tennessee. The logical place to begin was the settlement of French Lick on the Cumberland River, which was a French trading post settled in 1692 by Martin Chartier and his Shawnee wife.

Under the direction of Henderson in October 1779, James Robertson left Fort Patrick Henry, where Kingsport is today, leading a party of men driving livestock overland through Cumberland Gap into Kentucky and down to French Lick. Two months later, John Donelson, a cohort of Richardson and Robertson, launched a flotilla of boats carrying the wives and children of the men on a harrowing journey down the Tennessee River to the Ohio, up that river to the Cumberland, and down to French Lick. Henderson, arriving about the same time as Donelson, took the lead in establishing a frontier government and selected the name Nashborough for Gen. Francis Nash, who had been clerk of the court over which Henderson had been judge and who was killed in the Revolutionary War. The settlers built a fort, similar to this replica, for protection from the Native Americans, many of whom did not recognize Henderson's claim to the land. Robertson is most credited with leading the settlement through the turbulent years of Chickamauga attacks and eventual recognition by North Carolina.

Head west on Broadway through the city. To the right, Fifth through Eighth Avenues lead north to the **Tennessee State Capitol,** which crowns the highest hill in the town. The Greek Revival structure was built in the years 1845 to 1859.

At Eighth Avenue, turn south on what is also US 31. At a fork, bear right to stay on Eighth Avenue to pass under I–40, which runs through the city. At the corner of Chestnut Street, turn left to cross over I–65 and turn left on Fort Negley Road. On the right at the top of the hill was **Fort Negley,** the Union fort that opened fire to begin the Battle of Nashville.

After the Confederate defeat at Atlanta in 1864, Gen. John Bell Hood decided to make a last attempt at regaining the momentum for the Confederacy with an offensive against Nashville. With the fall of Forts Henry and Donelson to the north in 1862, the Confederates had withdrawn from Nashville and Union forces had occupied the city. Marching north from Alabama in 1864, Hood threw his 38,000-man army against Union forces at Franklin in one of the bloodiest battles of the war; in just five hours of fighting on November 30, the Confederates lost 6,252 men killed, wounded, or missing, including six generals killed, while the Union side lost 2,326 killed, wounded, or missing. During the night, the Union forces retreated to Nashville. Not ready to give up, Hood followed with his battered forces. But the Union side had more than enough reinforcements. On December 15 and 16, in one of the last battles of the war, an overwhelming federal force decisively defeated the Confederate Army, which retreated south. A few months later, the Confederacy surrendered at Appomattox Courthouse, Virginia. Fort Negley was built in 1862, mostly by freed African Americans, of stone, logs, and railway iron. Unfortunately, the site of the fort is undeveloped city land that is not open to the public.

Also along Fort Negley Road is the **Cumberland Science Museum** with science exhibits and demonstrations, including planetarium shows. Return to US 31 and turn south to continue the drive.

BELMONT AND TRAVELER'S REST

In 0.6 mile turn right on Wedgewood Avenue. In 1 mile turn left on Magnolia Boulevard and left again on Eighteenth Avenue and left again on Acklen Avenue to enter Belmont University and reach **Belmont Mansion.**

Completed in 1853, Belmont was the summer home of Adelicia and Joseph Acklen. Adelicia Hayes had earlier married Isaac Franklin and upon his death in 1846, she inherited a fortune that included a Louisiana plantation and lands in Tennessee and Texas. She and Acklen married in 1849. The Italian villa-style house they built here was set among elaborate gardens with fountains, gazebos, and a greenhouse. The gardens still contain marble statues and a large collection of nineteenth-century cast-iron ornaments. Joseph Acklen was murdered during the Civil War, and the house was occupied by federal troops. During the war, Adelicia managed to get 2,800 bales of cotton shipped to England and sold for $960,000, thus saving her fortune. Moving to Washington, D.C., in the 1880s, Adelicia sold Belmont to a land development company that in turn sold the house for a women's school that later merged with Nashville's Ward School and became Ward-Belmont. In 1951 the school relocated into the city and sold the Belmont location to the Tennessee Baptist Convention, which opened Belmont University. In cooperation with the Baptist Convention, the Belmont Mansion Association manages the house and conducts tours.

From Belmont, return to US 31 and continue south, traveling the route of the old Franklin Pike. In 1.3 miles pass under I–440, which circles Nashville on the south. In 1 mile **Glen Leven** stands on the left. Built in 1857 by John Thompson, it has a large white-columned portico and spacious grounds that still surround the house.

In 2.2 miles farther south turn left on Farrell Road and then right on Farrell Parkway to **Traveler's Rest.** John Overton purchased this site in 1796. He built a home in 1799 and at first called it Golgotha, meaning "Hill of Skulls," for the number of prehistoric Native American remains that were exposed when the cellar was dug. It has since been determined that this was the site of a Mississippian village. Overton, who served as a circuit court judge and supreme court justice for the newly established State of Tennessee later changed the name to Traveler's Rest to reflect his relief at arriving home at the end of many circuit travels.

Arriving in Tennessee as a young man, Overton roomed with Andrew Jackson, who came to be a lifelong friend. The two, along with James Winchester, founded the city of Memphis in 1819 and developed West Tennessee. Overton is credited with later guiding Jackson to the U.S. presidency.

Traveler's Rest was a working plantation, growing corn, cotton, and fruit and reportedly making Overton the richest person in the state at that time. Late in life, Overton married Mary White, the daughter of James White, the founder of Knoxville. Their son, John Overton, Jr., who inherited the house, strongly supported the Confederacy during the Civil War and so had to flee Nashville when federal troops occupied the city. He returned in 1864, when Gen. Hood brought his army to try to recapture the city. Hood used Traveler's Rest as his headquarters prior to the Battle of Nashville.

Return to Franklin Pike and continue south. In 0.4 mile you can turn right on Otter Creek Road to reach **Radnor Lake State Natural Area** and access hiking trails that lead along Radnor Lake. The visitor center for the natural area is on the west side of the park on Otter Creek Road off Granny White Pike.

ANTEBELLUM MANSIONS

South on Franklin Pike in 2.3 miles, pass through the bustling community of Brentwood. The highway crosses the Little Harpeth River in 1.7 miles and enters plantation country with horse farms and mansions shrouded in trees. In 0.8 mile watch on the right for **Mountview,** a Greek Revival home with early Italianate influences. Built in 1861 on the brink of the Civil War by William A. Davis, this was the last of the antebellum mansions to be constructed.

Across from Mountview stands **Ashlawn,** an 1835 Georgian home with Greek Revival influences. It was built by Richard Christmas and his wife, Mary Emeline Smith. Mary had inherited this land that was originally part of a Revolutionary War land grant to her grandfather, Capt. James Leiper.

In another 0.4 mile south on Franklin Pike, **Owens Chapel** stands on the right. Built in 1859, this small brick building of the Church of Christ still contains the original pews and the partitions that separated women from the men. In another 0.3 mile, the imposing **Isola Bella** stands on the left, built in 1840 by James and Narcissa Johnson. General Hood met with his officers here before the Battle of Nashville.

Other antebellum homes dot the landscape as Franklin Pike travels south. In 4.4 miles approach Franklin. In another 0.6 mile, on the left, stands **Truett Place,** built in 1846 by Alpheus Truett, a nurseryman who established Truett Floral Company, which remained in the family until 1969. The frame mansion with narrow, square-columned portico was the headquarters for Union Gen. John M. Schofield during the Battle of Franklin. In 0.8 mile on the right stands **Riverview,** built in 1902 by Henry Hunter Mayberry, who was one of the founders and president of the Franklin–Nashville Interurban Railway that carried people between the two cities from 1908 to 1941.

FRANKLIN

Franklin Pike crosses the Harpeth River into the **Franklin Downtown Historic District,** entering as Main Street. To the left on Second Avenue stands the **Hiram Masonic Lodge,** built in the Gothic style in 1823. This is the first three-story building in Tennessee and the first Masonic Lodge in the state. Here the Protestant Episcopal Church was organized by Bishop James H. Otey, who later was one of the founders and the first chancellor of the University of the South in Sewanee. Pres. Andrew Jackson led the negotiations here for the Chickasaw Treaty of 1830, which would exchange the Chickasaws' remaining lands in Tennessee for lands in the West and force them to relocate to Oklahoma. The lodge is a National Historic Landmark.

Continuing into downtown Franklin on Main Street, watch on the left for the **Mcphail Office,** built in 1817. Dr. Daniel Mcphail purchased the small brick building in 1839 for his medical practice. The building is now the Franklin Visitor Information Center where you can get maps and information for a walking tour of the 15-block historic district.

The town is centered on the public square where a statue of a Confederate soldier stands on a high pedestal in the center. The **Williamson County Courthouse** on the east side of the square was built in 1859 and has four cast iron columns for its portico. Outside of the square, the surrounding neighborhoods contain historic homes, churches, and commercial buildings.

Stay south on US 31, now called Columbia Avenue as it passes through the town. In 0.6 mile, the **Carter House** stands on the right; the brick neoclassical farmhouse, built in 1830 by Fountain Branch Carter, stood north of Union lines during the Battle of Franklin in 1864 and was used as a federal command post. With the Carter family hiding in the basement, the Confederates surged into the Union position and the battle raged around the house. The fight claimed their youngest son, Capt. Tod Carter. Once the battle was over, his commanding officer led the Carter family to where Tod lay wounded, just 175 yards from the house. They took him back to his home, where he died. The house and farm buildings still show the scars of battle and are judged to be the most heavily damaged structures still standing from the Civil War. The house is now a National Historic Landmark.

Across Columbia Avenue from the Carter House stands the **Lotz House,** which was also at the center of the battle. Built in 1858 by Johann Albert Lotz, a German immigrant, the house is also open to the public. Civil War and Old West artifacts are on display.

Columbia Avenue soon becomes Columbia Pike. Turn left on Cleburne Street to its end and turn right on Lewisburg Avenue. Then turn right on Carnton Lane toward **Carnton Plantation.** The tree-shrouded lane was obviously the entrance to the plantation, but now modern housing incongruously lines the road. At a junction, stay straight on a drive that circles left to the plantation house. This neoclassical home was built in 1826 by Randal and Sarah McGavock and named for the McGavock family's ancestral home in Ireland. Their son, John McGavock, lived here with his wife, Carolyn, by the time of the Battle of Franklin. They opened their home as a hospital for the Confederate wounded who filled the house and overflowed onto the yard. The bodies of four Confederate generals lay on the back porch. The dead on the battlefield were buried where they lay. In 1866 the McGavocks dedicated two acres of land for the reinterment of Confederate dead; 1,481 soldiers found a final resting place there. Caroline McGavock carefully recorded the names, ranks, and home states of the dead, but 225 were unknown. Return down the drive to the junction and turn right to reach **McGavock Cemetery** beneath the trees, the largest private Confederate cemetery in the country.

BATTLE OF FRANKLIN

Return from Carnton to Columbia Pike and continue south. In 1.9 miles the highway begins to climb Winstead Hill. Turn right at that point into **Winstead Hill Park.** Here was where Gen. John Bell Hood commanded Confederate troops during the Battle of Franklin. Across the road is **Breezy Hill,** where Union troops were positioned before the battle. Climb the path to the left of the parking area past several interpretive signs to a sheltered overlook with a map of the battlefield.

General Hood had expected better conditions for the battle. As he marched from the south, Hood had intended to place his army between Maj. Gen. John Schofield's 30,000-man Union army that had ventured as far south as Pulaski and the remaining 30,000 Union troops in Nashville. Hood thought that with his 38,000 men he could defeat the divided Union army in separate battles.

Schofield had been ordered to engage Hood but to gradually fall back to Nashville, while the troops there fortified the city. As Hood tried to go around the Union troops at Pulaski, Schofield retreated to the crossing of the Duck River at Columbia. Leaving a force there to hold the attention of the federal troops, on November 29 Hood took the main contingent of his army in a second flanking maneuver around Columbia to Spring Hill in an attempt to cut off Schofield's escape to Nashville.

Realizing he was about to be trapped, Schofield retreated, still trying to get to Nashville. Inexplicably, the Confederates bivouacked for the night just short of the Columbia Pike, and so when Schofield's troops retreated up the road, they passed right by the Confederates. On the morning of November 30, Hood became infuriated when he realized Schofield had escaped. At the age of thirty-three, Hood was the youngest full general in the Confederate Army; he had already lost a leg at Chickamauga and suffered a mangled arm at Gettysburg. He was not a man to show patience and understanding. He blamed his subordinate generals and ordered his troops to attack Schofield, who was now entrenched at Franklin. Hood's generals tried to dissuade him from such a foolhardy attempt, but he was insistent, wanting to stop Schofield from reaching Nashville and foiling his plan. At 4:00 P.M. that afternoon, the

Confederate troops hurled themselves against the Union troops in what would later be described as the "five tragic hours" of the Battle of Franklin. The Confederates lost nearly three times as many men as the Union side. Schofield retreated to Nashville, where on December 16 the remainder of Hood's army was soundly defeated in the Battle of Nashville.

South of Winstead Hill, the **Harrison House** stands on the right, built in 1848 by William Harrison, who was at one time a sheriff of Williamson County. The brick mansion with white columned portico was where General Hood planned the Battle of Franklin on the afternoon of November 30. Gen. Nathan Bedford Forrest objected to a frontal attack and suggested a flanking maneuver. The two generals argued, with Hood asserting his position as the commanding general and Forrest stalking off to rejoin his cavalry. One of the six Confederate generals killed at the Battle of Franklin died in this house where he had been taken.

In 3.1 miles **Laurel Hill** on the right was begun in the early 1800s but not completed until 1854 by James P. Johnson. The brick mansion once commanded a progressive plantation of harness horses and purebred cattle. The slim-columned portico differs from the massive porticos of other ante-bellum homes.

In 0.7 mile cross the West Harpeth River. Passing other large farmhouses, watch on the left in 1 mile for **Lea Farm,** a two-story frame building now gutted by fire; it was built in 1816 and later operated as an inn here on Columbia Pike.

Roderick stands on a hill to the left in another 0.7 mile. A federal-style brick home built in 1815 by Spenser Buford, it was later named for Gen. Nathan Bedford Forrest's favorite mount, which was shot from under him in the 1863 Battle of Thompson's Station. The horse was brought to this plantation for burial. The home is now part of a cattle farm, and a large addition has been attached to the back of the original house.

In 0.7 mile on the right is **Homestead Manor,** a two-story brick inn completed in 1819 by Francis Giddens. The 1863 Battle of Thompson's Station was fought in front of the old inn on March 5. Alice Thompson, the teenaged daughter of Dr. Elijah Thompson for whom Thompson's Station is named, took refuge in the basement of the manor, which had become the home of the Thomas Baker family. Confederate forces under Gens. Nathan Bedford Forrest and Earl Van Dorn were thrown back several times by a larger federal force. During one charge, a flag bearer was shot down in front of the house. Alice ran from the basement and went outside to pick up the banner. Seeing the girl waving the flag over her head, the Confederates charged the

Union line with renewed courage while General Forrest's cavalry attached the flank. They overwhelmed the Federals, taking 1,220 prisoners along with munitions. It was during the flanking charge that Forrest's mount, Roderick, was killed.

You can turn right on Thompson's Station Road to enter the small community and see the reconstructed **Thompson's Station Depot,** which now houses the library.

SPRING HILL

Continue south on Columbia Pike, and in 3.2 miles enter Maury County. In another 0.4 mile enter the small community of Spring Hill and watch for the **McKissack Home** on the right. Built in 1841–45, this was the first brick house in Spring Hill and was the girlhood home of Jessie McKissack, who married Dr. George B. Peters in 1863. Soon after, Confederate soldiers under Gen. Earl Van Dorn occupied the town. The notorious Van Dorn soon had an affair going with the new Jessie Peters. Later in the war, prior to the Battle of Franklin, Union General Schofield's troops crept past the Confederates who thought they had cut off his retreat. Schofield took up temporary headquarters in the McKissack home. Upon leaving, he left his sword with Mrs. McKissack so he would not have to surrender the weapon if captured by the Confederates under General Hood, a former West Point classmate.

At the corner of Depot Street stands the town library where you can pick up driving tours of historic Spring Hill. To the west lies **Ewell Farm,** established by Gen. Richard Ewell, who brought the first Jersey cows here in 1867 and developed the "Hal" line of Tennessee pacers, which helped create the sport of harness racing. The old white frame Ewell Home sits on a hill to the left a half mile down Depot Street.

South on Columbia Pike stands **Ferguson Hall,** a huge brick mansion built in the early 1850s by Dr. John Haddock; in 1854, the local physician sold the home to Martin Cheairs. Here Gen. Earl Van Dorn established his headquarters in 1863. Soon Jessie McKissack Peters' carriage was seen frequently at the back of the mansion, and Van Dorn visited the Peters' home when her husband was away. On May 7, Dr. Peters came to the headquarters to accuse Van Dorn of having an affair with Jessie. Peters shot Van Dorn in the back of the head, who died without regaining consciousness. Peters fled the scene and was never prosecuted. Van Dorn, who had quite a reputation as a ladies' man, was little missed in the Confederacy, which prided itself on chivalry. Ferguson Hall is today part of Tennessee Children's Home.

Rippavilla

South from Spring Hill on Columbia Pike in 1.8 miles, you can catch a glimpse of the Saturn Plant to the right where Saturn cars are made. In another 0.4 mile on the left stands **Rippavilla,** built in 1852 by Nathaniel Cheairs, the brother of Martin Cheairs of Ferguson Hall. The brothers' two mansions are almost identical, Nathaniel probably having copied Ferguson Hall. Nathaniel Cheairs was married to Susan McKissack, the sister of Jessie M. Peters. In 1864, on the morning of the Battle of Franklin, November 30, Nathaniel and Susan Cheairs invited General Hood and several of his generals to have breakfast before pursuing Union General Schofield to Franklin. Five of Hood's generals gathered around the table that morning would die in the Battle of Franklin that afternoon. Rippavilla is today the headquarters of the Tennessee Antebellum Trail and is open for tours.

Another 0.9 mile south on Columbia Pike, turn left on Denning Lane to see **Oaklawn.** The narrow lane wanders through farmland for 2.4 miles to the brick mansion with white portico that sits at the end of a long drive. On November 29, 1864, General Hood spent the night here after making his flanking maneuver around Union General Schofield. Hood thought that his troops, including the cavalry of General Forrest, held the Columbia Pike, but Schofield's army passed by the Confederates in the night.

COLUMBIA

Return to Columbia Pike and continue south. In 6.1 miles **Mountview** stands on the right, an 1836 Greek Revival that was constructed around an older log cabin. In 1.2 miles the highway crosses the Duck River and in another 1.2 miles reaches TN 7 to the right. You can turn on TN 7 for a side trip to **Chickasaw Trace Park** in 4.2 miles. This county park contains picnic areas, mountain bike trails, and boat access to the Duck River.

Return to Columbia Pike and continue south to enter the downtown of Columbia on Garden Street. At Seventh Street turn left and travel 1 block to the town square centered on the **Maury County Courthouse.** The chamber of commerce on the east side of the square has maps and information about historic sites in the city.

Return to Garden Street. Notice on the far corner the 1839 **Bank of Tennessee Building,** a Greek Revival temple-style construction that figured prominently in the economic boom of the planter society of Middle Tennessee.

Here you can turn south for a side trip to **Elm Springs.** In 1.7 miles turn left on TN 50 and in 0.7 mile turn right on Mooresville Pike. Drive 1.2 miles to the magnificent Greek Revival mansion on the right built in 1837 by James Dick, a New Orleans businessman, for his sister, Sarah. The home today is the headquarters of the Sons of Confederate Veterans, the oldest organization for male descendants of Confederate soldiers, and is open for tours.

Return to the intersection of Seventh Street and continue west. At the corner of High Street stands the **Samuel Polk House,** built in 1816 by the father of James K. Polk, the eleventh U.S. president. Born in North Carolina but still a boy when his family moved to Tennessee, James was in law school at the time this house was built. After graduation and service as a law clerk in Nashville for Judge Felix Grundy, who was later U.S. senator and then attorney general under Martin Van Buren, Polk came to his parents' home and lived with them while setting up a law practice in Columbia. Since this is the only surviving residence that Polk lived in, other than the White House, this family residence is considered the ancestral home of the president. Preserved by the James K. Polk Memorial Association, the home contains personal and household items of the president and his wife, Sarah, and is open for tours.

Today Polk is considered one of the country's best presidents; he worked diligently to accomplish specific stated aims, including expansion to the Pacific. After office he returned to Middle Tennessee, residing in the old Felix Grundy home in Nashville that came to be called Polk Place; he died a few months later of cholera, but Sarah lived on for many years in the house, which no longer stands.

Near the Polk Houses on Seventh Street is **St. Peter's Episcopal Church,** constructed in 1860, and across the street are several historic homes. Turn left on Athenaeum Street to the **Athenaeum Rectory** on the right. This unusual Gothic and Moorish-style home was begun in 1835 for Samuel Polk Walker, a nephew of James K. Polk, but Walker never lived in the home. Completed in 1837, it became the home of Rev. Franklin G. Smith, who had come to Columbia to be president of the Columbia Female Institute, an Episcopal school for girls. In 1851 Smith founded the Columbia Athenaeum School for girls. The Smith family and their descendants continued to live in the rectory until 1973 when family members donated it to the Association for the Preservation of Tennessee Antiquities, which now maintains the house as a museum open for tours. Tradition is maintained at the rectory with the "1861 Athenaeum Girls' School" for a week in July, in which girls fourteen to eighteen years old, adorned in nineteenth-century dresses, participate in classes of etiquette, penmanship, art, music, dance, and social graces. In May, a two-day version of the school is offered to women nineteen and older.

Return to Seventh Street and continue west to turn left on TN 243 to once more enter a countryside of antebellum homes. In 4.4 miles **Clifton Place** resides in the trees to the left. This 1839 mansion was the home of Gen. Gideon J. Pillow, hero of the Mexican War who later shared the blame for the defeat of the Confederates at Fort Donelson. The remaining house and lands are now one of the most intact plantations in the South.

RATTLE AND SNAP

In another 1.6 miles **St. John's Episcopal Church** stands on the left. Built in 1840, it is one of the few remaining plantation churches in the South. The four sons of Col. William Polk erected the church at the juncture of their properties. Three of the brothers—Lucius, Rufus, and George—are buried in the church cemetery. The fourth, Leonidas—Bishop of the Diocese of Louisiana and Confederate General—was killed at the Battle of Pine Mountain, Georgia. The grounds of the church are open to the public. A pull-out on the left allows you to park in front of the church, and stone steps take you over the rock wall lining the grounds.

Just past St. John's, you can turn right on Zion Road and travel 1.8 miles for a side trip to **Zion Church.** This Greek Revival church building with its slave gallery was constructed in 1849 by a group of Scotch-Irish Presbyterians from South Carolina who settled this area. The church cemetery contains the graves of veterans of every war from the Revolutionary War through World War II.

Continue south on TN 243. In 0.8 mile **Hamilton Place** is on the right. It was the 1834 home of Lucius Polk, who became a noted breeder of cattle and horses; the home is named for a fifth brother who died when he was twenty. Polk married Mary Jane Eastin, a niece of Rachel and Andrew Jackson.

Then on the left in another 0.3 mile is the entrance to **Rattle and Snap,** perhaps the grandest antebellum mansion of them all.

Colonel William Polk, a Revolutionary War veteran, became a successful land speculator, even winning a 5,600-acre tract of land in a gambling match with the governor of North Carolina. Similar to dice, the game involved the shaking of dried beans and tossing them with a snap of the fingers, so Polk called his property the Rattle and Snap tract. William was the cousin of Samuel Polk, the father of the president; their fathers, Thomas and Ezekiel, were brothers and early settlers of Tennessee. William Polk divided Rattle and Snap among his four sons, and for his portion, George retained the name. In the 1840s George and his wife, Sally Hilliard, built the mansion that came to be called Rattle and Snap, a monumental Greek Revival home with ten 26-foot Corinthian columns. Commanding a hill at the end of a sweeping drive, the home has been meticulously restored by private owners and is now open to the public.

You can continue southwest on TN 243 for another 3.3 miles to Mt. Pleasant, which has a number of historic homes. On the corner with Main Street, **Lumpy's Malt Shop** serves up malts and shakes from a 1950s soda fountain. To the right of the malt shop is the **Mt. Pleasant/Maury Phosphate Museum.** In the late 1800s phosphate rock was discovered in the Mount Pleasant area and the town boomed with the creation of a dozen or more mining companies. Mount Pleasant became known as the "Phosphate Capital of the World," shipping phosphate rock worldwide. The period of phosphate mining lasted until the mid-1980s.

Natchez Trace

NASHVILLE TO MISSISSIPPI STATE LINE

GENERAL DESCRIPTION: This 136-mile drive follows the approximate route through Tennessee of the old Natchez Trace, which once connected Nashville with Natchez, Mississippi.

SPECIAL ATTRACTIONS: Nashville, Belle Mead Plantation, Warner Parks, Harpeth Scenic River, Natchez Trace Parkway, Leipers Fork, Gordonsburg, Hohenwald, Meriwether Lewis Park, Buffalo River, historic homes and buildings, scenic views, fall color, hiking, biking, boating, fishing, and wildlife viewing.

LOCATION: Middle Tennessee. Begin the drive in downtown Nashville on Broadway.

DRIVE ROUTE NUMBERS: TN 100 and 46, Natchez Trace Parkway, US 412, and TN 20.

CAMPING: Meriwether Lewis Park (no hookups) and David Crockett State Park.

SERVICES: All services at Nashville and Hohenwald.

NEARBY ATTRACTIONS: Laurel Hill Wildlife Management Area and David Crockett State Park.

THE DRIVE

As early as 1785, farmers and merchants of Middle Tennessee and Kentucky transported their products on flatboats down the Cumberland and the Mississippi Rivers for sale at Natchez and New Orleans. Since this was before the advent of steam power, there was no easy way to get the boats back upriver, and so the boats were dismantled and the lumber sold. The way home was then overland by foot or horseback through hundreds of miles of Choctaw and Chickasaw lands. Treaties with these Native Americans in the early 1800s allowed the United States to establish a road through their lands linking Natchez with Nashville. Soon after, the Natchez Trace was designated a post road and the U.S. Army made improvements, widening the track and bridging streams as the trace became a busy thoroughfare.

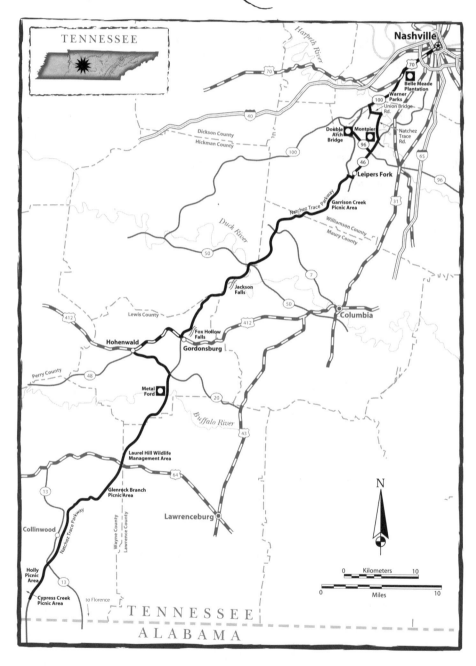

BELLE MEADE

This drive follows the approximate route of the old Natchez Trace, joining the Natchez Trace Parkway, a 442.3-mile national scenic road between Nashville and Natchez, Mississippi. Begin this drive on Broadway Avenue in downtown Nashville. At the corner of Eighth Avenue, the Antebellum Drive heads south while this drive continues west on Broadway. Crossing Ninth Avenue, notice on the left the magnificent **Union Railroad Station,** now the Union Station Hotel, a Richardsonian Romanesque structure built in 1900 by the L & N Railroad; a train shed still stands beside the building.

Broadway first crosses I–40; then, when Broadway bears left at a fork, stay to the right on West End Avenue. In 1.4 miles on the right is **Centennial Park,** which contains the **Parthenon,** built in 1897 for Tennessee's Centennial Exposition. A full-scale exact replica of the fifth-century B.C. Athenian temple in Greece, this massive columned structure incorporates an art museum. The park also contains plenty of open space for walking and picnicking by the park lake.

Continue west, crossing over I–440, which circles the city to the south, and enter the West End neighborhood. In 0.9 mile on the left stands **Montgomery Bell Academy,** endowed by Bell, a wealthy ironmaster during the early 1800s.

The avenue becomes Harding Road, which is also US 70S. It generally follows the route of the Natchez Trace traveling southwest from Nashville. The road enters the Belle Meade neighborhood and, in 2.7 miles, passes in front of **Belle Meade Plantation.** Continue to Leake Avenue and turn left to the entrance for tours that start from the visitor center.

In the 1780s a log cabin was erected on this site by Daniel Dunham, who had been one of John Donelson's party that arrived by river in 1780 to settle what would become Nashville. In 1788 Dunham was killed by Indians, who considered the whites trespassers on their land. His family stayed on, but the Indians burned the cabin in 1790. His son, Daniel A. Dunham, rebuilt the cabin that became known as **Dunham Station,** one of the stops along the Natchez Trace.

Coming from Virginia in 1798, John Harding bought Dunham Station in 1807 and erected an addition on the west side of the cabin with a dogtrot between. By 1816 Harding had established a horse farm where a stallion of Montgomery Bell "stood the season." Sometime after 1819, Harding built a larger federal-style brick home that he called Belle Meade, meaning "beautiful meadow." His son, William Giles Harding, became a noted turfman, breeding and racing horses; at one time the Belle Meade farm had more thoroughbred horses than any other stud farm in the country. William's first wife,

Belle Meade Plantation

Selena, died and in 1840, he married Elizabeth McGavock, the daughter of Randal and Sarah McGavock of Carnton Plantation. William and Elizabeth completed the present Belle Meade in 1853, a Greek Revival mansion incorporating the former house; the portico is supported by six columns of limestone quarried by slaves on the plantation.

During the Civil War, Harding was imprisoned by the Federals for his support of the Confederacy—support that included a half million dollars he donated to the cause. After the war, Harding and General William H. Jackson, a son-in-law who had married a Harding daughter, Selene, revived the plantation and horse farm, which once again became a recognized thoroughbred nursery and stud farm. The entire plantation once contained 5,400 acres. Today, Belle Meade Mansion and the remaining thirty acres of the plantation are owned by the Association for the Preservation of Tennessee Antiquities, which conducts tours. On the grounds stands a huge 1892 carriage house and stable that contains a collection of antique carriages. The grounds also include a smokehouse, creamery, and garden house along with the cabin that was Dunham Station.

WARNER PARKS

In 0.6 mile past Belle Meade, where US 70S forks to the right, stay left on TN 100. In 0.7 mile you can turn left to **Cheekwood Museum of Art and Botanical Gardens,** which occupies the mansion and estate of the Cheek family.

Then along the left is **Warner Parks,** a combination of Percy Warner Park and Edwin Warner Park. In 1926 Percy Warner, chairman of the Nashville Park Board, persuaded his son-in-law, Luke Lea, who had acquired much of the Belle Meade Plantation, to donate an 868-acre tract for a city park. When Warner died the next year, Lea recommended the park be named for his father-in-law. Percy's brother, Edwin, succeeded Percy on the park board and donated funds for the expansion of the park. Miles of trails and one-lane roads wander through the 2,058 acres. In 2.5 miles Old Hickory Boulevard to the left provides access to the park, including the stables and equestrian center where the **Iroquois Steeplechase Track** is located. The track was built in 1941 by the WPA, which also constructed roads, trails, and picnic areas. The track is named for the Belle Meade horse that won the English Derby in 1881.

Just beyond Old Hickory Boulevard, you can turn left to the **Warner Parks Nature Center** with nature exhibits and trail access. This additional section of 623 acres west of Old Hickory is named for Edwin Warner.

As TN 100 leaves Warner Parks, a driveway on the left leads to **Devon Farm,** which unfortunately cannot be seen from the road. This was the house of David Morris Harding, brother of Belle Meade's John Harding. In 1816, David married Fanny, the daughter of John and Dorcus Davis, who originally settled the land in 1795.

NATCHEZ TRACE

Continuing west, the highway enters the countryside. In 0.7 mile cross the **Harpeth Scenic River.** In 2.7 miles the **Loveless Cafe** on the right has been a landmark west of Nashville for more than fifty years; the eatery serves up fried chicken, country ham, southern biscuits, and homemade preserves that draw folks from out of the city. Soon after, TN 100 intersects the **Natchez Trace Parkway.**

You can enter the parkway here at this northern terminus and begin a scenic drive to the southwest. But for a more historic drive, return along TN 100 for 0.4 mile to a turn to the south on Pasquo Road. Curve left on Union Bridge Road as Pasquo continues straight. Enter Williamson County, cross Trace Creek, and in 1.5 miles turn right onto Natchez Trace Road, which follows the government-constructed route along the Harpeth River rather than the traditional trace that traverses Backbone Ridge to the west.

This is one of the most scenic drives in the state and is a popular bicycle route past old homes, rock walls, and historic sites. The Harpeth River is on the left. In 2.3 miles watch for a historical marker for **Old Town** at a crossing of Brown Creek, a tributary of the Harpeth. Look down to the creek on the right to see bridge abutments left from the Natchez Trace. Andrew Jackson's army crossed this bridge on its way south during the War of 1812. This place is called Old Town because it is the site of a Mississippian village, characterized by ceremonial and residential mounds; the remains of some of the mounds can be seen in the field to the right just after the bridge crossing of Brown Creek. The two-story white frame home on the right, past the field, was built by Thomas Brown around 1842; the home is also called Old Town.

In 0.7 mile stay with Natchez Trace Road as it bends to the left where a right fork enters Montpier Farms, a residential development on the old plantation of **Montpier,** the 1822 two-story brick home of Nicholas Bigbee Perkins and his wife, Mary. The old home stands to the right in another 0.3 mile. Perkins gained notoriety in 1807 when he helped capture Aaron Burr, who was on the run from charges of treason for working with the Spanish to set up a new colony in the Southwest, with himself in charge. Perkins, a major in the militia, was given the task of taking Burr to Richmond, Virginia, for trial, where Burr was acquitted. Perkins acquired the 12,000 acres that made up Montpier Plantation after returning to Tennessee.

In 0.6 mile Natchez Trace Road reaches a junction with TN 46 in the community of Forest Home, thought to be named for Confederate cavalry general Nathan Bedford Forrest; Forrest retreated to this community after a raid on Union-occupied Brentwood in 1863. A stone marker at the junction commemorates this route of the Natchez Trace.

Turn right on TN 46. In 0.4 mile you can turn left on Del Rio Pike and travel 0.6 mile to see **Meeting of the Waters** on the left. Named for the confluence of the West Harpeth River with the Harpeth, the home was built in the early 1800s by Thomas Perkins, whose daughter, Mary, married her cousin Nicholas Bigbee Perkins. Mary and Nicholas moved from Montpier to this fine Georgian-style home in 1838 when she inherited the house upon the death of her father.

Return to TN 46 and continue south. In 2 miles, the highway crosses TN 96. You can turn to the right and drive 3.2 miles to where TN 96 intersects with the Natchez Trace Parkway; the scenic highway crosses on the 1,648-

foot long TN 96 **Double-Arch Bridge,** one of only two post-tensioned, segmental concrete arch bridges in the world. Completed in 1995 as this northern end of the parkway was constructed, the bridge has been selected as one of the top engineering projects in the last 125 years.

For this drive, continue south on TN 46, still following the route of the government road built for the Natchez Trace, passing old homes and horse farms for 4.3 miles into the community of **Leipers Fork.** Named for the nearby tributary of the West Harpeth River that in turn was named for Hugh Leiper, an early pioneer surveyor, the community was the home of Thomas Hart Benton, who began his political career here as a state senator. Benton moved to Missouri and in 1821 was elected to the U.S. Senate where he served for thirty years; a grandnephew by the same name became a noted American painter. This was also the home of Dick Poynor, a free African American in the 1800s who was an outstanding wood craftsman known for the chairs he made. The heart of historic Leipers Fork is now a crafts and art center, with shops carrying items varying from flintlock rifles and handcrafted chairs to fine art and interior design.

THE PARKWAY

Through Leipers Fork, TN 46 continues to the south and, in 1.3 miles, turns to the right to intersect with the Natchez Trace Parkway. Get on the Trace and head south. The parkway is a limited access road that provides for leisurely car touring with minimal traffic, passing through hardwood forests and scattered fields with only occasional glimpses of civilization. For the most part, the original Trace followed ridges instead of valleys because the high places were drier, more easily cleared, and had fewer streams to cross.

In 1.8 miles **Garrison Creek Picnic Area** lies on the left. This is also the northern trailhead for the Natchez Trace National Scenic Trail, which parallels the parkway for 25 miles, following some of the original route of the Natchez Trace and ending at TN 50 near the Duck River. Backcountry camping is by special use permit only; contact the Leipers Fork District Office for the parkway.

In another 1.3 miles along the parkway, **Old Trace Picnic Area** on the left gives additional access to the national scenic trail; the segment of trail between Garrison and Old Trace is the longest remaining section of the original Trace in Tennessee.

In 0.9 mile the **Burns Branch Picnic Area** on the left also gives access to the national scenic trail. It's approximately in this area that the government road passing through Old Town and Leipers Fork joined the traditional route

View from Natchez Trace Parkway

as it ascends Duck River Ridge. In 1.5 miles the parkway tops the ridge at the **Tennessee Valley Divide.** Duck River Ridge is part of a long ridge dividing Middle Tennessee east to west; streams to the south flow into the Duck and Tennessee Rivers while water to the north flows into the Cumberland River. This divide once marked the boundary of Chickasaw lands to the south.

Continue south on the parkway, passing into Maury County. In 8.2 miles TN 7 leads to Columbia to the east. In another 3.9 miles a side road left off the parkway leads to **Water Valley Overlook** with a view to the east.

In 4.0 miles the parkway intersects TN 50. A parking area and trailhead just to the west is the southern terminus of the Natchez Trace National Scenic Trail. Just beyond the junction lies the **Gordon House Historic Site** on the left. In 1802 John Gordon reached an agreement with Chickasaw Chief George Colbert to establish a trading post and ferry here on the Duck River. Gordon was also a scout and military man and so accompanied Andrew Jackson on several expeditions. While Gordon was away, his wife, Dorathea, saw to the construction of the two-story brick home that still stands. Gordon died soon after the house was completed in 1818, but Dorathea continued to live here until her death in 1859. A quarter-mile trail leads from the house to the Duck River where Gordon's ferry operated. While smaller streams could be easily bridged, rivers required ferries to transport travelers to the other side.

Beyond the Gordon House, the parkway crosses the Duck River. In 2.8 miles **Baker Bluff Overlook** on the left offers a view east across the valley of the Duck River. In 0.4 mile parking on the left gives access to a steep, quarter-mile path that leads to the base of **Jackson Falls** on Jackson Branch, a tributary of the Duck River named for Andrew Jackson; the two-step waterfall makes a right-angle turn as it skips 50 feet down the bluff.

In 1 mile south on the parkway, a pull-out on the left gives access to a 2,000-foot-long segment of the **Old Trace.** Along the parkway, signs direct you to remaining sections of the original Natchez Trace.

In 0.6 mile pass a road emerging on the left. In another 1.7 miles an old tobacco barn stands on the left, remaining from an early 1900s tobacco farm; these old barns have plenty of space between the wallboards to allow air to dry the tobacco that is hung from rafters in the barn. A narrow gravel road behind the barn is the beginning of a 2-mile drive along a section of the original Trace, emerging on the parkway at the road you just passed.

In 1.2 miles, at **Sheboss Place** on the left, another inn, or "stand," stood on the trace, run by the widow Cranfield. Her second husband, a Native American, spoke little English, and when asked about lodging, he would point to his wife and say, "She boss."

The parkway passes into Lewis County. Then in 7.7 miles **Swan View Overlook** on the right offers a view of forested hills across the valley of Big Swan Creek. In another 0.5 mile parking on the left gives access to a quarter-mile trail that descends steeply to the bottom of 25-foot **Fall Hollow Falls.**

GORDONSBURG AND HOHENWALD

The parkway crosses Big Swan Creek and in 0.8 mile reaches an exit for US 412. Leave the parkway here. On US 412, first head east into Gordonsburg; in 1.6 miles the **Gordonsburg Farm Market** on the right offers Tennessee crafts and produce. In another 0.6 mile the **Blackburn Farmstead and Pioneer Museum** lies on the left. Around 1806 Capt. Ambrose Blackburn, a Revolutionary War veteran, built the home here along with several outbuildings; now covered in weatherboard, the house was originally a log cabin. His son, John Porter Blackburn, who served with Andrew Jackson in the War of 1812, became an influential person, and when the county was formed, the county court met in the Blackburn house. Needing a secluded place to deliberate, the court jury would gather in the corn crib. Ambrose Blackburn is buried on the property. John Blackburn later moved to Texas.

Return west along US 412 and pass under the Natchez Trace Parkway to continue west 7.8 miles to Hohenwald, a railroad town settled by Germans and Swiss. On the left in the center of town stands the **Hohenwald Depot,** built in 1896; this region was the site of iron and phosphate mines, and railroads were a necessary link in the transportation of products out of the area. The depot now contains the chamber of commerce. Adjacent to the depot is the **Lewis County Museum of Natural History.**

GRINDER'S INN AND THE PARKWAY

Just beyond the depot, US 412 reaches a junction with TN 48. Turn left, and in 0.4 mile bear left on TN 20. In 5.9 miles turn left to get back on the Natchez Trace Parkway that's just ahead. In 0.1 mile you'll turn right to the parkway, but first stay straight into **Meriwether Lewis Park** with picnic areas, a campground, and hiking trails. Stay straight to the reconstructed **Grinder's Inn.** Here on the night of October 10, 1809, gunshots took the life of Meriwether Lewis, the famed explorer of the 1804–06 Lewis and Clark Expedition that investigated the then little-known western part of North America. President Jefferson and the U.S. Congress named Lewis governor of the Louisiana Territory as a reward for his successful expedition. In 1809 Lewis set out from St. Louis to head back east to Washington, D.C., traveling at first by river. He and his party disembarked at Fort Pickering, which was located at present-day Memphis, and continued traveling east. Lewis and his group next intersected the Natchez Trace and headed northeast, stopping at this stand operated by Robert Grinder. During the night two shots were heard, and Lewis was found wounded in the head and chest. He said to his slave, John Pernier, "I have done the business, my good Servant; give me some water." He died on October 11. Lewis had had bouts of depression throughout his life and seemed especially restless the evening of October 10; so it is thought he committed suicide. He was buried in the nearby cemetery. In 1848 the state erected over his grave a monument resembling a broken shaft, symbolizing an untimely end.

Return from Grinder's Inn and turn left to get back on the Natchez Trace Parkway and continue to the south. In 2.5 miles cross a bridge over the Buffalo River, and soon after, turn right to **Metal Ford** where the Trace made a shallow river crossing; travelers noting the stone river bottom said the crossing reminded them of stone-covered roadways, which they referred to as "metaled." A short walk leads along the scenic river and returns by way of a mill race that was once part of an ironworks that was located here; a charcoal-burning furnace was used to manufacture pig iron. Metal Ford is a major put-in on the Buffalo River for canoeists.

One mile farther south on the parkway, a pull-out on the right lies adjacent to **Napier Mine,** an open-pit mine where iron ore was dug from the ground to supply an iron-making operation begun by John Catron in the early 1800s; Catron was later an associate justice of the U.S. Supreme Court. The Napiers took over the operations and in the 1890s had a huge blast furnace located nearby. The ironworks continued here until 1923.

The parkway continues south for 4 miles to **Jacks Branch Picnic Area** on the left, where steep steps lead down beside the shaded creek. In 0.2 mile pass an exit onto gravel roads, and in 1.8 miles reach **Old Trace Drive** to the left, a narrow 2.5-mile one-way gravel road that follows a section of the Old Trace and emerges back on the parkway at the exit you just passed.

In 3.9 miles, as the parkway passes through a corner of Lawrence County, Brush Creek Road to the left leads 1.7 miles to **Laurel Hill Wildlife Management Area** on the left, which contains fishing lakes and picnic areas.

In another 2.8 miles, entering Wayne County, the parkway intersects US 64, which leads east 14.5 miles to **David Crockett State Park,** which has camping. In 0.7 mile farther, an interpretive site on the right tells about **Dogwood Mudhole,** where the Trace traveled through a dogwood-covered depression that became virtually impassable after heavy rains as wagons mired in the mud.

In 2.8 miles at **Glenrock Branch Picnic Area,** a path leads down to a stream with a balanced rock atop a rock ledge. In 0.8 mile cross Sweetwater Branch and in another 0.7 mile a pull-out on the right gives access to the Sweetwater Branch Nature Trail, which wanders through the forest along the small stream.

In 10.1 miles the parkway passes on the right the site of **McGlamery Stand,** an inn established by John McGlamery in 1849; it only lasted until the Civil War but the nearby community took the name.

In 2.4 miles farther south is an interpretive site for the **Sunken Trace.** The old Natchez Trace was often muddy in places, and so people would go around the mud holes, creating new paths. Here, three separate paths were created by travelers avoiding muddy ruts.

Then in 4.3 miles the **Holly Picnic Area** lies on the right on Cypress Creek. The **Cypress Creek Picnic Area** also lies on the right in another 2.7 miles. Then in 1.7 miles the parkway crosses the state line into Alabama. From here you can continue on the Natchez Trace Parkway, crossing the northwest corner of Alabama and entering Mississippi to reach Natchez in another 342 miles.

23

cumberland River

NASHVILLE TO LAND BETWEEN THE LAKES

GENERAL DESCRIPTION: A 110-mile drive travels along the Cumberland River, passing historic Clarksville and ending at Land Between the Lakes National Recreation Area.

SPECIAL ATTRACTIONS: Cumberland River, Harpeth Scenic River, Ashland City, Cheatham Lake, Clarksville, Dover, Fort Donelson National Battlefield, Land Between the Lakes, historic homes and buildings, scenic views, fall color, hiking, biking, fishing, hunting, boating, and wildlife viewing.

LOCATION: Northwest Middle Tennessee. Begin the drive from exit 201 on I-40 west of Nashville.

DRIVE ROUTE NUMBERS: TN 251, 249, and 12, US 41A Bypass and 79, and the Trace.

CAMPING: Harpeth River Bridge Campground (no hookups), Cheatham Lake Campground, Land Between the Lakes National Recreation Area, and Paris Landing State Park.

SERVICES: All services at Ashland City, Clarksville, and Paris.

NEARBY ATTRACTIONS: Confluence of the Harpeth, Dunbar Cave State Natural Area, the Post House, Cross Creeks National Wildlife Refuge, Tennessee National Wildlife Refuge, and Paris.

THE DRIVE

On its way west, the Cumberland River dips into Tennessee to pass north of Nashville. It then heads northwest to Clarksville and reenters Kentucky before joining the Ohio River, nearly adjacent to where the Tennessee River also joins the Ohio. The strip of land between the two rivers is now a national recreation area called Land Between the Lakes because the rivers are dammed to create Lake Barkley on the Cumberland and Kentucky Lake on the Tennessee. Between Nashville and Land Between the Lakes, the Cumberland River flows through a countryside of small farms and small towns on Tennessee back roads.

CUMBERLAND RIVER

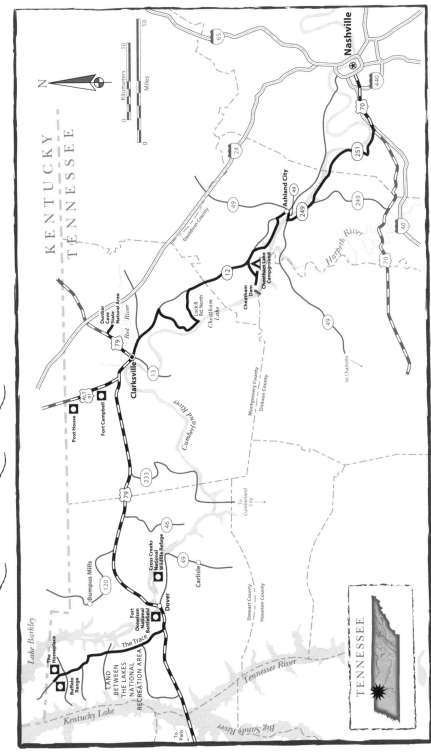

CHEATHAM LAKE

Begin the drive west of Nashville from I–40. Take Exit 201 onto US 70 (this is also the beginning of the Civil War Railroad and the Iron Industry drive). In 0.3 mile River Road branches off to the right, but stay straight here on US 70 to avoid an industrial area. In 1.3 miles at a junction with TN 251, turn right. In 0.4 mile at a junction with Old Charlotte Pike, turn left, and in a few yards turn right on River Road Pike, which is the continuation of TN 251. In 1.1 miles River Road joins from the right. River Road winds through forests and fields and passes occasional houses while paralleling the **Cumberland River** to the northeast. The river is at a distance still, but bluffs on the far side of the river are occasionally visible.

In 11.4 miles leave Davidson County and enter Cheatham County. Soon the river is visible on the right. Here it is wide and deep because it is part of **Cheatham Lake,** backed up by the Army Corps of Engineers Cheatham Dam farther downstream. In 3.4 miles TN 251 leads straight ahead into TN 249, which joins the road from the left.

Cheatham Dam

In another 0.9 mile **Brush Creek Recreation Area** lies on the right, just after the road crosses Brush Creek. This recreation area at the edge of Cheatham Lake has a boat launch, picnic area, and fishing.

Continue northwest on TN 249. Fields lead down to the river, where cattle graze at the river's edge. Ahead, you can see a bridge crossing of the Cumberland River on TN 49, which will be the route to Ashland City. The road veers away from the river to climb over a ridge and descend to a junction with TN 49 in 2.7 miles.

The drive turns right here, but you can turn left for a side trip to the confluence of the Harpeth Scenic River. In 1.3 miles a sharp right turn leads to **Bluff Creek Launching Ramp** in the Hudgen's Slough area of Tennessee's **Cheatham Lake Wildlife Management Area.** This 5,000-acre stretch of land on both sides of Cheatham Lake is administered by the Tennessee Wildlife Resources Agency (to the southwest there is another 20,000 acres in **Cheatham Wildlife Management Area).** The one-lane, tree-shrouded road to the launching ramp dips along the Bluff Creek embayment, which is frequented by waterfowl, especially in winter; herons stand along the creek bank and ducks paddle out onto Cheatham Lake. There are picnic spots along the road, which ends at the boat ramp.

After Bluff Creek, TN 49 reaches **Harpeth River Bridge Campground** on the right in 2.5 miles. The campground (no hookups) sits at the edge of the Harpeth Scenic River just below the Montgomery Bell Bridge crossing of the river. TN 49 then crosses the bridge.

In 0.8 mile turn right up Dozier Boat Dock Road. In 1 mile the road ends at **Pardue Recreation Area,** which sits at the confluence of the Harpeth Scenic River. The recreation area has a boat ramp and picnic tables. Across the Harpeth, **Indian Town Bluff** stands on the point of land between the two rivers; mounds and graves are evidence of an ancient Mississippian Indian occupation. This is also the site of a 1710 battle between the Shawnees and the Chickasaws. The Chickasaws had joined the Cherokees in driving the Shawnees and their French allies out of Tennessee. Most had left by then, but a straggling Shawnee band was defeated here in a last battle. The Shawnees thereafter lived to the north along the Ohio River and its tributaries.

Return to the junction of TN 249 and continue on TN 49 to cross the highway bridge over the Cumberland River and enter Ashland City at a junction with TN 12 in 1 mile. Directly across the street stands the **Cheatham County Courthouse.** A newer addition in front was built in 1914, but walk or drive around the square to see the original courthouse attached in back; it was constructed in 1869. The drive continues left on TN

12, but a right turn on TN 12 will take you through town a block and a half to **Stratton's Restaurant and Soda Shop;** this establishment has been serving old-fashioned milk shakes and hamburgers since 1954.

Turn west on TN 12 to continue the drive along the Cumberland River, now on the northeast side of the waterway. In 1 mile turn left on Chapmansboro Road just after crossing Marks Creek. An old railroad trestle stands to the left and just beyond is a parking area on the right for the **Cumberland River Bicentennial Trail.** This rail-to-trail project has converted the old railbed of the Tennessee Central route from Nashville to Clarksville into a trail for hikers and bicyclists. Currently the trail runs from this Marks Creek Trailhead 4 miles northwest to another trailhead on Chapmansboro Road, passing rock bluffs, skirting wetlands, and crossing Sycamore Creek on an old railroad trestle.

Continue on Chapmansboro Road, which curves right to parallel the Cumberland River downstream with nice views of the placid river. In 3.1 miles the road reaches **Sycamore Creek Recreation Area,** which sits on the embayment of Sycamore Creek. It has picnic tables and boat access down the creek to Cheatham Lake. The road crosses Sycamore Creek on a high bridge. Immediately on the other side, turn right to stay on Chapmansboro Road. In 1 mile the Cumberland River Bicentennial Trail emerges on the right at a trailhead in the Dyson Ditch area of the Cheatham Wildlife Management Area. The trail will eventually continue across the road and travel all the way to Cheatham Dam.

In 1.1 miles Chapmansboro Road rejoins TN 12. Turn left to the small community of Cheap Hill in 0.6 mile. Here you can turn left on Cheatham Dam Road to Cheatham Dam, descending to the river in 2.8 miles. At a junction with a road along the river, **Cheatham Lake Campground** lies to the left. Boat access to the lake is also here. A right turn along the river leads 1.5 miles to **Cheatham Lock and Dam,** an Army Corps of Engineers project. The low dam stretches across the river, creating Cheatham Lake, an impoundment that stretches all the way back to Nashville. Below the dam is the beginning of Lake Barkley, created by Barkley Dam on the Cumberland River in Kentucky. Beyond the dam is a picnic shelter and playground and, at the end of the road, a boat ramp for river access below the dam.

Return to Cheap Hill and turn left on TN 12 to continue the drive. At the corner stands the **Pardue House,** a large, two-story, white frame house that was constructed around 1840; white fences roam across rolling fields. The old estate settled by Littleton John and Martha Ann Pardue is now a horse farm with gamboling horse statuary at the entrance gate.

In 5.9 miles TN 12 passes through the community of Henrietta where Pat Head Summit played girls' high school basketball. As women's basketball coach at the University of Tennessee, Summit has guided her teams to several national titles and is the winningest coach in women's college basketball. TN 12 from Henrietta to Clarksville is the Pat Head Summit Highway. After Henrietta, the highway enters Montgomery County.

In another 2 miles turn left on Lock B Road North in the community of Fredonia. At a junction soon after, turn left and then immediately turn right to stay on Lock B Road, which passes through the community of Hickory Point, which contains the Holt Dairy Farm on the right. The road then descends to the river at **Holt Landing** in 4 miles, a boat ramp here gives access to the Cumberland River. The road bears right along the river for a short scenic drive. Watch for concrete walls on the far bank; these are the remains of the old Lock B. On the right, the remains of a railroad trestle can be seen; it was part of the old Tennessee Central route. The road becomes Gholson Road as it turns away from the river and climbs back out of the river valley past small farms with a number of silos. In 4.6 miles **Bethlehem United Methodist Church** stands on the left; it was built in 1899 in a Gothic style used by the Methodists around the turn of the century.

CLARKSVILLE

At a junction with Hickory Point Road in 1.7 miles, turn left a short distance to reconnect with TN 12. Turn left and travel 2.1 miles to a junction with the US 41A/TN 12 Bypass at Clarksville. Turn left to circle south around the city, passing between concrete piers that once supported a Tennessee Central railroad trestle over the highway.

In 4.3 miles the highway becomes Riverside Drive as it joins the Cumberland River to bypass Clarksville. On the west side of the city, the drive passes under an L & N Railroad overpass that bridges the Cumberland River to the left; the stone piers of this bridge were constructed in 1859. At Commerce Street in 1.4 miles, turn right to enter Clarksville, which occupies the hill at the confluence of the Red River with the Cumberland. The city was founded in 1784 and named for George Rogers Clark, a general in the Revolutionary War and a brother of William Clark, who with Meriwether Lewis explored the western part of the continent in the Lewis and Clark Expedition of 1803.

Stop in at the **Clarksville-Montgomery County Museum** at the corner of Commerce and Second Street. The museum is housed in a grand building with Italianate ornamentation and a slate roof. Constructed in 1889, it was originally a U.S. Post Office and Customs House. From the museum, walking and driving tours wander through the historic town that includes the 1878 **Montgomery County Courthouse** on Public Square; many of the buildings of the downtown were constructed after an 1870 fire destroyed many original structures. At the corner of Commerce and Tenth Streets sits the **L & N Train Station,** built in 1890 and recently renovated; the nearby railroad still carries freight but no passengers.

While in Clarksville, you can take a side trip to **Dunbar Cave State Natural Area.** Take Second Street to the north to intersect with College Street and turn right. **Austin Peay State University** stands to the left; this liberal arts college grew from Austin Peay Normal School, founded in 1929 and named for a Tennessee governor. College Street becomes US 79N and soon crosses the Red River; this stretch of US 79 is also called Wilma Rudolph Boulevard, named for the three-time gold medalist runner in the 1960 Olympics whose home was Clarksville. In 1 mile, turn right on Dunbar Cave Road and drive another 1.2 miles to the Dunbar Cave State Natural Area.

Dunbar Cave was a mineral springs resort around the turn of the century; the visitor center is housed in the restored swimming pool bathhouse. Country music star Roy Acuff purchased the property in 1948 and continued a tradition of weekend dances here. He also broadcast a country music radio show from the area. Dunbar Cave was designated a state natural area in 1973. Trails loop through the property, passing Swan Lake and leading to the cave. Rockwork, railings, and platforms at the cave entrance remain from the resort days. Ranger-led tours of the cave are available but are limited, so call ahead for reservations.

Return to Riverside Drive and continue along the Cumberland River. At **McGregor Park,** the paved **Cumberland Riverwalk** offers a stroll along the river. Picnic areas and a boat ramp are available here. The **Cumberland River Center,** also at this site, houses displays about the history of the river.

At a junction of US 41A Bypass and US 79, bear left as the two highways merge. Cross a bridge over the Red River and turn left on B Street for a short trip to **Fort Defiance.** At an intersection, turn left on Walker Street. On the right is **Sevier Station,** a stone building that's the oldest structure in the county, built in 1792 by Valentine Sevier, a brother of John Sevier, Tennessee's first governor. At a junction with A Street, turn left to Fort Defiance on the right. This site contains some of the best preserved Civil War earthworks in the state. The fort was constructed by Confederate forces and slaves; it overlooks the confluence of the Cumberland and Red Rivers. Following the

Union capture of Forts Henry and Donelson to the west in 1862, the Confederates abandoned the fort without a battle.

Return to US 79/41A, and continue to the northwest. At a junction where the highways separate in 0.6 mile, the scenic drive follows US 79 to the left, but you can stay straight on US 41A for a side trip to historic sites. In 3.3 miles you can turn right on Old Mill Road down to Ringgold Creek and the waterpowered **Ringgold Mill,** a large white building. This is the third mill at this location. The present mill, built in 1874, continued operation, grinding grain, until 1971. The dam on the creek was built in 1859.

Continuing north, US 41A crosses Ringgold Creek. To the left is **Fort Campbell,** a 105,000-acre U.S. Army installation that is the home of the 101st Airborne Division, the only air assault division in the army. The history of the "Screaming Eagles" is told at the **Don F. Pratt Memorial Museum** located on the army base.

In 2.0 miles **Patriots Park** lies in the median of the four-lane highway and contains **Bethel United Methodist Church** and the **Post House.** The Bethel Meeting House, a log structure built in 1812, once stood where the present church now stands. It is said that after a Sunday sermon preached at the Meeting House, Tennessee's famous Bell Witch could be heard repeating the sermon word for word at supper that evening. The log structure was later replaced by a frame construction that burned; the church was then reconstructed, using slave labor, as a brick building. At the front of the church, the older brick structure on the right is easily distinguished from later additions.

The Post House, a small brick building constructed in 1830, served as a relief station along the stagecoach route between Nashville and Hopkinsville, Kentucky; here the coach horses were changed. Since these coaches carried the U.S. mail, such roads were known as "Post Roads," and so the name Post House was given to this resting spot. Now fully renovated, the building houses a U.S. Post Office and tourist information center and serves as a bus stop for Clarksville Transit System.

Return to US 79 and turn west. In 2 miles a left turn leads to **Smiths Landing Launch Site** on the Cumberland River. In another 5.3 miles pass through the small community of Woodlawn. Then on the left in 1.9 miles, TN 233 gives access to the **River Bend Launching Area.**

Continuing west, the highway borders the vast Fort Campbell compound to the north; while farmland and houses lie to the left, virtually unbroken forest stands to the right. In 1.4 miles pass through the small community of Oakwood, and in another 3.1 miles enter Stewart County.

Cumberland River

DOVER AND FORT DONELSON

Continue straight on US 79 another 13.1 miles, passing through farmland and eventually paralleling Dover Creek, a tributary of the Cumberland. The **Dover Creek Recreation Area** lies just to the left as the highway approaches the Cumberland River and crosses on a bridge into the community of Dover.

At a junction with TN 49 in Dover, turn left on TN 49 (this is also called Spring Street), and turn left again on Petty Street to **Dover Hotel,** also called Surrender House. Here Confederate Gen. Simon B. Buckner surrendered his forces to Union Gen. Ulysses S. Grant after the fall of Fort Donelson.

At the beginning of the Civil War, with Tennessee siding with the Confederacy and Kentucky remaining in the Union, it was inevitable that Tennessee, as a border state, would become a major battleground. More battles were fought in Tennessee than in any other state except Virginia.

The Confederates desperately needed to hold West Tennessee, otherwise Nashville and the railroads in Middle Tennessee used to transport troops and supplies would be exposed. And if Tennessee were lost, the Confederate forces would have to withdraw to Mississippi, Alabama, and Georgia.

Any invasion of West Tennessee would occur up the two rivers that flowed from Tennessee into Kentucky—the Cumberland and the Tennessee. The Confederates quickly moved to fortify these rivers just below the Tennessee-Kentucky border. Fort Henry was constructed on the east side of the Tennessee River, and Fort Donelson was built on the west bank of the Cumberland.

The invasion occurred in February 1862 under the command of Flag Officer Andrew H. Foote and Brig. Gen. Ulysses S. Grant. Union ironclad gunboats under Foote's direction sailed down the Tennessee River while Grant's men marched south; the two would converge in an attack on Fort Henry. On February 6, the Union gunboats opened fire on the fort. After more than an hour of battle, Confederate Brig. Gen. Lloyd Tilghman realized he could not hold the fort with Union troops approaching. He ordered most of his men—nearly 2,500—to withdraw to Fort Donelson. Tilghman remained behind with less than one hundred men. He allowed his army time to get away and then surrendered.

With Fort Henry in Union control, Foote and Grant turned their attention to Fort Donelson. By February 13, Union troops surrounded the fort, and on the morning of February 14, Union gunboats on the Cumberland began a bombardment. The Confederates had a stronger position at Fort Donelson with entrenchments and earthworks stretching all the way to

Dover. The fort's eleven big guns pounded the Union fleet, causing them to retreat. The Confederates, however, were hemmed in by Grant's forces, who continued to receive reinforcements. Needing to act quickly before the situation was hopeless, the Confederates attacked the Union right on February 15 in an effort to open a passageway for retreat to Nashville. At first the Federals were pushed back, but confusion among the Confederate generals resulted in an order for the Confederate troops to pull back to their entrenchments. Grant took advantage of the indecision and counterattacked, once more encircling the fort. With their position untenable, Confederate generals John Floyd and Gideon Pillow managed to slip away with 2,000 men, retreating toward Nashville. Col. Nathan Bedford Forrest refused to surrender and also escaped with his cavalry regiment, fording Lick Creek to the southeast of Dover. On the morning of February 16 Brig. Gen. Simon B. Buckner was left to surrender the 13,000 Confederate troops that remained.

The Dover Hotel had served as Buckner's headquarters, and it was from here that he asked for Grant's terms of surrender. Grant replied, "No terms except an unconditional and immediate surrender can be accepted," which is how the general came to be called "Unconditional Surrender" Grant. The two-story, white frame Dover Hotel, built around 1852 and restored to its appearance at the time of the surrender, sits on the bank high above the Cumberland River.

On TN 49, you can take a side trip south to **Cross Creeks National Wildlife Refuge.** Leaving Dover, the highway crosses Lick Creek in 0.9 mile. In another 1.3 miles turn left on Wildlife Road to enter the wildlife refuge; at the visitor center on the left, you can get information about the 8,862-acre refuge that stretches for 12 miles along the Cumberland River. It provides feeding and resting habitat for migrating waterfowl, wintering ducks, and geese that stop off here in the thousands.

Back to TN 49, you can continue another 2.7 miles to see the **Bear Spring Furnace.** An iron industry once thrived in Stewart County, and in this spot Joseph and Robert Woods and Thomas Yeatman built the first furnace. The iron produced was shipped by rail line along the route of the present highway. The furnace was destroyed by Union troops during the Civil War. The existing structure was built in 1873 and operated until 1901.

Back in Dover, continue west on US 79 and turn right on Church Street. The **Rice House** on the left was the headquarters for Confederate General Gideon Pillow during the Fort Donelson battle. In 0.3 mile turn right into the **Fort Donelson National Cemetery** where 655 Union soldiers who fell at the battle of Fort Donelson are buried. Beside the cemetery, Crow Lane leads to a restored Civil War-era plantation house that is now the **Riverfront Plantation Inn.**

Continue on Church Street to reemerge on US 79 and turn right, continuing west. In 0.7 mile turn right into the **Fort Donelson National Battlefield** where you can take a 3-mile driving tour of the battlefield, passing by the earthworks of the fort and reaching the river batteries where the Confederates had a commanding view of the river as they pounded the Union gunboats. With the fall of Fort Donelson, the Confederate line of defense across the South was broken, and the heartland was open to Union invasion. Two attempts were made in 1862 and 1863 to retake the area, but both failed. The second attempt, led by Confederate General Joseph Wheeler, resulted in the Battle of Dover in which most of the town's buildings were burned.

LAND BETWEEN THE LAKES

From Fort Donelson, continue west on US 79 for 1.4 miles and turn right on the Trace and, in 2.9 miles, enter **Land Between the Lakes National Recreation Area.** This area encompasses 170,000 acres with 300 miles of undeveloped shoreline between the Tennessee Valley Authority's Kentucky Lake on the Tennessee River and the Army Corps of Engineers' Lake Barkley on the Cumberland River. The lakes are created by TVA's Kentucky Dam on the Tennessee and the Corps' Barkley Dam on the Cumberland, both across the state line in Kentucky near where both rivers flow into the Ohio. TVA established Land Between the Lakes, but recently management was transferred the U.S. Forest Service. Camping, hiking, backpacking, horseback riding, hunting, and fishing are the primary activities.

Upon entering Land Between the Lakes, at the **South Entrance Station,** you can turn left on Fort Henry Road that leads 7.8 miles to **Piney Campground.** Two miles before the campground is a right turn that leads 1.4 miles to **Boswell Landing Lake Access** to Kentucky Lake. At 0.3 mile down that road, where the road curves right downhill toward Kentucky Lake, stay straight on a gravel road for access to the **Fort Henry Hiking Trails.** These trails wander over the vicinity of Fort Henry, the Confederate fort that was the first defense against the Union invasion along the Tennessee River. The site of the fort is now under the water of Kentucky Lake.

From the intersection at the South Entrance Station, the Trace continues north in the recreation area, with side roads leading to lake access on either side. In 9.2 miles the **Great Western Iron Furnace** stands on the right, constructed in 1854 of limestone blocks by Brian, Newell and Co. The furnace was loaded with iron ore, charcoal, and limestone. The charcoal was ignited, and as it burned, the limestone combined with impurities and molten iron flowed out into sand molds. The iron solidified into crude casts called "pigs" because they resembled baby pigs lying side by side suckling a mother sow, thus the term "pig iron." The furnace ceased operation in 1854 because of a depletion of iron ore and a revolt by the slave laborers.

Beyond the furnace, the Trace passes the **Buffalo Range** where a herd of American bison range across pastures. Commonly called "buffalo," the American bison population was reduced from millions to only a few hundred by the turn of the twentieth century. Conservation efforts have saved the animal from extinction. The Trace then reaches **The Homeplace,** a living history museum depicting an 1850 farmstead. Historic houses, barns, and cribs were brought from other locations and rebuilt on-site. Start your tour at the interpretive center where admission is purchased.

Beyond the Homeplace, this scenic drive ends in 2.4 miles at **Cedar Pond Picnic Area,** where picnic tables nestle among trees at the edge of Cedar Pond. You can continue north on the Trace to explore the Kentucky portion of Land Between the Lakes or return along the Trace to US 79.

The Homeplace

PARIS

You can take a side trip to the community of Paris by continuing west on US 79, crossing the Tennessee River to **Paris Landing State Park** in 5.4 miles; the state park has a marina, fishing piers, campground, inn/restaurant, and a picnic area on the shore of Kentucky Lake. The **Tennessee National Wildlife Refuge** stretches south along the Tennessee River. In 5.9 miles you can turn left to the **Big Sandy Unit** of the refuge. In 3.6 miles turn left on Elkhorn Road, and where Elkhorn turns right, stay straight on a dead-end road. In 0.5 mile, where the road curves to the left, stay straight onto a side road that soon becomes a single lane. In another 0.5 mile the road enters the wildlife refuge and reaches a junction with a gravel road; turn left to an observation platform that overlooks the Big Sandy River, a tributary of the Tennessee. Waterfowl and shorebirds congregate: sandpipers, terns, herons, several duck species, and maybe even a white pelican or an American avocet.

Another 10.7 mile along US 79 is Paris, a historic railroad town. In the 1850s, railroads were constructed connecting Memphis to the west with Louisville to the north, passing through Paris; after the Civil War, the L & N Railroad took control of the lines and in 1898 established a division yard here that contained machine shops and roundhouses where locomotives were repaired. On Poplar Street, visit the **Paris-Henry County Heritage Center,** a museum located in the 1914 yellow-brick Renaissance Revival mansion of O. C. Barton; the mansion is part of the **North Poplar Street Historic District** containing the large homes built by professionals and businessmen, including the railroad executives. The last full week in April, Paris holds the World's Biggest Fish Fry. The annual event includes pageants and parades, in addition to fish dinners in which six tons of catfish are cooked and served. Paris even has its own 65-foot Eiffel Tower in Memorial Park.

Civil War Railroad and the Iron Industry

NASHVILLE TO PARKERS CROSSROADS

GENERAL DESCRIPTION: This 176-mile drive follows the route of the Nashville and Northwestern Railroad constructed during the Civil War for transporting supplies from the Tennessee River to Nashville.

SPECIAL ATTRACTIONS: Newsome's Mill, Kingston Springs, Mound Bottom, Narrows of the Harpeth State Historic Area, Harpeth Scenic River, Montgomery Bell State Park, Dickson, Charlotte, Cumberland Furnace, McEwen, Johnsonville State Historic Area, Waverly, Camden, Nathan Bedford Forrest State Park, Huntingdon, Parkers Crossroads, historic homes and buildings, scenic views, fall color, hiking, biking, boating, fishing, hunting, and wildlife viewing.

LOCATION: Middle Tennessee. Begin the drive from Exit 201 on I-40 west of Nashville.

DRIVE ROUTE NUMBERS: US 70; and TN 46, 48, and 22.

CAMPING: Montgomery Bell State Park, Loretta Lynn's Ranch, and Nathan Bedford Forrest State Park.

SERVICES: All services at Nashville, Dickson, Waverly, Camden, and Huntingdon.

NEARBY ATTRACTIONS: Enochs's Farm, Loretta Lynn's Ranch, Duck River Unit of the Tennessee National Wildlife Refuge, Patsy Cline Memorial, and McKenzie Depot.

THE DRIVE

The Nashville and Northwestern Railroad was intended to link Nashville with the Mississippi River at Hickman, Kentucky. But only a segment from Nashville to Kingston Springs had been constructed east of the Tennessee River by the time Union troops occupied Nashville following the fall of Fort Donelson. Since rivers and railroads were the key routes for transporting troops and supplies during the Civil War, the decision was made to extend the rail line west from Kingston Springs to the Tennessee River at

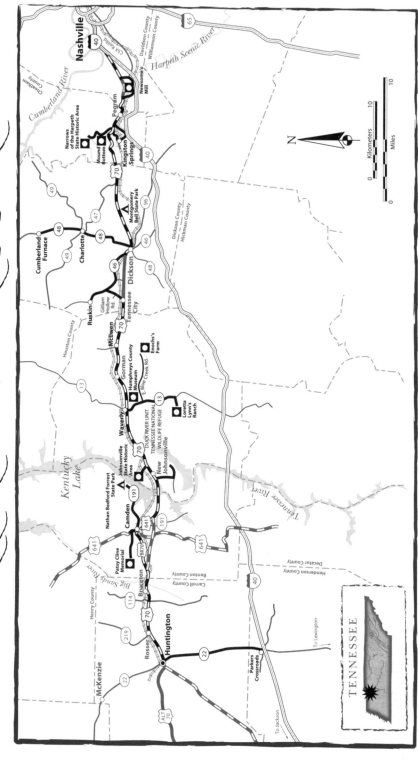

Johnsonville. Supplies could then be brought down the Tennessee River from Kentucky to Johnsonville and shipped overland by train to Nashville and then, by other railroads, farther into the South to support the invading Union forces that would soon fight at Shiloh, Stones River, and Chattanooga.

African Americans who had fled to Nashville to seek protection under the occupying Union forces were conscripted to build the rail line. In addition to miles of track, they constructed trestles and bridges with accompanying blockhouses and earthen fortifications to protect these vulnerable links along the route. When they had completed the construction of the rail line, the African-American laborers formed the infantry regiments that guarded the railroad at strategic positions along the route.

HARPETH SCENIC RIVER

US 70 west from Nashville generally parallels the route of the Nashville and Northwestern Railroad, now the CSX Railroad. Begin the drive at Exit 201 off I–40 west of Nashville, exiting onto US 70 (this is also the beginning of the Cumberland River Drive). The road travels over a forested ridge. In 6.1 miles turn left on Newsome Station Road. In 0.8 mile the road curves right and descends into bottomlands along the **Harpeth Scenic River,** a tributary of the Cumberland. Cross a bridge over the river and glance to the left to see the ruins of **Newsome's Mill.** The road curves left after the bridge and reaches a junction where Newsome Station Road turns right to pass under a low railroad overpass. Stay straight to parking for Newsome's Mill, constructed in 1862 by Joseph M. Newsome. The interior of this stone mill consisted of walnut and poplar beams supporting the milling machinery, which was powered by a side-shot waterwheel and used to grind wheat and corn to produce flour and cornmeal. The mill was the center of a bustling community beside the tracks of the Nashville and Northwestern Railroad. In 1905 James B. Ezell bought the mill and replaced the waterwheel with turbines that more efficiently used the waterpower. In 1960 the roof and the interior of the old mill burned.

Return to Newsome Station Road and turn left under the railroad overpass of the CSX Railroad, which occupies the old right-of-way of the Nashville and Northwestern. This is a short overpass, only 9 feet high. If your vehicle will not go under this overpass, return the way you came to US 70 and turn left to continue west on this drive.

Under the overpass along Newsome Station Road in 2.2 miles, turn right on McCrory Lane; I–40 runs by just to the left. Cross the Harpeth and then railroad tracks to rejoin US 70. Turn left to continue west. In 0.9 mile leave

Davidson County and enter Cheatham County. In 2.1 miles turn left on TN 249, again crossing the railroad tracks paralleling the highway and then the Harpeth Scenic River.

The highway becomes East Kingston Springs Road and enters the old community of Kingston Springs, founded in the 1840s when Samuel M. Kingston purchased lands and established the Sulphur Springs Resort. Kingston donated land for the railroad, which became the principal means of transportation for those coming to the resort from Nashville. In 3.2 miles, as you enter the community, watch for a white house on the left; behind it, you can glimpse one of the old cottages from the **Sulphur Springs Resort,** which operated until the early 1900s.

The road makes a sharp curve right to pass through the town. At an inter-section, West Kingston Springs Road turns left, but stay straight to cross the railroad tracks that run through town and curve right on Pinnacle Hill Road. The road becomes one lane beside the tracks. Cross the Harpeth with the railroad bridge to the right and an old Nashville and Northwestern railroad bridge to the left. You can turn left into **Kingston Springs City Park** and walk down to the river's edge and the old bridge, which is still supported by the original stone piers. Several other sites along the rail line to the west still have original stonework and earthen fortifications dating from the Civil War, but this is the only site that is easily accessible.

From the city park, continue up Pinnacle Hill Road, which climbs a ridge above Kingston Springs and descends to a junction with US 70 in 1.9 miles. Turn left to continue west. In 0.6 mile, just before a crossing of the Harpeth Scenic River, turn right on Cedar Hill Road. At 1.3 miles, near the Scott Cemetery, look left across the river to see the earthen mounds of **Mound Bottom,** an 800-year-old site of the Mississippian culture. These Native Americans built their towns with a central plaza surrounded by a large temple mound and smaller mounds and all enclosed in a palisade. The village at Mound Bottom stands at a bend in the Harpeth and occupies more than 300 acres, making it one of the largest Mississippian towns in North America. Public access is only available by arrangement with rangers at nearby Montgomery Bell State Park. A volunteer group, Friends of Mound Bottom, hopes to develop a state historic area that will be open for tours and educa-tional programs.

Continue up Cedar Hill Road while circling Mound Bottom across the river. In 2.8 miles turn left on a small road toward the **Narrows of the Harpeth State Historic Area.** Turn left again and then stay right at a junc-tion to reach a parking area below a rock wall with the river below on the left. Here you can take a wooden stairway down the bluff to the river's edge to see water flowing into a man-made tunnel.

In 1802, Montgomery Bell arrived in Tennessee from Pennsylvania and went to work at Cumberland Iron Works for James Robertson, one of the founders of Nashville; iron production was just becoming a major industry in Middle Tennessee. Bell bought out Robertson in 1804 and soon became a leader in the industry, building iron forges at several locations. Here where the Harpeth River nearly folds back on itself in a 5-mile bend in the river, Bell established the Pattison Forge, named for his mother. Needing waterpower to drive the hammers of the forge, Bell directed his slaves to dig a tunnel through the narrow ridge separating the two sections of river. They began in 1819 and completed the 209-foot-long tunnel in about a year. Because the downstream river on the other side of the ridge is lower, the water dropped out of the tunnel on the other end, thus providing the power Bell needed.

To get to the other end of the tunnel, walk back up the road. Notice on the right a wooden runner that provides canoe access to the river. At a trailhead on the left, turn up to a junction. A trail to the left leads to the top of the narrow ridge for panoramic views of the Harpeth Scenic River far below the bluffs. Past the ridge trail, a trail to the right at another junction leads to a boat take-out that is the endpoint for a 5-mile float trip. Stay left here one-quarter mile down to the edge of the river where water pours from Bell's tunnel.

To leave the state historic area, drive back up the road from the parking area to the last junction you encountered on the way in. Turn right on a one-way road and emerge back on Cedar Hill Road. You can turn left here to drive past the entrance to the state historic area and reach a crossing of the Harpeth in a beautiful valley; the canoe take-out is on the right at the bridge crossing.

Return to US 70; across the highway is **Tip-A-Canoe Harpeth River Outpost** where you can rent canoes for a float on the river. Turn right to continue west on US 70, crossing the **Harpeth Scenic River,** one of the prettiest rivers in the state; the stream is thought to be named for brothers Big and Little Harp, who were infamous robbers and murderers terrorizing the region around 1800.

MONTGOMERY BELL STATE PARK AND DICKSON

In 4.6 miles enter Dickson County, and in 6.2 miles turn left into **Montgomery Bell State Park,** which has a lodge/restaurant, campground, and fishing on three lakes. Drive into the park for 0.5 mile, and at a fork, stay right to cross a bridge over a small creek and turn right; at the corner on the left is a small mound of rocks that is all that remains from Laurel Furnace, which once operated beside a small creek. Continue to parking at the end of the road, and walk a short distance to a chapel and a replica log home that is on the site of the house of Rev. Samuel McAdow. Here McAdow, with Rev. Finis Ewing and Rev. Samuel King, founded the Cumberland Presbyterian Church, rejecting the traditional doctrine of predestination and embracing the gospel of "whosoever will."

From Montgomery Bell State Park, continue west on US 70. In 1.8 miles the **Broadway Drive-In Theater** on the left is still in operation. In 1.9 miles turn left on US 70 Business (also College Street) to enter the town of Dickson. In 1.4 miles, you'll reach a junction in the center of downtown with TN 48, which is also Main Street. On the far right corner sits **Ragan's Friendly Neighbor Store;** this furniture and appliance store contains on its walls an archive of photographs from Dickson County history collected by Henry Ragan.

Turn left on Main to pass several older commercial buildings, and bear left to the old **Dickson Depot,** which sits beside the railroad tracks running through town. Across the tracks stands the **Halbrook Hotel,** an old railroad hotel built in 1912. It was the birthplace of Frank G. Clement, three-time governor of Tennessee in the 1950s and '60s.

CHARLOTTE AND CUMBERLAND FURNACE

Return to the junction of College and Main Street, and continue north on TN 48. Pass over US 70, which bypasses the city on the north, and continue into the countryside with forest and small farms. In 6.9 miles enter the town of Charlotte, named for the wife of James Robertson. At a junction at this point, turn right to reach the **Charlotte Courthouse Square Historic District.** On the square stands the **Dickson County Courthouse;** built in 1833, it is the oldest courthouse still in use in Tennessee. Broad streets circle this lovely square with buildings dating from 1804 to 1920. The City Hall resides in an old Masonic Lodge on the east side of the square; stop by to pick up a walking tour of the twenty historic structures in town. On the southeast corner, notice the large **Mallory and Leach General Merchandise Store,** built in 1860. The **L. L. Leach General Merchandise Store** on the west side of the square is a three-story building built in 1849. The **Voorhies-James House,** also on the west is the oldest house remaining in Charlotte, built between 1806 and 1812; the two-story brick building was both a store and a residence. The **Hickerson Hotel** on the north, built in 1853, was the Union headquarters during the occupation of Charlotte during the Civil War. East of the square on Robertson Street, the **Old Jailer's House** now contains the **Dickson County History Museum.** The town spring, on Spring Street to the east, still flows from a cave; noted by James Robertson in his early survey of the region, the spring was the reason this site was chosen for the town.

Return to TN 48 and continue north, once more in a countryside with barns, old silos, and farmhouses. In 6.1 miles turn left to descend into **Cumberland Furnace Historic Village.** Here is where Robertson with William Sheppard established Cumberland Iron Works in 1793 with the construction of an iron furnace and a village to support the workers. Montgomery Bell joined Robertson and later purchased the enterprise. Bell built a second furnace and supplied cannon shot for Andrew Jackson's army during the War of 1812. In 1825 Anthony Wayne Van Leer purchased the ironworks and continued operation until the Civil War, becoming a wealthy industrialist in the process. In 1863, when Van Leer's granddaughter, Mary Florence Kirkman, married a Yankee soldier, Maj. James P. Drouillard, she was shunned by Nashville society; no one came to her wedding. Having recently inherited the ironworks from her father, Hugh Kirkman, who had married Van Leer's daughter, Eleanora, Mary Drouillard with husband James moved to Cumberland Furnace where in 1870 they built **Drouillard House,** an Italianate mansion now magnificently restored on a hill above the town. The home is not visible from the street; used as a site for workshops, the house is open to the public only at certain times by appointment and during a fall historic tour of the city.

The short road that drops into Cumberland Furnace intersects with the old road to Charlotte. Make a sharp left to reach **St. James Episcopal Church,** a small white frame church in the country gothic style. It was built in 1879 by the Drouillards. Just beyond stands the **Van Leer Academy,** a school built in 1880, also by the Drouillards. The building later became a public grade school that operated until 1948.

Turn around at the church and school and drive back toward the center of the village. Just beyond the road access down from TN 48 on the right, the drive up the hill to Drouillard House lies to the left. Pass through the center of town where small homes and stores that were part of the iron village still stand along the street.

In 1889 the Southern Iron Company purchased the ironworks and constructed a new coke furnace. In 1891 the L & N Railroad built a spur line

Drouillard House

from Clarksville to Cumberland Furnace for hauling in the coke to fuel the operations and carrying away the pig iron produced. The Buffalo Iron Company took over in 1896, and then by 1900 the Warner Iron Company stepped in to operate the furnace until 1938. It was reopened briefly during World War II but was then dismantled and sold for scrap.

At a junction with Dry Hollow Road stands an old brick building to the left that probably dates from Montgomery Bell's time. A two-story brick building to the right contained an iron company office, store, and hotel. Bell's furnace was behind the company office building. You can turn left on Dry Hollow Road to tour more of the village. Among the sights are the **Cumberland Furnace Depot,** built in 1920 after the original burned, and the sites of the other two furnaces, the Warner and the Robertson.

RUSKIN AND MCEWIN

To continue the drive, turn right on Dry Hollow Road to a junction with TN 48 and turn south, returning to Dickson. Exit onto the US 70 Bypass to stay north of the city. In 1 mile pass the other end of US 70 Business emerging from Dickson, which is also the crossing of TN 46. Just ahead the highway crosses a bridge over the railroad tracks that continue to parallel US 70 to the west. But at the intersection, turn right on TN 46, also known as Yellow Creek Road, for a side trip to the site of the old Ruskin utopian community. In 7.4 miles watch for Gilliam Hollow Road on the left. Then in another 3.4 miles look to the left for the site of the community, still marked by a three-story frame building that was the **Commonwealth House.**

In 1894 socialist Julius Wayland from Indiana established a colony at nearby Tennessee City, which had become a small village on the Nashville and Northwestern Railroad. Within a few months, a hundred colonists had arrived at the community, which Wayland named for John Ruskin, an English socialist writer. The colonists joined economically and socially in the Ruskin Cooperative Association. Wayland published a widely distributed paper, *The Coming Nation,* with more than 75,000 subscribers. Internal dissension soon disrupted the colony, and Wayland abandoned the enterprise after only a year. But the colony survived, moving to this location on Yellow Creek. The colonists were economically successful, at one time having seventy-five buildings and residences for their 250 members. There were businesses in printing, agriculture, and several home industries. But internal disputes continued to undermine the community. Several court cases over control of the colony settled nothing, and in 1899 a judge ordered the corporation dissolved and the colony's assets sold at public auction; most of the colony moved to Georgia. The Commonwealth House, which was the location of the printing business, is all that remains of Ruskin.

Return down Yellow Creek Road and turn right on Gilliam Hollow Road; travel 2.6 miles to cross the railroad tracks and reach US 70 in Tennessee City. Turn right to continue west, crossing into Humphreys County. In 7.0 miles enter the railroad town of McEwen. This small town is known for its **St. Patrick Irish Picnic and Homecoming,** billed as one of the world's oldest and largest outdoor barbecues, held the last Friday and Saturday in July; proceeds benefit the local St. Patrick School. The picnic dates to 1854 when the townspeople held a fundraising barbecue to purchase a bell for St. Patrick Church; the event has been held every year since, hosted by members of the church. The tons of slow-cooked pork are seasoned with a secret barbecue sauce brought by the Walsh family from Ireland; the recipe is passed down from generation to generation with only one family member knowing the ingredients.

WAVERLY AND ENOCHS'S FARM

Continue west on US 70, reaching Waverly in another 8.5 miles. Turn left on US 70 (Main Street) as US 70 Bypass continues straight to pass north of the downtown. Entering Waverly on Main Street, you'll reach the Humphreys County Chamber of Commerce on the left occupying the old **Greyhound Bus Station;** built between 1938 and 1939, the blue-enamel Art Moderne building is one of only two remaining in the state. Just beyond, Main Street intersects with TN 13 to the north. You can turn right here to pass the brick **McAdoo House** on the right, an Italianate Victorian home built in 1878 by Capt. H. M. McAdoo, a Union officer who returned to Waverly after the Civil War to live and became president of the Tennessee State Senate. Stay on TN 13 to the north to cross a viaduct over the US 70 Bypass and the railroad tracks to see the **Nolan House** on the left. The white frame house was built in 1870 by James N. Nolan, a Union lieutenant during the Civil War. Nolan commanded a battery at Fort Hill overlooking Waverly. Settling here after the war, he became a successful businessman. Descendants of the Nolan family lived in the house until 1979; today it is a bed-and-breakfast.

Return to Main Street, and continue west a short distance to the town square, site of the **Humphreys County Courthouse.** Turn left on TN 13 and ascend Fort Hill. Turn left on Hillwood Drive and make an immediate turn left onto Fort Hill Road that leads to the **Humphreys County Museum** in the Butterfield House, constructed in 1922 by Archibald and Lyda Butterfield. The museum contains Civil War and Native American artifacts. Beside the house stands an old white frame post office from the nearby community of Denver; these traditional small white frame buildings once served as post offices throughout the South. The grounds of the museum also contain the earthenworks of the Union fort that protected the Nashville and Northwestern Railroad where it passed through the town; here Lieutenant Nolan was stationed with his battery.

Return to TN 13, where you can turn left for a side trip to **Enochs's Farm** with an operating gristmill. In 1.5 miles, turn left on East Blue Creek Road and travel for 0.7 mile and turn left on Little Blue Creek Road. Pass through the lovely valley of Little Blue Creek for 3 miles to a right turn on Enochs Road a short distance to Enochs Mill. In the early 1900s Enoch and Allie Enochs came from Ohio to settle in the Little Blue Creek Community; later, their son, Wilbert, with his wife, Anne Davis, took over operation of the farm. In the 1930s, electricity had not yet reached the community, but Wilbert Enochs knew its benefits. He constructed a pond to supply waterpower, erected a small mill house, and installed a gristmill from Pennsylvania. He ground corn into meal and produced electricity that lighted four houses on the farm. Today, the Enochs's daughter, Joyce Enochs Bullington, and her son-in-law, Dorris Davis, still operate the mill.

Back on TN 13, you can continue south to reach **Loretta Lynn's Ranch** at Hurricane Mills; the highway is also called Loretta Lynn Parkway in honor of the country music star. In 5.6 miles cross Hurricane Creek and turn right into the ranch on Hurricane Mills Road. The grounds contain a campground, cabins, Loretta's mansion, and a museum housed in the old mill that sits on Hurricane Creek. There is also a re-creation of the Butcher Holler House in Kentucky where Loretta grew up. Her father, Ted Webb, was a Kentucky coal miner, and so the movie about Loretta's life was *Coal Miner's Daughter.*

Return to Waverly and turn left on Main Street to leave town, reaching a junction with the US 70 Bypass in 2.3 miles. Continue west on US 70. In 3 miles the **Valley Drive-In Theater** is on the left. In another 2.2 miles pass through the small community of Denver.

JOHNSONVILLE

In 1.9 miles turn right on a side road to head toward the **Johnsonville State Historic Area.** The road crosses the railroad tracks and climbs a ridge to pass under a multitude of power lines running east from TVA's New Johnsonville Steam Plant on the Tennessee River. Then drop into a bottomland along Trace Creek at a junction with Old Johnsonville Road in 2.3 miles. Turn left to enter the state historic area, which once contained the old depot that was the end of the Nashville and Northwestern Railroad at Johnsonville. Named for Andrew Johnson, governor of Tennessee and later president of the United States, the town no longer exists because TVA purchased the land for Kentucky Lake and moved the people out when the agency constructed Kentucky Dam on the Tennessee River.

On a knoll in the park is a museum and a circular redoubt that was a Union fortification during the Civil War protecting the Johnsonville Depot. On a higher knoll is the Crockett Cemetery where you can access the Johnsonville Redoubt Trail. Normally, you cannot climb on the remains of Civil War earthworks, but in this case the trail wanders along the top of the serpentine wall of the fort, providing a unique vantage point for viewing this upper redoubt that Union troops also used to guard the rail depot below.

Since this river-rail connection was an important link in the Union supply lines during the Civil War, the Confederacy's leaders ordered Nathan Bedford Forrest north with his cavalry in the fall of 1864 on one of his famous raids. Positioning his 3,000-man army with ten cannon on the west bank of the Tennessee River, he intended to break the rail-river link at Johnsonville; at the time this transportation route was supplying Sherman's march to the sea in Georgia. The battle began on October 29, when the Confederate troops opened fire on Union steamboats and gunboats trying to move north on the river. Over the next few days, the Confederates captured several boats and formed their own navy, which challenged the remaining Union gunboats. In the meantime Forrest had established his batteries directly across from Johnsonville. He opened fire on November 4 and quickly destroyed the town, sinking boats and exploding warehouses; a liquor warehouse spilled hundreds of barrels of burning alcohol through the town. With the situation lost, the Union quartermaster completed the job of burning the town to keep the Confederates from confiscating any supplies. The loss to the Union was three gunboats, eleven transports, eighteen barges, and supplies worth more than eight million dollars. Some of these boats still remain on the bottom of Kentucky Lake in the river channel; TVA has documented their locations and condition. Forrest lost only two killed and nine wounded. While this was a great victory for the Confederates—in fact, a unique battle in which a cavalry defeated a naval force—it did little to slow Sherman in Georgia, who had decided to live off the land as he cut a swath through the state to Savannah.

Return from the Johnsonville State Historic Area to US 70 and continue west, entering the community of New Johnsonville, which was settled when old Johnsonville was flooded by Kentucky Lake. In 1.1 miles you can turn left for a side trip to the **Duck River Unit** of the Tennessee National Wildlife Refuge. In 2.5 miles at a junction with Old State Route 1, turn left; then turn right on Hickman Road, and in 0.6 mile turn left on Refuge Lane. The road enters the wildlife refuge where the road becomes gravel. November through February is a good time to see migrating waterfowl here along the Duck River where it joins the Tennessee River. Wood ducks, mallards, and black ducks breed here each year, and the refuge has one of the largest rookeries in Tennessee for great blue heron.

Return to US 70 and continue west. In 0.9 mile the entrance to TVA's **New Johnsonville Steam Plant** is on the right; guided tours explain how electricity is made from steam power. US 70 then crosses the broad Tennessee River; barges ply the waters and to the right stands the steam plant. On the other side in Benton County, the highway continues west on a berm through lowlands along the river, passing through the state's **Camden Wildlife Management Area.**

CAMDEN AND HUNTINGDON

In 3.4 miles, at a junction with US 70 bearing left to bypass Camden, stay straight on US 70 Business toward the town. In 0.7 mile TN 191 turns south toward **Birdsong Marina** on Kentucky Lake, which hosts tours of a working freshwater pearl farm. This is one of the last places in Tennessee where pearls are harvested. Pearls from freshwater mussels once created a thriving industry in Tennessee, until the construction of dams flooded the rivers and released water below the dams that is too cold for mussels to survive.

The highway crosses the CSX Railroad tracks generally following the route of the Nashville and Northwestern as it continued west toward the Mississippi River. In 1.7 miles enter Camden at the town square where the **Benton County Courthouse** stands. Turn right to go around the square to the opposite corner and turn right on TN 191 to head for **Nathan Bedford Forrest State Park.** In 6.3 miles pass through the community of Eva, and enter the park in another 1.5 miles; a campground is there. The park road ascends Pilot Knob to the **Tennessee River Folklife Interpretive Center,** a museum with exhibits on life and customs along the Tennessee River, including information and artifacts on musseling and commercial fishing. A deck at the back of the center offers a grand view of the Tennessee River from this highest point in West Tennessee. An obelisk on the hill is a monument to Nathan Bedford Forrest.

Return to Camden and circle the town square to the opposite corner and turn right to take US 70 west out of town. In 1 mile at a junction with US 641, you can turn right to take a side trip to the **Patsy Cline Memorial.** After turning right on US 641, make an immediate left on Mt. Carmel Road, and in 2.7 miles turn right into a small park. Here, country-music star Patsy Cline died in a plane crash with several other performers on March 5, 1963. Newspaper articles from the time of the accident are mounted on a display board. A short walk down a steep slope leads to a stone monument at the crash site.

On US 70, continue to the west. In 5.9 miles enter Carroll County. In 0.8 mile cross the Big Sandy River, a tributary of the Tennessee. In 0.9 mile pass through the old railroad town of Bruceton, which is still a junction of railroads with a line extending south from Paris to an intersection with the CSX running east-west.

Continue west on US 70. In 7.7 miles enter Huntingdon on East Main Street. **Thomas Park** on the right occupies the site of the old Huntingdon train depot beside the railroad tracks. Huntingdon boasts several historic homes along East Main and on Browning Street, which turns right just past Thomas Park. Up Browning, the **Enochs House** stands on the right; this Gothic Revival home with three gables across the front was built in 1905 by Circuit Judge Wilson Enochs. On East Main, just before the town square, the **Huntingdon Historical Museum** occupies an old commercial building on the right; it has photographs and artifacts about the local history.

At the town square, with the **Carroll County Courthouse,** you can take a side trip to McKenzie by turning right on Paris Street to cross the railroad tracks and pass through a historic residential district to take TN 22 northeast. In 10.3 miles in McKenzie the **Governor Gordon Browning Museum** resides in an old post office building on the town square; Browning practiced law in Huntingdon and was twice governor of Tennessee. Also in McKenzie, you can go by the **McKenzie Depot,** an L-shaped Italian Renaissance train station in red brick with a tile roof. It sits beside the railroad tracks at what used to be a junction of rail lines.

PARKERS CROSSROADS

In Huntingdon take TN 22 south from the town square to complete this drive. In 12.6 miles enter Henderson County and reach the small community of Parkers Crossroads in 1.7 miles. The city park on the left is the first stop on a driving tour for the **Battle of Parkers Crossroads.** Here Union forces sought to entrap Nathan Bedford Forrest and his cavalry as they returned from an 1862 raid through Union-occupied West Tennessee; they had torn up rail lines, destroyed bridges, and seized munitions and supplies. Always on the offensive, Forrest attacked the Union position at Parkers Crossroads, causing the federal troops to pull back to a small hill called Red Mound, where they were surrounded. While Forrest negotiated for the surrender of the troops, Union reinforcements arrived from the north. Informed that he was now between two Union forces, Forrest gave the order to "Charge them both ways." The surprise action slowed the Union attack long enough for Forrest and his men to withdraw and continue their escape to the south. Forrest later returned to Tennessee on several daring raids, including the 1864 raid on the Johnsonville Depot.

TN 22 soon reaches I–40. South of the interstate, a log house visitor center on the left has brochures describing the driving tour of the battlefield.

25

Shiloh

NATCHEZ TRACE STATE PARK TO SHILOH BATTLEFIELD

GENERAL DESCRIPTION: This 106-mile drive passes through backcountry along the Tennessee River to the historic battlefield of Shiloh.

SPECIAL ATTRACTIONS: Natchez Trace State Park, Tennessee National Wildlife Refuge, Mousetail Landing State Park, Saltillo Ferry, Savannah, Shiloh National Military Park, Shiloh Indian Mounds National Historic Landmark, iron furnaces, historic homes, scenic views, fall color, hiking, biking, boating, fishing, hunting, and wildlife viewing.

LOCATION: Where the Tennessee River divides West and Middle Tennessee. Begin the drive from Exit 116 on I–40 at Natchez Trace State Park.

DRIVE ROUTE NUMBERS: TN 114; US 412; TN 438, 100, 69, and 128; US 64; and TN 22.

CAMPING: Natchez Trace State Park, Mousetail Landing State Park, and Pickwick Landing State Park

SERVICES: All services at Lexington and Savannah.

NEARBY ATTRACTIONS: Lady Finger Bluff Small Wild Area, Cedar Grove Iron Furnace, Brownsport Furnace, Buford Pusser Home.

THE DRIVE

Throughout the South, the name *Shiloh* rings across the subconscious like a distant pealing church bell. Nearly all know this was one of the most important Civil War battles and that both Union and Confederates soldiers here participated in heroic efforts. Gathered around a small church meeting house called "Shiloh," more than 80,000 troops clashed in the largest engagement of the war up to that time, the spring of 1862. The Union victory, coupled with the recent fall of Forts Henry and Donelson, severed the Confederacy in the west and foreshadowed the defeat of the South.

NATCHEZ TRACE STATE PARK

Start this drive at **Natchez Trace State Park and Forest.** On I–40, 35 miles east of Jackson and 95 miles west of Nashville, take Exit 116 onto TN 114 and head south.

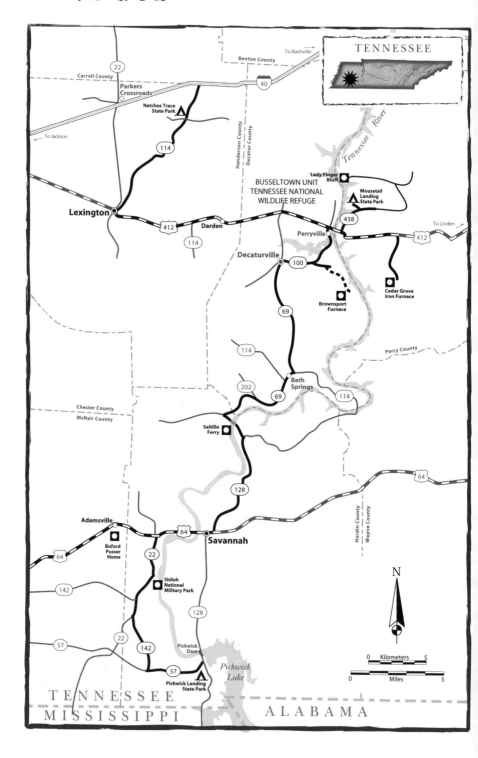

The area of Natchez Trace State Park was settled in the 1830s by Joseph Morris and other immigrants from North Carolina seeking fertile lands west of the Appalachians. Here they and later settlers established farms in what had always been a woodland, and for the next hundred years the land was cleared of trees, crops were grown, and livestock raised. With the tree cover gone, the land began to erode, so that by the early 1900s the land was spent and scarred with ditches and gullies, no longer suitable for farming.

At 0.5 mile into the park, Fairview Gullies on the left remain from the settlement days, a reminder of the damage caused by farming without any attention to conservation of the land. A 3-mile hiking trail travels through the area.

In the mid-1930s the Resettlement Administration, part of the New Deal Program, purchased thousands of acres while relocating the people who lived here and began a demonstration project to reclaim the land. Soon after, the State of Tennessee leased the land to continue the work and was eventually given the area for the creation of a state park. Because a western branch of the old Natchez Trace that ran from Nashville to Natchez, Mississippi, once passed through this area, the park was given the name Natchez Trace.

TN 114 travels through regenerated forest that now covers the eroded farmland. The task of managing this recovered land is shared by agencies; the Department of Environment and Conservation runs the state park facilities, while the Division of Forestry manages the forests and the Tennessee Wildlife Resources Agency oversees wildlife. The state forest lands extend north of I–40, while most visitor facilities are south of I–40. At times in the fall, visitor use is restricted to the lodges and campground areas because hunting is allowed in designated seasons; during these times, the state park hiking trails are closed.

Continuing south from Fairview Gullies on TN 114, the state park visitor center is on the right in 1.1 miles. In another 0.5 mile, **Bucksnort Campground** lies on the right; this wrangler's camp has tethering sites for horses in addition to the usual amenities at campgrounds.

TN 114 reaches a junction of roads in the center of the park in 1.6 miles. A grocery store is on the right, and straight ahead is the Five Points Group Lodge on Browns Lake. To the far left, a road leads into the **Cub Creek Recreation Area,** which has camping, rustic cabins, and a swimming area on Cub Creek Lake. Just to the left, Corinth Road leads past a fire tower to exit the park and connect with US 412 to the south. Take the road to the right at the junction to continue through the state park.

In 3.2 miles a left turn leads to **Pin Oak Lodge** and **Pin Oak Campground,** both on Pin Oak Lake. This new area of the park was made available by the Tennessee Valley Authority and brings the total land area to 48,500 acres.

LEXINGTON AND BUSSELTOWN

In another 1.4 miles TN 114 exits the park and continues south, reaching a junction with US 412 in 6.6 miles. Downtown Lexington lies to the right at a junction with US 22 where the **Beech River Heritage Museum** is located in the old brick Colonial Revival post office. The Beech River flows south and east around Lexington on its way to the Tennessee River.

At the junction with US 412, turn left to head east. Pass large fields of soybeans and corn on a drive of 9.2 miles to a junction with Corinth Road to the left. Continue east on US 412 through the small community of Darden and leave Henderson County, entering Decatur County. In another 9.2 miles Perryville Road turns to the right to enter the small community of Perryville. The drive will turn right here to head south, but first stay straight on US 412. In 0.8 mile turn left on Bunch Chapel Road to reach the **Tennessee National Wildlife Refuge Busseltown Unit.** This backcountry road offers a drive through forest along the west side of the Tennessee River. In 2.9 miles join Mousetail Road near the small community of Busseltown and bear right to enter the wildlife refuge. This southernmost unit of the Tennessee National Wildlife Refuge preserves wetlands habitat for migrating ducks, geese, and shorebirds that pass through in fall and winter; an occasional bald eagle glides into the treetops. The road becomes gravel as it enters the refuge, where fields of corn and soybeans support the migrating birds. In 1.3 miles the road reaches the river with boat access and great views from the river bank. Across the water stands Lady Finger Bluff, a TVA small wild area you can access later on this drive.

MOUSETAIL LANDING
AND LADY FINGER BLUFF

Return to US 412, and continue east. Cross a long highway bridge spanning the Tennessee River and offering expansive views; barges ply the waters, moving to ports up and down the river. The river is wide here because it is still part of Kentucky Lake, which stretches north to TVA's Kentucky Dam. On the east side of the river, in Perry County, turn left on TN 438. In 0.9 mile a left turn drops steeply toward the river to a primitive camping area and a boat launch for **Mousetail Landing State Park.** Continue straight another 0.8 mile, and turn left in the main entrance for the state park which has a campground and hiking trails. This small state park occupies a place along the Tennessee River that was a river port, locally called a "landing"; goods were shipped by river to ports as far as St. Louis. The products of the region included timber, iron, and tanned hides. The tanneries at the landing were constantly filled with animal hides waiting to be tanned, which attracted mice. When one of these tanneries burned during the Civil War, so many mice came running out with their tails in the air, it was thereafter called Mousetail Landing.

Just upstream from the state park, TVA's **Lady Finger Bluff Small Wild Area** offers great views from the bluff above the Tennessee River. For this side trip, exit the park and turn left, continuing north on TN 438. The road climbs a ridge and drops steeply into the valley of Lick Creek before reaching a junction in 5.5 miles. Turn left on Bunker Hill/Standing Rock Road. In 4.1 miles turn left on a side road, and in another 0.2 mile turn left on a gravel road. This cedar-lined backcountry lane travels along an embayment on Lick Creek where water from the river has backed into the creek channel. In 0.6 mile a pull-out on the right provides access to the trailhead. The 1.5-mile trail dips through bottomland and climbs to the limestone bluff overlooking the river; across the way is the Busseltown Unit of the Tennessee National Wildlife Refuge.

Return to Mousetail Landing State Park and continue south on TN 438 to return to US 412. You can continue east for a side trip to **Cedar Grove Iron Furnace.** In 6.2 miles turn right on Cedar Creek Road and travel 6.3 miles. This rare double-stack furnace built in 1834 and rebuilt in 1846 produced pig iron until 1862. There was once an entire village of cabins, barns, and blacksmith shops surrounding the furnace; only the stone stack remains.

Go back out on US 412, return to TN 438, and continue west to recross the Tennessee River. Travel 1.7 miles to a junction with Perryville Road to the left. Turn left to enter Perryville in 1 mile; on the river, piles of gravel, sand, and logs wait to be loaded on barges. The road curves right to a junction with TN 100. Turn left to continue south.

BEECH RIVER AND SALTILLO

In 0.1 mile cross the Beech River, a tributary of the Tennessee River. In another 0.4 mile, the **Beech River Recreation Area** lies among trees on the left beside the confluence of the Beech River with the Tennessee. The area has a picnic area, boat ramp, and campground. In 2.6 miles a small side road leads to the Cypress Pond Wetlands Area; there is little public access other than for hunters at this TWRA area. But if you are especially interested in the iron industry of the 1800s, you can get to the **Brownsport Furnace.** In 1.6 miles at a fork, stay to the right another 2 miles to the iron furnace, which operated from 1848 to 1878. Some of the outside rock and brick has fallen away to reveal the brick-lined chimney inside the stack.

Back out on TN 100, continue south along a stretch of forested highway. In 1.6 miles cross Rushing Creek, a tributary of the Beech River. In another 1.7 miles pass through the town of Decaturville, with the **Decatur County Courthouse** on the right. In another 0.8 mile arrive at junction with TN 69 and turn left to continue south through another stretch of forest. In 3.3 miles cross TN 202 and continue 7.9 miles to a junction with TN 69. Turn right and in 3 miles pass through the small community of Bath Springs, and in 8.1 miles enter Hardin County.

In 1.1 miles enter the town of Saltillo at a junction with TN 69 turning to the right. This small river town contains several historic homes dating from before the Civil War. To the right is the **Meady White House,** a Greek Revival with Italianate influences built with slave labor around 1847. White was a local businessman, sheriff, and justice of the peace and had a hand in the founding of Saltillo, which was named by soldiers returning from the Mexican War of 1846–48. The **Parker House** was built around 1906 by Dr. Luther Parker, a local physician, the house is now a bed-and-breakfast. Turn left through the town to Saltillo Ferry Landing. **Saltillo Ferry** is one of the few operating ferries left in Tennessee. This drive crosses the Tennessee River here; if the ferry is not on this side of the river, just honk your horn for the tug-pulled barge to cross the river to pick you up. Hardin County operates the ferry Monday through Friday. (Any ferry operation these days is a money-losing venture, so there is always a chance the ferry will stop running. If that's the case, you must drive east on TN 69 10 miles to Milledgeville and turn south on TN 22 and travel another 10 miles to a junction with US 64, and turn back east 9 miles to Savannah, crossing the river on a highway bridge, to pick up this drive.)

Taking the ferry across, pull up the bank on the other side of the river and turn right on Wilkinson Ferry Road to parallel the river. The road curves left away from the river and reaches a junction with Russell Chapel Road in 1.8 miles; **Russell Chapel,** an old country church, sits at the top of the hill to the left. Turn right. In 0.6 mile join TN 128 straight ahead. In 9.9 miles, stay with the highway curving left, and in 0.7 mile reach a junction with US 64; turn right. In another 0.7 mile turn right again as TN 69 joins from the left.

SAVANNAH AND ADAMSVILLE

Stay straight on US 64, which is Main Street, to enter the historic river town of Savannah. **Hardin County Courthouse** with its clock tower stands on the left. Just past the courthouse on the left is the **Tennessee River Museum** located in a 1939 post office. The museum has a fine collection of

Saltillo Ferry

artifacts and exhibits about the Tennessee River. Included in the artifacts of the Native Americans who once used the river as a trade route is the important Shiloh Effigy Pipe found in 1898 at Shiloh Mounds, which lie to the south later on this drive; the pipe's image is a kneeling human figure. Exhibits also tell about the steamboat days on the Tennessee River in the early 1800s and explain the river's role as a transportation route in the Civil War.

The museum building is also the location for the Hardin County Tourism Information Center. Here you can pick up a brochure for a walking tour of the **Savannah Historic District** turn-of-the-century homes. The **Welch-Nesbitt House,** a Queen Anne-style home built around 1900 on Church Street, is now the White Elephant Bed and Breakfast; Church turns north off Main before the courthouse.

From the museum, continue west on Main Street. The grand **Ross House** stands on the right, a 1909 brick Colonial Revival with a two-story portico and wraparound porches. Soon after, US 64 bears to the left, but stay straight on Main to its end at the Tennessee River. The **Cherry Mansion** stands to the left; the oldest home in Savannah, it was built by slaves for David Robinson in 1821; he gave the house as a wedding present to his daughter, who married Edgar Cherry. At the end of the road, you may walk around the gate and down a drive to a landing on the Tennessee River.

Savannah was once an important junction of the east-west road to Memphis with the Tennessee River. The road crossed the river here on a ferry, first operated by James Rudd in 1815. In 1900 the ferry was operated by Alec Haley, the grandfather of noted author Alex Haley; Alex's grandmother, Queen, who was the subject of his book by the same name, is buried in Savannah. In 1838 several hundred Cherokee Indians crossed the river on their way west. The federal government had banished them from this part of the country with the Indian Removal Act of 1830; in addition to Cherokees, nearly 100,000 Native Americans were sent west between 1830 and 1850.

From the river overlook, Cherry Mansion stands to the left with a commanding view of the river. Here Ulysses S. Grant headquartered for a time during the Civil War. The Tennessee River was the Union invasion route into the heart of the Confederacy. After the fall of Fort Henry on the Tennessee River and Fort Donelson on the Cumberland River, both near the Kentucky border, the Union forces moved south along the Tennessee, bringing with them the armored gunboats they used to fight Confederate shore batteries. Grant stayed at Cherry Mansion only for a short time; to the south, Shiloh awaited. On the morning of April 6, 1862, those at the house could hear the gunfire that inaugurated the battle. Grant boarded his boat here at the landing and quickly sailed south to the confrontation.

Return along Main Street to the junction with US 64 and turn right. The highway crosses a high bridge over the river. In another 3.6 miles TN 22 turns left. The drive turns south here, but before making the turn, you can continue straight to Adamsville on a side trip to the **Buford Pusser Home.** US 64 crosses into McNairy County and, in Adamsville in 3.5 miles, reaches a junction with Walnut Street; turn left. Turn right on Pusser Street to the Pusser Home on the right; parking is in back. This house museum is a modern rancher, typical of the region, but it's filled with newspaper clippings, photographs, and artifacts from Pusser's life. He served three years as Adamsville's Chief of Police before becoming the McNairy County Sheriff; his heroic efforts to clean up illegal activities in his county were documented in three *Walking Tall* movies. Most days, Pusser drove from his home in Adamsville west to the McNairy County Courthouse in Selmer where his office was located.

SHILOH

Return east to the junction with TN 22 and turn south. In 4.8 miles turn left into **Shiloh National Military Park,** which encompasses Shiloh Battlefield. The visitor center stands to the left with information and exhibits;

Shiloh Battlefield

be sure to see the very helpful interpretive film that reveals the significance of the sites along the park's 9.5-mile auto tour. The drive itself is a beautiful journey through forests and open fields. Monuments and interpretive signs are scattered along the route. A solemn silence hangs over the battlefield where Confederates engaged Union forces in a desperate attempt to halt the North's advance into the Confederacy.

After the capture of Fort Henry on the Tennessee River and Fort Donelson on the Cumberland River in February 1862, the Union forces moved south along the Tennessee. One goal was the capture of the important rail link formed by the Memphis and Charleston Railroad that ran along the southern border of West Tennessee before dipping south to a rail junction in Corinth, Mississippi; the Confederates had withdrawn south to the railroad after their defeat. General Albert Sidney Johnston concentrated troops at Corinth for a counteroffensive against Gen. U. S. Grant's Army of the Tennessee moving south down the river past Savannah to Pittsburg Landing. Here, Grant had his 40,000 men camp around a small church called the Shiloh Meeting House. (Today that one-room log church is gone, but another church building stands on the site.) Here they waited to be joined by

Maj. Gen. Don Carlos Buell and his Army of the Ohio. Grant bided his time at Cherry Mansion in Savannah.

Johnston's force of 44,000 men moved north from Corinth to within striking distance of Grant's army, and on the morning of April 6, 1862, the Southern troops attacked. Grant's breakfast was interrupted with the news that the battle had begun. He hurried downriver to the engagement.

The Confederates pushed the Union troops back until the Federals regrouped at a well-worn dirt road called the "Sunken Road." Here they held the ground, repulsing repeated Confederate attempts to overrun the position. The fighting was so fierce that whizzing bullets filled the air, and so the place was thereafter called the Hornets' Nest. After seven hours of fighting, the Confederates finally brought up sixty-two cannon that bombarded the position while Southern troops surrounded and captured the Union force. This delay in the Confederate advance allowed Grant time to establish a line just inland from Pittsburg Landing where he would attempt to halt the Confederate advance.

General Johnston was killed while trying to cut off the Union escape route at the river landing; he was the highest ranking Confederate officer killed in the war. Second in command, Gen. P. G. T. Beauregard, assumed control of the Confederate forces.

Union General Buell's force in the meantime had made its way overland and now crossed the Tennessee River to reinforce Grant's army. The Union side had become 55,000 strong. Confederate attacks on the Union defense line were repulsed, and so the Southern troops pulled back to regroup for the night.

On the morning of April 7, the Confederates attacked with renewed vigor. The larger Union force finally began to push them back. The Confederates counterattacked in an attempt to halt the Union advance. Although they stopped the advance, the Confederates could not break the Union line. Low on ammunition and with 15,000 men dead, wounded, or missing, General Beauregard withdrew and headed back toward Corinth. The next day Grant sent Gen. William T. Sherman after the Confederates, but when they encountered the retreating troops, they were turned back by a cavalry rear guard under Col. Nathan Bedford Forrest.

In late April and into May, the Union troops marched on Corinth, eventually capturing the city while other federal forces took Memphis. Both forces then headed to Vicksburg, Mississippi. Their protracted siege of that city, coupled with the fall of Port Hudson in Louisiana, gave the Union side complete control of the Mississippi River. Although the Civil War continued for another three years, the outcome was now determined.

Across from the Shiloh Visitor Center, the **Shiloh National Cemetery** contains the graves of 3,643 known and unknown Union soldiers killed in the Battle of Shiloh and in other battles along the Tennessee River. The 1,728 Confederates killed at Shiloh, however, were buried en masse by the Union troops in several trenches across the battlefield. To the victors go the good burial sites.

The driving tour of the battlefield starts from Pittsburg Landing overlooking the Tennessee River. It loops through the battlefield with stops that include Grant's final defensive line, the Hornets' Nest on the Sunken Road, a Confederate burial trench, and the place where General Johnston was killed. The park road also gives access to the **Shiloh Indian Mounds National Historic Landmark,** a group of mounds dating from the Late Woodland to Late Mississippian prehistoric cultures; Riverside Drive, which gives access to the mounds, is closed at this writing because of erosion problems along the river, but you can walk along the road a half mile to the mounds on the bluff above the Tennessee River. A stairway to the top of Mound A offers a view of the river below the bluff.

On TN 22, you can continue south to reach **Pickwick Landing State Park** for camping and lodging. In 3.1 miles, where TN 22 bears to the right, stay left on TN 142. At a junction with TN 57 in 4.6 miles, turn left to reach the state park in another 5.2 miles.

26

changing the Landscape

JACKSON TO PICKWICK LANDING STATE PARK

GENERAL DESCRIPTION: A 101-mile drive south from Jackson passes the range of human influence on the landscape, from Indian mounds past nineteenth-century homes and onward to the modern Pickwick Dam on the Tennessee River.

SPECIAL ATTRACTIONS: Jackson, Pinson Mounds State Archaeological Area, Chickasaw State Park, Bolivar, Big Hill Pond State Park, Pickwick Landing State Park, historic homes and buildings, scenic views, fall color, hiking, biking, fishing, hunting, boating, and wildlife viewing.

LOCATION: Southern part of West Tennessee. Begin the drive in Jackson at the Convention and Visitors Bureau on East Main Street.

DRIVE ROUTE NUMBERS: US 45 and TN 100, 18, 125, and 57.

CAMPING: Chickasaw State Park, Big Hill Pond State Park, Pickwick Landing State Park, and Pickwick Dam Recreation Area.

SERVICES: All services at Jackson and Bolivar.

NEARBY ATTRACTIONS: Old Salem Cemetery, Cypress Grove Nature Park, Britton Lane Battlefield, Davis Bridge Battlefield, and Sheriff Buford Pusser's Office.

THE DRIVE

This drive demonstrates the historical range of human influence on Tennessee's landscape. The route passes from some of the earliest human manipulation of the environment by Middle Woodland Indians at Pinson Mounds, through antebellum houses constructed with slave labor that now still grace the neighborhoods of Bolivar, to the drastically changed landscape of Pickwick Lake created by TVA's Pickwick Dam.

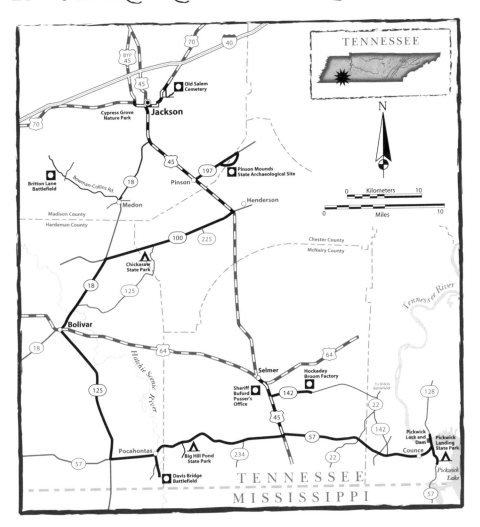

JACKSON

Start at the **Old Jackson City Hall** at 314 East Main Street in downtown Jackson, which houses the Arts Council and, on the second floor, the Jackson Convention and Visitors Bureau where you can gather information about the town and the region. Adjacent to the old building stands a new **McWherter Cultural Arts Center.** Across the street is the **Greyhound Bus Station;** this Art Modern building with blue porcelain exterior and flowing lines was built in 1938 and is the second oldest Greyhound station still operating.

From the old city hall, head east on Main Street to Royal Street. The drive turns south here, but first stay straight on Main to cross railroad tracks and pass through a brick gateway to enter the **POEMS Historic District;** the name is an acronym for Preservation of East Main and Surroundings. The elegant homes in this residential neighborhood date from the late 1800s; each house has a sign out front giving the name and date of construction. Watch on the left for the magnificent **Polk House,** a Queen Anne built in 1895. Some of the homes may be toured by appointment.

You can continue east on Main Street for a side trip to **Old Salem Cemetery,** site of a Civil War battle. At a junction with US 70 in 0.7 mile, turn left, and in 1.2 miles turn right on Bendix Drive. In 1 mile turn left on Cotton Grove Road. Old Salem Cemetery is soon on the left; it contains the graves of Madison County's early settlers and several unknown Confederate soldiers who died in the Battle of Salem Cemetery.

In December 1862, Confederate General Nathan Bedford Forrest entered West Tennessee on a notorious raid of Union supply lines after the fall of Fort Donelson. The Union side feared he was about to attack Jackson on his way north, and attempting to get the upper hand, they ordered two regiments east toward Cotton Grove. These forces met other Union forces retreating from Lexington where Forrest's cavalry had captured the city. These combined forces set up a battle line on December 19 around Salem Cemetery. Forrest sent some of his cavalry and troops against the outermost Union line to draw their attention while his detachments continued destroying railroad and telegraph lines to the north of Jackson and bridges to the south. In the fighting, the Union front fell back, with the Confederates approaching within 50 yards of Salem Cemetery. There, the main line of Union troops opened fire, killing a few Confederates. With more Union troops approaching from Jackson, Forrest called his troops back and continued north on his mission; it was probably never his intention to attack Jackson.

Return from Salem Cemetery and to Main and Royal, and turn south. In 0.5 mile stands the **Murphy Hotel** on the right, one of the few remaining railroad hotels in the state. Constructed by the Neely family in 1911 in a neo-classical style with a two-story portico, the brick structure accommodated salesmen and other travelers during Jackson's railroad boom. In 1946 the Murphy family purchased the hotel and renamed it; the Murphy operated into the early 1990s. In 1997 the old hotel was purchased by the City of Jackson and is being renovated to house the West Tennessee Children's Museum.

Just past the hotel on the left sits the restored **N. C. & St. L. Depot.** The Nashville, Chattanooga, & St. Louis Railroad once ran through Jackson, which was an important railroad junction with as many as four railroads operating in the city. The N. C. & St. L. Railroad constructed the depot in 1907. Eventually the L & N Railroad took over this smaller railroad, and later the L & N became part of the CSX Corporation. The old depot was used until 1985. In the 1990s the city purchased the building and renovated it as a museum, which now contains exhibits, artifacts, and a fascinating collection of photographs from the railroad days. Don't miss the working scale-model railroad in a back room of the depot. Built by the Jackson Model Railroad Club, the large display shows Jackson's four railroads.

The depot was constructed next to the city's old Lancaster Park, which once had a zoo and was a favorite picnic site on weekend afternoons. The park was developed around the **Electro Chalybeate Well,** which is just south of the depot. Iron-rich water has flowed from this spring for more than a century; probably both Confederate and Union soldiers camped nearby and drank from the spring. In the late 1800s the spring was rediscovered when Jackson's first modern waterworks was being constructed. Since this was a time when mineral-rich waters were believed to cure various ailments, the spring soon became a gathering place for people to sample the water. The spring still gushes from a fountain under a gazebo. Next door stands the old Art Deco waterworks building constructed in 1885 and now restored.

Continue south on Royal Street to join Highland Avenue, which is US 45. The drive continues south on US 45, but here you can also take a side trip to **Cypress Grove Nature Park.** Turn right on US 45 and travel 0.6 mile to a left turn on the US 45 Bypass. Drive another 1.5 miles and turn left on US 70. Cross the South Fork of the Forked Deer River and in 1.8 miles turn left into the nature park, a cooperative project between the City of Jackson and the National Park Service. The road into the park ends at a visitor center where an intricate system of boardwalk trails penetrates the cypress and tupelo bottomlands along the South Fork, ending at an observation tower overlooking a pond with occasional waterfowl. One segment of the boardwalk leads to a raptor center where eagles, owls, vultures, and hawks that can no longer survive in the wild are housed in large cages.

BRITTON LANE AND PINSON MOUNDS

Head south on US 45. The highway crosses the South Fork of the Forked Deer River in 0.7 mile and in another 2.5 miles reaches a junction with TN 18 to the right. Here you can take a side trip to the small **Britton Lane Battlefield.** Along TN 18 in 7.5 miles at the small community of Medon, turn right on Bowman-Collins Road and in 0.3 mile turn right on Collins Road. At a junction in 5.3 miles turn right on Steam Mill Ferry Road and soon turn left on Britton Lane. The battlefield is on the left in another 0.5 mile. In 1862 Confederate cavalry under Brig. Gen. Frank C. Armstrong were sent north from Mississippi to harass Union forces in Tennessee. On September 1, the Confederates engaged federal troops at Britton Lane in a four-hour battle. Although 213 Union soldiers were captured, Confederate losses were heavy. The battlefield contains several monuments and signs explaining the battle. A mass grave of unknown Confederates is also here. A dogtrot log cabin to the rear that was used as a field hospital has been furnished with period artifacts.

Continue south on US 45 from the junction with TN 18. In 6.6 miles enter the community of Pinson at a junction with TN 197 and turn left to reach the **Pinson Mounds State Archaeological Site;** the highway passes through a tree nursery of the Tennessee Division of Forestry. In 2.5 miles turn right into Pinson Mounds. The park road leads to a visitor center/museum, an earth-covered building constructed to resemble an Indian mound. A network of trails behind the visitor center leads through the Pinson complex of mounds, earthworks, and habitation areas. This village was constructed by Native Americans of the Middle Woodland Period. The tallest of the fifteen mounds is Sauls Mound; at 72 feet, it is the second highest in the United States. Large mounds were used to support ceremonial structures; smaller mounds were usually burial sites.

The Pinson site was discovered in 1820 by a survey crew, one of whom was Joel Pinson. The site remained mostly unknown and undisturbed until the 1880s when a Jackson newspaper editor, J. G. Cisco, began publicizing the mound complex. In the early 1900s the Smithsonian Institution came to investigate and map the area. The State of Tennessee later purchased the site at the urging of local citizens and today preserves it as an archaeological park. The importance of the site is recognized by its designation as a National Historic Landmark.

Saul's Mound

CHICKASAW STATE PARK AND BOLIVAR

The road into Pinson Mounds is a one-way circuit, so to leave the area, continue from the visitor center and exit through the state nursery, which is on the grounds of the park. The road rejoins TN 197 in 0.8 mile. Turn left to return to US 45 and turn left to continue south, entering Chester County. In 5.7 miles turn right at a junction with TN 100. In 7.2 miles reach **Chickasaw State Park and Forest** on the left. The park contains a restaurant and cabins as well as a campground and picnic areas. Swimming, boating, and fishing are enjoyed on the impounded Lake Placid; a scenic footbridge crosses the lake.

Continue west on TN 100 into Hardeman County. In 4.1 miles, at a junction with TN 18, turn left to continue south. In 7.1 miles cross the **Hatchie Scenic River.** Old Hatchie Town, originally a Chickasaw village, was located here along the river at the crossing of Fowler's Ferry. In 1824, because of frequent flooding, the town was moved a mile to the south and named after

Changing the Landscape

Simon Bolivar, the liberator of South America from the control of Spain. In 0.8 mile enter the town, which now has a Tennessee pronunciation with emphasis on the first syllable rather than the Spanish pronunciation. TN 18 enters town through the **North Main Historic District.** The 3-block area contains numerous homes dating from the 1800s. **Magnolia Manor** on the left is a Georgian-style English country home built in 1849 by Judge Austin Miller. During the Civil War, four Union generals stayed at the manor; among them were Grant and Sherman. The home is now a bed-and-breakfast. Emerging from the historic district in 0.1 mile, notice the **Luez Theater** on the right, an Art Deco theater still showing movies.

The **Hardeman County Courthouse** stands on the square in the center of town. Erected in 1868 to replace the courthouse burned by Union troops during the Civil War, the building combines Greek Revival and Italianate styles and is topped with a square bell and clock tower. On the south lawn of the courthouse stands an 1873 Confederate monument; it is the first carved memorial erected for Confederate dead. A monument on the west lawn was given to the county by the people of Venezuela in recognition of the name of the town.

Past the courthouse, at a junction with TN 125 straight ahead, turn right to stay on TN 18, which is Market Street. The Hardeman County Chamber of Commerce on the right resides in the **Water Treatment Plant,** which also housed the first electric generator in the county. This 1900 brick building is just one of 119 structures in Bolivar that are on the National Register of Historic Places; annually in April, the city and county host a Historic Tour of Buildings and Gardens. The magnificent homes in Bolivar reflect a growing economy in the 1800s based on steamboat trade on the Hatchie River; in the 1840s, as many as fourteen steamboats stopped regularly at Bolivar.

Tongue-and-groove paneling on the inside of the Water Treatment Plant is made from various trees that grow in Hardeman County, which is a leading producer of hardwood lumber. Each October, the county holds a Tennessee Forest Festival celebrating the lumber industry. The chamber building also contains various exhibits and photographs about local history.

Turn left up Union Street into the **Bills–McNeal Historic District.** Cross Lafayette, McNeal, and Bills Streets past the **McNeal House** on the left. This elaborate Italianate townhouse has wrought iron porch columns and railings. The house was built between 1858 and 1861 to help assuage the grief of the owner's wife over the death of their daughter. During the Civil War, Bolivar was occupied by Union troops, and the wife had to get permission to walk across the street to put flowers on her daughter's grave.

Past the McNeal House, the **Polk Cemetery,** established in 1845, lies on the right. Ezekiel Polk, the grandfather of Pres. James K. Polk, is buried here. Ezekiel with his brother, Thomas, played an important role in formulating the Mecklenburg Declaration of Independence, a 1775 proclamation by the citizens of Mecklenburg County, North Carolina. Made more than thirteen months before the Declaration of Independence was adopted in 1776 by the thirteen colonies, the anti-British resolutions of Mecklenburg actually did not mention independence. Ezekiel wrote his own epitaph prior to his death. In it he vilified Methodists, saying, "And Methodists with their camp bawling, Will be the cause of this down falling . . . ." This statement was removed from the gravestone during his grandson's campaign for the presidency. The candidate was apparently concerned that it might cost him some votes. The stone has since been repaired.

Return along Union from the Polk Cemetery to Bills Street and turn right. The **Wren's Nest** stands on the left; it is an 1870 Victorian cottage that is now an antique shop. The house was built by John Houston Bills as a wedding present for his daughter, Lucy, who was rather small; the architect, Fletcher Sloan, who designed many homes and buildings in Bolivar, compared her to a wren. Bills was a successful merchant, planter, and politician.

At the corner of Bills and Washington Streets, **The Pillars** stands on the left, facing Washington. This home was constructed in 1826 and is reported to be the first brick home in Bolivar. John Houston Bills purchased the original small Federal house here in 1837 and expanded it in a Greek Revival style. During the renovation, the fluted Doric columns on the front porch were installed upside down; the abacus, a square slab that usually forms the uppermost part of a column and supports the entablature of the roof, is here on the floor of the porch. Slaves left on their own to install the columns rightly thought the abacus would make a solid base. The Bills heirs deeded the house to the Association for the Preservation of Tennessee Antiquities (APTA), which has renovated the house and opens it for tours.

Across Washington to the right, lies **McAnulty Wood;** the only known stand of old-growth trees remaining in West Tennessee, the forest has been designated a National Natural Landmark. Turn left on Washington to pass in front of the Pillars, then turn left on McNeal Street. **The Columns** stands on the left on McNeal. This brick home with a massive classical portico was built in 1860 by Thomas Smith, Sr. Union forces used the home as a hospital during their occupation. In the 1800s the home had several owners, including Albert T. McNeal, for whom the street is named. George T. Ingram purchased the home in 1909 and added a south wing. Out of eight Ingram children, three daughters lived out their lives at the house; all were community leaders. The last, Elizabeth Ingram, had a private school in Jackson for forty-five years and operated a kindergarten in the basement of The Columns in the 1940s and '50s. Wanting to preserve her family home, she helped established the Bolivar Historical and Community Foundation and gave the foundation a lifetime lease on the house. Upon her death at age 102 in 1995, the foundation took possession and has since renovated the house. The Foundation now maintains the house with funds left by Elizabeth Ingram and makes it available for tours.

At the next corner, turn right on Lauderdale to return to Market Street, then turn right. Return to the court square and stay straight past the courthouse to the **Little Courthouse** on the left. Constructed in 1824, this was Hardeman County's original log courthouse; it was moved from the court square to this location to make way for the second courthouse that was burned by Union troops. Today it is a museum owned by the county and maintained by APTA. Among the many artifacts in the museum is the desk used by the county's first court clerk, Thomas Jones Hardeman, for whom the county is named.

Return to Main Street (the junction of TN 18 and 125) and turn left on TN 125 to leave Bolivar. The highway travels through timberland, where you are likely to notice lumber companies and trucks hauling lumber and logs from the surrounding hardwood forests. In the small community of Middleton in 14.3 miles, cross the tracks of the Norfolk–Southern, which follows the route of the old Memphis and Charleston Railroad, a strategic transportation link during the Civil War.

DAVIS BRIDGE AND BIG HILL POND

In another 1.5 miles turn left on TN 57, which parallels the rail line across the southern part of the state from Memphis. In 4.8 miles, at the small community of Pocahontas, turn right on Pocahontas Road for a side trip to **Davis Bridge Battlefield.** The road curves right to a fork in 0.4 mile. You can stay to the right to climb the ridge and arrive at Metamora Hill in 1.1 miles, which overlooks the valley leading to Hatchie River. Here Union troops gathered to support two batteries aimed toward Confederate forces gathered at Davis Bridge. Back at the fork stay to the left to reach the site of the bridge. In 1.1 miles pull into a gravel road on the left beside a house. Park here and walk down the road to the bank of the Hatchie River in a quarter mile.

In October 1862, Confederate forces marched on Corinth, Mississippi, in an effort to wrest the important railroad town from the occupying Union troops who had taken the city following the Confederate defeat at the Battle of Shiloh; Corinth lies to the west and just south of the Tennessee state line. Southern troops were left at this crossing of the Hatchie to keep a retreat route open to the west. In response to the Confederate attack on the Mississippi town, Union forces in Bolivar headed for Corinth. Approaching the Hatchie River at Davis Bridge on October 5, the Union forces encountered the defending Confederates on the west side of the river. The Union batteries on Metamora Hill soon routed the Southerners, who escaped across the bridge. The Union troops pursued the Confederates across the bridge where they encountered fire from Confederate guns mounted on a hill facing the river; in several desperate attempts to take the hill, the Union side suffered 570 dead and wounded; many Confederates were also killed. In the meantime, the Confederate attack on Corinth had been repulsed and the retreating Southerners approached Davis Bridge. With the river crossing in the hands of the Federals, the Confederate army turned south, where another bridge had just been repaired. The Southern troops at Davis Bridge pulled back and formed the rear guard as the Confederates escaped south.

Return to TN 57 and cross the highway into the small railroad town of Pocahontas. Cross the railroad tracks; a two-story, red-roofed brick mansion stands on the right, remaining from the prosperous days when Pocahontas was a railroad stop. At a junction with Peavine Road, turn right, and at a junction with TN 57, turn left to continue east.

Soon cross the Hatchie Scenic River, and in another 0.8 mile enter McNairy County. In 3.8 miles **Big Hill Pond State Park** lies on the left with a campground (no hookups) and boat ramp for access to the 165-acre impounded Travis McNatt Lake. The Big Hill Pond for which the state park is named is not accessible by improved road; the pond was created in 1853 when dirt was taken to build a levee for the Memphis to Charleston Railroad where it crossed bottomlands along the Tuscumbia River and Cypress Creek, both of which border the park. The pit that remained filled with water, creating a thirty-five-acre pond now surrounded by a cypress forest.

SELMER AND PICKWICK LANDING STATE PARK

On TN 57, continue east. In 6 miles, in the small community of Ramer, cross north-south railroad tracks, part of the Norfolk–Southern that heads south to a junction in Corinth with the old Memphis and Charleston that has turned south into Mississippi. In another 4.3 miles, at a junction with US 45, you can turn north for a side trip to Selmer and **Sheriff Buford Pusser's Office.** In 4.4 miles up US 45 you can turn east on TN 142 and travel 3 miles to

Hockaday Broom Factory. Here Jack Martin creates handmade brooms, growing his own broom corn and using the same equipment his great-grandfather Will Hockaday made to start the business in 1916. Each year, Hockaday Brooms hosts the Broomcorn Folk-Art Festival, usually the third weekend in September.

Continue north on US 45. At a junction with US 64, stay straight into Selmer to the town square with the **McNairy County Courthouse** on the left in 2.3 miles. The sheriff's office in the basement of the courthouse is now a museum featuring artifacts from the period when Buford Pusser was sheriff of McNairy County. From 1964 to 1970, Pusser broke up gambling, prostitution, and moonshine rings that operated in this region of the Tennessee-Mississippi stateline, arresting more than 7,500 persons. He survived an assassination attempt in which he was shot in the jaw and his wife was killed, only to die in a car accident in 1974. Three *Walking Tall* movies were made about his exploits. Across from the courthouse, turn right on Third Street to visit the **McNairy County Historical Museum** housed in the old Ritz Movie Theater.

Return from Selmer to TN 57 and continue east for 8.5 miles. There, TN 22 turns left to Shiloh National Military Park and a connection with the Shiloh Drive. Stay on TN 57 to the east for 3.8 miles more. Here TN 142 also turns north toward Shiloh. In 3.5 more miles pass through the small community of Counce. Watch for the **Tenneco Packaging Arboretum,** a small forest with trees identified along a paved walkway.

In another 1.7 miles at a four-way junction, you can turn left to reach **Pickwick Lock and Dam.** The Army Corps of Engineers operates the lock at this Tennessee Valley Authority dam on the Tennessee River. Pull in the parking area past the office building and enter the side of the building to the **Tennessee River Waterway Museum.** It has exhibits on the Tennessee River, its strategic importance during the Civil War, and TVA's later damming of the river.

Straight ahead from the four-way junction, TN 128 circles left to cross Pickwick Dam, forming Pickwick Lake. Across the dam, you can turn left into the **Powerhouse/River Recreation Area** with overlooks, boat access to the river, and a campground nestled among tall pines.

At the four-way junction, TN 57 turns to the right to enter **Pickwick Landing State Park,** which has lodging, a golf course, a campground, a marina, and a picnic area on the shore of Pickwick Lake.

Railroad, Teapots, and David Crockett

JACKSON TO UNION CITY

GENERAL DESCRIPTION: This drive follows the route of a branch of the Mobile and Ohio Railroad north from Jackson for 55 miles, passing through David Crockett country and visiting several historic towns.

SPECIAL ATTRACTIONS: Jackson, Humboldt, Trenton, Pioneer Homeplace, David Crockett House, Kenton white squirrels, farmland, and historic neighborhoods.

LOCATION: Upper West Tennessee. Begin the drive in Jackson at the Convention and Visitors Bureau on East Main Street.

DRIVE ROUTE NUMBERS: US 45W.

CAMPING: Private campgrounds near Jackson and Union City.

SERVICES: All services at Jackson, Humboldt, Trenton, and Union City.

NEARBY ATTRACTIONS: Casey Jones Home and Railroad Museum, West Tennessee Agricultural Museum, and Big Cypress Tree State Natural Area.

THE DRIVE

Much of the community organization and history of West Tennessee was determined by the railroads; communities congregated at rail junctions, and the economy grew with this faster transportation that allowed farmers to ship their crops more efficiently. David Crockett played a key role in local politics and folklore. And in later years, the region has benefited from the collection and donation of fine art, agricultural artifacts, and teapots that are showcased in museums along this drive.

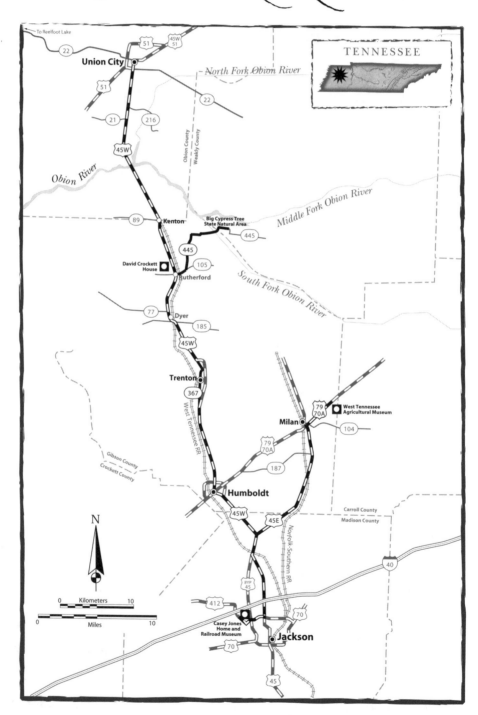

JACKSON AND CROCKETT

Start at the **Old Jackson City Hall** at 314 East Main Street in downtown Jackson; the Jackson Convention and Visitors Bureau is on the second floor (this is also the starting point for the Changing the Landscape drive). Head west on Main Street, crossing Church and Liberty to pass in front of the **Madison County Courthouse.** It was here, after losing reelection to the U.S. Congress, that David Crockett told the gathered crowd, "You can all go to hell; but I am going to Texas." Crockett had served as a Tennessee Representative to the U.S. Congress from 1827 to 1831 and from 1833 to 1835. His early frontier exploits, including fighting under Andrew Jackson in the Creek Wars, led to the image of a legendary Davy Crockett depicted in song, movies, and television, an image reinforced by several reputedly autobiographical books about his adventures. He was a renowned hunter, claiming to have killed 105 bears in just one year. He also seemed to be an honorable person, for he opposed Andrew Jackson's Indian Removal Act, calling it a "wicked, unjust measure."

Answering the call for volunteers, Crockett joined other Tennesseans in the fight for Texas' independence from Mexico. When 2,700 fighting men were requested from Tennessee to help the cause, thirty thousand volunteered, initiating a tradition of offering service in times of war that has earned Tennessee the title of "The Volunteer State." Joining the fight in Texas, Crockett died at the Alamo in 1836. Crockett County and the town of Alamo to the northwest are named in his honor.

At the next corner, turn right on Highland Avenue to head north. In 3.8 miles **Suede's Restaurant and Museum** on the left commemorates the life and music of Carl Lee Perkins, who had his home in Jackson. Born in Ridgely, Tennessee, in 1932, Perkins was the son of sharecroppers. Hearing both country music and rhythm-and-blues as he was growing up, Perkins taught himself how to play the guitar and combined the two music forms to create a sound called "rockabilly" that influenced such music greats as Elvis Presley and the Beatles. Soon after Perkins wrote the song "Blue Suede Shoes," a car accident put him on the sidelines long enough for the music industry to pass him by, so he never received the fame and recognition of those who played his music. He was inducted into the Rock and Roll Hall of Fame in 1987.

At I–40, you can head west 2 miles to the next exit and turn south to the **Casey Jones Home and Railroad Museum.** An Illinois Central railroad engineer and a native of Jackson, John Luther Jones died in a train wreck at Vaughan, Mississippi, on April 30, 1900; his nickname was "Casey" because he spent some of his childhood in Cayce, Kentucky. Rather than jumping from the out-of-control train, Casey stayed with his locomotive, applying the brakes and slowing the train enough to save his passengers; the story of his heroic effort was later told in a popular song and a movie. In addition to the Jones Home, which was moved to this location, the museum contains a replica of Jones' steam engine, No. 389, known as "The Cannonball Express."

MILAN AND HUMBOLDT

From the junction with I–40, continue north on US 45. In 4.6 miles, US 45 Bypass joins US 45; bear right to continue north. In 0.5 mile cross the Middle Fork of the Forked Deer River. The name of the river was changed from the Chickasaw name, Okeena, by an earlier explorer, Henry Rutherford, who thought the native deer had unusually forked antlers.

In 1.5 miles US 45E turns right toward Milan. Take that turn for a side trip to the **West Tennessee Agricultural Museum.** On your way to the museum, you will see the Milan Arsenal, which lies to the right about 10 miles from your turn onto US 45E. An army facility established in 1942 to produce ammunition during World War II, the center is still active as a munitions plant. After you pass the arsenal, US 45E enters Milan. At a junction with US 79/70A, turn right and head out of town on that road for 2.3 miles to the agricultural museum, which is part of the University of Tennessee's Milan Experiment Station, established in 1962 to conduct row crop research on the federal lands around the Milan Arsenal. Tom McCutchen worked here to develop a "no-till" system of planting in which seeds are plugged into the ground with no plowing of the soil. This method of farming prevents loss of topsoil by erosion; unfortunately, chemicals must be used to control weeds because they are not plowed under the topsoil. McCutchen also amassed farm tools and implements during his years at the experiment station; these now form the core collection of farming artifacts housed in the museum. The collection includes probably the world's largest assemblage of plows; it seems appropriate that the home of no-till farming should contain a large number of abandoned plows. The grounds of the museum include the log cabin that was the boyhood home of Gordon W. Browning, Tennessee governor from 1937 to 1939 and from 1949 to 1953. From the museum return on US 79 to its junction with US 45E in Milan. At that four-way intersection, go straight to continue southwest on US 79 12 miles to Humboldt.

Or, if you did not take the side trip to Milan on US 45E and US 79, just continue north on US 45W from the junction with US 45E. In 2.7 miles, enter Gibson County. In 1.2 miles, stay straight on US 45W Business when US 45W Bypass turns to the right to circle Humboldt. Named for Baron

Alexander von Humboldt, an early German explorer of Central and South America, the city of Humboldt obviously had founders with German ancestry. Enter Humboldt on Main Street. In 2 miles is a junction with Central Avenue, which is US 45W continuing north. On the left before the intersection notice the Art Deco **Plaza Theater.** Stay on Main Street through the intersection to the **Humboldt Old City Hall,** a neoclassical building constructed in 1912. This building now houses the **West Tennessee Regional Art Center,** which occupies the front lobby and the old courtroom on the upper floor. The courtroom gallery contains the Caldwell Collection of fine art, including oil and watercolor paintings, sculpture, and silk screens. The collection was donated to the city by Dr. Benjamin and Gertrude Sharp Caldwell. A Nashville physician, Dr. Caldwell is a Humboldt native who, with his wife, collected art from around the country and the world.

As you enter the lobby of the Old City Hall, the Chamber of Commerce is to the left, and to the right is the **West Tennessee Strawberry Festival/Historical Museum.** At one time Humboldt was the center of a thriving strawberry industry that played a large part in the region's economy. To celebrate its famed fruit, Humboldt held its first strawberry festival in 1934, an outpouring of local pride that became a major event each spring thereafter. Although strawberries are no longer grown as a major crop, Humboldt still holds its festival, crowning a Hostess Princess and a Territorial Queen and their courts, staging float parades, and drawing upwards of 100,000 people the first week of May. The museum documents the sixty-six-year tradition.

At the west end of Main, the old train depot sits on the right beside the railroad tracks. This rail line is part of what was once the Mobile and Ohio line that ran north from Jackson and is now the Norfolk–Southern line, which follows US 45E; a branch, now the West Tennessee Railroad, follows US 45W. Return to the intersection of Main with Central, and take Central (US 45W) 1.1 miles north out of town. At that point is a junction with US 79/45 Bypass around Humboldt. Stay straight on US 45W.

TRENTON AND DYER

In 7.1 miles, where US 45W bears right to bypass Trenton, stay straight on US 45W Business, which is also TN 367, to enter Trenton. In 1.7 miles, proceed into town on College Street, which passes through the residential **Trenton Historic District,** a neighborhood that contains a collection of houses dating from the 1850s to the 1940s. Writer Peter Taylor, who won the Pulitzer Prize for his novel, *A Summons to Memphis*, was born and lived as a child at 208 High Street. Stop in the City Hall on the right to visit the **Trenton Teapot Museum,** a collection of more than 500 nineteenth-century teapots and numerous other rare antique porcelains; used also as night lights, the teapots have small warmers that were used to brew the tea. Frederick Freed, a New York doctor, collected these teapots from around the world and donated them to his hometown. If you come by after hours, check in at the police station to gain admittance.

College Street reaches the town square where stands perhaps the prettiest courthouse in the state. **Gibson County Courthouse,** built in 1899, is a vivid Victorian/Italianate structure of red roof, tan brick, and white trim. On the southwest corner of the square sits a bust of David Crockett who in 1823, as a member of the state legislature, instituted the formation of Gibson County. To the right on Eaton Street (TN 77) stands the **Freed House,** the 1871 Victorian home of the Freed family. Julius Freed, a merchant, came to Trenton during Reconstruction following the Civil War; the family became leading citizens of the town.

Travel around the spacious Trenton square, and continue north on US 45W Business out of town. The highway enters cotton country immediately north of town. During harvest season cotton bolls that have dropped from trucks and trailers dust the sides of the highway. A shed on the right shelters open-air trailers full of cotton. Cross the North Fork of the Forked Deer River. In 1.5 miles US 45W joins this roadway from the right.

In 1.8 miles, Gibson County High School lies on the left; the grounds include the adjacent H. B. Yates Memorial Park, which contains the **Pioneer Homeplace,** a fine collection of log cabins and outbuildings you can wander through. In 3.4 miles, crossing the railroad tracks that have been paralleling the highway from Humboldt, enter the small community of Dyer. Grain elevators sit beside the tracks in the center of town. This branch of the old Mobile and Ohio line, now the West Tennessee line, runs only as far north as Kenton but once led to Union City.

This rail line was part of an important transportation system during the Civil War. After Union forces captured Forts Henry and Donelson as they invaded from Kentucky and occupied West Tennessee in early 1862, they used the rail system to transport troops and supplies. Having escaped with his cavalry before the fall of Fort Donelson, Gen. Colonel Nathan Bedford Forrest returned to West Tennessee in December 1862 in an attempt to disrupt this federal transportation system. While one detachment captured the railroads at Humboldt and destroyed track, trestles, and trains and burned Union supplies and munitions, Forrest captured the federal troops encamped around the railroad station in Trenton. He then moved north to capture federal forces here at Dyer, tore up railroad tracks at the Obion River, and moved on to the important junction of Union City where he captured the Union garrison and destroyed tracks. Then, turning southeast to McKenzie, he ripped up more tracks and again captured a federal garrison where he spent Christmas Eve.

BIG CYPRESS TREE AND RUTHERFORD

Continue north of Dyer on US 45W. In 4.3 miles, Rutherford lies at a junction with TN 105. For a side trip to **Big Cypress Tree State Natural Area,** turn right on TN 105 to pass through the small downtown extending to the rail line and cross the tracks. Then cross Rutherford Fork of the Obion River just west of town and in 0.9 mile, turn left on TN 445. In 3.3 miles turn right to stay on TN 445, and cross the South Fork of the Obion River and enter Weakley County. In another 4.1 miles, turn left into Big Cypress Tree State Natural Area. The natural area preserves bottomlands along the Middle Fork of the Obion River; unfortunately the big cypress tree for which the area is named fell some years ago.

David Crockett House

In Rutherford, continue north on US 45W and watch for the **David Crockett House** on the left, a log cabin reconstructed using some of the logs from the original house, which was located about 5 miles to the east. This was Crockett's last home in Tennessee; after losing his bid for reelection to the U.S. Congress he left for Texas, never to return. His mother, Rebecca Hawkins Crockett, lived with him at several locations in Middle and West Tennessee, then took up residence with a daughter near Rutherford. She was originally buried in a nearby cemetery but was later reinterred here beside the Crockett cabin.

KENTON AND UNION CITY

Traveling north from Rutherford, US 45W passes through farmland with big, open fields where corn, soybeans, and cotton grow. In 5.3 miles enter Obion County and reach Kenton. To the right, huge grain elevators for storing the grain stand beside the railroad tracks; the grain is loaded directly into train cars for shipping south to rail junctions in Jackson. Kenton calls itself the "Home of the White Squirrels." No one is sure how the white squirrels came to Kenton, but one account has them being left by wandering gypsies more than a hundred years ago. The squirrels are actually albino gray squirrels that have inbred long enough to produce an isolated population of about 200. You may catch a glimpse of the squirrels as you drive through town.

Heading north from Kenton, in 5.5 miles US 45W crosses the Obion River, a tributary of the Mississippi River. Huge fields blanket the land; when you top a rise along the highway, you can see for a mile across the clearings. Traveling north another 9.5 miles, US 45W reaches a junction with TN 22 at Union City. Take First Street to enter the historic downtown. In 0.7 mile Washington Street leads left to the **Obion County Courthouse.** The **Union City Post Office** is on the left down the street, a smaller but more elaborate building with columns and terraced roof constructed in 1913.

Continue up First Street, and notice the 1927 Art Deco **Capitol Theater** on the right in a block of commercial buildings. Touring shows and silent films appeared here in the theater's early years, and later talking movies came to the screen. The theater has been restored and is now the home of the Masquerade Theatre group. This row of buildings facing the street was once the back of the buildings. Turn right at the next block to reach the railroad tracks behind. Originally the front entrances faced the tracks. With the waning of railroad business and the routing of a highway through town on the other side in the 1920s, the businesses constructed entrances on their back side to take advantage of the traffic passing through town.

Ahead is the old **Union Depot** on East Church Street; it now houses the Chamber of Commerce. In 1855 George Washington Gibbs offered land for a junction between the Mobile and Ohio and the Nashville and Northwestern Railroads. He wanted to call the town Junction City, but since another town already claimed that name, he decided on Union City. The present depot dates from 1922.

Return to TN 22 and turn east. In 0.6 mile turn left on Russell Street to the **Obion County Museum** on the left in an old church; this fine collection on local history includes an exhibit of photographs of Reelfoot Lake and Union City. Taken by Verne and Nonie Sabin, these photos date from 1919 to 1924. The museum occupies the block between Russell and Edwards Streets. Exit the museum parking area on Edwards and turn right. Drive 0.3 mile to a junction with Summers Street. To the left stands the **Confederate Memorial;** erected in 1869, it is the earliest monument to unknown Confederate soldiers. On his raid into West Tennessee in late 1862, Gen. Nathan Bedford Forrest captured the federal garrison at Union City. The graves of Confederates who died in the raid are some of those grouped at four corners around the monument.

cotton, Blues, and Barbecue

MEMPHIS TO BROWNSVILLE LOOP

GENERAL DESCRIPTION: This 177-mile drive circles through West Tennessee cotton country, which gave rise to the blues and barbecue.

SPECIAL ATTRACTIONS: Memphis, Germantown, Collierville, LaGrange, Ames Plantation, Dancyville, Hatchie National Wildlife Refuge, Brownsville, Stanton, Arlington, Davies Plantation, Overton Park, Victoria Village Historic District, historic homes and buildings, scenic views, fall color, hiking, biking, fishing, hunting, and wildlife viewing.

LOCATION: West Tennessee. Begin the drive at the Tennessee Welcome Center on Riverside Drive in Memphis.

DRIVE ROUTE NUMBERS: US 72, TN 57, LaGrange Road, TN 76, and US 70/79.

CAMPING: T.O. Fuller State Park and private campgrounds near Memphis.

SERVICES: All services at Memphis, Germantown, Collierville, Somerville, Brownsville, and Bartlett.

NEARBY ATTRACTIONS: National Bird Dog Museum, Historic Williston, Cotton Museum of the South, and Gotten House.

THE DRIVE

Cotton, blues, and barbecue have long played a role in southern culture. Cotton was the principal crop that established the old plantations of the South and continues to be a major part of the economy in West Tennessee. Slaves, and then sharecroppers and cotton pickers after them, sang spirituals and other songs that often were lamentations about their lives and their lack of opportunity for improvement. Out of this tradition came the blues, a music style that embodies a regret over life's eccentricities and one's own foolhardy participation. And barbecue is a fitting complement to cotton and blues; it's a food that fortifies the soul.

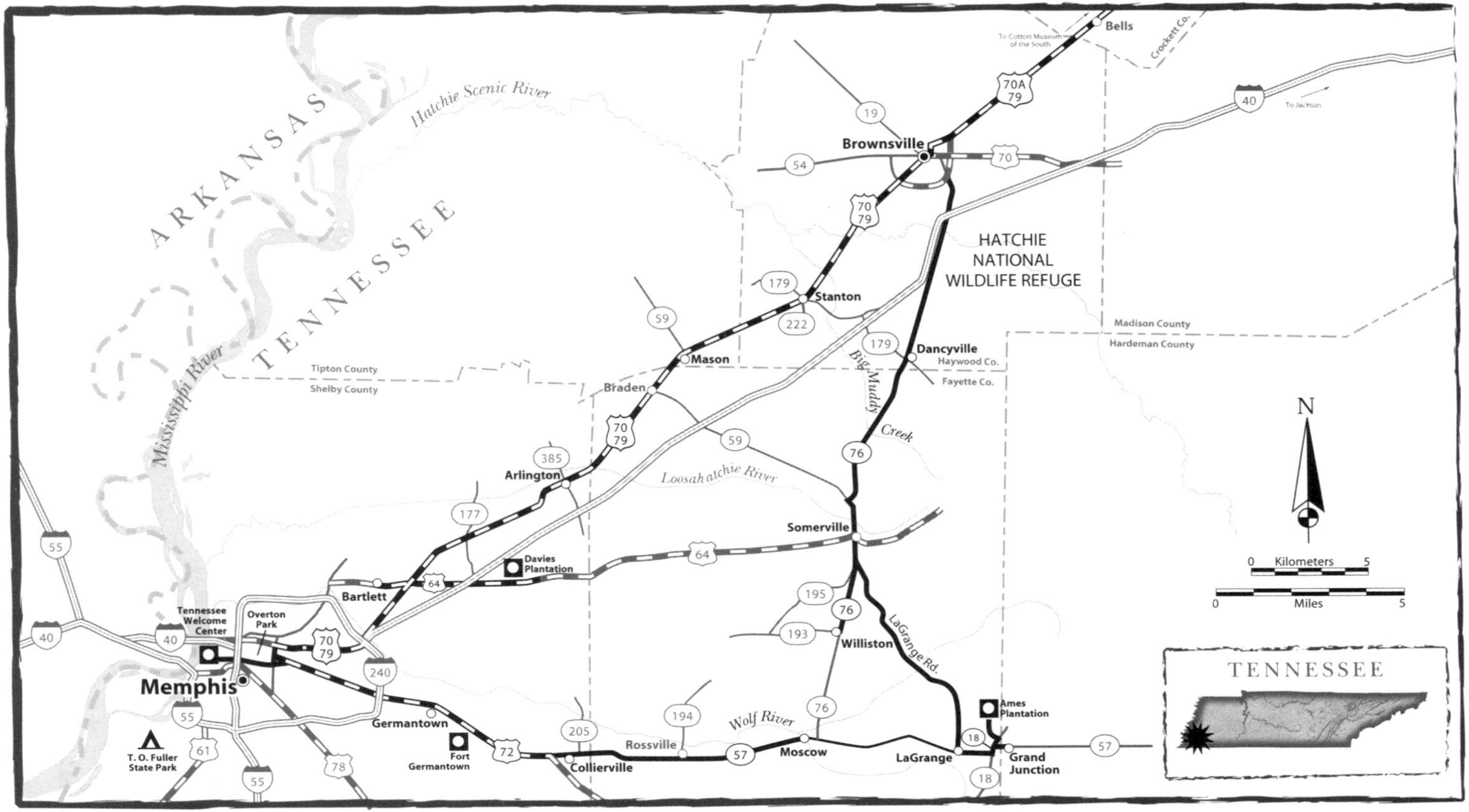
ARKANSAS
TENNESSEE
Mississippi River
Hatchie Scenic River
Tipton County
Shelby County
Bells
To Cotton Museum of the South
Crockett Co.
To Jackson
Brownsville
HATCHIE NATIONAL WILDLIFE REFUGE
Stanton
Mason
Braden
Dancyville
Haywood Co.
Fayette Co.
Madison County
Hardeman County
Big Muddy Creek
Loosahatchie River
Arlington
Somerville
Davies Plantation
Bartlett
Williston
LaGrange Rd.
Tennessee Welcome Center
Overton Park
Memphis
Germantown
Fort Germantown
T. O. Fuller State Park
Collierville
Rossville
Wolf River
Moscow
LaGrange
Ames Plantation
Grand Junction
N
0 Kilometers 5
0 Miles 5
TENNESSEE

MEMPHIS

Begin this drive at the **Tennessee Welcome Center** on Riverside Drive in Memphis, just south of the I–40 crossing of the Mississippi River. In 1819 Andrew Jackson, John Overton, and James Winchester founded a small community on these bluffs above the Mississippi River where Fort Pickering was located. Winchester selected the name Memphis after the Egyptian city on the Nile. This townsite had once been the home of a large Mississippian mound village, part of which is preserved at Chucalissa Historic Site, a National Historic Landmark located in **T. O. Fuller State Park** at the southwest corner of the city. The Chickasaw Indians later lived along the river bluffs but relinquished their claim to West Tennessee in 1818 with the Jackson Purchase, negotiated by Andrew Jackson.

Exit the Welcome Center to cross Riverside Drive and head up Jefferson Avenue to Front Street and turn right to enter the **Cotton Row Historic District.** Situated on the Mississippi River, Memphis grew to become one of the largest inland ports in the country. As settlers learned the land was good for growing cotton, the city became an important port for buying, selling and shipping cotton. The business still takes place in commercial buildings along Front Street dating from the 1800s to the early 1900s. Watch for **Howard's Row** on the right; these connected buildings constructed in 1843 are the oldest commercial buildings in the downtown district.

In 4 blocks, at the corner of Union and Front, stands the **Memphis Cotton Exchange** on the left, constructed in 1925. The first-floor lobby contains photographs and information on the cotton industry, including a display of various grades of cotton. In 1826, the year Memphis was incorporated, 300 bales of cotton were brought by horse-drawn wagons to be sold. By 1870, railroads and steamboats delivered 400,000 bales, and Memphis had become the largest inland cotton market in the country. The cotton dealers decided they needed a trade association, so they formed the Cotton Exchange in 1873 and began issuing crop reports. With more than five million bales now passing through the exchange, Memphis has become the world's largest spot market in cotton.

Two blocks north on Union stands the **Peabody Hotel,** constructed in 1925; magnificently restored, it is still the place to stay in Memphis. In 1932 the management put some ducks in the hotel's indoor fountain, and it soon became a tradition for the ducks to daily march from their rooftop homes to the fountain; the public is welcome to watch the ducks arrive at 11:00 A.M. and depart at 5:00 P.M. Near the hotel on Second Street, the **Rendezvous** has served up West Tennessee pork barbecue and their famous dry ribs since 1948.

Continue on Front Street to Beale Street and turn left into the **Beale Street Historic District.** Urban renewal has destroyed much of the African-American community that gave rise to a music form known as "the blues," but the street still has a number of the original commercial buildings, blues clubs, and cafes to give a representative sampling of the neighborhood. Travel 1 block to the corner of Beale and Main Street, where the **Orpheum Theater** stands on the right. Built in 1928 as theater for vaudeville acts, the Orpheum is now a performing arts center. At Second Street, you can turn right to visit the **National Civil Rights Museum** at the Lorraine Motel on Mulberry Street. Dr. Martin Luther King Jr. was assassinated at the motel on April 4, 1968.

Continuing east on Beale Street, notice **A. Schwab's General Merchandise Store** on the right; established in 1876, it is still in operation. Across Third Street, the **W. C. Handy Park** lies on the left, with a statue of W. C. Handy, the father of the blues; Handy was one of the first to formalize blues by writing it down, composing such classics as "Memphis Blues," "St. Louis Blues," and "Beale Street Blues." Notice on the right the **Old Daisy Theater** built in 1914. At the corner of Beale and Fourth Street on the left is a small house that is the **W. C. Handy House Museum;** Handy's home-place was moved to this location and now houses artifacts and memorabilia about his life and music.

Across Fourth Street on the right lies **Church Park** established in 1899 by Robert R. Church Sr. as a public space for the community. A former slave and later a businessman, Church became the first African-American million-aire in the South.

Across Danny Thomas Boulevard on the right stands the **Hunt-Phelan Home,** a grand two-story brick home with a massive, white-columned por-tico, built in the years 1828 to 1832. During the Civil War, Gen. U. S. Grant used the home as his headquarters while he planned the capture of Vicks-burg. After the war, a frame building constructed behind the house was one of the first schools established by the Freedman's Bureau, a federal agency established to help newly freed slaves.

At the next corner, turn left on Lauderdale Street and travel 1 block to Union Street. Directly across Union is **Sun Studio,** where Sam Phillips opened a recording studio in 1950. Music legends got their start here, from B. B. King to Johnny Cash and Elvis Presley. The studio is open for tours; a cafe and a gallery are upstairs. Elvis had his home at **Graceland** to the south on Elvis Presley Boulevard, also open for tours.

Turn right on Union Street and drive 3.6 miles to a junction with East Parkway. Turn right and travel 0.7 mile and turn left on Central Avenue. In

1.5 miles the **Pink Palace** stands on the left. Founder of the Piggly Wiggly Grocery Stores, Clarence Saunders was the first businessman to provide self-service stores so customers could personally pick out their grocery items instead of a clerk gathering groceries from a shopping list. Saunders started construction of his home in 1922 using pink marble from Georgia. The building was not yet finished when his finances collapsed. A developer who bought the property gave the structure to the city, which turned it into a museum with exhibits on the natural and cultural history of the area.

Continue east on Central and in 1.9 miles turn left on Goodlett Road. Continue to Poplar Avenue and turn right. In 2.5 miles watch for the original **Corky's Bar-B-Q,** which has been so successful serving up West Tennessee pork barbecue that it has expanded into a chain of restaurants. Aficionados claim only West Tennessee style is the proper way to fix barbecue—slow roasted and pulled, not cut; the sauce added only at the table before eating, not during the cooking. And in this part of the country, don't bother asking for beef.

In 1.3 miles pass a junction with I–240 that circles the southern half of Memphis, and continue out of town on Poplar, which is also US 72/TN 57. In 0.6 mile you can turn right on Ridgeway Road to reach **Lichterman Nature Center** on Quince Road. This sixty-five-acre wildlife sanctuary is an environmental education facility; walking trails wander through a variety of habitats.

GERMANTOWN AND COLLIERVILLE

Continuing east on US 72, enter Germantown, now part of the urban area surrounding Memphis. The town was named for the many German immigrants who settled here in the 1830s. In 2.1 miles turn right on Germantown Road to enter the old section of Germantown. Where the road crosses railroad tracks, the **Germantown Depot** stands on the right in a small town park. Germantown became a thriving community around the Memphis and Charleston Railroad, which was constructed across the southern portion of West Tennessee to connect the cotton markets of Memphis and ports along the Mississippi River with ports on the Atlantic shore. When the Memphis and Charleston was completed in 1853, it became an important rail corridor that played a strategic role during the Civil War. Today the line is part of the Norfolk–Southern Railway.

Turn left on Poplar Pike to continue east. On the right is **Oaklawn Garden Historic Site.** In 1918 Fritz Hussey and Mamie Cloyes purchased the 1854 house. Two generations later, Harry Cloyes, their grandnephew, along with wife Becky, established a botanical garden and outdoor museum containing an eclectic collection of historical items from Germantown's past.

Continue east on Poplar Pike. In 1 mile you can turn right on Honey Tree Drive to reach **Fort Germantown.** The Union Army built this Civil War fortification in 1863 to guard the Memphis and Charleston Railroad; by then, federal forces were occupying Middle and West Tennessee and used the railroads to transport troops and supplies. The fort was a post, sapling, and earth construction; now only the earthworks remain.

Return to Poplar Pike and continue east, paralleling the railroad tracks on the right. In 2.6 miles Poplar Pike joins US 72 as you leave the urban area outside of Germantown.

Where US 72 turns to the right in 2.7 miles, continue straight on TN 57. In 1.2 miles turn right on Main Street to enter the **Collierville Historic District.** Collierville started as a small settlement but quickly grew into a railroad town with the coming of the Memphis and Charleston in the 1850s. During the Civil War, Collierville was a important Union supply base along the railroad. On October 11, 1863, a Confederate raiding party under Gen. James R. Chalmers attacked the rail station. Just as the battle began, Maj. Gen. William T. Sherman arrived by train, having been sent from Memphis to start his march to the sea. The Confederates captured the train along with Union supplies and horses, including Sherman's favorite horse, Dolly. After three hours of fighting and with Union reinforcements on their way, the Confederates withdrew. The battle claimed fifty-one Confederate and one hundred Union casualties. In his anger over the losses, Sherman ordered the town burned. Today's Collierville has commercial buildings dating from 1895 to 1930 on three sides of the square, one of the most picturesque town squares in the state. On the north, the **Silver Caboose Restaurant** occupies an old pharmacy building and contains the original soda fountain. The center of the square is a park with a gazebo, walkways, and benches. The **Collierville Depot** stands on the south side of the square next to the railroad tracks; originally the depot was in LaGrange to the east but was moved here in 1944. The train cars gathered around the depot form an outdoor museum.

LAGRANGE AND AMES PLANTATION

Return to TN 57 from the town square, and turn right to continue east out of Collierville. In 1.1 miles pass from Shelby County into Fayette County, crossing the railroad tracks again while paralleling the state line to the south. The highway passes through rural countryside with large farms and spreading fields; cotton and soybeans are harvested by the end of October. Soybeans are legumes used as a foodstuff. The cotton plant is an annual that produces pods, called "bolls," at the end of the stems. The bolls contain seeds packed with white fibers used to make thread since prehistoric times. For ages, cotton was picked by hand, but the introduction of mechanical pickers in recent times greatly speeded up the harvest. Prior to harvest you may see the plants turned to a rust-colored brown and the bolls opened to reveal the white cotton; the crop is treated with a defoliant to rid the plant of leaves before picking. After harvest, light fluffs of cotton feather the sides of the road where they have blown off the trucks and trailers hauling the harvest to cotton gins.

In 13.7 miles cross a bridge over the Wolf River and enter the community of Moscow, another railroad town along the Memphis and Charleston. On the left sits **Lewis' Restaurant,** which has been serving West Tennessee pork barbecue since 1938.

Continue straight on TN 57 another 8.8 miles to **LaGrange,** established in 1819 on the site of an Indian trading post. The town is named for the ancestral home of the Marquis de Lafayette, the Frenchman who fought in the American Revolution. On his triumphal tour of the U.S. in 1824, he visited LaGrange, calling it *La Belle Village,* "the beautiful village." The town contains a fine collection of antebellum homes. An annual walking tour takes you past many of the two-story white frame houses; nearly every home is white and many have porches and white picket fences, features that make the town one of the most charming small communities in the state.

In the center of town, turn right on Main Street to see the small commercial district. Just beyond on the right is an old cotton gin. Before cotton fibers can be spun into thread, they must be separated from the seeds. This was a painstaking process until Eli Whitney invented the cotton engine in 1793. Better known by its shortened name of "cotton gin," the machine consisted of a toothed cylinder that pulled the fibers through a grate the seeds could not pass through. More modern gins use circular saws that pull the fibers through a grid. The extracted seeds contain cottonseed oil that is processed for use in foods. In recent years most small gins were abandoned as cotton ginning became concentrated in a few modern, computer-operated gins. These older gins, now deserted and rusting, dot the countryside throughout the cotton country.

Continue east on TN 57 to leave LaGrange. Watch for **Woodlawn Mansion** sitting grandly on a hill to the left; the brick Greek Revival home was built in 1828 by Maj. Charles Michie, who fought in the War of 1812. The huge portico on the east side of the home was added later. During the Civil War, the house was the headquarters of Union Gen. William Sherman for a short time and was used as a hospital by both sides.

At a junction with TN 18, turn left to cross the railroad tracks and reach a junction with TN 57 continuing right. You can turn right here to enter Hardeman County and the community of Grand Junction and find the **National Bird Dog Museum,** founded by the Bird Dog Foundation to preserve and promote the sport of using bird dogs for hunting and field trials. The exhibits feature more than forty breeds of dogs grouped into pointers, retrievers, and setters.

Grand Junction has its old cotton gin, and the old **Grand Junction Depot** awaits renovation. **Tennessee Pewter Company** still turns out utensils made of pewter, a metal alloy containing mostly tin; items include tableware and jewelry.

Return along TN 57 into Fayette County to the junction with TN 18 and turn right. Then turn left on Buford Ellington Road to enter **Ames Plantation** along a cedar-lined lane. You'll reach the grand manor house in 3.8 miles. You may walk around the grounds; the house is occasionally open for visitors. It is not by coincidence that the National Bird Dog Museum is located in this part of Tennessee; for nearly one hundred years, the National Field Trial Championship has been held at this plantation.

When this region was settled in the early 1800s, several plantations and homesteads were staked out for the growing of cotton; this economy, almost totally based on cotton and with slaves doing most of the work, flourished until the Civil War. Eventually more than 200 families lived in the area. The white Greek Revival manor house was built in 1847 for John Walker Jones and was called Cedar Grove. In 1901 the house and 400 acres were purchased by Hobart C. Ames, Boston industrialist and quail hunter who wanted to establish a home for the national field trials for bird dogs. Ames eventually expanded his holdings to the 18,567 acres that make up the present Ames Plantation, which is managed by the Hobart Ames Foundation in cooperation with the University of Tennessee College of Agriculture. The university conducts experimental research in agriculture, continuing a tradition started by Ames, who bred Black Angus cattle. The bird dog field trials are held here annually in February.

WILLISTON, SOMERVILLE, AND HATCHIE SCENIC RIVER

Return to LaGrange, and in the center of town, turn right on LaGrange Road to continue this drive to the north. The road passes along the back side of Ames Plantation and enters farmland; large cotton fields lie on both sides of the road with occasional soybean and cattle fields. In 6.1 miles cross the

North Fork of the Wolf River. The highway joins TN 76 in another 8.2 miles just south of Somerville. You can turn left onto TN 76 for a 4.3-mile side trip to Williston. Turn right on TN 193 to get to the old town center. The 1860s **W. C. Crawford General Merchandise Store** stands along the route of an old railroad spur that once passed through town, connecting Somerville to the north with the Memphis and Charleston line to the south; Williston grew up as a railroad stop about halfway between Somerville and the M & C Line. The old railroad right-of-way has now been converted into a town park. The town contains the 1850 **Walker-Crawford House,** a beautifully restored farmhouse—painted gray with green shutters, it has flower boxes and red-brick chimneys.

On TN 76 continue north into Somerville. The **Somerville Historic District** contains several houses and buildings constructed before the Civil War; the oldest is **Frogmore,** a residence built in 1829. In 1.3 miles, the **Fayette County Courthouse** with clock tower stands on a square. To the right from the square is **The Hut,** which has served up some of the finest West Tennessee pork barbecue since 1952. Across the street stands Somerville's old cotton gin.

Pass around the square to continue north on TN 76. You can turn left on North Main to reach the **Hanum-Reah House;** built in 1832, the home is being restored by the Association for the Preservation of Tennessee Antiquities and will serve as the Fayette County Museum and Cultural Center. To the right on TN 76 rests **Yancy Park,** celebrating Tennessee's longest serving mayor, whose term ran from 1940 to 1978.

In 2.1 miles bear right to stay on TN 76 where TN 59 turns to the left. Back into countryside, the road passes cotton fields, grain silos holding soybeans, and rolls of hay sitting in pastures. In 5 miles cross Big Muddy Creek. This bottomland of water and cypress trees contrasts with the surrounding farmland. In 4.1 miles enter Haywood County, and in another 0.6 mile enter Dancyville with the **Dancyville United Methodist Church** to the left. The white frame church was built in 1850 of hand-sawed lumber from trees that were on the church grounds. The adjacent cemetery that spreads down the hill dates from 1830 and contains several Civil War dead. Continue north on TN 76; a small cotton gin, abandoned, stands on the left just before reaching the Dancyville town square.

Through Dancyville, the road reenters farmland with fields and small farms. In 4.7 miles TN 76 begins to parallel I–40 to the left, entering the **Hatchie National Wildlife Refuge** along the Hatchie Scenic River. The road skims the top of a berm that lifts the highway out of the wetlands along

W. C. Crawford General Merchandise Store

the river. Despite surrounding development and farmland, the Hatchie still has a hardwoods bottomland little changed from when white men first entered the region. The refuge protects 9,400 acres that support birds, mammals, reptiles, amphibians, and fish. Hunting, fishing, and wildlife observation are popular activities. In 1.7 miles turn right on a gravel road for a 2-mile scenic drive around **O'Neal Lake.** This man-made lake is the site for Project Fish, a demonstration project for developing boardwalks and platforms at the water's edge for the disabled; fishing is limited to special permit. Watch for wood ducks, mallards, hooded mergansers, and Canada geese.

Back on TN 76, continue north. The highway crosses bridge after bridge after bridge that spans openings in the berm that allow the waters to move freely back and forth through this bottomland. In 1.2 miles a gravel road turns off to the right; it passes through the refuge along the Hatchie Scenic River through bottomland forest with opportunity for wildlife viewing.

TN 76 then crosses a larger bridge over the **Hatchie Scenic River.** This beautiful river stretches for 200 miles through three states before emptying into the Mississippi River to the west. It is the longest unchannelized tributary in the Mississippi Valley and the largest forested river floodplain in Tennessee. The Nature Conservancy has named the Hatchie one of the seventy-five Last Great Places in the world that need protection; the Tennessee chapter of the conservancy is working diligently with government agencies and landowners to protect the river from loss of habitat and a high sedimentation rate.

BROWNSVILLE

The national refuge headquarters lies on the right of TN 76. You can stop here for information on the area. Soon after TN 76 crosses I–40 turn right on Sunnyhill Cove Lane to reach the **West Tennessee Delta Heritage Center.** It features displays for each surrounding county plus special exhibit rooms for the three primary concerns of the region: wildlife, cotton, and blues.

Outside the heritage center stands the **"Sleepy" John Estes House,** the old homeplace of John Adam Estes. (It was originally on Bradford Street in nearby Brownsville.) Estes began playing blues at an early age; the usually mournful tones and melancholy lyrics grew out of songs sung by workers in the cotton fields. Estes, who liked to take naps, wrote and sang of his own experience and the hard life many in the South endured in songs such as "Brownsville Blues" and "Someday Baby." Estes teamed with fellow Brownsville blues artists harmonica player Hammie Nixon and James "Yank" Rachell on the mandolin to play at dances and picnics and later at clubs in

Memphis. In 1931 Estes and Nixon moved to Chicago and recorded with Decca and Bluebird Records. Eventually Estes returned to West Tennessee, recording at Memphis's Sun Studio in the early 1950s. In the early 1960s, with a resurgence in folk and blues music, Estes was rediscovered living in Brownsville and embarked on the most successful part of his career—making more recordings, performing at the Newport Jazz Festival and the Smithsonian, and touring Europe and Japan. He continued to perform until his death in 1977. During this latter phase, he was rejoined many times by Nixon and Rachell who had also become famous blues musicians. In mid-September Brownsville holds the annual **Brownsville Blues Fall Festival,** celebrating the three Brownsville bluesmen and their music with performances by bluesmen and women from around the country.

Return to TN 76 and turn right, heading into Brownsville. In 2.4 miles the road intersects the US 70/79 Bypass around the city. Before entering Brownsville, you can turn right for a side trip to see operating cotton gins and a restored steam-operated cotton gin. On the bypass in 1.1 miles, you can turn right on US 70 to pass through large farms. During the fall harvest, trailer loads of cotton sit in fields, waiting to be taken to the gin. Haywood County is usually the largest producer of cotton in Tennessee; the harvest is something like 150,000 bales a year. In 3.6 miles is **Zion Gin Company,** a modern cotton gin on the right. In another 3 miles the **Union Cotton Gin,** older but still operating, sits on the left in the community of Union. Return to the US 70/79 Bypass and turn right to continue around Brownsville another 1 mile, then turn right on US 79 to the northeast to continue this side trip. Passing through more cotton fields, the highway parallels the railroad tracks that lead into Brownsville; this is part of the CSX Railroad running northeast to southwest through West Tennessee to Memphis, following the old route of the Memphis and Ohio that connected Paris and Memphis. In 9.8 miles cross into Crockett County and enter the community of Bells in 0.7 mile. In this old railroad town, granaries and an old cotton gin sit beside the railroad tracks. At a junction with US 412, turn left to head northwest 2.3 miles to the **Cotton Museum of the South** at Green Frog Village. John and Nancy Freeman, who operate the village, have brought a 1915 Continental four-stand cotton gin from Alabama and are restoring it as the centerpiece of the Cotton Museum, a nonprofit foundation. When fully restored and attached to a steam generator, the gin will be used to demonstrate the ginning and baling of cotton.

Return to Brownsville and enter the town on US 79 if you went to the cotton museum. If you did not take the side trip, continue on TN 76 across the US 70/79 Bypass to enter Brownsville, and reach a junction with East Main Street (US 70 Business) in another 1.3 miles. Turn left to reach the town square where the blues festival is held each year. The **Haywood County Courthouse** stands on the center. Pass around the town square and out West Main; the Brownsville-Haywood County Chamber of Commerce is housed in the old **Carnegie Library** on the right. The library was built in 1910 with a grant from industrialist and philanthropist Andrew Carnegie, who funded more than 2,800 libraries in the U.S., many in Tennessee. At the chamber, you can pick up a 1.5-mile walking/driving tour of the **Brownsville Historic District** of homes and churches.

Continue west from the town square to a junction where US 70 turns to the left. Here you can turn right on North Grand to enter the **College Hill Center Historic District,** which contains College Hill, an old school that today houses the **Haywood County Museum** and the **Felsenthal Lincoln Collection** of books, photos, and artifacts about Abraham Lincoln and the Civil War.

Return to Main and cross the street to head out of town on US 70 Business. Back into cotton country, the highway passes through fields and farms. In 6.6 miles cross the Hatchie Scenic River. In 1824 Hiram and Miles Bradford established Bradford's Landing here on the Hatchie as a stop for river transportation; Hiram Bradford had the first gin and store in Brownsville.

STANTON, MASON, ARLINGTON

In 3.7 miles the highway crosses the Big Muddy Creek tributary of the Hatchie River. In 1.4 miles, enter Stanton at a junction with TN 179. You can turn right on Covington Street to the old **Stanton Baptist Church,** and just beyond is the white frame Greek Revival **Stanton Masonic Lodge and School.** Built in 1871, it had a school for the local children on the first floor and a Masonic hall on the second floor. Masonry, or freemasonry, grew out of sixteenth-century craft guilds of masons and architects that protected trade secrets with a practice of rituals and passwords; the members were called Free and Accepted Masons. In more modern times, being a stoneworker or builder was no longer a requirement for membership. Today, it is an international secret fraternal organization based on religion, charity, and obedience to custom. George Washington was a member.

Return down Covington to cross US 70/79 and enter the center of the community. Turn right on Main Street, paralleling the railroad tracks that run through town on the left; old commercial buildings are lined up on the right facing the tracks. To the left beside the railroad is an operating cotton gin. Past

Arlington Historic Post Office

Oak Street stands the **Stanton Presbyterian Church.** This Gothic church was built in 1870 on land donated by Grace Stanton Adams, the daughter of Joseph B. Stanton for whom the town is named, and her husband, Nathan. With its spires and arches, it is a replica of a church the couple had seen in Scotland. When the Presbytery closed the church and proposed moving the structure, local citizens formed the Stanton Preservation Trust, which purchased the building; community events are now held in the old church.

Main Street reaches a junction with TN 222; turn right to return to US 70/79 and turn left to continue traveling on US 70/79 to the southwest. Beyond Stanton, the highway passes through field after field of cotton. In 4.2 miles enter Tipton County. Four miles farther in the community of Mason, **Bozo's Restaurant** has served up fine West Tennessee barbecue since 1923. In another 0.5 mile enter Fayette County while paralleling the CSX Railroad tracks on the left, again passing through huge fields of cotton, but also corn, soybeans, and cattle. In 5.7 miles on US 70/79, reenter Shelby County. Passing through lowlands to both sides of the road, cross the Loosahatchie River. In 2 more miles you reach Arlington, where you can turn left on

Chester Street to reach the old town center, crossing the railroad tracks that run through town with an old depot to the right; an old cotton gin also stands to the right. Bear right to stay on Chester and pass in front of the **Arlington Historic Post Office** on the left; the small white frame building opened in 1885 and is reminiscent of small-town post offices throughout the South. Just beyond, at the corner of Walker Street, stands the small white frame Arlington Bank and Trust Company building. Constructed in 1905, it is now the **Rachel H. K. Burrow Museum,** named for a local schoolteacher and historian. Walker Street to the right passes through an old commercial district where the fourth generation of **S. Y. Wilson and Co.** operates a general merchandise store that has stood here since 1893.

DAVIES PLANTATION AND BARTLETT

Return to US 70/79, and continue to the southwest, crossing the CSX Railroad tracks running toward Memphis. In 12 miles turn left on US 64 to head for **Davies Plantation.** In 3.2 miles turn left on New Brunswick Road and make an immediate right on Brunswick Road. In 2.2 miles turn right on Davies Plantation Road. In 0.5 mile, the **Tennessee Genealogical Society Research Center and Library** resides in a parklike setting. In another 0.4 mile Davieshire Road turns off to the left. Then the entrance to Davies Plantation on the left leads up a long lane to Davies Manor, a two-story colonial-style log house. The west portion of the house was constructed by a Chickasaw farmer in 1807. Joel W. Royster acquired the property in 1831 and added the eastern half of the house with a dogtrot between that is now a closed hallway. Logan Davies purchased the house in 1851 and with his brother, James, established a plantation that grew to 2,000 acres. The house is now managed by the Davies Manor Association as a museum and contains artifacts from its early years. Tours begin at offices off Davieshire Road.

Return to US 70/79, where you can take a side trip into Bartlett by staying straight on Stage Road, which was once the route of a stagecoach road that ran east from Memphis to Nashville; Bartlett was originally a stop on the stagecoach route. Today, Stage Road passes through a modern commercial area. In 1.9 miles turn right on Court Street to the **Gotten House,** which now houses the Bartlett Museum. The New England salt-box style, two-story residence was built in 1871 by Nicholas and Julia Gotten. Nicholas had immigrated to the U.S. from Prussia in 1832; he settled in this region and became a prominent blacksmith, merchant, and cotton ginner, and served in the Confederate Army during the Civil War.

OVERTON PARK AND VICTORIAN VILLAGE

Return to US 70/79 and continue southwest. In 4.6 miles pass under I–40, which circles north of Memphis. The highway then enters the city as Summer Street. In 5.5 miles turn left on East Parkway at the corner of **Overton Park.** In 1.3 miles turn right on Poplar Avenue to reach the entrance to the city park on the right in 1 mile. In addition to the Brooks Museum of Art, the Memphis Zoo, picnic areas, a golf course, and ball fields, Overton Park contains 170 acres of climax oak-hickory forest, one of the finest urban forests in the nation. Established in 1901, the park is named for one of the city's founders, John Overton. In the 1960s and '70s, controversy raged over whether to complete Interstate 40 through Memphis, passing through the heart of Overton Park. Citizens to Preserve Overton Park fought the proposal, going all the way to the U.S. Supreme Court. In the end the preservation group stopped the construction of I–40, which now turns north when it reaches the I–240 bypass and travels around the city before resuming its east-west route.

Continue west on Poplar Avenue, and in 1.5 miles turn left on Watkins Street and then turn right on Jefferson Avenue. In 1.4 miles, where Jefferson bears to the left, stay right on Adams Avenue to enter the **Victorian Village Historic District,** which contains a number of historic homes. Several are open to the public as house museums. The **James Lee House** is a Second Empire-style mansion built in the years 1848 to 1871. The **Woodruff-Fontaine House,** also a Second Empire style mansion, was built between 1870 and 1871. The **Massey House,** a Greek Revival cottage built in 1847, is the oldest house in the village. The **Mallory-Neely House** is an Italian Villa built in the 1850s. Other historic homes lie within the historic district, but some of them are still private residences. Among these is the **Pillow-McIntyre House,** which was the home of Gen. Gideon J. Pillow, one of the generals at the fall of Fort Donelson.

Continue west on Adams. Watch for the **Magevney House** on the right in 0.8 mile; a white frame house built about 1836, it is the oldest middle-class residence remaining in Memphis. Originally it was a two-room house; then Eugene Magevney enlarged the home after he became the owner in 1837. An Irish immigrant, Magevney was one of the first schoolteachers in Memphis. The house is open to the public.

Adams Avenue runs into Riverside Drive at the **Tennessee Welcome Center** where this drive ends.

Mississippi River

MEMPHIS TO REELFOOT LAKE

GENERAL DESCRIPTION: This 166-mile drive follows the Mississippi River north from Memphis, occasionally dropping off Chickasaw Bluffs into the floodplain of the river and ending at Tennessee's only large natural lake.

SPECIAL ATTRACTIONS: Mud Island River Park, Meeman-Shelby Forest State Park, Covington, Alex Haley Boyhood Home, Fort Pillow State Historic Park, Reelfoot Lake, historic homes and buildings, scenic views, fall color, hiking, biking, fishing, hunting, and wildlife viewing.

LOCATION: West Tennessee. Begin the drive at the Tennessee Welcome Center on Riverside Drive in Memphis.

DRIVE ROUTE NUMBERS: TN 388 and 59; US 51; TN 87, 209, 88, 181, 79, 78, 22, and 21.

CAMPING: Meeman-Shelby Forest State Park, Fort Pillow State Historic Park, and Reelfoot Lake State Park.

SERVICES: All services at Memphis and Covington.

NEARBY ATTRACTIONS: Sunk Lake State Natural Area, Lower Hatchie National Wildlife Refuge, Lauderdale Waterfowl Refuge, Chickasaw National Wildlife Refuge, and Reelfoot National Wildlife Refuge.

THE DRIVE

The Plateau of West Tennessee ends at Chickasaw Bluffs, a series of headlands standing 200 feet above the Mississippi floodplain. The river beyond forms the western boundary of the state. The Chickasaw Indians lived along the river bluff, which stretches along the floodplain of the river north to south through the state. In 1818 Andrew Jackson and Isaac Shelby negotiated the purchase of these lands in what came to be known as the Jackson Purchase. The county in the southwest corner of the state was named for Shelby. The following year Jackson, along with John Overton and James Winchester founded the town of Memphis. As this western part of the state developed, the Mississippi River became a primary transportation route and Memphis

TENNESSEE

KENTUCKY
TENN

To Union City

157

22

Grassy Island

212

Reelfoot Lake

22

Tiptonville

Samburg

REELFOOT WILDLIFE
MANAGEMENT AREA

601

21

21

Reelfoot Lake
State Park

Lake Co.

78

Mississippi River

Ridgely

LAKE ISOM
NATIONAL WILDLIFE
REFUGE

79

Obion County

Dyer County

181

Obion River

155

51

20

Dyersburg

MISSOURI

181

MOSS ISLAND
WILDLIFE MANAGEMENT
AREA

Forked Deer River

ARKANSAS

LAUDERDALE
WATERFOWL REFUGE

88

Eden-Nankipoo Rd.

Halls

210

CHICKASAW
NATIONAL WILDLIFE
REFUGE

51

South Fork Forked Deer River

Ripley

Three
Point

Sunk Lake
State Natural Area

209

Henning

87

Lauderdale Co.

Haywood Co.

Fort Pillow
State Historic Park

51

LOWER HATCHIE
NATIONAL WILDLIFE
REFUGE

Gilt Edge

59

Covington

Burlison

Hatchie River

178

Tipton County

Shelby County

51

N

Meeman-Shelby
Forest State Park

388

Loosahatchie River

Mississippi River
Greenbelt Park

240

40

Mud
Island

Wolf River

Tennessee
Welcome Center

Memphis

55

240

0   Kilometers   10

0   Miles   10

became an important inland port. The river also proved to be an important invasion route for Union forces during the Civil War.

MISSISSIPPI RIVER

Begin this drive at the **Tennessee Welcome Center** on Riverside Drive, just south of the I–40 crossing of the Mississippi River. Exit the Welcome Center to cross Riverside Drive and head up Jefferson Avenue to Front Street. To the right, the Cotton, Blues, and Barbecue Drive enters the Cotton Row Historic District. For this drive, turn left on Front Street. The entrance to **Mud Island River Park** is on the left. From here, visitors take a monorail across the Wolf River to Mud Island, the peninsula of land at the confluence of the Wolf and Mississippi Rivers. On the island you can visit the **Mississippi River Museum,** with exhibits and galleries about life on the Mississippi, and stroll along the **River Walk,** which wanders beside a flowing replica of the lower Mississippi.

Pass under I–40 where **The Pyramid** stands on the left. This structure is an arena contained in a 321-foot-high stainless steel pyramid, the shape obviously reflecting the Egyptian origin of the city's name. Turn left on Auction Avenue to cross a bridge over the Wolf River to Mud Island, and turn right on Mud Island Road, which passes in front of **Harbortown,** a planned residential development that has become a model for creating a pleasing living environment within a densely populated area. To the left is the **Mississippi River Greenbelt Park** where a paved walkway leads along the bluff just above the river floodplain. At a parking area on the left, you can stop for a stroll along the river.

In 1.4 miles, at the end of the island, a parking area down to the left provides access to the river where the channelized Wolf River joins the Mississippi. Mud Island Road turns right, away from the river, following the route of the **Mississippi River Trail,** a 177-mile bicycle route following backcountry roads through forests, farmlands, and small communities while paralleling the Mississippi River north. This drive will periodically follow the bike route in Tennessee, marked by MRT signs along the way.

The road crosses an earthen berm over the old channel of the Wolf River. At a junction with Second Street, turn left to cross the river, now flowing east to west through the Wolf River Diversion Channel, which cuts off Mud Island from the mainland and makes it an actual island. Where Second Street curves to the right, the road becomes Whitney Avenue. From that point, travel 1.8 miles to the place where the MRT turns left on Benjistown Road, but stay straight on Whitney to US 51. Turn left on the four-lane highway and travel 2.2 miles to a left turn on TN 388, which is part of the Great River Road, a series of roads that parallel the Mississippi River north; here TN 388 is North Watkins Road.

MEEMAN-SHELBY AND COVINGTON

In 1.5 miles cross the Loosahatchie River, which flows through a wet bottomland with cypress trees. North Watkins ends at a junction in 5.7 miles. Turn left on Lock Cuba Road and drive 0.7 mile to a right turn on Bluff Road. Travel another 0.7 mile to the entrance on the left for **Meeman-Shelby Forest State Park.**

Edward J. Meeman was a Memphis newspaper editor and conservationist who played a role in establishing Shelby Forest, which eventually became a state park with camping, cabins, picnicking, swimming, fishing, horse riding, and occasional managed hunts. Twenty miles of trails wander through the park, including a 5-mile bicycle trail and an 8-mile segment of the Chickasaw Bluff State Scenic Trail.

Turn left into Meeman-Shelby to a visitor center where you can get maps and information. Just beyond the visitor center, turn right to pass the campground and stay straight on a one-way scenic drive that penetrates a hardwood forest; the bluff and river bottomlands do not support any pine trees, in contrast to most other areas of Tennessee. In fall, Shelby Forest is ablaze with color. In 1.6 miles, the one-way drive intersects with a two-way road. You can turn left here to descend Chickasaw Bluff and travel through the bottomlands forest for 3.7 miles. The road then curves left to parallel the river another 1.2 miles. It ends at a boat ramp and a view of the wide Mississippi.

Return the way you came to the junction with the one-way road, and continue up the road to Bluff Road; turn left. The road almost becomes a single lane as it leaves the park. In 2.3 miles at a junction with Herring Hill Road, turn left. The road drops off Chickasaw Bluff into the floodplain of the Mississippi River. Continue along the bottom of the bluff with broad fields to the left. Herring Hill becomes a well-maintained gravel road as it crosses into Tipton County. In 3.5 miles, the road becomes paved again and reaches a junction in 1.4 miles just after crossing Bear Creek, a small tributary of the Mississippi River. Stay straight on Pryor Road. In 2.9 miles at a junction with Richardson Landing Road, turn left. In 1.1 miles descend into the floodplain where broad fields stretch across the fertile soil. Then rise back out of the bottomland to a junction with TN 59 in 1.3 miles. Turn right on TN 59 to head east.

In 2.9 miles Glen Springs Road to the right leads 2 miles to **Glen Springs Lake,** a family fishing lake with fishing pier and picnic shelters; the lake is stocked with bass, bluegill, crappie, and catfish. Stay straight on TN 59 to pass through cotton fields. In 5.2 miles in the community of Gilt Edge, the **Gilt Edge Cafe** is known for its barbecue and ribs. Travel 4.1 miles farther to the small community of Burlison and notice the old cotton gin on the left. In another 6.6 miles, TN 59 reaches a junction with US 51 in Covington; notice some old Art Deco commercial buildings lining the highway. Turn right on US 51 and then left on TN 54, which is West Pleasant Street, to enter the old downtown. On the right is the **Ruffin Theater,** an Art Deco movie house built in 1937 by William F. Ruffin, who had a chain of movie theaters in West Tennessee and Kentucky. The theater today hosts live performances and plays.

The town square has the **Tipton County Courthouse,** a Victorian building constructed in 1889. Large hickory trees adorn the historic square. You can turn right on Main Street to enter the **South Main Historic District** of residences built between 1870 and 1940. The growth of the neighborhood began with the coming of the Newport News and Mississippi River Valley Railroad, which ran along the route of what is now US 51. The **Palmer-Sherrod House** is the oldest residence on South Main, built in 1853. On Roper Street, you'll find the **Hamilton Log House,** constructed in 1820.

Return along South Main to the town square and stay straight past the courthouse. Turn left on Liberty Street and stay straight to leave the downtown area. On the right just after the square stands the **Hotel Lindo,** a three-story brick structure built in 1901 and now containing law offices.

Rejoin US 51 and turn right. This four-lane highway travels to the north, paralleling the Mississippi River far to the west. It also parallels the Illinois Central Railroad tracks that can often be seen to the right-hand side of the road. The original Newport News and Mississippi River Valley Railroad was constructed in the 1880s. In 1893 the Illinois Central expanded and purchased the smaller railroad.

HENNING AND FORT PILLOW

In 5.4 miles, cross the Hatchie River into Lauderdale County. In 1.8 miles, turn right on TN 209. In 1.5 miles in the community of Henning, turn left on Haley Avenue and drive 2 blocks to Church Street and the **Alex Haley Boyhood Home.** Haley lived here with his grandparents, the Palmers, from 1921 to 1929, and later spent many summers here listening to the generational stories told by his grandmother and aunts. These stories became the basis for his Pulitzer Prize winning novel, *Roots,* which became a best-seller and the subject of a television miniseries that riveted the nation in 1977.

Return to TN 209, and stay north through the downtown of Henning where old commercial buildings line the street. At a junction with TN 87, turn left to return to US 51. Stay straight across the highway and keep going west on TN 87 through small farms and cotton fields. In 7.2 miles, enter the small community of Three Point. Here you can turn right on Sunk Lake Road for 2.5 miles on a side trip to **Sunk Lake State Natural Area,** a complex of small lakes created during the New Madrid earthquake that also created Reelfoot Lake to the north; the bottomland hardwood forest around these lakes contain large bald cypress and water tupelo.

Return to TN 87 and continue west. In 8.3 miles turn right on TN 207 to enter **Fort Pillow State Historic Park** in 1 mile. Stay straight on the park road to pass a campground. An overlook on the left provides a view of the Mississippi River in the distance. Over time, the river meanders from side to side in the floodplain; during the Civil War era, the river channel was closer, running just below Chickasaw Bluff.

The road dips to cross an earthen berm holding back a lake. At the top of a hill, earthworks lie to the right among the trees, built by Confederate troops and slaves when Fort Pillow was constructed in 1861–62. The road reaches the park interpretive center at the end of the road in 2.1 miles.

During the Civil War, rivers served as main transportation routes into Tennessee. To protect the invasion route along the Mississippi River, Confederate fortifications were built at Island No. 10, a bend in the river in the extreme northwest corner of the state, and here at Fort Pillow, named for Gen. Gideon J. Pillow, a Mexican War hero and one of the Confederate generals at the fall of Fort Donelson on the Cumberland River.

As expected, Union gunboats moved south on the Mississippi in the spring of 1862. After a long bombardment and siege, Island No. 10 was surrendered to the Federals on April 8. Only Fort Pillow stood between the Union forces and Memphis. In May, a Confederate squadron of gunboats attacked the Union fleet just north of Fort Pillow as the fleet made its way south. The Confederates were successful in damaging the Union boats, but then had to withdraw to Memphis for repairs. The federal gunboats soon began a bombardment of Fort Pillow, which was evacuated on June 4. Federal troops soon occupied the fort.

The Union boats continued south and met the Confederate gunboats at Memphis on June 6. In front of thousands of people watching from atop Chickasaw Bluff, the Confederate fleet was destroyed. Using Memphis as a command center, the Union Army proceeded to secure the Memphis and Charleston Railroad that ran east to the important rail junction of Corinth,

Mississippi, and stretched its control farther down the Mississippi River to Vicksburg, where a long siege would end in the surrender of the city.

But Fort Pillow was not forgotten. Now a Union post guarding the Mississippi River, the fort was too important for the Confederates to leave in the hands of federal forces. In 1864, on one of his daring raids into West Tennessee, Confederate Gen. Nathan Bedford Forrest and 1,500 troops attacked Fort Pillow on April 12. With the Union forces outnumbered three to one, Forrest soon gained control of the battle and asked for the fort's surrender. Maj. William F. Bradford refused. The Confederates then attacked, easily taking the fort with the Union troops suffering high casualties.

Controversy still surrounds this battle due to the unexplained high number of Union troops killed. Half the federal troops were African Americans. The month before in Forrest's raid at Paducah, Kentucky, Union African-American troops refused to surrender and successfully turned back the Confederate attack. Perhaps Forrest revenged his earlier defeat. But perhaps the responsibility lies with Major Bradford, who refused to surrender in an impossible situation.

You can tour the battlefield by following a trail system that leads from the interpretive center. The reconstructed fort, a palisade with gun holes, is a half-mile walk. The fortifications faced inland, which is where an attack would come. The 15-mile trail system that explores the battle site and fort includes a segment of the Chickasaw Bluff State Scenic Trail.

Return from Fort Pillow to the junction with TN 87. You can turn right and travel 1.8 miles for a side trip to the **Lower Hatchie National Wildlife Refuge.** Here where the Hatchie Scenic River joins the Mississippi, these refuge lands protect a riverine forest inhabited by numerous wading birds and frequented by songbirds.

Return along TN 87 and cross US 51 to reenter Henning, then turn left on TN 209. This backcountry route passes through Ripley in 5.6 miles. Like Covington and Henning, Ripley lies along the route of the old Newport News and Mississippi Valley Railroad and later the Illinois Central. Travel another 13.6 miles north to the place where TN 209 intersects TN 88 in the community of Halls, another railroad town along the train route. The drive turns left on TN 88, but you can continue straight on TN 210 for 2.7 miles to the **Lauderdale Waterfowl Refuge** on the right. The Tennessee Wildlife Resources Agency and Ducks Unlimited maintain flooded fields along the South Fork of the Forked Deer River to create a wetlands. From atop an observation tower beside the road, you can look out over the marsh in late fall and winter to see a multitude of ducks—black, ring-necked, pintails, mallards, hooded mergansers, and blue-winged and green-winged teal.

In Halls, turn west on TN 88 for 1.5 miles to cross US 51. Soon after, you can turn left on Edith-Nankipoo Road for a side trip to the **Chickasaw National Wildlife Refuge,** traveling through farmland and cotton fields for 6.3 miles to a place where the road drops off Chickasaw Bluff and descends into the Mississippi floodplain. A road to the right leads into the refuge that shelters white-tailed deer, wild turkey, soaring hawks, and a variety of migrating waterfowl and shore birds. Farther along, you can turn right on gravel Sand Bluff Road to reach the refuge headquarters, where you can pick up a map for exploring the area. The refuge is closed in winter.

Return to TN 88 and continue west from US 51. In 5.5 miles the highway descends Chickasaw Bluff into the floodplain of the Mississippi. In 5.9 miles from that point, after you cross several channels of the Forked Deer River, turn right onto TN 181, another segment of the Great River Road. In 0.5 mile cross the Obion River into Dyer County. In another 2.5 miles a gravel road leads right into the **Moss Island Wildlife Management Area** that occupies a bend in the Obion; you can enter in search of wildlife, including migrating birds; there is hunting in season.

Continue north on TN 181 along the floodplain of the river, passing through farmland with large fields. Ponds are ringed with trees. In 12.6 miles, cross I–155. Continue north along the highway, which is on a berm running through the bottomlands; egrets and herons frequent the wet areas below the level of the road. Now farmland, this area is protected from flooding by a levee running along the river to the west. This section of the Great River Road is part of the Mississippi River Trail and has ample shoulders for bicycling.

In 7.2 miles, cross into Lake County. In another 2.7 miles, TN 181 ends at a junction. Turn left on TN 79 and bear north on the Tiptonville-Obion Levee Road, paralleling the levee to the left, an obvious earthen berm. In 2.7 miles the road curves away from the levee and then curves back north. In another 0.4 mile turn right to stay on Levee Road, crossing railroad tracks and entering Ridgely in 1.7 miles. Turn right through the old downtown; the **Ridgely Historical Museum** is in an old commercial building on the right. At the next block, turn left and in 1.6 miles reach a junction with TN 78.

REELFOOT LAKE

Turn left to head north for 8.3 miles to enter Tiptonville. Watch on the right for the **Carl Perkins Boyhood Home,** a wooden cabin moved to this location from Ridgely. In his music, Perkins combined country music and rhythm and blues as a precursor of rock 'n' roll; he lived his adult life in Jackson. At a junction with TN 21 on the east end of Tiptonville, the massive silos of the **Lake County Oil Mill** stand abandoned to the left; the mill once produced cottonseed oil. **Reelfoot Lake** lies to the right and straight ahead.

The 15,500-acre lake was created in the New Madrid earthquake that consisted of 1,874 recorded tremors from December 16, 1811 until March 8, 1812; New Madrid was a nearby Spanish/French settlement in what is now Missouri. These were some of the most powerful quakes to ever hit North America. The most violent tremor occurred on February 7, 1812 and was felt from Canada to New Orleans and east to the Atlantic coast. At the time, this was a sparsely settled region, still Chickasaw lands. The few witnesses who were around told of the rolling land and water and fumes spewing from fissures. The Mississippi River erupted, the water rising like a mountain, flowing upstream for a time and spilling over its banks. When the water settled, a lake had formed to the east along the channel of the Reelfoot River, named for a Chickasaw chief who had a deformed foot that caused him to walk unsteadily, or to "reel." In contrast to other lakes in Tennessee that are man-made, backed up by dams on the Tennessee and Cumberland Rivers and their tributaries, Reelfoot Lake is a natural lake, the only large one in the state.

At the junction with TN 21, you can continue north on TN 78 to travel along the west side of Reelfoot Lake; the water is at a distance and so is not visible, however. The highway passes the **Reelfoot Wildlife Management Area** in 3 miles and the **Black Bayou Waterfowl Refuge** in another 3 miles. Then, 1.3 miles farther, turn right onto Airport Road (TN 213) to reach the **Reelfoot Lake Airpark Inn** on the Upper Blue Basin of Reelfoot Lake. The inn/restaurant stands on a pier over marsh waters at the edge of the lake. The area also includes a campground, picnic area, boat launch, and an air strip, which is why the inn has the name "Airpark." Tours for observing eagles are offered from December through mid-March. Up to 200 bald eagles spend the winter here, flying south from the Great Lakes and Canada. They have come to Reelfoot Lake for generations, constituting the largest population of wintering bald eagles outside of Alaska. The park maintains a live cam on nesting eagles that can be accessed on the Internet (www.eaglewatch.com).

For this drive, turn east on TN 21 in Tiptonville. In 2.5 miles on the left is the **Reelfoot Lake State Park Visitor Center,** which offers information about the state park; pontoon boat cruises leave daily from May through September. Out back is a boardwalk that wanders among cypress trees growing at the edge of the lake; the widespread roots of the tree send up woody growths called "knees" that aid in providing air to the submerged roots. Although a member of the pine family, the cypress sheds its needles in winter, and so is called "bald cypress."

The visitor center houses a museum on local history, including a display on the Reelfoot Lake Stumpjumper, a wooden boat built by the Calhoun family for four generations. Across the highway from the visitor center sits **Calhoun Boat Works.** Joseph Calhoun came to Reelfoot Lake in the early 1900s; he was a farmer, brick mason, and blacksmith, and he built boats on the side. His great-grandson Dale continues the tradition today. Made of cypress planks and oak ribbing, the stumpjumper comes to a point on both ends and so is able to slide over or around stumps, logs, and cypress knees that stick up from the water of Reelfoot Lake. An innovation was bow-facing oars; these hinged oars allow a person to row in the direction he or she is facing, avoiding stumps and watching for wildlife more easily, instead of moving backwards as with traditional oars. In 1998 Dale Calhoun was awarded a National Heritage Fellowship by the National Endowment for the Arts for keeping a traditional craft alive.

Adjacent to the boat works, **Boyette's** started in 1921 as a grocery store that offered lunches to fishermen and hunters. The store has since expanded to a 300-seat restaurant known for its fish dinners.

Continue east along the southern edge of Reelfoot Lake. Several day-use areas offer picnicking, fishing, and boat access. In 1.1 miles TN 21 enters Obion County. In another 0.5 mile cross the **Reelfoot Lake Spillway,** which allows excess water from Lower Blue Basin to empty into Running Reelfoot Bayou that drains south to the Obion River. This spillway and flood-control levees along the Mississippi River stabilize the lake level. To the south, **Lake Isom National Wildlife Refuge** surrounds Lake Isom, a small body of water off the bayou.

In another 0.5 mile, **Reelfoot Lake State Park Campground** lies on the left at the lakeside. You can continue around the lake by staying with TN 21 to a junction with TN 22 and turning northeast.

In 2.3 miles you can turn right on Old Samburg Road for a side trip to **Flippen's Fruit Farm.** The road ascends from the Mississippi floodplain. In 0.4 mile, a small park on the right has a short trail leading to a small Indian mound on a point of the bluff; the mound was likely built by members of the Mississippian culture who lived along the great river before the Chickasaws. In 3 miles, Old Samburg Road reaches a junction with Shawtown Road and just to the left is the fruit farm. Forty years ago the Flippen family planted the

Boardwalk and Observation Tower, Reelfoot Lake

orchard that produces the apples and peaches sold at the farm. The family continues to operate the business, which includes a restaurant where their famous fried pies are sold; try the chocolate.

Return to TN 22 and continue north. In 4.6 miles turn left on TN 157. In 1 mile on the left is the visitor center for the **Reelfoot National Wildlife Refuge,** a 10,428-acre preserve around the northeast end of the lake. In another 1.2 miles, you can turn left on Walnut Log Road to drive the **Grassy Island Auto Tour,** a tree-shrouded lane that passes along a bayou. At the end of the 3-mile road, a boardwalk leads to an observation tower where you can look out over the lake waters.

The formation of Reelfoot Lake created a wetland that is now a major component of the Mississippi Flyway, serving as a stopover and wintering area for waterfowl. Mallards, gadwall, American widgeon, and ringneck ducks begin arriving in October. By midwinter, the mallards alone can reach 400,000. Canada geese gather in January, ranging from 50,000 to 100,000. In spring and summer, watch for blue herons and wood ducks. During the year, roughly 250 different bird species are in and around Reelfoot Lake.

Suggested Reading

Anderson, Truman D., and Jere Hall, eds. *A Guidebook to Historic Places in Roane County, Tennessee.* Kingston, Tenn.: Roane County Heritage Commission, 1997.

Brandt, Robert. *Touring the Middle Tennessee Backroads.* Winston-Salem: John F. Blair, 1995.

———. *Middle Tennessee on Foot.* Winston-Salem: John F. Blair, 1998.

Corlew, Robert E. *Tennessee, A Short History,* 2nd Edition. Knoxville: The University of Tennessee Press, 1990.

Crockett, David. *A Narrative of the Life of David Crockett of the State of Tennessee.* Knoxville: The University of Tennessee Press, 1973.

Dykeman, Wilma. *The French Broad.* Newport, Tenn.: Wakestone Books, 1955.

Fink, Paul. *Jonesborough, The First Century of Tennessee's First Town.* Johnson City: Overmountain Press, 1989.

Govan, Gilbert E., and James W. Livingood. *The Chattanooga Country, 1540–1976.* Knoxville: The University of Tennessee Press, 1977.

Hamel, Paul. *Tennessee Wildlife Viewing Guide.* Helena, Mont.: Falcon Press, 1993.

Luther, Edward T. *Our Restless Earth, The Geologic Regions of Tennessee.* Knoxville: The University of Tennessee Press, 1977.

Manning, Russ. *An Outdoor Guide to the Big South Fork National River and Recreation Area.* Seattle: The Mountaineers Books, 2000.

———. *100 Trails of the Big South Fork National River and Recreation Area.* Seattle: The Mountaineers Books, 2000.

———. *100 Hikes in the Great Smoky Mountains.* Seattle: The Mountaineers Books, 2000.

———. *40 Hikes in Tennessee's South Cumberland.* Seattle: The Mountaineers Books, 2000.

———. *The Historic Cumberland Plateau, An Explorer's Guide,* 2nd Edition. Knoxville: The University of Tennessee Press, 1999.

——— and Sondra Jamieson. *Historic Knoxville and Knox County, A Walking and Touring Guide.* Norris, Tenn.: Mountain Laurel Place, 1990.

Mathews, Paul A., and James B. Jones, Jr. *Passport to Tennessee History, A Guide to Selected Historic Sites, Historic Areas, and Museums.* Nashville: Tennessee Historical Commission, 1996.

McDonough, James Lee. *Chattanooga—A Death Grip on the Confederacy*. Knoxville: The University of Tennessee Press, 1984.

——— and Thomas L. Connelly. *Five Tragic Hours, The Battle of Franklin*. Knoxville: The University of Tennessee Press, 1983.

———. *Stones River—Bloody Winter in Tennessee*. Knoxville: The University of Tennessee Press, 1980.

———. *Shiloh—In Hell before Night*. Knoxville: The University of Tennessee Press, 1977.

Means, Evan. *Hiking Tennessee Trails*. Old Saybrook, Conn.: Globe Pequot Press, 1994.

O'Brien, Tim. *Tennessee Off the Beaten Path, A Guide to Unique Places*. Old Saybrook, Conn.: Globe Pequot Press, 1996.

Patrick, James. *Architecture in Tennessee, 1768–1897*. Knoxville: The University of Tennessee Press, 1981.

Raulston, J. Leonard, and James W. Livingood. *Sequatchie, A Story of the Southern Cumberlands*. Knoxville: The University of Tennessee Press, 1974.

Rothrock, Mary U., ed. *The French Broad-Holston Country, A History of Knox County, Tennessee*. Knoxville: East Tennessee Historical Society, 1946.

Sakowski, Carolyn. *Touring the East Tennessee Backroads*. Winston-Salem: John F. Blair, 1993.

Satz, Ronald N. *Tennessee's Indian Peoples*. Knoxville: The University of Tennessee Press, 1979.

Skelton, Will, ed. *Wilderness Trails of Tennessee's Cherokee National Forest*. Knoxville: The University of Tennessee Press, 1992.

Smith, Reid. *Majestic Middle Tennessee*. Gretna, La.: Pelican Publishing Co., 1982.

Summerlin, Cathy and Vernon. *Traveling the Trace, A Complete Tour Guide to the Historic Natchez Trace from Nashville to Natchez*. Nashville: Rutledge Hill Press, 1995.

Tennessee Department of Tourist Development. *Tennessee Heritage Trails, Arts & Crafts, History and Music*. Nashville: State of Tennessee, 1999.

Tennessee Historical Commission. *Tennessee Historical Markers*, 8th Edition. Nashville, 1996.

West, Carroll Van. *Tennessee's Historic Landscapes, A Traveler's Guide*. Knoxville: The University of Tennessee Press, 1995.

Williamson County Bicentennial Committee. *Portraits in Time, Williamson County Bicentennial, 1799–1999*. Franklin, TN, 1999.

Woodward, Grace Steele. *The Cherokees*. Norman, Okla.: University of Oklahoma Press, 1963.

For More Information

1: THE OVERHILL COUNTRY

Cherokee National Forest
P.O. Box 2010
Cleveland, TN 37320
(800) 204–6366
www.r8web.com/cherokee

Ocoee/Hiwassee Ranger District
Route 1, Box 348D
Benton, TN 37307
(423) 338–5201

Tellico Ranger District
250 Ranger Station Road
Tellico Plains, TN 37385
(423) 253–2520

Coker Creek Village
P.O. Box 98
Coker Creek, TN 37314
(423) 261–2310

Company House Bed & Breakfast Inn
P.O. Box 154
Ducktown, TN 37326
(800) 343–2909

Ducktown Basin Museum
P.O. Box 458
Ducktown, TN 37326
(423) 496–5778

Fort Loudoun State Historic Area
338 Fort Loudoun Road
Vonore, TN 37885
(423) 884–6217
www.state.tn.us/enviroment/parks/loudoun

Lake Ocoee Inn & Marina
Route 1, Box 347
Benton, TN 37307
(800) 272–7238

Monroe County Tourism Council
4765 Highway 68
Madisonville, TN 37354
(800) 245–5428
www.monroecountychamber.org

Museum Center at Five Points
200 Inman Street East
Cleveland, TN 37311
(423) 339–5745

Ocoee Whitewater Center
Route 1, Box 285
Copperhill, TN 37317
(423) 496–5197
www.r8web.com/ocoee

Polk County Chamber of Commerce
P.O. Box 560
Benton, TN 37307
(800) 633–7655
www.polkcotn.com

Red Clay State Historic Area
1140 Red Clay Park Road Southwest
Cleveland, TN 37311
(423) 478–0339
www.state.tn.us/environment/parks/redclay

Sequoyah Birthplace Museum
P.O. Box 69
Vonore, TN 37885
(423) 884–6246
www.sequoyahmuseum.org

Tennessee Overhill Heritage Association
P.O. Box 143
Etowah, TN 37331
(423) 263–7232
www.tennesseeoverhill.com

2: RAILROADS AND HIWASSEE RIVER

Carmichael Inn Tourist Information Center
P.O. Box 303
Loudon, TN 37774
(423) 458–1442

Englewood Textile Museum
P.O. Box 253
Englewood, TN 37329
(423) 887–5455

Etowah Area Chamber of Commerce
P.O. Box 458
Etowah, TN 37331
(423) 263–2228
www.etowahcoc.org

Hiwassee State Scenic River
P.O. Box 5
Delano, TN 37325
(423) 263–0050
www.state.tn.us/environment/parks/hiwassee

Lost Sea
140 Lost Sea Road
Sweetwater, TN 37874
(423) 337–6616
www.monroecounty.com/lost.
html

Loudon County Visitors Bureau
1075 Highway 321 North
Lenoir City, TN 37771
(423) 986–6822

Majestic Mansion Bed & Breakfast
202 East Washington Avenue
Athens, TN 37303
(423) 746–9041

Mayfield Dairy Farms
4 Mayfield Lane
Athens, TN 37303
(423) 745–2151

McMinn County Living History Museum
P.O. Box 889
Athens, TN 37371
(423) 745–0329

Sweetwater Valley Farm
17988 West Lee Highway
Philadelphia, TN 37086
(877) 862–4332
www.sweetwatervalley.com

Woodlawn Bed & Breakfast
110 Keith Lane
Athens, TN 37303
(800) 745–8213

3: GREAT SMOKY MOUNTAINS

Blount County Chamber of Commerce
201 South Washington Street
Maryville, TN 37804-5728
(865) 983–2241
www.chamber.blount.tn.us

Gatlinburg Chamber of Commerce
P.O. Box 527
Gatlinburg, TN 37738
(800) 568–4748
www.gatlinburg.com

Great Smoky Mountains National Park
107 Park Headquarters Road
Gatlinburg, TN 37738
(865) 436–1200
Backcountry Reservation
Office: (865) 436–1231
www.nps.gov/grsm

Great Smoky Mountains Institute at Tremont
Great Smoky Mountains
National Park
9275 Tremont Road
Townsend, TN 37882
(865) 448–6709
www.nps.gov/grsm/tremont.
htm

LeConte Lodge
250 Apple Valley Road
Sevierville, TN 37862
(865) 429–5704

Little River Railroad & Lumber Company Museum
P.O. Box 211
Townsend, TN 37882
(865) 448–2211

Sam Houston Schoolhouse
3650 Sam Houston School
Road
Maryville, TN 37804
(865) 983–1550

Townsend Visitors Center
7906 East Lamar Alexander
Parkway
Townsend, TN 37882
(800) 525–6834
www.smokymountains.org

Tuckaleechee Caverns
825 Cavern Road
Townsend, TN 37882-4505
(865) 448–2274

4: NORTH CHEROKEE

Butler House Bed & Breakfast
309 North Church Street
Mountain City, TN 37683
(423) 727–4119

Nolichucky/Unaka Ranger District
124 Austin Street, Suite 3
Greeneville, TN 37745
(423) 638–4109

Watauga Ranger District
P.O. Box 400
Unicoi, TN 37692
(423) 735–1500

Elizabethton–Carter County Chamber of Commerce
P.O. Box 190
Elizabethton, TN 37644
(888) 542–3852
www.tourelizabethton.com

Johnson City Convention & Visitors Bureau
P.O. Box 180
Johnson City, TN 37605
(800) 852–3392
www.johnsoncitytn.com

Johnson County Welcome Center
P.O. Box 1
Mountain City, TN 37683
(423) 727–5800
http://pages.preferred.com/
~jcwc

Roan Mountain State Park
1015 Highway 143
Roan Mountain, TN 37687
(800) 250–8620
www.state.tn.us/environment/
parks/roanmtn

Sycamore Shoals State Historic Area
1651 West Elk Avenue
Elizabethton, TN 37643
(423)543–5808
www.state.tn.us/environment/
parks/sycamore

Tipton-Haynes Historic Site
P.O. Box 225
Johnson City, TN 37605
(423) 926–3631

Unicoi County Heritage Museum
Federal Fish Hatchery Site
P. O. Box 317
Erwin, TN 37650
(423) 743–9449

5: EARLY SETTLEMENTS

Andrew Johnson National Historic Site
P.O. Box 1088
Greeneville, TN 37744
(423) 638–3551
www.nps.gov/anjo/index.htm

Blair–Moore House Bed & Breakfast
201 West Main Street
Jonesborough, TN 37659
(888) 453–0044
www.netta.com/blair.html

Davy Crockett Birthplace State Park
1245 Davy Crockett Park Road
Limestone, TN 37681-5825
(423) 257–2167
www.state.tn.us/environment/
parks/davyshp

Doak House Museum
Highway 107
Tusculum College
Greeneville, TN 37743
(423) 636–8554
www.tusculum.edu/museum/
doak.html

General Morgan Inn
111 North Main Street
Greeneville, TN 37743
(800) 223–2679
http://greene.xtn.net/com/
genmorgan

Greeneville–Greene County Chamber of Commerce
115 Academy Street
Greeneville, TN 37743
(423) 638–4111
www.gcp.xtn.net

Hawley House Bed & Breakfast
114 East Woodrow Avenue
Jonesborough, TN 37659
(423) 753–8869

Jefferson County Chamber of Commerce
532 Patriot Drive
Jefferson City
TN 37760-3216
(423) 397–9642
www.jefferson-tn-chamber.
org

Jonesborough Bed & Breakfast
P.O. Box 722
Jonesborough, TN 37659
(423) 753–9223

Jonesborough/Washington County History Museum & Visitor Center
117 Boone Street
Jonesborough, TN 37659
(423) 753–1010
jonesborough.tricon.net/
museum.html

May-Ledbetter House Bed & Breakfast
130 West Main Street
Jonesborough, TN 37659
(423) 753–7568
www.bbonline.com/tn/mlh

Newport/Cocke County Chamber of Commerce
433-B Prospect Avenue
Newport, TN 37821
(423) 623–7201
http://cockecounty.org

Pres. Andrew Johnson Museum & Library
Gilland Street
Tusculum College
Greeneville, TN 37743
(423) 636–7348
www.tusculum.edu/museum/
johnson.html

Rocky Mount Museum
P.O. Box 160
Piney Flats, TN 37686
(888) 538–1791

6: FORKS OF THE RIVER

Blount Mansion
P.O. Box 1703
Knoxville, TN 37901
(865) 525–2375

Confederate Memorial
Hall (Bleak House)
3148 Kingston Pike
Knoxville, TN 37919
(865) 522–2371
www.kornet.org/bhpa

Gateway Regional Visitor
Center
900 Volunteer Landing Lane
Knoxville, TN 37915
(800) 727–8045
www.knoxville.org

Ijams Nature Center
P.O. Box 2601
Knoxville, TN 37901
(865) 577–4717
www.ijams.org

James White's Fort
205 East Hill Avenue
Knoxville, TN 37915
(865) 525–6514

Knoxville Convention &
Visitors Bureau
601 West Summit Hill Drive
Suite 200B
Knoxville, TN 37902
(800) 727–8045
www.knoxville.org

Marble Springs State
Historic Farmstead
1220 West Gov. John Sevier
Highway
Knoxville, TN 37920
(865) 573–5508

Museum of East Tennessee
History
600 Market Street
Knoxville, TN 37902
(865) 215–8732
www.east-tennessee-history.
org

Ramsey House
2614 Thorngrove Pike
Knoxville, TN 37914
(865) 546–0745

Women's Basketball Hall
of Fame
700 Hall of Fame Drive
Knoxville, TN 37915
(865) 633–9000
www.WBHOF.com

7: MINERAL WATER, FLYING MACHINES, AND MELUNGEONS

Crockett Tavern
2002 Morningside Drive
Morristown, TN 37814
(423) 587–9900

Glenmore Mansion
P.O. Box 403
Jefferson City, TN 37760
(865) 475–5014

Grainger County Chamber
of Commerce
P.O. Box 101
Rutledge, TN 37861
(865) 828–4222
www.grainger.k12.tn.us/
chamber.htm

Homeplace Bed &
Breakfast
132 Church Lane
Mooresburg, TN 37811
(800) 521–8424

House Mountain State
Natural Area
P.O. Box 109
Corryton, TN 37721
(865) 933–6851
www.state.tn.us/environment/
parks/house

Morristown Chamber of
Commerce
825 West First North Street
Morristown, TN 37814
(423) 586–6382
www.morristownchamber.com

Panther Creek State Park
2010 Panther Creek Park
Road
Morristown, TN 37814
(423) 587–7046
www.state.tn.us/environment/
parks/panther

Rose Center
P.O. Box 1976
Morristown, TN 37816-1976
(423) 581–4330
www.rosecenter.org

8: COUNTRY MUSIC, BOATYARDS, AND JOURNALISM

Allandale Mansion
4444 West Stone Drive
Kingsport, TN 37660
(423) 229–9422

Bays Mountain Park
853 Bays Mountain Road
Kingsport, TN 37660
(423) 229–9447

Bristol Caverns
P.O. Box 851
Bristol, TN 37621
(423) 878–2011

Bristol Chamber of
Commerce
20 Volunteer Parkway
Bristol, TN 37620
(423) 989–4850
www.bristolchamber.org

Exchange Place
4812 Orebank Road
Kingsport, TN 37664
(423) 288-6071

Kingsport Chamber of
Commerce
P.O. Box 1403
Kingsport, TN 37660
(423) 392-8800
www.kingsportchamber.org

Netherland Inn
P.O. Box 293
Kingsport, TN 37660
(423) 246-6262

Rogersville/Hawkins
County Chamber of
Commerce
107 East Main Street
Suite 100
Rogersville, TN 37857
(423) 272-2186
http://welcome.to/hawkins
county

Warrior's Path State Park
P.O. Box 5026
Hemlock Road
Kingsport, TN 37663
(423) 239-8531
www.state.tn.us/environment/
parks/warrior

9: TVA AND
CUMBERLAND GAP

Abraham Lincoln Museum
Lincoln Memorial University
Harrogate, TN 37752
(423) 869-6235

Anderson County
Conservation Park
P.O. Box 41
Andersonville, TN 37705
(865) 494-9352

Anderson County Tourism
Council
P.O. Box 147
Clinton, TN 37717
(800) 524-3602
www.andersoncountychamber.
org

Appalachian Community
Craft Center
P.O. Box 608
Norris, TN 37828
(865) 494-9854
www.korrnet.org/comcraft

Big Ridge State Park
1015 Big Ridge Road
Maynardville, TN 37807-1727
(865) 992-5523
www.state.tn.us/environment/
parks/bigridge

Campbell County Tourism
Council
P.O. Box 795
Jacksboro, TN 37757
(423) 506-0329
http://co.campbell.tn.us

City of Norris
P.O. Box 1090
Norris, TN 37828
(865) 494-7645

Claiborne County Tourism
Committee
P.O. Box 332
Tazewell, TN 37879
(800) 332-8164
www.claibornecounty.com

Cove Lake State Park
110 Cove Lake Lane
Caryville, TN 37714
(423) 566-9701
www.state.tn.us/environment/
parks/covelak

Cumberland Gap National
Historical Park
P.O. Box 1848
Middlesboro, KY 40965
(606) 248-2817
www.nps.gov/cuga

Cumberland Trail
Conference
19 East Fourth Street
Crossville, TN 38555
(931) 456-6259
www.cumberlandtrail.org

Museum of Appalachia
P.O. Box 1189
Norris, TN 37828
(865) 494-7680

Norris Dam State Park
125 Village Green Circle
Lake City, TN 37769-5932
(865) 426-7461
www.state.tn.us/environment/
parks/norris

Tennessee Valley Authority
400 West Summit Hill Drive
Knoxville, TN 37802-1499
(865) 632-2101
www.tva.gov

10: TENNESSEE RIVER

Booker T. Washington
State Park
5801 Champion Road
Chattanooga, TN 37416
(423) 894-4955
www.state.tn.us/environment/
parks/bookert

Bowater, Inc.
Calhoun Woodlands
Operations
5020 Highway 11 South
Calhoun, TN 37309-5249
(423) 336-7205

Chattanooga Area
Convention & Visitors
Bureau
2 Broad Street
Chattanooga, TN 37402
(800) 322–3344
www.chattanoogafun.com

Dayton Chamber of
Commerce
305 East Main Avenue
Dayton, TN 37321
(423) 775–0361
www.rheacounty.com/
welcome.html

Fort Southwest Point
1226 South Kentucky Street
Kingston, TN 37763
(865) 376–3641

Harrison Bay State Park
8411 Harrison Bay Road
Harrison, TN 37341
(423) 344–2272
www.state.tn.us/environment/
parks/harrison

Meigs County Tourism
P.O. Box 611
Decatur, TN 37322
(423) 334–5850

Roane County Visitors
Bureau
P.O. Box 1033
Kingston, TN 37763
(800) 386–4686

11: TENNESSEE RIVER GORGE

Battles for Chattanooga
1110 East Brow Road
Lookout Mountain
TN 37350
(423) 821–2812

Chickamauga &
Chattanooga National
Military Park
P.O. Box 2128
Fort Oglethorpe, GA 30738
(706) 866–9241

Chattanooga Area
Convention & Visitors
Bureau
2 Broad Street
Chattanooga, TN 37402
(800) 322–3344
www.chattanoogafun.com

Chattanooga Choo Choo
1400 Market Street
Chattanooga, TN 37402
(800) TRACK 29
www.choochoo.com

Chattanooga Nature
Center/Reflection Riding
400 Garden Road
Chattanooga, TN 37419
(423) 821–1160 or
(423) 821–9582
www.naturecenter.cjb.net

Lookout Mountain Incline
Railway
827 East Brow Road
Lookout Mountain
TN 37350
(423) 821–4224
www.lookoutmtnattractions.
com

Prentice Cooper State
Forest
Route 5
North Chattanooga
TN 37405
(423) 658–5551

Raccoon Mountain
Caverns
319 West Hills Drive
Chattanooga, TN 37419
(423) 821–9403

Ruby Falls
Scenic Highway
Lookout Mountain
TN 37409
(423) 821–2544
www.rubyfalls.com

Southern Belle
Chattanooga Riverboat Co.
201 Riverfront Parkway
Pier 2
Chattanooga, TN 37402-1616
(800) 766–2748
www.chattanoogariverboat.
com

Tennessee Aquarium
One Broad Street
Chattanooga, TN 37401-2048
(800) 262–0695
www.tnaqua.org

Tennessee Civil War
Museum
Tennessee Avenue
Chattanooga, TN 37550
(423) 821–4954

Tennessee River Gorge
Trust
25 Cherokee Boulevard
Suite 104
Chattanooga, TN 37405
(423) 266–0314

12: THE OBED RIVER

Anderson County
Chamber of Commerce
245 North Main Street
Suite 200
Clinton, TN 37716
(865) 457–2559

Frozen Head State Park
964 Flat Fork Road
Wartburg, TN 37887
(423) 346–3318
www.state.tn.us/environment/
parks/frzhead

Garden Inn at Bee Rock
Bed & Breakfast
1400 Bee Rock Road
Monterey, TN 38574
(931) 839–1400

Lone Mountain State
Forest
302 Clayton Howard Road
Wartburg, TN 37887
(423) 346–6655

Morgan County Resource
Development Council
P.O. Box 325
Wartburg, TN 37887
(423) 346–3000

Oak Ridge Convention &
Visitors Bureau
302 South Tulane Avenue
Oak Ridge, TN 37830-6726
(800) 887–3429
www.visit-or.org

Obed Wild & Scenic River
P.O. Box 429
Wartburg, TN 37887
(423) 346–6294
www.nps.gov/obed

13: SEQUATCHIE
VALLEY

Bledsoe County Chamber
of Commerce
P.O. Box 205
Pikeville, TN 37367
(423) 447–2791

Canoe the Sequatchie
Box 211
Dunlap, TN 37327
(423) 949–4400

Club House Bed &
Breakfast
512 Mountain View Road
Dunlap, TN 37327
(423) 949–4983

Colonial House Bed &
Breakfast
303 Main Street
Pikeville, TN 37367
(423) 447–7183

Cumberland County
Chamber of Commerce
34 South Main Street
Crossville, TN 38555
(800) 987–7772
www.crossville.com/
thechamber

Cumberland County
Playhouse
P.O. Box 484
Crossville, TN 38557
(931) 484–5000
www.ccplayhouse.com

Cumberland Homesteads
Museum
96 Highway 68
Crossville, TN 38555
(931) 456–9663

Cumberland Mountain
State Park
24 Office Drive
Crossville, TN 38555
(931) 484–6138
Reservations: (800) 250–8618
www.state.tn.us/environment/
parks/cumbmtn

Dunlap Coke Ovens
Historic Site
Sequatchie Valley Historical
Association
114 Walnut Street
Dunlap, TN 37327
(423) 949–3483

Fall Creek Falls State
Resort Park
Route 3, Box 300
Pikeville, TN 37367
(423) 881–5298
Nature Center:
(423) 881–5708
www.state.tn.us/environment/
parks/fallcrek

Homestead Bed &
Breakfast
1165 Highway 68
Crossville, TN 38555
(888) 782–9987
www.bbonline.com/tn/
homestead

Jasper–Marion County
Chamber of Commerce
P.O. Box 789
Jasper, TN 37347
(423) 942–5103
http://marioncountychamber.
com

Ketner's Mill Country Fair
P.O. Box 322
Lookout Mountain
TN 37350

Sequatchie County/Dunlap
Chamber of Commerce
13 Rankin Avenue North
P. O. Box 1653
Dunlap, TN 37327
(423) 949–7608
www.sequatchie.com

South Cumberland
Recreation Area
Route 1, Box 2196
Monteagle, TN 37356
(931) 924–2980
Savage Gulf Ranger Station:
(931) 779–3532
Stone Door Ranger Station:
(931) 692–3887
www.state.tn.us/environment/
parks/socumb

Victoriana Bed & Breakfast
P.O. Box 1045
Pikeville, TN 37367
(423) 447–2231

14: ROCK ISLAND AND CUMBERLAND CAVERNS

Cumberland Caverns
1437 Cumberland Caverns
Road
McMinnville, TN 37110
(931) 668–4396

Cumberland County
Playhouse
P.O. Box 453
Crossville, TN 38557
(931) 484–5000

Falcon Manor
2645 Faulkner Springs Road
McMinnville, TN 37110
(931) 668–4444
http://falconmanor.com

McMinnville–Warren
County Chamber of
Commerce
P.O. Box 574
McMinnville, TN 37111
www.warrentn.com

Rock Island State Park
82 Beach Road
Rock Island, TN 38581-4200
(931) 686–2471
www.state.tn.us/environment/
parks/rockis

Sparta–White County
Chamber of Commerce
16 West Bockman Way
Sparta, TN 38583
(931) 836–3552
www.sparta-chamber.net

15: HERO, STATESMAN, AND ROLLY HOLE

Big South Fork National
River & Recreation Area
4564 Leatherwood Road
Oneida, TN 37841
(931) 879–3625
www.nps.gov/biso

Cookeville/Putnam County
Chamber of Commerce
302 South Jefferson Avenue
Cookeville, TN 38501
(800) 264–5541
www.cookeville.com/
chamber

Cookeville Depot Museum
P.O. Box 998
Cookeville, TN 38503-0998
(931) 528–8570

Cordell Hull Birthplace &
Museum State Park
1300 Cordell Hull Memorial
Drive
Byrdstown, TN 38549
(931) 864–3247
www.state.tn.us/environment/
parks/cordell

Cornucopia Bed &
Breakfast
303 Mofield Street
Livingston, TN 38570
(931) 823–7522
www.bbonline.com/tn/
cornucopia

Dale Hollow Lake & Dam
U.S. Army Corps of Engineers
Resource Managers Office
5050 Dale Hollow Dam
Road
Celina, TN 38551
(931) 243–3136
www.orn.usace.army.mil

Fentress County Chamber
of Commerce
P.O. Box 1294
Jamestown, TN 38556
(931) 879–9948
www.jamestowntn.org

Holly Ridge Winery &
Vineyard
486 O'Neal Road
Livingston, TN 38570
(931) 823–8375

Livingston–Overton
County Chamber of
Commerce
222 East Main Street
Livingston, TN 38570
(931) 823–6421
www.overtonco.com

Pickett County Chamber
of Commerce
P.O. Box 447
Byrdstown, TN 38549
(931) 864–7195
www.dalehollow.com

Sgt. Alvin C. York State
Historic Site
General Delivery
Highway 127
Pall Mall, TN 38577
(931) 879–6456
www.state.tn.us/environment/
parks/sgtyork

Standing Stone State Park
1674 Standing Stone Park
Highway
Hilham, TN 38568-6610
(931) 823–6347
www.state.tn.us/environment/
parks/standstn

Upper Cumberland Tourist
Association
P.O. Box 2411
Cookeville, TN 38502
(800) 868–7237
www.uppercumberland.org

16: UPPER CUMBERLAND RIVER

Armour's Red Boiling Springs Hotel
321 East Main Street
Red Boiling Springs
TN 37150
(615) 699–2180

Avery Trace Association
P.O. Box 177
Gainesboro, TN 38562
(931) 268–0971

Clay County Chamber of Commerce
P.O. Box 69
Celina, TN 38551
(931) 243–3338

Cordell Hull Lake & Dam
Route 1, Box 62
Carthage, TN 37030-9710
(615) 735–1034
Defeated Creek Campground:
(615) 774–3141
Indian Creek Campground:
(615) 897–2233
Salt Lick Creek Campground:
(615) 678–4718

Dixona
TN Highway 25
Dixon Springs, TN 37057
(615) 735–1862

Donoho
500 East Main Street
Red Boiling Springs
TN 37150
(615) 699–3141

Gibbs Landing Bed & Breakfast
136 Gibbs Landing Road
Carthage, TN 37030
(615) 735–2198
www.gibbslanding.com

Hartsville–Trousdale County Chamber of Commerce
240 Broadway
Hartsville, TN 37074
(615) 374–9243

Jackson County Chamber of Commerce
101 East Hull Avenue
Gainesboro, TN 38562
(931) 268–0971

Smith County Chamber of Commerce
P.O. Box 70
Carthage, TN 37030
(615) 735–2093
www.smithcounty.net

Thomas House
P.O. Box 408
Red Boiling Springs
TN 37150
(615) 699–3006

17: CENTER HILL LAKE AND CEDARS OF LEBANON

Appalachian Center for Crafts
Route 3, Box 430
Smithville, TN 37166
(615) 597–6801

Burgess Falls State Natural Area
4000 Burgess Falls Drive
Sparta, TN 38583-8456
(931) 432–5312
www.state.tn.us/environment/
parks/burgess

Cedars of Lebanon State Park
328 Cedar Forest Road
Lebanon, TN 37090
(615) 443–2769
www.state.tn.us/environment/
parks/cedars

Center Hill Lake
Resource Manager
Lancaster, TN 38569
(615) 858–3125
Long Branch Recreation Area:
(615) 548–8002
Floating Mill Recreation Area:
(615) 858–4845
Holmes Creek Recreation Area:
(615) 597–7191

DeKalb County Chamber of Commerce
P.O. Box 64
Smithville, TN 37166
(615) 597–4163
www.dekalbtn.com

Edgar Evins State Park
1630 Edgar Evins State Park Road
Silver Point, TN 38582-7917
(800) 250–8619
www.state.tn.us/environment/
parks/edgar

Green Brook Inn
810 South College Street
Smithville, TN 37166
(615) 597–2998
www.smithvilletn.com/green
brookinn

Long Hunter State Park
2910 Hobson Pike
Hermitage, TN 37076
(615) 885–2422
www.state.tn.us/environment/
parks/longhunt

18: STONES RIVER AND WALKING HORSES

Bell Buckle Chamber of Commerce
P.O. Box 222
Bell Buckle, TN 37020
(931) 389–9371

Bridlewood Farm
P.O. Box 909
Shelbyville, TN 37160
(931) 389–9388

Henry Horton State Park
4358 Nashville Highway
Chapel Hill, TN 37034
(931) 364–7724
www.state.tn.us/environment/
parks/henry

Marshall County Chamber
of Commerce
227 Second Avenue North
Lewisburg, TN 37091
(931) 359–3863
www.lewisburgtn.com

Oaklands
P.O. Box 432
Murfreesboro, TN 37133
(615) 893–0022

Rutherford County
Chamber of Commerce
501 Memorial Boulevard
Murfreesboro, TN 37129
(800) 716–7560
www.rutherfordchamber.org

Sam Davis Home
1399 Sam Davis Road
Smyrna, TN 37167
(888) 750–9524

Shelbyville–Bedford
County Chamber of
Commerce
100 North Cannon Boulevard
Shelbyville, TN 37160
(888) 662–2525
www.shelbyvilletn.com

Stones River National
Battlefield
3501 Old Nashville Highway
Murfreesboro
TN 37129-3094
(615) 893–9501
www.nps.gov/stri

Tennessee Walking Horse
National Celebration
P.O. Box 1010
Shelbyville, TN 37162
(931) 684–5915
www.twhnc.com

Walking Horse and
Eastern Railroad
Shelbyville–Bedford County
Chamber of Commerce
(800) 695–8995
http://homestead.juno.com/
lnrr/whoe.html

Walking Horse Hotel
101 Spring Street
Wartrace, TN 37183
(931) 389–7050

19: THE WHISKEY TRAIL

The Antebellum Inn
974 Lynchburg Highway
Winchester, TN 37398
(931) 967–5550

David Crockett State Park
P. O. Box 398
Lawrenceburg, TN 38464
(931)762–9408
www.state.tn.us/environment/
parks/davidsp

Elk River Canoe Rental
190 Smithland Road
Kelso, TN 37348
(931) 937–6886

Falls Mill
134 Falls Mill Road
Belvidere, TN 37306
(931) 469–7161
www.fallsmill.com

Franklin County Chamber
of Commerce
P.O. Box 280
Winchester, TN 37398
(931) 967–6788
www.fccc-tn.org

Franklin County Old Jail
Museum
400 Dinah Shore Boulevard
Winchester, TN 37398
(931) 967–0524

George Dickel Distillery
P.O. Box 1448
Tullahoma, TN 37388
www.georgedickel.com

Giles County Chamber of
Commerce
100 South Second Street
Pulaski, TN 38478
(931) 363–3789
www.public.usit.net/gilecofc

Granville House Bed &
Breakfast
229 Pulaski Street
Lawrenceburg, TN 38464
(931) 762–3129

Holly Berry Inn
302 North Atlantic Street
Tullahoma, TN 37388
(931) 455–4445
www.hollyberryinn.com

Jack Daniel Distillery
Tullahoma-Lynchburg
Highway 55
Lynchburg, TN 37352
(931) 759–6180
www.jackdaniels.com

James D. Vaughn Museum
c/o Mainstreet Lawrenceburg
P.O. Box 607
Lawrenceburg, TN 38464
(931) 762–8991

Lawrence County
Chamber of Commerce
1609 North Locust Avenue
Lawrenceburg, TN 38464
(931) 762–4911
www.usit.net/lawrence

Ledford Mill Bed &
Breakfast
Route 2, Box 152B
Wartrace, TN 37183
(931) 455–2546
www.bbonline.com/tn/
ledfordmill

Lincoln County Chamber
of Commerce
208 South Elk Avenue
Fayetteville, TN 37334
(931) 433–1234
www.vallnet.com/chamberof
commerce

Lynchburg/Moore County
Chamber of Commerce
P.O. Box 421
Lynchburg, TN 37352
(931) 759–4111
www.lynchburgtn.com

Manchester Area Chamber
of Commerce
110 East Main Street
Manchester, TN 37356
(931) 728–7635
www.manchester-tn.com

Milky Way Farm
1864 Milky Way Road
Pulaski, TN 38478
(931) 363–9769

Miss Mary Bobo's
Boarding House
Main Street
Lynchburg, TN 37352
(931) 759–7394

Old Stone Fort State
Archaeological Park
732 Stone Fort Drive
Manchester, TN 37855
(931) 723–5073
www.state.tn.us/environment/
parks/stoneft

Tims Ford State Park
570 Tims Ford Drive
Winchester, TN 37390-4136
(931) 962–1183
www.state.tn.us/environment/
parks/timsford

Tullahoma Chamber of
Commerce
P.O. Box 1205
Tullahoma, TN 37388
(931) 455–5497
mscc.cc.tn.us/~ccrawford/
tullahoma.html

20: BLEDSOE'S LICK, MANSKER'S STATION, AND PORT ROYAL

Bledsoe Creek State Park
400 Zieglers Fort Road
Gallatin, TN 37807-1727
(615) 452–3706
www.state.tn.us/environment/
parks/bledsoe

Cragfont
200 Cragfont Road
Castalian Springs, TN 37031
(615) 452–7070

Gallatin Chamber of
Commerce
P.O. Box 26
Gallatin, TN 37066
(615) 452–4000
www.gallatintn.org

The Hermitage
4580 Rachel's Lane
Hermitage, TN 37076
(615) 889–2941
www.thehermitage.com

Mansker's Station
P.O. Box 1779
Goodlettsville, TN 37070
(615) 859–FORT

Port Royal State Historic
Park
3300 Old Clarksville
Highway
Adams, TN 37010
(931) 358–9696
www.state.tn.us/environment/
parks/proyal

Rock Castle State Historic
Site
139 Rock Castle Lane
Hendersonville, TN 37075
(615) 824–0502

Springfield–Robertson
County Chamber of
Commerce
100 Fifth Avenue West
Springfield, TN 37172-0307
(615) 384–3800
www.springfield-tennessee.
com

Sumner County Museum
183 West Main Street
Gallatin, TN 37066
(615) 451–3738

Sumner County Tourism
P.O. Box 957
Gallatin, TN 37066
(615) 230–8474
www.sumnertn.org

Trousdale Place
183 West Main Street
Gallatin, TN 37066
(615) 452–5648

Wynnewood State
Historic Site
210 Old Highway 25
Castalian Springs, TN 37031
(615) 452–5463

21: THE ANTEBELLUM TRAIL

Athenaeum Rectory
808 Athenaeum Street
Columbia, TN 38401
(931) 381–4822

Belmont Mansion
Belmont University
1900 Belmont Boulevard
Nashville, TN 37212
(615) 460–5459
www.citysearch.com/nas/
belmontmansion

Carnton Plantation
1345 Carnton Lane
Franklin, TN 37064
(615) 794–0903

Carter House
1140 Columbia Avenue
Franklin, TN 37046
(615) 791–1861

Cumberland Science Museum
800 Fort Negley Boulevard
Nashville, TN 37203-4899
(615) 862–5160
www.csmisfun.com

Elm Springs
National Headquarters
Sons of Confederate Veterans
740 Mooresville Pike
Columbia, TN 38401
(931) 380–1844

Lotz House
1111 Columbia Avenue
Franklin, TN 37046
(615) 791–6533

Maury County Convention & Visitors Bureau
8 Public Square
Columbia, TN 38401
(888) 852–1860
www.antebellum.com

Mount Pleasant/Maury Phosphate Museum
108 Public Square
Mount Pleasant, TN 38474
(931) 379–9511

Nashville Convention & Visitors Bureau
211 Commerce Street
Suite 100
Nashville, TN 37201
(615) 259–4700
www.nashvillecvb.com

Polk Home
P.O. Box 741
Columbia, TN 38402
(931) 388–2354
www.jameskpolk.com

Radnor Lake State Natural Area
1160 Otter Creek Road
Nashville, TN 37220-1700
(615) 373–3467
www.state.tn.us/environment/
parks/radnor

Rattle & Snap Plantation
1522 North Main
Columbia, TN 38401
(800) 258–3875
www.rattleandsnap.com

Rippavilla Plantation
5700 Main Street
Spring Hill, TN 37174
(931) 486–9037

Tennessee Antebellum Trail
P.O. Box 877
Spring Hill, TN 37174
(800) 381–1865

Traveler's Rest
636 Farrell Parkway
Nashville, TN 37220
(615) 832–8197
http://travrest.home.
mindspring.com

Williamson County Tourism
P.O. Box 156
Franklin, TN 37065
(800) 356–3445

22: NATCHEZ TRACE

Belle Meade Plantation
5025 Harding Road
Nashville, TN 37205
(800) 270–3991

Blackburn Farmstead & Pioneer Museum
121 John Sharp Road
Hampshire, TN 38461
(931) 796–7264

Cheekwood Botanical Garden & Museum of Art
1200 Forrest Park Drive
Nashville, TN 37205
(615) 356–8000
www.cheekwood.org

Lewis County Chamber of Commerce
112 East Main Street
Hohenwald, TN 38462
(931) 796–4084
www.visitlewis.com

Lewis County Museum
108 East Main Street
Hohenwald, TN 38462
(931) 796–1550

Loveless Cafe
8400 Highway 100
Nashville, TN 37221
(615) 646–9700

Natchez Trace Parkway
2680 Natchez Trace Parkway
Tupelo, MS 38804
(662) 680–4025
Leipers Fork District Office:
(615) 790–9323
www.nps.gov/natr

The Parthenon Centennial
Park
25th at West End Avenue
Nashville, TN 37201
(615) 862–8431
www.parthenon.org

Warner Park Nature
Center
7311 Highway 100
Nashville, TN 37221
(615) 352–6299

23: CUMBERLAND
RIVER

Cheatham County
Chamber of Commerce
P.O. Box 354
Ashland City, TN 37015
(615) 792–06722

Cheatham Lake
Campground
Reservations: (877) 444–6777

Cheatham Lake Wildlife
Management Area
(615) 792–4510

Tennessee Wildlife
Resources Agency
Ellington Agriculture Center
P.O. Box 40747
Nashville, TN 37204

Clarksville–Montgomery
County Museum
200 South Second Street
Clarksville, TN 37040
(931) 648–5780

Clarksville/Montgomery
County Tourist
Commission
P.O. Box 883
Clarksville, TN 37041-0883
(800) 530–2487
www.clarkesville.tn.us

Cross Creeks National
Wildlife Refuge
643 Wildlife Road
Dover, TN 37058
(931) 232–7477
www.fws.gov/~r4eao

Don F. Pratt Memorial
Museum
Tennessee Avenue, Bldg. 5702
Fort Campbell, KY 42223
(502) 798–3215

Dunbar Cave State
Natural Area
401 Old Dunbar Cave Road
Clarksville, TN 37043
(931) 648–5526
www.state.tn.us/environment/
parks/dunbar

Fort Donelson National
Battlefield
P.O. Box 434
Dover, TN 37058
(931) 232–5706

Harpeth River Bridge
Campground
(615) 792–4195

Land Between the Lakes
100 Van Morgan Drive
Golden Pond, KY 42211-9001
(800) LBL–7077
www.lbl.org

Paris–Henry County
Chamber of Commerce
P.O. Box 8
Paris, TN 38242
(800) 345–1103
www.paris.tn.org

Paris–Henry County
Heritage Center
614 North Poplar Street
Paris, TN 38242
(731) 642–1030

Paris Landing State Park
16055 Highway 79–N
Buchanan, TN 38222-4109
Office: (731) 644–7359
Inn: (731) 642–4311
Reservations: (800) 250–8614
www.state.tn.us/environment/
parks/paris

The Post House
3190 Fort Campbell
Boulevard
Clarksville, TN 37042
(931) 431–5605

Stewart County Chamber
of Commerce
P.O. Box 147
Dover, TN 37058
(931) 232–8290

Tennessee National
Wildlife Refuge
P.O. Box 849
Paris, TN 38242
(731) 642–2091
southeast.fws.gov/wildlife/
nwrtns.html

U.S. Army Corps of
Engineers
Cheatham Lake
1798 Cheatham Dam Road
Ashland City, TN 37015
(615) 792–5697

24: CIVIL WAR
RAILROAD AND THE
IRON INDUSTRY

Benton County Chamber
of Commerce
202 West Main Street
Camden, TN 38320
(731) 584–8395

Birdsong Marina
255 Marina Road
Camden, TN 38320
(800) 225–7469

Carroll County Chamber
of Commerce
P.O. Box 726
Huntingdon, TN 38344
(731) 986–4664

Cumberland Furnace
Historic Village, Inc.
P.O. Box 242
Cumberland Furnace
TN 37051
(615) 446–1655

Dickson County Chamber
of Commerce
P.O. Box 339
Dickson, TN 37055
(615) 446–2349

Enochs's Farm
3072 Little Blue Creek Road
McEwen, TN 37101
(931) 582–3385

Gordon Browning Museum
640 North Main Street
McKenzie, TN 38201
(731) 352–3510
www.gbmuseum.tn.org

Harpeth Scenic River &
Narrows Historic Area
Kingston Springs, TN 37887
(615) 797–9051
www.state.tn.us/environment/
parks/harpeth

Humphreys County
Chamber of Commerce
124 East Main Street
Waverly, TN 37185
(615) 296–4865

Humphreys County
Museum
201 Fort Hill Drive
Waverly, TN 37185
(615) 296–1099

Irish Picnic &
Homecoming
175 Street Patrick Street
McEwen, TN 37101
(931) 582–3493

Johnsonville State Historic
Area
Route 1 Box 374
New Johnsonville
TN 37134
(931) 535–2789
www.state.tn.us/environment/
parks/johnson

Loretta Lynn's Ranch
44 Hurricane Mills Road
Hurricane Mills, TN 37078
(931) 296–7700
www.lorettalynn.com

Montgomery Bell State
Park
P.O. Box 39
Burns, TN 37029
(615) 797–9052
Inn Reservations:
(800) 250–8613
www.state.tn.us/environment/
parks/montbell

Nathan Bedford Forrest
State Park
1825 Pilot Knob Road
Eva, TN 38333
(731) 584–6356
www.state.tn.us/environment/
parks/forrest

Nolan House Bed &
Breakfast
375 Highway 13 North
Waverly, TN 37185
(931) 296–2511

25: SHILOH

Buford Pusser Home and
Museum
P.O. Box 301
Adamsville, TN 38310
(731) 632–4080

Hardin County Chamber
of Commerce
P. O. Box 996
Savannah, TN 38372
(731) 925–2363
www.hardincountytn.com

Mousetail Landing State
Park
Route 3, Box 280B
Linden, TN 37096
(731) 847–0841
www.state.tn.us/environment/
parks/mouse

Natchez Trace State Park
24845 Natchez Trace Road
Wildersville, TN 38388-8329
Office: (731) 968–3742
Inn: (731) 968–8176
Reservations: (800) 250–8616
www.state.tn.us/environment/
parks/natchez

Parker House Bed &
Breakfast
Saltillo, TN 38370
(731) 687–3456

Shiloh National Military
Park
1055 Pittsburg Landing
Shiloh, TN 38376
(731) 689–5696
www.nps.gov/shil

Tennessee River Museum
507 Main Street
Savannah, TN 38372
(731) 925–2364
www.tourhardincnty.org

Trail of Tears National
Historic Trail
Long Distance Trails Group
Office
National Park Service
P.O. Box 728
Santa Fe, NM 87504
(505) 988–6888

White Elephant Bed &
Breakfast
304 Church Street
Savannah, TN 38372
(731) 925–6410
www.bbonline.com/tn/
elephant/

26: CHANGING THE LANDSCAPE

Big Hill Pond State Park
1435 John Howell Road
Pocahontas, TN 38061
(731) 645–7967
www.state.tn.us/environment/
parks/bighill

Chickasaw State Park
20 Cabin Lane
Henderson, TN 38340
(731) 989–5141
www.state.tn.us/environment/
parks/chickasaw

Hardeman County
Chamber of Commerce
500 West Market Street
P.O. Box 313
Bolivar, TN 38008
(731) 658–6554
www.bolivarnet.com/
Hardeman/Chamber/default.
html

Hockaday Handmade
Brooms
2074 Highway 142
Selmer, TN 38375
(731) 645–4823

Magnolia Manor Bed &
Breakfast
418 North Main Street
Bolivar, TN 38008
(731) 658–6700

McNairy County Chamber
of Commerce
P.O. Box 7
Selmer, TN 38375
(731) 645–6360
www.centurytel.net/mccc

N. C. & St. L. Depot and
Railroad Museum
582 South Royal Street
Jackson, TN 38301
(731) 425–8223

Pickwick Landing State
Park
Park Road
Pickwick Dam
TN 38365-0015
Office: (731) 689–3129
Inn: (731) 689–3135
Reservations: (800) 250–8615
www.state.tn.us/environment/
parks/pickwick

Pinson Mounds State
Archaeological Park
460 Ozier Road
Pinson, TN 38366
(731) 988–5614
www.state.tn.us/environment/
parks/pinson

27: RAILROADS, TEAPOTS, AND DAVID CROCKETT

Big Cypress Tree State
Natural Area
297 Big Cypress Road
Greenfield, TN 38230
(731) 235–2700
www.state.tn.us/environment/
parks/cypress

Casey Jones Village
Jackson, TN 38305
(800) 748–9588
www.caseyjonesvillage.com

David Crockett House
219 North Trenton Street
Rutherford, TN 38369
(731) 665–7166

Gibson County Chamber
of Commerce
P.O. Box 464
Trenton, TN 38382
(731) 855–0973
www.gibsoncountynet.com

Humboldt Chamber of
Commerce
1200 Main Street
Humboldt, TN 38343
(731) 784–1842

Jackson Area Chamber of
Commerce
P.O. Box 1904
Jackson, TN 38302-1904
(731) 423–2200

Jackson Convention and
Visitors Bureau
314 East Main Street
2nd Floor
Jackson, TN 38301
(731) 425–8333
www.jacksontncvb.com

Obion County Museum
1004 Edwards Street
Union City, TN 38261
(731) 885–6774

Trenton Teapot Museum
City Hall
309 South College
Trenton, TN 38330
(731) 855–2013

West Tennessee
Agricultural Museum
3 Ledbetter Gate Road
Milam, TN 38358
(731) 686–8067

West Tennessee Regional
Arts Center
1200 Main Street
Humboldt, TN 38343
(731) 784–1842

28: COTTON, BLUES, AND BARBECUE

Ames Plantation
P.O. Box 389
Grand Junction
TN 38039-0389
(901) 878–1067
www.amesplantation.org

Bartlett Chamber of
Commerce
P.O. Box 34193
Bartlett, TN 38134
(901) 372–9457
www.bacofc.com

Brownsville–Haywood
County Chamber of
Commerce
121 West Main Street
Brownsville, TN 38012
(731) 772–2193
www.brownsville-
haywoodtn.com

Chucalissa Museum
1987 Indian Village Drive
Memphis, TN 38109
(901) 785–3160

Collierville Chamber of
Commerce
125 North Rowlett
Collierville, TN 38017
(901) 853–1949

Corky's Bar-B-Q
5259 Poplar Avenue
Memphis, TN 38119
(901) 685–9771

Cotton Museum of the
South
Green Frog Village
P.O. Box 474
Bells, TN 38006
(731) 663–3319

Davies Manor Plantation
9336 Davies Plantation Road
Brunswick, TN 38014
(901) 386–0715

Fayette County Chamber
of Commerce
P. O. Box 411
Somerville, TN 38068
(901) 465–8690
www.fayettecountychamber.
com

Germantown Chamber of
Commerce
2195 Germantown Road
South
Germantown, TN 38138
(901) 755–1200
www.germantownchamber.
com

Graceland
P.O. Box 16508
Memphis, TN 38186
(800) 238–2000
www.elvis–presley.com

Hatchie National Wildlife
Refuge
4172 Highway 76 South
Brownsville, TN 38012
(901) 772–0501
www.fws.gov/~r4eao

Haywood County Museum
College Hill
127 North Grand Avenue
Brownsville, TN 38012
(731) 772–2193

Magevney House
198 Adams Avenue
Memphis, TN 38103
(901) 526–4464

Mallory-Neely House
652 Adams Avenue
Memphis, TN 38105
(901) 523–1484

Memphis Convention &
Visitors Bureau
47 Union Avenue
Memphis, TN 38103
(901) 543–5300
www.memphistravel.com

National Bird Dog
Museum
P.O. Box 774
Grand Junction, TN 38039
(731) 764–2058

National Civil Rights
Museum
450 Mulberry Street
Memphis, TN 38103
(901) 521–9699
www.civilrightsmuseum.org

Oaklawn Garden Historic
Site
7831 Old Poplar Pike
Germantown, TN 38138

Peabody Hotel
149 Union Avenue
Memphis, TN 38103
(800) PEABODY
www.peabodymemphis.com

Pink Palace Museum
3050 Central Avenue
Memphis, TN 38111
(901) 320–6320

Rendezvous
52 South Second Street, Rear
Memphis, TN 38103
(901) 523–2746

Sun Studio
706 Union Avenue
Memphis, TN 38103
(901) 525–8055
www.sunstudio.com

T. O. Fuller State Park
1500 Mitchell Road
Memphis, TN 38109
(901) 543–7581
www.state.tn.us/environment/
parks/tofuller

West Tennessee Delta
Heritage Center
121 Sunny Hill Cove
Brownsville, TN 38012
(731) 779–9000

Woodruff-Fontaine House
680 Adams Avenue
Memphis, TN 38105
(901) 526–1469

29: MISSISSIPPI RIVER

Alex Haley Boyhood
Home
201 Church Street
P.O. Box 500
Henning, TN 38041
(731) 738–2240

Calhoun Boat Works
Route 1, Box 440
Tiptonville, TN 38079
(731) 253–7777

Chickasaw National
Wildlife Refuge
Lower Hatchie National
Wildlife Refuge
1505 Sand Bluff Road
Ripley, TN 38063-6085
(731) 635–7621

Fort Pillow State Historic
Park
3122 Park Road
Henning, TN 38041
(731) 738–5581
www.state.tn.us/environment/
parks/pillow

Meeman–Shelby Forest
State Park
910 Riddick Road
Millington, TN 38053
(901) 876–5215

Mississippi River Trail
7777 Walnut Grove Road
Box 27
Memphis, TN 38120

Mud Island River Park
125 North Front Street
Memphis, TN 38103
(800) 507–6507
www.mudisland.com

Reelfoot Lake State Park
Route 1, Box 2345
Tiptonville, TN 38079-9799
(731) 253–7756
Reservations: (800) 250–8617
www.state.tn.us/environment/
parks/reelfoot

Reelfoot & Lake Isom
National Wildlife Refuges
4343 Highway 157
Union City, TN 38261
(731) 538–2481

Index

Index   **363**

About the Author

Russ Manning began as a science writer but for the last ten years has concentrated on writing about the outdoors. He has authored several books on the Southeast, including *100 Hikes in the Great Smoky Mountains*, *The Historic Cumberland Plateau*, *75 Hikes in Shenandoah National Park*, and *An Outdoor Guide to the Big South Fork*. He has also written more than 200 articles for such publications as *Blue Ridge Country*, *Southern Living*, *Backpacker*, *Outside*, *Environment*, *The Tennessee Conservationist*, and *Environmental Ethics*.